THE CAPTIVE IMAGINATION

Charlotte Perkins Gilman, 1860–1935

THE CAPTIVE IMAGINATION

IMAGINATION

A Casebook on
The Yellow Wallpaper

Edited by Catherine Golden

THE FEMINIST PRESS
at The City University of New York
New York

Published 1992 by The Feminist Press at The City University of New York,
311 East 94 Street, New York, NY 10128
Distributed by The Talman Company, 150 Fifth Avenue,
New York, NY 10011

Permission Acknowledgments begin on page 339.

96 95 94 93 92 5 4 3 2 1

Library of Congress Cataloging-in-Publication Data

The Captive Imagination : a casebook on The yellow wallpaper / edited
  by Catherine Golden.
    p.   cm.
  Includes bibliographical references.
  ISBN 1-55861-047-2 (alk. paper) : $35.00.—ISBN 1-55861-048-0
(pbk. : alk. paper) : $14.95
  1. Gilman, Charlotte Perkins, 1860-1935. Yellow wallpaper.
I. Golden, Catherine.
PS1744.G57Y453   1992
813'.4—dc20   91-4796
                                                                   CIP

This publication is made possible, in part, by public funds
from the New York State Council on the Arts.

Cover design: Gilda Hannah
Text design: Paula Martinac

Printed in the United States on acid-free paper
by McNaughton & Gunn, Inc.

To the Memory of Robin I. Thevenet

An Obstacle

Charlotte Perkins Gilman

I was climbing up a mountain-path
    With many things to do,
Important business of my own,
    And other people's too,
When I ran against a Prejudice
    That quite cut off the view.

My work was such as could not wait,
    My path quite clearly showed,
My strength and time were limited,
    I carried quite a load;
And there that hulking Prejudice
    Sat all across the road.

So I spoke to him politely,
    For he was huge and high,
And begged that he would move a bit
    And let me travel by.
He smiled, but as for moving! —
    He didn't even try.

And then I reasoned quietly
    With that colossal mule:
My time was short — no other path —
    The mountain winds were cool.
I argued like a Solomon;
    He sat there like a fool.

Then I flew into a passion,
 And I danced and howled and swore.
I pelted and belabored him
 Till I was stiff and sore;
He got as mad as I did—
 But he sat there as before.

And then I begged him on my knees;
 I might be kneeling still
If so I hoped to move that mass
 Of obdurate ill-will—
As well invite the monument
 To vacate Bunker Hill!

So I sat before him helpless,
 In an ecstasy of woe—
The mountain mists were rising fast,
 The sun was sinking slow—
When a sudden inspiration came,
 As sudden winds do blow.

I took my hat, I took my stick,
 My load I settled fair,
I approached that awful incubus
 With an absent-minded air—
And I walked directly through him,
 As if he wasn't there!

Contents

CRITICISM   **121**

Preface

Over the years I have felt compelled to reread, teach, discuss, and debate "The Yellow Wallpaper" with my colleagues and students at Skidmore College. I was initially drawn to this late American Victorian tale by its intensity, and my interest in Gilman's story has not waned. A focal point for analysis and lively discussion, "The Yellow Wallpaper" continues to captivate, puzzle, and perplex new readers and Gilman specialists alike.

As I began to explore the sociocultural, psychological, and linguistic dimensions of "The Yellow Wallpaper" and to write my own critical interpretation about Gilman's story, I found myself as engaged in reading the criticism about "The Yellow Wallpaper" as in reading the story itself. This book grew out of my fascination with the way in which critics from different disciplines have used a range of theoretical perspectives to read "The Yellow Wallpaper." The extensive scholarly attention to the story in recent years suggests that critics and students of literature alike still feel compelled to engage actively with the text and to debate it. Paralleling the feat the narrator achieves at the end of the story, Gilman's "The Yellow Wallpaper" remains "out" and cannot be "put . . . back": it is now included in the syllabi of high school, undergraduate, and graduate courses in literature and women's studies and is readily found in personal and public libraries and bookstores. Marking the centenary of the story's first publication in the January 1892 issue of *New England Magazine*, this critical edition of "The Yellow Wallpaper" offers historical background and literary criticism to draw readers into "The Yellow Wallpaper" and to encourage further readings, research, and teaching of this rich and complex short story.

While the book grew out of my own interest in "The Yellow Wallpaper," the support of other individuals and my home institution helped bring it to fruition. I wish to thank Skidmore College for awarding me several Faculty Research Grants. I am grateful to Rosemary DelVecchio, Humanities Librarian of the Lucy Scribner Library, for completing a number of bibliographic searches through a growing field of Gilman scholarship to insure that I had located all the past and current criticism on "The Yellow Wallpaper." I also wish to thank the Reference Assistants at the Lucy Scribner Library, Marilyn Sheffer and Shirley Webb, for quickly obtaining many articles and books on Gilman that proved vital to the creation of this book. I also appreciate the assistance of Betty Allen, Librarian at the Schaeffer Library of Union College, and Marie-Hélène Gold, Photograph Assistant at the Schlesinger Library of Radcliffe College. Betty Allen made arrangements for me to view and photograph the original illustrations accompanying "The Yellow Wallpaper" in the 1892 issue of *New England Magazine*. Marie-Hélène Gold directed my attention to a number of engaging photographs of Charlotte Perkins Gilman.

I wish to thank the community of feminist scholars at large and particularly at Skidmore College whose insights about Gilman have shaped my own. I am especially appreciative of my colleagues Susan Kress, Charlotte Goodman, and Phyllis Roth, who served as readers of my own critical interpretation of "The Yellow Wallpaper" and shared with me an informed response to Gilman's story. Susan Kress particularly acted as a thorough and supportive reader who helped me to crystallize my argument about the tension between the muted text of Gilman's writing and the dominant text of the character's descent into madness in "The Yellow Wallpaper." It was Phyllis Roth who suggested that I take my work further and create a casebook of criticism on the story; I am indebted to her for sparking the idea for this book. I am also extremely grateful to Charlotte Goodman for reading the drafts of my Introduction and Headnotes of this book. Her insights into American literature, feminism, and Gilman's story helped to shape my work and supported me throughout this entire project.

I very much appreciate the many enthusiastic students in my classes at Skidmore College who, over the years, helped me think about my ideas and interpretation of "The Yellow Wallpaper." I particularly wish to thank my students Erin Senack and Helene Schneider who did resourceful work as Research Assistants. Erin Senack tracked down bibliographic references and helped me to assemble the materials included in the book. Guiding Erin Senack on an independent study on "The Yellow Wallpaper" and working with her on a collaborative research grant from Skidmore College helped me to clarify my own ideas about Gilman as we engaged in lively discussion of the criticism of "The Yellow Wallpaper." Helene Schneider also helped to compile the acknowledgments and bibliography; she cheerfully typed, proofread, and assisted me in completing the final details as I sent the book to press.

I have had the good fortune of working with Florence Howe, Director of The Feminist Press, and Susannah Driver, Senior Editor of The Feminist Press. I have benefited by consulting with the intelligent, dedicated, and lively staff of The Feminist Press, which has long been invested in Gilman's landmark story. Attentive and committed to this book, Florence Howe and Susannah Driver supported me throughout this entire project and offered informed, helpful advice in every stage of this book. I also wish to thank Kathy Casto, who graciously supervised the final stages of the book's production.

Finally, I want to thank my husband and colleague, Michael Steven Marx. From the initial proposal to the final completed manuscript, Michael tirelessly served as a springboard for my ideas about "The Yellow Wallpaper." He acted as an informed, critical, and understanding reader of my work on Gilman. I could never have completed this book without his endless support, faith, and encouragement.

THE CAPTIVE IMAGINATION

One Hundred Years of Reading "The Yellow Wallpaper"

Catherine Golden

The redefinition of the literary canon has directed attention to a number of overlooked works by late nineteenth- and early twentieth-century women writers. Prominent among this group is Charlotte Perkins Gilman's "The Yellow Wallpaper." From its first publication in the January 1892 issue of *New England Magazine*[1] until the early 1970s, "The Yellow Wallpaper" was virtually unknown; it found its way into only a few collections of short fiction between 1892 and 1972.[2] A cursory glance at the chronologically arranged Table of Contents and Bibliography of this book reveals the critical attention this complex and controversial story has received since it was republished in 1973. Along with *Herland*, "The Yellow Wallpaper" has gained distinction among the fiction produced by Gilman, a leading turn-of-the-century feminist lecturer and writer;[3] her fictional account of a psychological breakdown offers a chilling Poe-esque plot, a well-crafted and powerful style, and a feminist perspective on the sociocultural situation confronting women in the late nineteenth century. It has now been incorporated into the contemporary canon of American literature and hailed in the feminist canon.

The selections included in the Backgrounds and Criticism sections demonstrate multiple ways of looking at "The Yellow Wallpaper" and, specifically, of reading the dominant symbol of the wallpaper and understanding the story's protagonist. The essays within this critical edition represent the breadth of theoretical perspectives that scholars have used

1

to approach "The Yellow Wallpaper"—principally reader response, bio-graphical, psychological (for example, Lacanian, Freudian, Adlerian), feminist, and linguistic. Although much of the criticism is feminist in its orientation, selections from the Backgrounds section convey the original response to the story as a horror tale, and several essays from the Criticism section suggest the need to extend the feminist perspective.[4]

Overlap occurs between essays, particularly those that read "The Yellow Wallpaper" through a given critical lens. However, critics often approach the story from a combination of theoretical perspectives and typically take notice of different dimensions of the story within their essays. In fact, the experience of following all the criticism of "The Yellow Wallpaper" begins to mimic that of the fictional narrator as she struggles to read the everchanging text of the wallpaper and follow it to some sort of conclusion: the story evolves before our eyes and gains new definition.

Interpretations from scholars representing different disciplines and articulating distinct and, at times, dissimilar points of view have increased the recognition of Gilman and her story. The now privileged status of "The Yellow Wallpaper" conflicts with the reception it received in the 1890s as well as the conclusion Gilman realistically reached about her literary career following the publication of "The Yellow Wallpaper" and numerous poems: "All these literary efforts providing but little, it was well indeed that another avenue of work [lecturing] opened up to me at this time" (*Living* 65).[5] Within this critical edition, scholars fre-quently make reference to the autobiographical roots of the story because of the striking parallels between the narrator's and Gilman's creative life. Revisiting the climate and situation that the author con-fronted in 1890 through 1892 continues to serve as a reminder of the distance the story has traveled over the past one hundred years.

To recall the apt title of one of Gilman's own poems, it took the overcoming of "An Obstacle"[6] for "The Yellow Wallpaper" to achieve recognition. Editors and readers were not ready to receive "The Yellow Wallpaper" when Charlotte Perkins Gilman (then Stetson)[7] sent it to the well-established novelist, critic, and editor William Dean Howells in 1890. Gilman records in her autobiography, *The Living of Charlotte Perkins Gilman*, that Howells had earlier initiated a correspondence; his "unforgettable letter" made her feel "like a 'real' author at last" (D. Appleton-Century, 113). In this letter dated June 9, 1890, Howells praised two of her poems, "Similar Cases" and "Women of To-day," and concluded of both: "It ["Women of To-day"] is as good almost as the other ["Similar Cases"], and dreadfully true" (1935; 113). Thus, it is not surprising that in an effort to publish another work that was also "dreadfully true," Gilman sent Howells, the major proponent of American realism, her consciously autobiographical "The Yellow Wallpaper."[8]

Gilman's difficulty in getting her now acclaimed story published is not unique in literary history. But the reaction to her landmark story informs its long-lasting and virtual neglect. Howells, a former editor of the prestigious *Atlantic Monthly*, recommended the story to his friend Horace Scudder, then serving as editor. Scudder's often quoted reply bears repeating:

> DEAR MADAM,
>   Mr. Howells has handed me this story.
>   I could not forgive myself if I made others as miserable as I have made myself!
>
> > Sincerely yours,
> > H.E. SCUDDER.

Gilman concluded of her rejection: "I suppose he would have sent back one of Poe's on the same ground" (*Living* 64). In appraising why Scudder rejected the story, Gilman draws a salient parallel between her fiction and Edgar Allan Poe's that has illuminated the original responses to her story as a horror tale. Many have considered Gilman's tale of a woman's descent into madness a continuation of a genre made popular by Poe. Gilman's first husband, Walter Stetson, found the story more disturbing than Poe's tales of horror.[9] As recently as 1973, horror writer H. P. Lovecraft included it as a "classic example in subtly delineating the madness which crawls over a woman dwelling in the hideously papered room"[10] in a collection titled *Supernatural Horror in Literature*. Nonetheless, the climate of Victorian America and its expectations for literature suggest that Scudder might well have accepted one of Poe's tales of madness yet rejected "The Yellow Wallpaper"—on different grounds. Of consequence, the story did not offer the kind of uplifting ending to which *Atlantic Monthly* stories typically adhered. More provocatively, the protagonist who descends into madness is a middle-class wife and mother. As Annette Kolodny has noted: "Those fond of Poe could not easily transfer their sense of mental derangement to the mind of a comfortable middle-class wife and mother; and those for whom the woman in the home was a familiar literary character were hard-pressed to comprehend so extreme an anatomy of the psychic price she paid" (154–5). No doubt Gilman's uncomfortable depiction of a familiar literary figure succumbing to madness within the sacrosanct Victorian domestic circle made Scudder "miserable." He may well have rejected the story in an attempt to protect his late nineteenth-century readers from the story's attack on the appropriate sphere for dutiful women: husband, child, and home.

"The Yellow Wallpaper" eventually found a literary residence if not a home in 1892. Gilman employed Henry Austin, a literary agent, who placed it in *New England Magazine*, a relatively conservative periodical offering a range of nonfiction (travel, history, and biographical spotlights), stories, and poems accompanied by photographs and black-and-white illustrations.[11] The story appeared with three illustrations and a decorative pictorial capital designed by Jo H. Hatfield, a staff illustrator for the magazine. Gilman never received any payment for the initial publication of the story although the editor of *New England Magazine* claimed that he paid Austin forty dollars for it. Nonetheless, she did receive ample compensation in reader response, which proved opinionated and mixed. One antagonistic review entitled "Perilous Stuff" (1892), appearing in the Boston *Transcript*, called it: "a sad story of a young wife passing the gradations from slight mental derangement to raving lunacy" (*Living* 64). This protester, an anonymous male physician, argued to censure the story of "deadly peril";[12] but he betrayed his own curiosity when he fearfully admitted that it held the reader "in morbid fascination to the end" (*Living* 64). While the story made this doctor as miserable as the editor of the *Atlantic Monthly*, it evoked praise from another doctor, Brummel Jones, who in 1892 sent Gilman a congratulatory letter. Jones complimented the story's authentic depiction of mental derangement and argued in a self-congratulatory tone: "From a doctor's standpoint, and I am a doctor, you have made a success. So far as I know, and I am fairly well up in literature, there has been no detailed account of incipient insanity" (*Living* 65).

When I read "The Yellow Wallpaper" in the original periodical, I was surprised to discover how the illustrations, along with Poe's literary influence, encouraged the original responses to the story as a horror tale of a wife and mother's mental derangement. Heretofore no critic has discussed the illustrations accompanying the story in *New England Magazine*. It was customary to illustrate both fiction and nonfiction pieces printed in *New England Magazine*, and Hatfield's pen-and-ink drawings are realistic, typical of the style of illustration the late century tended to produce.[13] However, these illustrations, corresponding to specific lines of the story, deserve attention because they draw out, to use Brummel Jones's words, a "detailed account of incipient insanity."

Below the first illustration appears the caption "I am sitting by the Window in this Atrocious Nursery," a paraphrase of a line from the early pages of Gilman's diary-like story written from the point of view of a first-person narrative.* Prominently placed as a headpiece, this illustration shows the narrator as a respectable-looking Victorian woman engaged in writing. Although the narrator writes only in secret and hides her journal when she senses John's entry, in this illustration Hatfield captures the narrator in an act that directly confronts the opinion of those who prescribe her rest cure: her physician-husband, John, who "hates to have [her] write a word" (26); S. Weir Mitchell, the foremost specialist in nervous diseases for women; and even John's sister Jennie, an "enthusiastic housekeeper" who "thinks it is the writing which made [her] sick" (30). Pen in hand and inkwell by her side, she is drawn acting deceitfully but not looking so. Seated in a decorative rocking chair by the window,[14] dressed demurely, and hair swept back in a neat bun, she looks like the narrator describes John: "practical" (24). Smiling contentedly, she truly believes that "congenial work, with excitement and change, would do [her] good" (25).

The narrator's facial expression appears not contented but composed and almost rigid in the second, marginal let-in illustration whose caption reads "She didn't know I was in the Room." This illustration responds to the narrator's discussion of how Jennie (and earlier John) suspects her obsession with the paper and is puzzled by it. Less effective than the first illustration, this drawing realizes Jennie's look of alarm and confusion as well as the narrator's consciously "restrained manner" (35) as she asks Jennie to explain why she is inspecting the wallpaper. Hatfield also lightly indicates the sprouting and flamboyant curves and "sprawling outlines" (31) of the yellow wallpaper in the portion of the paper framing Jennie. No major changes occur in the narrator's dress or hairstyle although a peculiar expression clouds her too-tight composure

---

*The illustrations are reprinted in the text of "The Yellow Wallpaper" in this edition.

and conveys the very beginning of her hallucinatory state—well established at this point in the story.

The final illustration, dynamically positioned as an endpiece, appears below the line it illustrates: "I had to creep over him every time."[15] The dramatic shift in the portrayal of the narrator between the first two drawings and the third suggests that the narrator succumbs to full-blown madness at an alarming rate and passes through "the gradations from slight mental derangement to raving lunacy," much as the anonymous Boston reviewer describes. The illustration captures the narrator in an act very different than covert writing: creeping on the floor in front of and over John. Conveying a decrepit eeriness, her long and wild dark hair has been freed from the constraints of its late Victorian-style coiffure to accentuate her madness.[16] Although there are no indications of a change in the narrator's appearance in the text (or discussion of her appearance in the text at all for that matter), Hatfield's depiction responds to the traditional conception of the long- and wild-haired madwoman in literature, *Jane Eyre*'s Bertha Mason a prime example.

The narrator's thick and slightly frizzled mane now masks the demure details of her high-necked, long-sleeved Victorian gown. Her hair drapes down her back, in front of her shoulder, and over John, who lies prostrate underneath her in a dead faint. Alongside him lie the tattered strips of the wallpaper that the narrator has torn from the wall. John's three-quarter pose allows the reader-viewer to see the extent of his swoon, leaving his face blank, his hands limp, and his body in a fetal position. The narrator's hands, placed directly on top of John's head and back, facilitate her crawling over her husband. These graphic depictions of John in a position of extreme vulnerability as well as of the narrator in a state of total madness create a visual climax that may have encouraged the traditional response that this tale of "incipient insanity" was of "deadly peril." Totally self-absorbed in her actions, the narrator conveys disregard for and detachment from "that man" (41), who, to recall Gilman's own poem, is reduced to "An Obstacle" across her path: "And I walked directly through him/ As if he wasn't there."

Anthologizing the story without the illustrations nearly thirty years later, Howells continued this line of interpretation of the story's chilling portrayal of insanity in "A Reminiscent Introduction" to his 1920 collection of *The Great Modern American Stories*: "It wanted at least two generations to freeze our young blood with Mrs. Perkins Gilman's story of

'The Yellow Wall Paper' " (55).[17] Howells was well aware of the polemical intent permeating Gilman's fiction and her feminist principles; in fact, in the Biography and Bibliography section at the end of his collection, he emphasized the latter when he said of Gilman: "She is deeply interested in labor problems and the advance of women."[18] However, Howells did not remark in his very brief introduction that "The Yellow Wallpaper" also "wanted [more than] two generations" for its feminist thrust or its polemical intent to be appreciated. Gilman emphasized the latter in her discussions of the story appearing in the *Forerunner* (1909–16) as well as in her autobiography.

In *The Living of Charlotte Perkins Gilman*, Gilman records that when Howells asked her if he might include the story in his collection, she replied, "I was more than willing, but assured him that it was no more 'literature' than my other stuff, being definitely written 'with a purpose' " (65). Her purpose for writing this story has led some critics to call it a polemic against Mitchell's treatment:[19] "the real purpose of the story was to reach Dr. S. Weir Mitchell, and convince him of the error of his ways" (*Living* 65). In 1887 Silas Weir Mitchell treated Gilman at his Philadelphia sanitarium with his well-known rest cure of enforced passivity and confinement, a treatment which is presented by Mitchell, Gilman, and critic Ann Douglas Wood in the Backgrounds section. A leading nineteenth-century neurologist[20] and specialist in women's nervous disorders, Mitchell diagnosed Gilman's condition as "nervous prostration" or "neurasthenia," a breakdown of the nervous system, in her case brought on by a postpartum depression. Overwhelmed by the demands of marriage and motherhood, she willingly entered into the rest cure treatment, but Mitchell's methods and his therapeutic advice at the close of her treatment proved disastrous.

Gilman—who gave way to tremors and weeping when caring for her infant daughter—attempted to follow Mitchell's prescription: "Live as domestic a life as possible. Have your child with you all the time" (*Living* 62). She made a rag doll baby that she hung on a doorknob and began to crawl into dark corners in a state of mental despair. As Jeffrey Berman notes, "In contrast to Mitchell's dictum to return to her husband and presumably expand her family, Gilman chose the only form of pregnancy she could imagine—literary creation" (229). After nearly losing her mind by rigidly following his remaining injunction "never [to] touch pen, brush or pencil as long as you live" (*Living* 62, Gilman, a commercial artist and writer, defied Mitchell and transformed him into a minor but memorable character in her fiction. In describing the nature of her story, Gilman records: "It is a description of a case of nervous breakdown beginning something as mine did, and treated as Dr. S. Weir Mitchell treated me with what I considered the inevitable result, progressive insanity" (*Living* 63). No doubt to advance her "purpose" as well as to establish medical authenticity, Gilman directly implicated Mitchell by naming the doctor in one salient reference in which the nameless narrator, undergoing a three-month rest cure for a postpartum depression, protests about her physician/husband, "John says if I don't pick up faster he shall send me to Weir Mitchell in the fall. But I don't want to go there at all. I had a friend who was in his hands once, and she says he is just like John and my brother, only more so!" (30). The narrator's "friend" serves as a shadowed reference to the author herself and further exposes the autobiographical roots of the story.

"The Yellow Wallpaper" reveals the consequences of following Mitchell's treatment and his therapeutic advice, which Gilman rigidly did for three months. The nameless narrator, like Gilman herself, initially defies the rest cure by writing, much as Hatfield's opening illustration depicts her. Once submissive, the protagonist pursues her ambition to find out the pattern of the wallpaper and to tear the wallpaper to free the woman trapped behind the pattern. She gains a forceful sense of self only as she acts out of madness. As she creeps on the floor, her actions move beyond the realm of sanity where Gilman had also found herself moving before defying her cure; in her words, "I had been as far as one could go and get back" (*Living* 65). Gilman managed not only to "get back" but to turn her sickness into a creative work of art that exposed Mitchell. She sent her doctor a copy of "The Yellow Wallpaper" to urge him to rethink his treatment of nervous prostration. Learning secondhand that Mitchell changed his methods upon reading her story, she proudly remarked: "If that is a fact, I have not lived in vain" (*Living* 65).

Gilman conceived of her work only as a story with a mission, a point that many of the critics within this book also note. Although "The Yellow Wallpaper" remains compatible with her other fiction in its attention to women's issues and women's problems, it appears distinctive from her oeuvre of fiction, which even Gilman enthusiasts consider too didactic, too ideological, and often hastily crafted. "The Yellow Wallpaper" has been singled out as the best of Gilman's creative writing. It is read today, to quote Ann Lane, as "a genuine literary piece."[21] This representative selection from scholarship over the past two decades examines Gilman's rich and complex short story as a work of art. Critics illuminate the sociocultural, psychological, and linguistic dimensions of Gilman's literary piece as well as explore its place within the literary tradition.

The sociocultural importance of the story took nearly eight generations of readers to be appreciated; until the 1970s, as Elaine Hedges notes, "No one seems to have made the connection between insanity and the sex, or sexual role, of the victim, no one explored the story's implications of male-female relationships in the nineteenth century" (125). In her 1973 Afterword to the Feminist Press edition, Hedges reintroduced the story as "one of the rare pieces of literature we have by a nineteenth-century woman which directly confronts the sexual politics of the male-female, husband-wife relationship" (124). Connecting "The Yellow Wallpaper" to Kate Chopin's *The Awakening* (1899) for its frank presentation of the submission of the middle-class wife, she links the destruction of both heroines to the climate of their times. Gail Parker initiated this sociocultural line of argument in her 1972 Introduction to *The Oven Birds: American Women on Womanhood, 1820–1920*. This anthology includes Gilman's "The Yellow Wallpaper" as well as poetry and excerpts from *The Home* and her autobiography, alongside letters, diary excerpts, memoirs, and fiction and nonfiction writings by leading feminist thinkers, notably Elizabeth Cady Stanton, Jane Addams, Sarah Orne Jewett, and Gilman's famous Beecher relatives, her great aunts Catharine Beecher and Harriet Beecher Stowe. In her historical anthology, Parker aimed to connect the history of American feminism and literary history; the inclusion of "The Yellow Wallpaper" in Parker's collection placed this work of fiction firmly within the context of the history of American feminism. Although Parker's discussion of the story is brief and largely autobiographical, she cast "The Yellow Wallpaper" in a feminist context in suggesting that it forces the reader to "recognize what happens to a woman who is denied the right to be an adult" (85). Through Parker's and Hedges's feminist readings, the story became not simply a Poe-esque horror story of mental derangement "chilling" to the blood but a fictional arena in which Gilman voiced and questioned the submissive role prescribed to women.

"The Yellow Wallpaper" does not provide an alternative, feasible female model to guide women readers of future generations as Gilman's fiction typically does. Rather, through her depiction of a rest cure, it plays out the extreme restrictions and limitations confronting women in their society in order to accentuate the fatal consequences of making a woman totally dependent on her male protectors and returning her to an infantile state. The narrator's progressive descent into madness further comments upon the doubly authoritative role of the male protagonist in this late Victorian climate: husband and doctor of "high standing" (24). In contrast, the woman trapped behind the barred pattern of the yellow wallpaper with whom the nameless narrator attempts to identify has been read not only as her literary double but as a symbol of the woman's social condition. The story touches on sensitive questions and worries that haunted Gilman and the women of her time, many of which are also raised in the selections included in the Backgrounds section by Barbara Ehrenreich and Deirdre English, Ann Douglas Wood, Jill Conway, and Gail Parker. The story encourages us to ponder: might a woman feel confined in the home and constricted by her male protector much as the narrator does by her paternalistic husband who, despite his well-meaning intentions, drives her into madness in administering a Mitchell-like rest cure? Might the unending demands of caring for a husband and a child she desperately loves drive a woman to a nervous breakdown, especially if she has an imaginative mind and also desires meaningful work, as the narrator does in "The Yellow Wallpaper"? The questions Gilman's story raises about the limited sphere for women in the nineteenth century readily engage audiences today as equally as they baffled or bothered Gilman's contemporary readers who, as Kolodny argues, either lacked an awareness of the conventions of women's writing or were unprepared for the uncomfortable depiction of the middle-class housewife it revealed; the narrator's problems were presented as sociocultural rather than idiosyncratic, as was customary in the tales of Poe. More consciously autobiographical than any of her other fictional works, the story expresses Gilman's deep sadness over the lost opportunities for women not allowed to fulfill their own purpose in life.

Although Gilman's own mental illness and personal indictment of S. Weir Mitchell have often been read into "The Yellow Wallpaper," the story's psychological importance apart from Gilman's own life has not gone undetected. The yellow wallpaper lining the walls of the former nursery whose color is "hideous" and "unreliable" and whose pattern is "torturing" (34) functions as the primary symbol of the story. The wallpaper filled with "flamboyant patterns committing every artistic sin" (26) soon becomes "an interminable string of toadstools, budding and sprouting in endless convolutions" (34). Her hallucinations evoke night-mare images revealing of the narrator's own distraught mental state. At any given moment in the story the narrator looks at the paper in disparate ways: "Looked at in one way" (31), the narrator tells us, the principle design appears as a " 'debased Romanesque' with delirium tre-mens . . . But, on the other hand, they connect diagonally, and the sprawling outlines run off in great slanting waves of optic horror, like a lot of wallowing seaweeds in full chase" (31). As the story unfolds, the wallpaper continues to evolve from "delirium tremens" to "wallowing seaweed" into a human form as it gains a personality, odor, and movement.

These changes have provoked a plethora of psychological readings interpreting the changes in the once abhorrent and then obsessively mesmerizing wallpaper as a psychological indicator of the narrator's mental state. Beate Schöpp-Schilling applies the psychoanalytical princi-ples of Alfred Adler to "The Yellow Wallpaper" to appreciate the narra-tor's situation at the end of the story as well as Gilman's grasp of psychological processes. In her reading, the narrator's mental deteriora-tion manifested through an excessive preoccupation with wallpaper importantly demonstrates the active characteristics of mental illness, "a perverted attempt of a human being to overcome his feelings of inferior-ity" (143). Jeffrey Berman interprets the changing patterns of the bud-ding, sprouting paper as a reflection of the narrator's own fragmented state and calls it "a projection screen or Rorschach test of the narrator's growing fright" (232), particularly of her morbid fears of marriage, pro-creation, and motherhood.[22] The dominant/muted pattern of the paper has led critics such as Judith Fetterley to read the wallpaper as a "palimp-sest." The longer the narrator looks at the paper, the more definition she sees in both parts of the paper—a front pattern of bars and a muted back pattern that first looks "like" a woman (33) and then "is" a woman (34). The wallpaper becomes more than personified. As the woman behind the wallpaper becomes the narrator's sole preoccupation, she also becomes the narrator's state of mind, in Loralee MacPike's psychological interpretation. To MacPike the wallpaper, like the narrator, is "itself imprisoned in the nursery, with the humanoid heads, behind their intangible bars, denied the sexuality of bodies" (139). Not only trapped like the narrator, the wallpaper embodies contradictions and so mirrors the narrator as well as the larger social condition for women in which such contradiction remains inherent. Her identification with the formless figure, born of an hallucination, leads the narrator to free the woman and that part of herself trapped by the restrictive pattern of her own society.

Examining the psychology of the wallpaper reveals that its meaning cannot simply be fixed. Likewise, the form and language of the text lead the reader deep into the complex psyche of the narrator and invite a multiplicity of readings. The story is comprised of ten diary-like entries and written in the first person, thus giving the impression that the narrator is writing her own story in which she is also the protagonist. Critics have not typically distinguished the narrator/journalist from the protagonist who stops writing, a point of contradiction which Paula Treichler and Richard Feldstein have raised and explored. As Feldstein poses: "If the protagonist stops writing, how do we explain the completion of her journal?" (315). Answering this question invites a range of disparate interpretations and importantly maintains the multiple meanings of this richly ambiguous story that defies one reductive explanation. Has the narrator written the final entry after the fact? Has she done so consciously to prove her recovery? Both of these interpretations deny any disjunction between the narrator/narrated. But perhaps Gilman wanted to direct our attention to this very disjunction. Gilman may have called upon modernist techniques purposefully to show the narrator to be both fused with and distinct from the narrated much as she consciously shows the narrator to be separate from and joined with the woman trapped behind the wallpaper.

Particularly, the pronoun usage in the opening of the tenth entry suggests the narrator's temporary fusion of identity with the woman behind the wallpaper, which Kolodny and I note in our respective essays: "I pulled and she shook, I shook and she pulled, and before morning we had peeled off yards of that paper" (39). Following this dramatic liberation of the woman behind the paper, the narrator emerges independent and resumes writing in the first person singular. Focusing on the narrator's linguistic struggle to defy the physician's "sentence" that condemns her to silence, Treichler argues that the narrator becomes an involved language user who authors her own sentences in a defiant, "impertinent" language. Nonetheless, the narrator who speaks defiantly remains trapped in a room, creeping.

Revising the way she reads the wallpaper, the narrator, although mad, writes in a way that no longer matches her thoughts and actions or conveys one consistent characterization of an oppressed figure who is fearful and fanciful. Interpreting the entire story as well as its main symbol of the wallpaper as a "palimpsest" allows for further examination of the linguistic features of the story. As I argue in my essay, the thoughts and actions of the narrator logically comprise its dominant text, but the writing through which the narrator expresses them (assuming the narrator/narrated is one) comprises a second, muted text informing the narrator's final characterization. Precisely at the point when she dramatically creeps on the floor, tears the wallpaper, and seemingly condemns herself to madness, the narrator increasingly uses and prominently places the nominative case pronoun in the defiant sentences she authors. Nonetheless, the forcefulness of her language, which both Treichler and I recognize, permits her only a dubious victory over patriarchal control. These discussions of the relationship between the mental and social condition of the narrator and language continue to open the multiplicity of meanings in the text and to invite further systematic examination of the style and syntax of the narrator as a language user.

Whether "The Yellow Wallpaper" should be regarded a short story or a novella also remains in dispute. While many critics consider it a short story, others call it a novella, a term that some might think increases its literary stature but that also conflicts with its brevity. Echoing the ambiguity surrounding all aspects of the text, the title shifted from being placed in quotation marks when it first appeared as a "short story" in *New England Magazine* in 1892 to being underlined when it was reissued as a single volume "novella" edition first in 1899 by Small, Maynard and again in 1973 by The Feminist Press. While its treatment as a single volume edition has increased attention to "The Yellow Wallpaper" as a work of fiction in its own right, its first inclusion in Howells's anthology, *The Great Modern American Stories*, importantly placed Gilman's landmark story alongside the short fiction of her noted female and male American contemporaries, Sarah Orne Jewett, Edith Wharton, Mark Twain, and Henry James. The story's inclusion in Howells's collection also paved the way for its acceptance in the contemporary American literary canon.

Conrad Shumaker discusses "The Yellow Wallpaper" in relation to central concerns of nineteenth-century American literature, particularly the work of Nathaniel Hawthorne. Shumaker compares Gilman's John to Hawthorne's Aylmer in "The Birthmark," and he argues that Gilman explores an issue central to American literature and culture when she reveals how the imagination becomes destroyed by a world view that leaves no room for anything that is not useful. John embodies this world view on the opening page of the story when the narrator confides: "John is practical to the extreme. He has no patience with faith, an intense horror of superstition, and he scoffs openly at any talk of things not to be felt and seen and put down in figures" (24). The narrator, in contrast, has a strong imagination leading her to invent stories about things that cannot really be "felt and seen." John urges her to check this inclination by exerting self-control. John does not believe his wife is sick, treats her fancy as a "defect," and represses her imaginative nature, as Shumaker notes, "only to find he has destroyed her in the process" (246). The woman's more poetic world view presented through Gilman's narrator conflicts with the extremely "practical" approach of her sensible physician/husband John, who misreads her much as Henry James's Winterbourne crucially misreads Daisy in "Daisy Miller."

Although Shumaker finds the feminist readings of "The Yellow Wallpaper" instructive, he raises a concern that such approaches isolate "The Yellow Wallpaper" from what he considers to be the "dominant tradition" of Hawthorne, James, Twain, and Wharton, of which it is a part. But in her feminist interpretation Fetterley focuses on the theme of reading about reading, a central concern of the "classics" of American literature, and she reads "The Yellow Wallpaper" alongside Susan Glaspell's "A Jury of Her Peers" and Edgar Allan Poe's "The Murders in Rue Morgue." Building upon Kolodny's work, Jean Kennard has argued that the rise of literary conventions of women's writing not available to readers of the 1890s has allowed a feminist reading of the story to be voiced and accepted. The plethora of such feminist readings published between 1973 and 1980 has brought the story its acclaim and has led to its inclusion in the contemporary canons of both American literature and feminist literature. Collectively the work of Hedges, Kennard, Kolodny, Sandra Gilbert and Susan Gubar, and Fetterley helped the text to achieve a privileged status among literature by women. In *The Madwoman in the Attic* (1979), Gilbert and Gubar call "The Yellow Wallpaper" "a striking story of female confinement and escape, a paradigmatic tale which (like *Jane Eyre*) seems to tell *the* story that all literary women would tell if they could speak their 'speechless woe'" (145). Through this context, "The Yellow Wallpaper" came to be included among those long-neglected works of nineteenth-century women writers which these authors resurrected and reinterpreted.

Along with other overlooked late nineteenth-century works of fiction such as Kate Chopin's *The Awakening*, "The Yellow Wallpaper" has been reprinted in numerous mainstream fiction anthologies as well as anthologies of women writers, such as the *Norton Anthology of Literature By Women* (1985), edited by Gilbert and Gubar. Its widespread inclusion in anthologies today demonstrates that the story has become a literary staple in courses in fiction and particularly in those with an emphasis on women's literature. The way in which the story is introduced within these anthologies has also changed. Unlike Howells, who praised the tale for its chilling qualities without reference to its feminist appeal, Gilbert and Gubar connect it to this context in their introduction: "Charlotte Perkins Gilman's story *The Yellow Wallpaper* (1892) analyzed female madness in terms of women's ambivalent attitudes toward men and maternity."[23]

The now frequent appearance of the story in anthologies is but one indication of its firm place in the feminist literary canon, a point that has not gone without reproach. Janice Haney-Peritz reconsiders the influential feminist criticism of the story by Hedges, Gilbert and Gubar, Kolodny, and Kennard. She raises some of the troubling implications of this criticism in which "Gilman's short story has assumed monumental proportions" (262) and "functions as a feminist monument" (262). Mary Jacobus, also reviewing the work of feminist critics Kolodny and Kennard, points out that their feminist thematic readings importantly contradict the tendency to see women as unstable or hysterical. However, she questions whether such feminist readings may prove too "rationalist" (simply positing that confinement drives the woman mad) and suggests a need to consider dimensions of the story that feminist readings had heretofore barely explored: signs pointing to an "irrationalist, Gothic" reading (the wallpaper drives the narrator mad),[24] the importance of the yellow color of the wallpaper (a color of sickness and decay), and the uncanny creepiness of Gilman's story. In her own essay in feminist criticism, she illuminates the uncanny and reads the disturbing color and odor of the yellow wallpaper as a symbol of the narrator's repressed sexuality, a point that Berman also makes in his more traditionally Freudian psychoanalysis, published just prior to Jacobus's.[25]

Critics continue to debate the ambiguous and controversial ending, particularly the narrator's fate. The ending of the story defies a reductive explanation, no doubt as Gilman intended. Opinions range along a spectrum marked by extremes: liberation versus entrapment, triumph versus defeat. The pioneering studies appearing in the 1970s similarly read "The Yellow Wallpaper" as a story of a woman attempting to free herself from her restrictive, patriarchal nineteenth-century society. But these early complementary and sympathetic interpretations disagree somewhat about the degree of triumph and liberation the narrator achieves at the end of the tale. Most optimistic are the readings of Gilbert and Gubar, Kennard, and Schöpp-Shilling. Gilbert and Gubar argue that the narrator, "a supposedly 'mad' woman has been sentenced to imprisonment in the 'infected' house of her own body" (148); however, through identification with the double trapped on the other side of the wallpaper, the woman — whom society perceives as mad — escapes from her textual and architectural confinement into "the open space of [her] own authority" (147). Through Kennard's eyes, the narrator's madness can be seen even more optimistically as "a form of higher sanity, as an indication of a capacity to see truths other than those available to the logical mind" (180). Furthermore, to Kennard the narrator's discomfort in ancestral halls becomes a healthy expression of a desire for freedom and space, and her descent into madness a spiritual quest "if we agree to read madness as sanity" (182). In Schöpp-Schilling's positive reading, the narrator defies her husband, who forbids her to write, by turning to another form of paper — the wallpaper. The heroine's final descent into madness becomes a supreme defiance, "which ultimately enables her to creep triumphantly over her husband" (143). Of these early readings, Hedges and Kolodny, in contrast, emphasize the limitations of the narrator's situation at the end of the story. Through Hedges's lens, the narrator achieves temporary insight but "is destroyed" (132), completely mad. Kolodny similarly interprets the narrator's situation as a liberation into madness only "for in decoding her own projections onto the paper, the protagonist has managed to reencode them once more, and now more firmly than ever, within" (158).

Swinging across this spectrum, the narrator is allowed a partial victory by some critics of the mid-1980s, who place her between the extremes of finding meaning or self-definition in her state of madness to retreating into an inhuman or inanimate state. To Fetterley, the narrator achieves a "temporary sanity"; although this state enables her to express feelings that John represses, these emotions inevitably energize her to act out her madness rather than merely imagine it. Although Fetterley argues that the narrator does not escape the patriarchal text when she "got out at last" (41), she allows that the narrator's choice of literal madness may be preferable to John's confining prescription for sanity. Placing the narrator midway along the spectrum of entrapment versus liberation, Treichler concludes that "the story only hints at possibilities for change. Woman is both passive and active, subject and object, sane and mad" (207). She argues that the social conditions must change before the narrator and other women can truly be free. Writing in the late 1980s, I similarly permit the narrator a "dubious victory" because "Only at the point at which she acts out of madness does she find a place within the patriarchal language she uses, although not yet within her larger social reality" (304).

Not all critics perceive the narrator in limbo between madness and sanity or on the road to victory as some of the pioneering studies do. Marking a turning point in the literary criticism of "The Yellow Wallpaper," the mid-1980s favored a darker reading of the story and a more pessimistic view of the narrator's fate. In opposition to Gilbert and Gubar, Haney-Peritz asserts that "the narrator does not move out into open country; instead, she turns an ancestral hall into a haunted house and then encrypts herself therein as a fantasy figure" (271). Considering the story a "memento mori that signifies the death of (a) woman rather than as a memorial that encloses the body essential to a viable feminist criticism" (271), she suggests that a "memento mori" invokes sympathy for what may happen when a repressed woman can express herself only by encasing herself within an imaginary realm.

Emphasizing the narrator's animalness rather than her inanimateness, Jacobus describes how "The narrator of 'The Yellow Wallpaper' enacts her abject state first by timorousness and stealth (her acquiescence in her own 'treatment,' and her secret writing), then by creeping, and finally by going on all fours over the supine body of her husband" (286). She expands upon the animalhood of the hysterical narrator by likening her to Brontë's madwoman in the attic of Thornfield Hall, an association with *Jane Eyre* far different than Gilbert and Gubar's. To Jacobus, "The woman on all fours is like Bertha Mason, an embodiment of the animality of woman unredeemed by (masculine) reason" (287–8). Whereas the act of crawling becomes a condition of animalhood through Jacobus's 1986 reading, the same act serves as the triumphant overcoming of John (the narrator creeps over him) in Kennard's 1981 essay, or as a purposeful exertion of self-control—a means to shock John into a faint—in Feldstein's more recent 1989 reading. John's fainting has become a subject for discussion, some critics pointing to it as a sign that the narrator has outwitted John and others arguing that he will recover and commit his wife in the end. Feldstein also proposes that the narrator's action of crawling be seen as a form of self-expression: "Prohibited from writing in her journal, the narrator embodies herself as a stylus writing the line, her body being written in the process" (313) or, one might argue, giving birth to itself. The evolution in the way the narrator and the story itself have been read continues to defy a reductive pattern as does the story itself. Moving from the pioneering studies that appeared in the 1970s to the new historicist and cultural studies readings of the late 1980s, Hedges, in her concluding essay, explores the ways critics within and beyond this collection have looked at the story over the last two decades. Returning to examine the criticism following her Afterword accompanying the story's 1973 republication, she provocatively notes what aspects of "The Yellow Wallpaper" subsequent readings have highlighted or shadowed and points out the implications of some of the most recent criticism.

The gathering of many of these essays into a single book foregrounds the discussion among critics who have read "The Yellow Wallpaper" over the past two decades, a conversation that becomes increasingly more complex as critics openly debate central aspects of the story with each other. This aspect of literary criticism is not exclusive to "The Yellow Wallpaper." However, the increasingly dialogic quality of the literary criticism about Gilman's story, however, reveals that scholars are as actively engaged in reading and responding to each other's interpretations of "The Yellow Wallpaper" as they are in reading the story itself. For example, Schöpp-Schilling begins her psychological approach to the story by criticizing the work of feminist scholars Wood, Parker, and Hedges who, in her opinion, read Gilman's biography and personal motivations into the story and so fall prey to the biographical fallacy. In presenting her own feminist interpretation of the story as a woman's quest for identity within an oppressive patriarchy, Kennard draws upon three previously published feminist readings by Hedges, Kolodny, and Gilbert and Gubar. In an explanatory note, Fetterley acknowledges the influence of Kolodny's and Kennard's interpretations on her own feminist reading of the gender dynamics of the story. Although Shumaker finds the feminist approaches of Kolodny and Kennard persuasive, he attempts to broaden discussion of the story by reading it in relation to central concerns of American literature. The critical exchange becomes most striking in the debate occurring among three feminist critics that appeared in *Tulsa Studies in Women's Literature* in 1984 and 1985. Carol Neely and Karen Ford responded to Treichler's essay "Escaping the Sentence: Diagnosis and Discourse in 'The Yellow Wallpaper'" (included in this book), and Treichler, in turn, wrote a rejoinder to both critics printed alongside their pieces.[26]

As the essays in this book show, "The Yellow Wallpaper" continues to prompt an interactive and productive exchange of opinion because it seems to raise more questions than it answers. The nature of the story, the meaning of the wallpaper, the narrator's fate, her act of crawling, and whether or not the narrator has outwitted John and "got out at last" (41) emerge as some of the salient issues critics debate, often in conversation with each other. This critical edition serves as a reminder of the ways Gilman's story has been read but also as an invitation for new readings of it. The essays that follow also encourage teachers, students, and Gilman specialists to respond actively to the work of critics who read "The Yellow Wallpaper" and to entertain the questions that this complex and richly ambiguous story poses.

NOTES

1. Although the story first appeared in volume 5, no. 5 (January 1892) of *New England Magazine* (New Series) under the name of Charlotte Perkins Stetson, critics have variously noted the story's original date of publication as May 1891, January 1892, and May 1892. Critics within this collection list the date of the story's first publication most often as May 1892. The confusion surrounding the date no doubt stems from the way in which journals were bound at that time. While today we bind volumes by year, *New England Magazine* at the turn of the century did not. Volume 5 contains six volumes, beginning with September 1891 through February 1892. Had the magazine bound issues by year of publication, volume 5, no. 5 would have been May 1892. Compounding this confusion, Gilman in her autobiography reprints a letter written to *New England Magazine* that suggests that the publication date was May 1891 (*The Living of Charlotte Perkins Gilman* [New York: D. Appleton-Century Co., 1935], p. 119). (All further references will be taken from the reprint here, unless otherwise indicated, and cited in the text.) Gilman does have other inaccuracies in her autobiography. For example, she lists the year she founded a gymnasium for women as 1891 instead of 1881 (D. Appleton-Century, p. 66) and notes that the title of Howells's anthology that reprinted her story was *Masterpieces in American Fiction* instead of *Great Modern American Stories* (p. 65).

2. Small, Maynard reprinted the story as a single-volume edition in 1899. The following anthologies published between 1892 and 1972 reprint the story: William Dean Howells, ed. *The Great Modern American Stories* (New York: Boni & Liveright, 1920); Leslie Y. Rabkin, ed. *Psychopathology and Literature* (San Francisco: Chandler Publications, 1966); Elaine Gottlieb Hemley and Jack Mathews, eds. *The Writer's Signature: Idea in Story and Essay* (Glenview, Ill.: Scott, Foresman & Co., 1972); Seon Manley and Gogo Lewis, eds. *Ladies of Horror: Two Centuries of Supernatural Stories by the Gentle Sex* (New York: Lothrop, Lee, & Shepard, 1971); Gail Parker, ed., *The Oven Birds: American Women on Womanhood, 1820–1920* (Garden City, N.Y.: Anchor Books, 1972).

3. In her essay " 'Out at Last'? 'The Yellow Wallpaper' after Two Decades of Feminist Criticism" (in this volume), Elaine Hedges provides useful statistics on the story's widespread republication and recognition. She notes that nearly two decades since its 1973 reissue, "The Yellow Wallpaper" has been reprinted in England, Iceland, the Netherlands, Spain, Sweden, and Germany. Gilman's landmark story has also inspired several film versions, plays, an opera, and a "Masterpiece Theatre" adaptation, resulting in wider public recognition of Gilman and this important work.

4. The texts of essays included in this volume are reprinted as they appeared originally. Thus, references to editions of "The Yellow Wallpaper" vary as does spelling of the title. For discussion of these and other variations within criticism of the story, see "Reader, Text, and Ambiguous Referentiality in 'The Yellow Wallpaper' " by Richard Feldstein in this volume.

5. For further discussion of Gilman's literary frustrations see the autobiography.

6. This poem is reprinted as an epigram to the critical edition. It also appears in Zona Gale's Foreword to *Living*, pp. xxxiii–xxxiv.

7. Gilman was then Charlotte Perkins Stetson. She also published "The Yellow Wallpaper" under that name. For consistency, I refer to her as Gilman throughout the Introduction.

8. Thus, many critics argue that to read "The Yellow Wallpaper" requires biographical background. Within this book, see, for example, essays by Hedges (her Afterword) and Berman.

9. See Mary A. Hill, *Charlotte Perkins Gilman: The Making of a Radical Feminist 1860–1896* (Philadelphia: Temple University Press, 1980), p. 186 for Gilman's account of Stetson's reaction to "The Yellow Wallpaper."

10. H. P. Lovecraft, "The Weird Tradition in America," *Supernatural Horror in Literature* (New York: Dover Books, 1973), p. 72. Lovecraft goes on to assert that the room confined a former madwoman. Jacobus also raises this idea in her essay in this volume. In the text, Gilman reveals that the room, rather, was a former nursery, then a playroom and gymnasium.

11. The other selections in the January 1892 issue are, in order: "Phillips

Brooks," by Julius H. Ward; "The Master of Raven's Woe," a poem by Arthur L. Salmon; "Mice at Eavesdropping," by A. Rodent; "Purification," a poem by George Edgar Montgomery; "The City of St. Louis," by Prof. C. M. Woodward; "Deposed," a poem by Florence E. Pratt; "George William Curtis," a poem by John W. Chadwick; "Salem Witch," a story by Edith Mary Norris; "Author of Old Oaken Bucket," by George M. Young; "Christmas Eve," a poem by Agnes Maule Machar; "Stories of Salem Witchcraft," by Winfield S. Nevins; "Abraham Lincoln," by Phillips Brooks; " 'Tis Better To Have Loved And Lost," a poem by Philip Bourke Marston. The periodical concluded with two regular features: "Omnibus," including short one or two stanza poems by a number of male and female authors; "Editor's Table." Of the stories included in the six issues of volume 5, "Dr. Cabot's Two Brains," by Jeanette B. Perry, also illustrated by Jo H. Hatfield (pp. 344–54), comes the closest to Gilman's in its portrayal of a patronizing male physician who has "a very poor opinion of the mental ability of women" (p. 347).

12. The anonymous male physician writes: "To others, whose lives have become a struggle against an heredity of mental derangement, such literature contains deadly peril. Should such stories be allowed to pass without severest censure?" The latter is reprinted on p. 64.

13. A black-and-white decorative square motif surrounds the letter "I." Although it appears that this motif was commonly used in pictorial capital designs for *New England Magazine*, the pictorial capital introducing "The Yellow Wallpaper" proves interesting in relation to the story. The top triangle is of a dark pattern, reminiscent of the designs of the yellow wallpaper, while the bottom triangle remains white. This part of the design appears almost as a Yin-Yang symbol suggesting other dichotomies in the story and its writing. For other examples of Hatfield's capitals, see, for instance, two stories illustrated by Hatfield: "Dr. Cabot's Two Brains," by Jeanette B. Perry, *New England Magazine* 5:344–54; "The Squire's Niece Maria," by Mary F. Haynes, *New England Magazine* 6:461–71.

14. On close examination of the illustration, the lines on the windows look like bars.

15. The caption does not appear in the actual story, but it is listed in the Table of Contents.

16. In the 1989 "Masterpiece Theatre" PBS presentation of "The Yellow Wallpaper," introduced by Alistair Cooke, the narrator in the final scene is similarly shown to be a madwoman with long and mangy hair as she creeps on the floor and crawls over her husband.

17. For further discussion of Howells's brief but informative response to the story, see the Header in the Backgrounds section.

18. William Dean Howells, *Great Modern American Stories* (New York: Boni & Liveright, 1920), p. 427. In these brief biographical entries, Howells also

notes Gilman's family background, specifically that she descended from Lyman Beecher and twice married. At the end of the entry he offers a list of Gilman's fiction and nonfiction.

19. In *The Female Malady: Women, Madness, and English Culture 1830–1980* (New York: Pantheon Books, 1985), Elaine Showalter writes, "Her story is a powerful polemic against Mitchell's methods" (p. 141).

20. Mitchell was trained as a neurologist, as was Sigmund Freud. Medical practice of his time considered nerves to be the link between body and mind. Mitchell explored the relationship between psychology and physiology and believed that by healing the body he was also healing the mind. For more thorough discussion, see the Headnote to the selections from Mitchell's *Fat and Blood: And How to Make Them* in the Backgrounds section.

21. Ann J. Lane, ed., "The Fictional World of Charlotte Perkins Gilman." *Charlotte Perkins Gilman Reader* (New York: Pantheon Books, 1980), p. xviii. Lane discusses the limitations of Gilman's writing style in her introduction.

22. For a similar interpretation, see Julian Evans Fleenor, "The Gothic Prism: Charlotte Perkins Gilman's Gothic Stories and Her Autobiography," *The Female Gothic*, ed. Julian Evans Fleenor (Montreal: Eden, 1983).

23. Sandra M. Gilbert and Susan Gubar, eds., *Norton Anthology of Literature By Women: The Tradition in English* (New York: W. W. Norton & Co., 1985), p. 966.

24. For a feminist Gothic reading of "The Yellow Wallpaper," see a 1990 article by Michelle A. Masse appearing in *Signs: Journal of Women in Culture and Society* 15, no. 4: 679–709, entitled "Gothic Repetition: Husbands, Horrors, and Things That Bump in the Night."

25. In a recent essay appearing in *Feminist Studies*, Susan Lanser discusses the relationship between the color of the wallpaper and racism in turn-of-the-century America and also makes an original case regarding the reproduction and repression of racism in "The Yellow Wallpaper." See, "Feminist Criticism, 'The Yellow Wallpaper,' and the Politics of Color in America," *Feminist Studies* 15, no. 3 (1989): 415–41.

26. Whereas Treichler sets her initial discussion of "women's discourse" in the context of medical diagnosis, Neely situates hers in the discourse of midwifery and childbirth, and Ford places hers in the context of female literary narratives. Neely begins her response, entitled "Alternative Women's Discourse," by openly disagreeing with Treichler's argument that the narrator escapes the patriarchal sentence to become an involved language user who authors her own sentences; however, she concludes that " 'women's discourse' proves difficult to define because it remains so intertwined with the patriarchal discourse it tries to displace that it is difficult to be sure such a female discourse is really there. Hence Paula Treichler's interpretation of the yellow wallpaper and mine are not, perhaps, as antithetical as they might first appear to be"

(*Tulsa Studies* 4, no. 2 [1985]: 321). In " 'The Yellow Wallpaper' and Women's Discourse," Ford pursues the apparent difficulties which Treichler's analysis raises. For example, she argues that the narrator does not escape male diagnosis as Treichler suggests but becomes more of a victim of it as she involves herself more actively in the wallpaper and begins "creeping on all fours like the child John has accused her of being" (*Tulsa Studies* 4, no. 2 [1985]: 310). Tearing down the wallpaper signals a retreat from discourse and a recognition that discourse is controlled by patriarchy. Treichler concedes to the logic and persuasiveness of both interpretations in her 1985 rejoinder, entitled "The Wall Behind the Yellow Wallpaper: Response to Carol Neely and Karen Ford," (*Tulsa Studies* 4, no. 2 [1985]: 323–30). Like Neely, she does not find their views incompatible with her own and builds from their dialogue on women's discourse. Specifically, Treichler uses their comments to clarify further her thinking about language and feminist literary analysis, the problems inherent in the terms "women's discourse" and "alternative discourse," and the difficulty of defining the metaphor of the yellow wallpaper. In summarizing this entire debate between Treichler, Neely, and Ford in the introduction to his own 1989 essay, Feldstein foregrounds this earlier dialogue and keeps it ongoing.

The Yellow Wallpaper

Charlotte Perkins Gilman

It is very seldom that mere ordinary people like John and myself secure ancestral halls for the summer.

A colonial mansion, a hereditary estate, I would say a haunted house, and reach the height of romantic felicity—but that would be asking too much of fate!

Still I will proudly declare that there is something queer about it.

Else, why should it be let so cheaply? And why have stood so long untenanted?

John laughs at me, of course, but one expects that in marriage.

John is practical in the extreme. He has no patience with faith, an intense horror of superstition, and he scoffs openly at any talk of things not to be felt and seen and put down in figures.

John is a physician, and *perhaps*—(I would not say it to a living soul, of course, but this is dead paper and a great relief to my mind)—*perhaps* that is one reason I do not get well faster.

You see he does not believe I am sick!

And what can one do?

If a physician of high standing, and one's own husband, assures

---

This text is a reprint of the 1899 edition, published by Small, Maynard in Boston. The original 1892 version published in *New England Magazine* contains numerous inconsistencies in spelling. The illustrations, however, are taken from the 1892 edition.

24

friends and relatives that there is really nothing the matter with one but temporary nervous depression—a slight hysterical tendency—what is one to do?

My brother is also a physician, and also of high standing, and he says the same thing.

So I take phosphates or phospites—whichever it is, and tonics, and journeys, and air, and exercise, and am absolutely forbidden to "work" until I am well again.

Personally, I disagree with their ideas.

Personally, I believe that congenial work, with excitement and change, would do me good.

But what is one to do?

I did write for a while in spite of them; but it *does* exhaust me a good deal—having to be so sly about it, or else meet with heavy opposition.

I sometimes fancy that in my condition if I had less opposition and more society and stimulus—but John says the very worst thing I can do is to think about my condition, and I confess it always makes me feel bad.

So I will let it alone and talk about the house.

The most beautiful place! It is quite alone, standing well back from the road, quite three miles from the village. It makes me think of English places that you read about, for there are hedges and walls and gates that lock, and lots of separate little houses for the gardeners and people.

There is a *delicious* garden! I never saw such a garden—large and shady, full of box-bordered paths, and lined with long grape-covered arbors with seats under them.

There were greenhouses, too, but they are all broken now.

There was some legal trouble, I believe, something about the heirs and coheirs; anyhow, the place has been empty for years.

That spoils my ghostliness, I am afraid, but I don't care—there is something strange about the house—I can feel it.

I even said so to John one moonlight evening, but he said what I felt was a *draught*, and shut the window.

I get unreasonably angry with John sometimes. I'm sure I never used to be so sensitive. I think it is due to this nervous condition.

But John says if I feel so, I shall neglect proper self-control; so I take pains to control myself—before him, at least, and that makes me very tired.

I don't like our room a bit. I wanted one downstairs that opened on the piazza and had roses all over the window, and such pretty old-fashioned chintz hangings! but John would not hear of it.

He said there was only one window and not room for two beds, and no near room for him if he took another.

He is very careful and loving, and hardly lets me stir without special direction.

I have a schedule prescription for each hour in the day; he takes all care from me, and so I feel basely ungrateful not to value it more.

He said we came here solely on my account, that I was to have perfect rest and all the air I could get. "Your exercise depends on your strength, my dear," said he, "and your food somewhat on your appetite; but air you can absorb all the time." So we took the nursery at the top of the house.

It is a big, airy room, the whole floor nearly, with windows that look all ways, and air and sunshine galore. It was nursery first and then playroom and gymnasium, I should judge; for the windows are barred for little children, and there are rings and things in the walls.

The paint and paper look as if a boys' school had used it. It is stripped off—the paper—in great patches all around the head of my bed, about as far as I can reach, and in a great place on the other side of the room low down. I never saw a worse paper in my life.

One of those sprawling flamboyant patterns committing every artistic sin.

It is dull enough to confuse the eye in following, pronounced enough to constantly irritate and provoke study, and when you follow the lame uncertain curves for a little distance they suddenly commit suicide—plunge off at outrageous angles, destroy themselves in unheard of contradictions.

The color is repellent, almost revolting; a smouldering unclean yellow, strangely faded by the slow-turning sunlight.

It is a dull yet lurid orange in some places, a sickly sulphur tint in others.

No wonder the children hated it! I should hate it myself if I had to live in this room long.

There comes John, and I must put this away,—he hates to have me write a word.

We have been here two weeks, and I haven't felt like writing before, since that first day.

"I am sitting by the Window in this Atrocious Nursery."

I am sitting by the window now, up in this atrocious nursery, and there is nothing to hinder my writing as much as I please, save lack of strength.

John is away all day, and even some nights when his cases are serious.

I am glad my case is not serious!

But these nervous troubles are dreadfully depressing.

John does not know how much I really suffer. He knows there is no *reason* to suffer, and that satisfies him.

Of course it is only nervousness. It does weigh on me so not to do my duty in any way!

I meant to be such a help to John, such a real rest and comfort, and here I am a comparative burden already!

Nobody would believe what an effort it is to do what little I am able,—to dress and entertain, and order things.

It is fortunate Mary is so good with the baby. Such a dear baby!

And yet I *cannot* be with him, it makes me so nervous.

I suppose John never was nervous in his life. He laughs at me so about this wall-paper!

At first he meant to repaper the room, but afterwards he said that I was letting it get the better of me, and that nothing was worse for a nervous patient than to give way to such fancies.

He said that after the wall-paper was changed it would be the heavy bedstead, and then the barred windows, and then that gate at the head of the stairs, and so on.

"You know the place is doing you good," he said, "and really, dear, I don't care to renovate the house just for a three months' rental."

"Then do let us go downstairs," I said, "there are such pretty rooms there."

Then he took me in his arms and called me a blessed little goose, and said he would go down to the cellar, if I wished, and have it whitewashed into the bargain.

But he is right enough about the beds and windows and things.

It is an airy and comfortable room as any one need wish, and, of course, I would not be so silly as to make him uncomfortable just for a whim.

I'm really getting quite fond of the big room, all but that horrid paper.

Out of one window I can see the garden, those mysterious deepshaded arbors, the riotous old-fashioned flowers, and bushes and gnarly trees.

Out of another I get a lovely view of the bay and a little private wharf belonging to the estate. There is a beautiful shaded lane that runs down there from the house. I always fancy I see people walking in these numerous paths and arbors, but John has cautioned me not to give way to fancy in the least. He says that with my imaginative power and habit of story-making, a nervous weakness like mine is sure to lead to all manner of excited fancies, and that I ought to use my will and good sense to check the tendency. So I try.

I think sometimes that if I were only well enough to write a little it would relieve the press of ideas and rest me.

But I find I get pretty tired when I try.

It is so discouraging not to have any advice and companionship about my work. When I get really well, John says we will ask Cousin Henry and Julia down for a long visit; but he says he would as soon put fireworks in my pillow-case as to let me have those stimulating people about now.

I wish I could get well faster.

But I must not think about that. This paper looks to me as if it *knew* what a vicious influence it had!

There is a recurrent spot where the pattern lolls like a broken neck and two bulbous eyes stare at you upside down.

I get positively angry with the impertinence of it and the everlasting-ness. Up and down and sideways they crawl, and those absurd, unblinking eyes are everywhere. There is one place where two breaths didn't match, and the eyes go all up and down the line, one a little higher than the other.

I never saw so much expression in an inanimate thing before, and we all know how much expression they have! I used to lie awake as a child and get more entertainment and terror out of blank walls and plain furniture than most children could find in a toy-store.

I remember what a kindly wink the knobs of our big, old bureau used to have, and there was one chair that always seemed like a strong friend.

I used to feel that if any of the other things looked too fierce I could always hop into that chair and be safe.

The furniture in this room is no worse than inharmonious, however, for we had to bring it all from downstairs. I suppose when this was used as a playroom they had to take the nursery things out, and no wonder! I never saw such ravages as the children have made here.

The wall-paper, as I said before, is torn off in spots, and it sticketh closer than a brother—they must have had perseverance as well as hatred.

Then the floor is scratched and gouged and splintered, the plaster itself is dug out here and there, and this great heavy bed which is all we found in the room, looks as if it had been through the wars.

But I don't mind it a bit—only the paper.

There comes John's sister. Such a dear girl as she is, and so careful of me! I must not let her find me writing.

She is a perfect and enthusiastic housekeeper, and hopes for no better profession. I verily believe she thinks it is the writing which made me sick!

But I can write when she is out, and see her a long way off from these windows.

There is one that commands the road, a lovely shaded winding road, and one that just looks off over the country. A lovely country, too, full of great elms and velvet meadows.

This wall-paper has a kind of sub-pattern in a different shade, a particularly irritating one, for you can only see it in certain lights, and not clearly then.

But in the places where it isn't faded and where the sun is just so—I can see a strange, provoking, formless sort of figure, that seems to skulk about behind that silly and conspicuous front design.

There's sister on the stairs!

Well, the Fourth of July is over! The people are all gone and I am tired out. John thought it might do me good to see a little company, so we just had mother and Nellie and the children down for a week.

Of course I didn't do a thing. Jennie sees to everything now.

But it tired me all the same.

John says if I don't pick up faster he shall send me to Weir Mitchell in the fall.

But I don't want to go there at all. I had a friend who was in his hands once, and she says he is just like John and my brother, only more so!

Besides, it is such an undertaking to go so far.

I don't feel as if it was worth while to turn my hand over for anything, and I'm getting dreadfully fretful and querulous.

I cry at nothing, and cry most of the time.

Of course I don't when John is here, or anybody else, but when I am alone.

And I am alone a good deal just now. John is kept in town very often by serious cases, and Jennie is good and lets me alone when I want her to.

So I walk a little in the garden or down that lovely lane, sit on the porch under the roses, and lie down up here a good deal.

I'm getting really fond of the room in spite of the wall-paper. Perhaps *because* of the wall-paper.

It dwells in my mind so!

I lie here on this great immovable bed—it is nailed down, I believe—and follow that pattern about by the hour. It is as good as gymnastics, I assure you. I start, we'll say, at the bottom, down in the corner over there where it has not been touched, and I determine for the thousandth time that I *will* follow that pointless pattern to some sort of a conclusion.

I know a little of the principle of design, and I know this thing was not arranged on any laws of radiation, or alternation, or repetition, or symmetry, or anything else that I ever heard of.

It is repeated, of course, by the breadths, but not otherwise.

Looked at in one way each breadth stands alone, the bloated curves and flourishes—a kind of "debased Romanesque" with *delirium tremens*—go waddling up and down in isolated columns of fatuity.

But, on the other hand, they connect diagonally, and the sprawling outlines run off in great slanting waves of optic horror, like a lot of wallowing seaweeds in full chase.

The whole thing goes horizontally, too, at least it seems so, and I exhaust myself in trying to distinguish the order of its going in that direction.

They have used a horizontal breadth for a frieze, and that adds wonderfully to the confusion.

There is one end of the room where it is almost intact, and there, when the crosslights fade and the low sun shines directly upon it, I can almost fancy radiation after all,—the interminable grotesques seem to form around a common centre and rush off in headlong plunges of equal distraction.

It makes me tired to follow it. I will take a nap I guess.

I don't know why I should write this.

I don't want to.

I don't feel able.

And I know John would think it absurd. But I *must* say what I feel and think in some way—it is such a relief!

But the effort is getting to be greater than the relief.

Half the time now I am awfully lazy, and lie down ever so much.

John says I mustn't lose my strength, and has me take cod liver oil and lots of tonics and things, to say nothing of ale and wine and rare meat.

Dear John! He loves me very dearly, and hates to have me sick. I tried to have a real earnest reasonable talk with him the other day, and tell him how I wish he would let me go and make a visit to Cousin Henry and Julia.

But he said I wasn't able to go, nor able to stand it after I got there; and I did not make out a very good case for myself, for I was crying before I had finished.

It is getting to be a great effort for me to think straight. Just this nervous weakness I suppose.

And dear John gathered me up in his arms, and just carried me upstairs and laid me on the bed, and sat by me and read to me till it tired my head.

He said I was his darling and his comfort and all he had, and that I must take care of myself for his sake, and keep well.

He says no one but myself can help me out of it, that I must use my will and self-control and not let any silly fancies run away with me.

There's one comfort, the baby is well and happy, and does not have to occupy this nursery with the horrid wall-paper.

If we had not used it, that blessed child would have! What a fortunate escape! Why, I wouldn't have a child of mine, an impressionable little thing, live in such a room for worlds.

I never thought of it before, but it is lucky that John kept me here after all, I can stand it so much easier than a baby, you see.

Of course I never mention it to them any more—I am too wise,—but I keep watch of it all the same.

There are things in that paper that nobody knows but me, or ever will.

Behind that outside pattern the dim shapes get clearer every day.

It is always the same shape, only very numerous.

And it is like a woman stooping down and creeping about behind that pattern. I don't like it a bit. I wonder—I begin to think—I wish John would take me away from here!

It is so hard to talk with John about my case, because he is so wise, and because he loves me so.

But I tried it last night.

It was moonlight. The moon shines in all around just as the sun does.

I hate to see it sometimes, it creeps so slowly, and always comes in by one window or another.

John was asleep and I hated to waken him, so I kept still and watched the moonlight on that undulating wall-paper till I felt creepy.

The faint figure behind seemed to shake the pattern, just as if she wanted to get out.

I got up softly and went to feel and see if the paper *did* move, and when I came back John was awake.

"What is it, little girl?" he said. "Don't go walking about like that—you'll get cold."

I thought it was a good time to talk, so I told him that I really was not gaining here, and that I wished he would take me away.

"Why darling!" said he, "our lease will be up in three weeks, and I can't see how to leave before.

"The repairs are not done at home, and I cannot possibly leave town just now. Of course if you were in any danger, I could and would, but you really are better, dear, whether you can see it or not. I am a doctor, dear, and I know. You are gaining flesh and color, your appetite is better, I feel really much easier about you."

"I don't weigh a bit more," said I, "nor as much; and my appetite may be better in the evening when you are here, but it is worse in the morning when you are away!"

"Bless her little heart!" said he with a big hug, "she shall be as sick as she pleases! But now let's improve the shining hours by going to sleep, and talk about it in the morning!"

"And you won't go away?" I asked gloomily.

"Why, how can I, dear? It is only three weeks more and then we will take a nice little trip of a few days while Jennie is getting the house ready. Really dear you are better!"

"Better in body perhaps—" I began, and stopped short, for he sat up straight and looked at me with such a stern, reproachful look that I could not say another word.

"My darling," said he, "I beg of you, for my sake and for our child's sake, as well as for your own, that you will never for one instant let that idea enter your mind! There is nothing so dangerous, so fascinating, to a temperament like yours. It is a false and foolish fancy. Can you not trust me as a physician when I tell you so?"

So of course I said no more on that score, and we went to sleep before long. He thought I was asleep first, but I wasn't, and lay there for hours trying to decide whether that front pattern and the back pattern really did move together or separately.

On a pattern like this, by daylight, there is a lack of sequence, a defiance of law, that is a constant irritant to a normal mind.

The color is hideous enough, and unreliable enough, and infuriating enough, but the pattern is torturing.

You think you have mastered it, but just as you get well underway in following, it turns a back-somersault and there you are. It slaps you in the face, knocks you down, and tramples upon you. It is like a bad dream.

The outside pattern is a florid arabesque, reminding one of a fungus. If you can imagine a toadstool in joints, an interminable string of toadstools, budding and sprouting in endless convolutions—why, that is something like it.

That is, sometimes!

There is one marked peculiarity about this paper, a thing nobody seems to notice but myself, and that is that it changes as the light changes.

When the sun shoots in through the east window—I always watch for that first long, straight ray—it changes so quickly that I never can quite believe it.

That is why I watch it always.

By moonlight—the moon shines in all night when there is a moon—I wouldn't know it was the same paper.

At night in any kind of light, in twilight, candle light, lamplight, and worst of all by moonlight, it becomes bars! The outside pattern I mean, and the woman behind it is as plain as can be.

I didn't realize for a long time what the thing was that showed behind, that dim sub-pattern, but now I am quite sure it is a woman.

By daylight she is subdued, quiet. I fancy it is the pattern that keeps her so still. It is so puzzling. It keeps me quiet by the hour.

I lie down ever so much now. John says it is good for me, and to sleep all I can.

Indeed he started the habit by making me lie down for an hour after each meal.

It is a very bad habit I am convinced, for you see I don't sleep.

And that cultivates deceit, for I don't tell them I'm awake – O no!

The fact is I am getting a little afraid of John.

He seems very queer sometimes, and even Jennie has an inexplicable look.

It strikes me occasionally, just as a scientific hypothesis, – that perhaps it is the paper!

I have watched John when he did not know I was looking, and come into the room suddenly on the most innocent excuses, and I've caught him several times *looking at the paper!* And Jennie too. I caught Jennie with her hand on it once.

She didn't know I was in the room, and when I asked her in a quiet, a very quiet voice, with the most restrained manner possible, what she was doing with the paper – she turned around as if she had been caught stealing, and looked quite angry – asked me why I should frighten her so!

Then she said that the paper stained everything it touched, that she had found yellow smooches on all my clothes and John's, and she wished we would be more careful!

Did not that sound innocent? But I know she was studying that pattern, and I am determined that nobody shall find it out but myself!

Life is very much more exciting now than it used to be. You see I have something more to expect, to look forward to, to watch. I really do eat better, and am more quiet than I was.

John is so pleased to see me improve! He laughed a little the other day, and said I seemed to be flourishing in spite of my wall-paper.

I turned it off with a laugh. I had no intention of telling him it was *because* of the wall-paper – he would make fun of me. He might even want to take me away.

I don't want to leave now until I have found it out. There is a week more, and I think that will be enough.

"She didn't know I was in the Room."

I'm feeling ever so much better! I don't sleep much at night, for it is so interesting to watch developments; but I sleep a good deal in the daytime.

In the daytime it is tiresome and perplexing.

There are always new shoots on the fungus, and new shades of yellow all over it. I cannot keep count of them, though I have tried conscientiously.

It is the strangest yellow, that wall-paper! It makes me think of all the yellow things I ever saw—not beautiful ones like buttercups, but old foul, bad yellow things.

But there is something else about that paper—the smell! I noticed it the moment we came into the room, but with so much air and sun it was not bad. Now we have had a week of fog and rain, and whether the windows are open or not, the smell is here.

It creeps all over the house.

I find it hovering in the dining-room, skulking in the parlor, hiding in the hall, lying in wait for me on the stairs.

It gets into my hair.

Even when I go to ride, if I turn my head suddenly and surprise it— there is that smell!

Such a peculiar odor, too! I have spent hours in trying to analyze it, to find what it smelled like.

It is not bad—at first, and very gentle, but quite the subtlest, most enduring odor I ever met.

In this damp weather it is awful, I wake up in the night and find it hanging over me.

It used to disturb me at first. I thought seriously of burning the house—to reach the smell.

But now I am used to it. The only thing I can think of that it is like is the *color* of the paper! A yellow smell.

There is a very funny mark on this wall, low down, near the mop-board. A streak that runs round the room. It goes behind every piece of furniture, except the bed, a long, straight, even *smooch*, as if it had been rubbed over and over.

I wonder how it was done and who did it, and what they did it for. Round and round and round—round and round and round—it makes me dizzy!

I really have discovered something at last.

Through watching so much at night, when it changes so, I have finally found out.

The front pattern *does* move—and no wonder! The woman behind shakes it!

Sometimes I think there are a great many women behind, and sometimes only one, and she crawls around fast, and her crawling shakes it all over.

Then in the very bright spots she keeps still, and in the very shady spots she just takes hold of the bars and shakes them hard.

And she is all the time trying to climb through. But nobody could climb through that pattern—it strangles so; I think that is why it has so many heads.

They get through, and then the pattern strangles them off and turns them upside down, and makes their eyes white!

If those heads were covered or taken off it would not be half so bad.

I think that woman gets out in the daytime!

And I'll tell you why—privately—I've seen her!

I can see her out of every one of my windows!

It is the same woman, I know, for she is always creeping, and most women do not creep by daylight.*

I see her on that long road under the trees, creeping along, and when a carriage comes she hides under the blackberry vines.

I don't blame her a bit. It must be very humiliating to be caught creeping by daylight!

I always lock the door when I creep by daylight. I can't do it at night, for I know John would suspect something at once.

And John is so queer now, that I don't want to irritate him. I wish he would take another room! Besides, I don't want anybody to get that woman out at night but myself.

I often wonder if I could see her out of all the windows at once.

But, turn as fast as I can, I can only see out of one at one time.

And though I always see her, she *may* be able to creep faster than I can turn!

---

*Here, the 1892 edition of "The Yellow Wallpaper" includes the following passage:
I see her in that long shaded lane, creeping up and down. I see her in those dark grape arbors, creeping all around the garden (*New England Magazine* 5, no. 5 (1892): 654).

I have watched her sometimes away off in the open country, creeping as fast as a cloud shadow in a high wind.

If only that top pattern could be gotten off from the under one! I mean to try it, little by little.

I have found out another funny thing, but I shan't tell it this time! It does not do to trust people too much.

There are only two more days to get this paper off, and I believe John is beginning to notice. I don't like the look in his eyes.

And I heard him ask Jennie a lot of professional questions about me. She had a very good report to give.

She said I slept a good deal in the daytime.

John knows I don't sleep very well at night, for all I'm so quiet!

He asked me all sorts of questions, too, and pretended to be very loving and kind.

As if I couldn't see through him!

Still, I don't wonder he acts so, sleeping under this paper for three months.

It only interests me, but I feel sure John and Jennie are secretly affected by it.

Hurrah! This is the last day, but it is enough. John to stay in town over night, and won't be out until this evening.

Jennie wanted to sleep with me—the sly thing! but I told her I should undoubtedly rest better for a night all alone.

That was clever, for really I wasn't alone a bit! As soon as it was moonlight and that poor thing began to crawl and shake the pattern, I got up and ran to help her.

I pulled and she shook, I shook and she pulled, and before morning we had peeled off yards of that paper.

A strip about as high as my head and half around the room.

And then when the sun came and that awful pattern began to laugh at me, I declared I would finish it to-day!

We go away to-morrow, and they are moving all my furniture down again to leave things as they were before.

Jennie looked at the wall in amazement, but I told her merrily that I did it out of pure spite at the vicious thing.

She laughed and said she wouldn't mind doing it herself, but I must not get tired.

How she betrayed herself that time!

But I am here, and no person touches this paper but me,—not *alive*!

She tried to get me out of the room—it was too patent! But I said it was so quiet and empty and clean now that I believed I would lie down again and sleep all I could; and not to wake me even for dinner—I would call when I woke.

So now she is gone, and the servants are gone, and the things are gone, and there is nothing left but that great bedstead nailed down, with the canvas mattress we found on it.

We shall sleep downstairs to-night, and take the boat home to-morrow.

I quite enjoy the room, now it is bare again.

How those children did tear about here!

This bedstead is fairly gnawed!

But I must get to work.

I have locked the door and thrown the key down into the front path.

I don't want to go out, and I don't want to have anybody come in, till John comes.

I want to astonish him.

I've got a rope up here that even Jennie did not find. If that woman does get out, and tries to get away, I can tie her!

But I forgot I could not reach far without anything to stand on!

This bed will *not* move!

I tried to lift and push it until I was lame, and then I got so angry I bit off a little piece at one corner—but it hurt my teeth.

Then I peeled off all the paper I could reach standing on the floor. It sticks horribly and the pattern just enjoys it! All those strangled heads and bulbous eyes and waddling fungus growths just shriek with derision!

I am getting angry enough to do something desperate. To jump out of the window would be admirable exercise, but the bars are too strong even to try.

Besides I wouldn't do it. Of course not. I know well enough that a step like that is improper and might be misconstrued.

I don't like to *look* out of the windows even—there are so many of those creeping women, and they creep so fast.

I wonder if they all come out of that wall-paper as I did?

But I am securely fastened now by my well-hidden rope—you don't get *me* out in the road there!

I suppose I shall have to get back behind the pattern when it comes night, and that is hard!

It is so pleasant to be out in this great room and creep around as I please!

I don't want to go outside. I won't, even if Jennie asks me to.

For outside you have to creep on the ground, and everything is green instead of yellow.

But here I can creep smoothly on the floor, and my shoulder just fits in that long smooch around the wall, so I cannot lose my way.

Why there's John at the door!

It is no use, young man, you can't open it!

How he does call and pound!

Now he's crying for an axe.

It would be a shame to break down that beautiful door!

"John dear!" said I in the gentlest voice, "the key is down by the front steps, under a plantain leaf!"

That silenced him for a few moments.

Then he said—very quietly indeed, "Open the door, my darling!"

"I can't," said I. "The key is down by the front door under a plantain leaf!"

And then I said it again, several times, very gently and slowly, and said it so often that he had to go and see, and he got it of course, and came in. He stopped short by the door.

"What is the matter?" he cried. "For God's sake, what are you doing!"

I kept on creeping just the same, but I looked at him over my shoulder.

"I've got out at last," said I, "in spite of you and Jane. And I've pulled off most of the paper, so you can't put me back!"

Now why should that man have fainted? But he did, and right across my path by the wall, so that I had to creep over him every time!

Backgrounds

From *Fat and Blood:*
And How to Make Them

S. Weir Mitchell

IN 1887 THE TWENTY-SIX YEAR OLD Charlotte Perkins Gilman (then Stetson) traveled to Dr. S. Weir Mitchell's Philadelphia sanitarium to undergo a one-month rest cure treatment for "nervous prostration" or "neurasthenia," a breakdown of the nervous system. Following the birth of her daughter, she had become depressed, spiritless, weak, and hysterical. This nervous condition was not unique to Gilman or the female population; men also suffered from it, as did Mitchell himself. Because of the strains on the American woman from the rigid ideals of Victorian femininity, debilitating nervous disorders were more common among upper- and middle-class women than men. The causes of neurasthenia were thought to be gender-specific: men from overwork and women from too much social activity, sustained or severe domestic trials (such as nursing a sick family member), or strain commonly brought on by pursuing higher education.

Mitchell was trained as a neurologist but earned special recognition as a nerve specialist for women. He treated prominent American women intellectuals including Jane Addams, Edith Wharton, and Gilman. Neurology in the mid-to-late nineteenth century explored the relationship between psychology and physiology. Nerves were considered the link between the mind and the body; the rest cure aimed to heal the mind by healing the physical symptoms of depression. Mitchell developed the rest cure by combining a number of accepted medical practices. His rest cure, in accordance with the most advanced neurological thinking of his day, earned him international acclaim; in fact, Sigmund Freud, who was also trained as a neurologist, favorably reviewed *Fat and Blood* (1877), approved of Mitchell's rest cure, and even adapted and used it for a period of time. Introduced in England in the

45

1880s, the rest cure was used to treat well-known figures such as Alice James and Virginia Woolf (see Elaine Showalter, *The Female Malady: Women, Madness, and English Culture* [New York: Pantheon Books, 1985]).

Written for the less experienced physician, *Fat and Blood* offers a comprehensive account of reviving "chiefly women of the class well known to every physician, – nervous women, who as a rule are thin, and lack blood" (J. B. Lippincott, 9). The book devotes a chapter to each of the five components of Mitchell's rest cure: rest (typically for 6 to 8 weeks the patient remained in bed and for prescribed periods was not permitted to sit up, sew, feed herself, read, or write), seclusion (from familiar surroundings and family to curtail harmful, "cherished" habits), diet (excessive feeding, beginning with milk, to improve the color and number of red corpuscles of the blood and to increase body volume and energy), massage, and electricity (to guard against muscular atrophy incurred by too much bed rest). The first selection from "Fat in Its Clinical Relations," a representative portrait of a nervous female patient, reveals Mitchell's patronizing manner toward women. The second selection from "Rest," which Mitchell revised for his *Doctor and Patient* (1887), lends insight into why the rest cure proved more debilitating to creative, intellectual women like Gilman than the actual nervous condition.

Preferable to the less expensive medical alternatives for nervous exhaustion – leeches and drugs – the rest cure had merits: similar to the water cure in vogue in nineteenth-century America and Europe, Mitchell's rest cure removed the individual from the tensions of his or her world and offered a sanctuary for rest. Many of the hundreds of women who traveled to Mitchell's sanitarium felt relieved that their complaints had been both validated and treated, and they left satisfied. *Fat and Blood* concludes with case histories of female patients documenting Mitchell's success. Nonetheless, to many women, including Gilman, Mitchell's rest cure resembled a form of punitive rest. These selections suggest that the treatment fictionalized in "The Yellow Wallpaper" was severe. More than in her autobiography, the language and imagery of "The Yellow Wallpaper" reveal the lasting negative impact of the author's treatment by S. Weir Mitchell.

FAT IN ITS CLINICAL RELATIONS

I see every week — almost every day — women who when asked what is
the matter reply, "Oh, I have nervous exhaustion." When further questioned, they answer that everything tires them. Now, it is vain to speak
of all of these cases as hysterical, or, as Paget has done, as mimetic. It is
quite sure that in the graver examples exercise quickens the pulse curiously, the tire shows in the face, or sometimes diarrhœa or nausea
follows exertion, and though while under excitement or in the presence
of some dominant motive they can do a good deal, the exhaustion
which ensues is in proportion to the exercise used.

I have rarely seen such a case which was not more or less lacking in
color and which had not lost flesh; the exceptions being those trouble-
some cases of fat anæmic people which I shall by and by speak of more
fully.

Perhaps a full sketch of one of these cases will be better than any list
of symptoms: A woman, most often between twenty and thirty, under-
goes a season of trial or encounters some prolonged strain. She undertakes the hard task of nursing a relative, and goes through this severe
duty with the addition of emotional excitement, swayed by hopes and
fears, and forgetful of self and of what every one needs in the way of air
and food and change when attempting this most trying task; or possibly
it is mere physical strain, such as teaching. In another set of cases an
illness is the cause, and she never rallies entirely, or else some local
uterine trouble starts the mischief, and although this is cured the doctor
wonders that his patient does not get fat and ruddy again.

But no matter how it comes about, the woman grows pale and thin,
eats little, or if she eats does not profit by it. Everything wearies her, — to
sew, to write, to read, to walk, — and by and by the sofa or the bed is her
only comfort. Every effort is paid for dearly, and she describes herself as
aching and sore, as sleeping ill, and as needing constant stimulus and
endless tonics. Then comes the mischievous rôle of bromides, opium,
chloral, and brandy. If the case did not begin with uterine troubles they
soon appear, and are usually treated in vain if the general means
employed to build up the bodily health fail, as in many of these cases

---

Selections from Chapter 2, "Fat in Its Clinical Relations" (28–30 and 34–35) and Chapter 5, "Rest" (42–46).

they do fail. The same remark applies to the dyspepsias and constipation which further annoy the patient and embarrass the treatment. If such a person is emotional she does not fail to become more so, and even the firmest women lose self-control at last under incessant feebleness. Nor is this less true of men, and I have many a time seen soldiers who had ridden boldly with Sheridan or fought gallantly with Grant become, under the influence of painful nerve-wounds, as irritable and hysterically emotional as the veriest girl. If no rescue comes, the fate of women thus disordered is at last the bed. . . .

The treatment I am about to describe consists in seclusion, certain forms of diet, rest in bed, massage (or manipulation), and electricity; and I desire to insist anew on the fact that it is the use of these means together that is wanted. The necessities of my subject will of course oblige me to treat of each of them in a separate chapter.

REST

As a rule, no harm is done by rest, even in such people as give us doubts about whether it is or is not well for them to exert themselves. There are plenty of these women who are just well enough to make it likely that if they had motive enough for exertion to cause them to forget themselves they would find it useful. In the doubt I am rather given to insisting on rest, but the rest I like for them is not at all their notion of rest. To lie abed half the day, and sew a little and read a little, and be interesting and excite sympathy, is all very well, but when they are bidden to stay in bed a month, and neither to read, write, nor sew, and to have one nurse,—who is not a relative,—then rest becomes for some women a rather bitter medicine, and they are glad enough to accept the order to rise and go about when the doctor issues a mandate which has become pleasantly welcome and eagerly looked for. I do not think it easy to make a mistake in this matter unless the woman takes with morbid delight to the system of enforced rest, and unless the doctor is a person of feeble will. I have never met myself with any serious trouble about getting out of bed any woman for whom I thought rest needful, but it has happened to others, and the man who resolves to send any nervous woman to bed must be quite sure that she will obey him when the time comes for her to get up.

I have, of course, made use of every grade of rest for my patients, from insisting upon repose on a lounge for some hours a day up to entire rest in bed. In carrying out my general plan of treatment it is my habit to ask the patient to remain in bed from six weeks to two months. At first, and in some cases for four or five weeks, I do not permit the patient to sit up or to sew or write or read. The only action allowed is that needed to clean the teeth. In some instances I have not permitted the patient to turn over without aid, and this I have done because sometimes I think no motion desirable, and because sometimes the moral influence of absolute repose is of use. In such cases I arrange to have the bowels and water passed while lying down, and the patient is lifted on to a lounge at bedtime and sponged, and then lifted back again into the newly-made bed. In all cases of weakness, treated by rest, I insist on the patient being fed by the nurse, and, when well enough to sit up in bed, I insist that the meats shall be cut up, so as to make it easier for the patient to feed herself.

In many cases I allow the patient to sit up in order to obey the calls of nature, but I am always careful to have the bowels kept reasonably free from costiveness, knowing well how such a state and the efforts it gives rise to enfeeble a sick person.

Usually, after a fortnight I permit the patient to be read to, — one to three hours a day, — but I am daily amazed to see how kindly nervous and anæmic women take to this absolute rest, and how little they complain of its monotony. In fact, the use of massage and the battery, with the frequent comings of the nurse with food and the doctor's visits, seem so to fill up the day as to make the treatment less tiresome than might be supposed. And, besides this, the sense of comfort which is apt to come about the fifth or sixth day, — the feeling of ease, and the ready capacity to digest food, and the growing hope of final cure, fed as it is by present relief, — all conspire to make most patients contented and tractable.

The moral uses of enforced rest are readily estimated. From a restless life of irregular hours, and probably endless drugging, from hurtful sympathy and over-zealous care, the patient passes to an atmosphere of quiet, to order and control, to the system and care of a thorough nurse, to an absence of drugs, and to simple diet. The result is always at first, whatever it may be afterwards, a sense of relief, and a remarkable and often a quite abrupt disappearance of many of the nervous symptoms with which we are all of us only too sadly familiar.

All the moral uses of rest and isolation and change of habits are not obtained by merely insisting on the physical conditions needed to effect these ends. If the physician has the force of character required to secure the confidence and respect of his patients he has also much more in his power, and should have the tact to seize the proper occasions to direct the thoughts of his patients to the lapse from duties to others, and to the selfishness which a life of invalidism is apt to bring about. Such moral medication belongs to the higher sphere of the doctor's duties, and if he means to cure his patient permanently, he cannot afford to neglect them. Above all, let him be careful that the masseuse and the nurse do not talk of the patient's ills, and let him by degrees teach the sick person how very essential it is to speak of her aches and pains to no one but himself.

Why I Wrote
"The Yellow Wallpaper"

Charlotte Perkins Gilman

CRITICS WHO READ GILMAN'S LIFE into her story commonly cite this brief but forceful one-page magazine article appearing in *Forerunner* in 1913. Gilman explains the autobiographical roots of "The Yellow Wallpaper" and her personal intentions for writing the story of a woman's breakdown, which she develops further in Chapter 8 of her autobiography, entitled "The Breakdown" (see 58–63).* In the *Forerunner* article, Gilman proudly cites the example of having "saved one woman from a similar fate" (53). However, in this article she glosses over the indirect manner in which she learned "the best result" (53) of writing her story: that Mitchell (to whom she sent a copy of the story) altered his treatment of neurasthenia after reading "The Yellow Wallpaper."

Gilman founded the *Forerunner* in 1909 because she felt constrained by the limited market for expressing "important truths, needed yet unpopular" (*Living*, D. Appleton-Century, 304). In her words, "If the editors and publishers will not bring out my work, I will" (*Living*, D. Appleton-Century, 304). Gilman was the sole author of the thirty-two page monthly magazine during its seven-year run (1909–16). Different from other one-person magazines, the *Forerunner* included a range of writings: editorials, articles, book reviews, comments and observations on current events, advertisements, poems, humor, short stories, and installments of serials. In addition to numerous short stories (nine of which have been reprinted in *The Charlotte Perkins Gilman Reader*, ed. Ann Lane [New

---

*Citations in headnotes to material included in this volume give page numbers in this volume, unless otherwise indicated.

51

neurasthenia- nervous exhaustion, nervous breakdown

York: Pantheon Books, 1980]), she brought out two full-length books in serial form each year, typically one fiction and one nonfiction. The magazine has a marked socialist slant and reflects Gilman's commitment to the rights of women. Although the circulation was small (Gilman had to lecture and publish outside the magazine to meet expenses), subscribers came from Europe, India, and Australia as well as across the United States. The *Forerunner* remains available today; in 1968 Greenwood Reprinting Corporation reissued the entire run of the *Forerunner* as part of their series of radical United States periodicals.

M any and many a reader has asked that. When the story first came out, in the *New England Magazine* about 1891, a Boston physician made protest in *The Transcript*. Such a story ought not to be written, he said; it was enough to drive anyone mad to read it.

Another physician, in Kansas I think, wrote to say that it was the best description of incipient insanity he had ever seen, and—begging my pardon—had I been there?

Now the story of the story is this:

For many years I suffered from a severe and continuous nervous breakdown tending to melancholia—and beyond. During about the third year of this trouble I went, in devout faith and some faint stir of hope, to a noted specialist in nervous diseases, the best known in the country. This wise man put me to bed and applied the rest cure, to which a still good physique responded so promptly that he concluded there was nothing much the matter with me, and sent me home with solemn advice to "live as domestic a life as far as possible," to "have but two hours' intellectual life a day," and "never to touch pen, brush or pencil again as long as I lived." This was in 1887.

I went home and obeyed those directions for some three months, and came so near the border line of utter mental ruin that I could see over.

Then, using the remnants of intelligence that remained, and helped by a wise friend, I cast the noted specialist's advice to the winds and went to work again—work, the normal life of every human being; work, in which is joy and growth and service, without which one is a pauper and a parasite; ultimately recovering some measure of power.

Being naturally moved to rejoicing by this narrow escape, I wrote *The Yellow Wallpaper*, with its embellishments and additions to carry out the ideal (I never had hallucinations or objections to my mural decorations) and sent a copy to the physician who so nearly drove me mad. He never acknowledged it.

The little book is valued by alienists and as a good specimen of one kind of literature. It has to my knowledge saved one woman from a similar fate—so terrifying her family that they let her out into normal activity and she recovered.

But the best result is this. Many years later I was told that the great specialist had admitted to friends of his that he had altered his treatment of neurasthenia since reading *The Yellow Wallpaper*.

It was not intended to drive people crazy, but to save people from being driven crazy, and it worked.

From "A Reminiscent Introduction"

William Dean Howells

BEST KNOWN AS THE AUTHOR of *The Rise of Silas Lapham* (1885), William Dean Howells was an influential, liberal editor of the prestigious *Atlantic Monthly* (1871–81) who later wrote the "Easy Chair" column for *Harper's Weekly*. A dominant figure in the history of American literature, Howells is often referred to as the forefather of American Realism, a genre that challenged romantic literary conventions. Howells's reputation, which declined in the 1920s and 1930s, has been restored; nonetheless, in the field of late nineteenth-century American literature today, Howells is eclipsed by his famous literary friends, Mark Twain and Henry James, whose works he promoted. James praised Howells for "painting what he sees" ("William Dean Howells," *Harper's Weekly* 30 [June 19, 1886]). Even his aesthetic adversary Ambrose Bierce respected his literary accomplishments when he exclaimed, "The Master of this detestable school of literature [American Realism] is Mr. Howells" ("Sharp Criticism of Mr. Howells," *New York Times*, May 23, 1892).

Gilman's relationship with Howells began in June 1890. "That was a joy indeed" (*Living*, D. Appleton-Century, 113), Gilman proclaimed in her autobiography when she received a letter from the prominent novelist, critic, and editor. Although Gilman confided in letters to her close friend Martha Luther Lane that Howells "never was a favorite of mine; His work . . . seems to me of small artistic value" (June 7, 1890; July 27, 1890), she recognized the importance of his support: "There was no man in the country whose good opinion I would rather have had. I felt like a real 'author' at last" (*Living*, D. Appleton-Century, 113). Howells, who described Gilman as "The best brains and the best profile of any woman in America,"[1] promoted Gilman's work throughout her creative life. He recommended "The Yellow Wallpaper" to his

54

friend Horace Scudder, then editor of the *Atlantic Monthly*. Howells reissued it as one of twenty-four stories in his 1920 anthology, *The Great Modern American Stories*. It appears alongside the stories of leading American authors: Edith Wharton's "The Mission of Jane," Sarah Orne Jewett's "The Courting of Sister Wisby," Theodore Dreiser's "The Lost Phoebe," Henry James's "A Passionate Pilgrim," and Mark Twain's "The Celebrated Jumping Frog of Calaveras County." Howells's placement of "The Yellow Wallpaper" alongside the stories of Gilman's contemporaries, some of whom remain well known today, paved the way for the story's acceptance into the current canon of American literature.

Howells's brief introductory remarks appear on the first page of his eight-page "A Reminiscent Introduction." Howells offers the original response to "The Yellow Wallpaper," considering it to be a horror tale of a wife and mother's mental derangement. He "shiver[s]" over the chilling story "to freeze our young blood" (55) and reiterates Horace Scudder's now famous response that "it was so terribly good that it ought never to be printed" (55). His reservations in reissuing "The Yellow Wallpaper" are often remarked in criticism, but his self-congratulatory tone and belief that he "corrupted the editor of *The New England Magazine* into publishing it" (55) have been overlooked. Howells's account contradicts Gilman's that her agent Henry Austin placed her story in *New England Magazine*.

Critics have speculated that more than literary and personal admiration for Gilman led Howells to anthologize her story. Howells's daughter Winifred was a patient of S. Weir Mitchell, Howells's close personal friend. Winifred suffered and died from nervous prostration. Howells's doubts about the severity of Mitchell's rest cure treatment expressed in a letter to Mark Twain suggest a personal investment in his support of "The Yellow Wallpaper."

I t wanted at least two generations to freeze our young blood with Mrs. Perkins Gilman's story of *The Yellow Wall Paper*, which Horace Scudder (then of *The Atlantic*) said in refusing it that it was so terribly good that it ought never to be printed. But terrible and too wholly dire as it was, I could not rest until I had corrupted the editor of *The New England Magazine* into publishing it. Now that I have got it into my collection here, I shiver over it as much as I did when I first read it in manuscript, though I agree with the editor of *The Atlantic* of the time that it was too terribly good to be printed.

NOTE

1. Ann J. Lane, *To Herland and Beyond: The Life and Work of Charlotte Perkins Gilman* (New York: Pantheon, 1990), p. 7.

From *The Living of Charlotte Perkins Gilman: An Autobiography*

Charlotte Perkins Gilman

THE PROMINENT AUTHOR Zona Gale fittingly begins her foreword to the 1935 edition of Gilman's autobiography with this tribute: "In the long, slow development of our social consciousness, Charlotte Perkins Gilman has flamed like a torch. This seems the right simile, for she has burned her way about the world, one message blazing from her spoken and written words, and from her living: 'Life is growth'" (D. Appleton-Century, xiii). The autobiography blazes with a rich self-portrait of this strong, self-reliant feminist lecturer and writer. Gilman describes her difficult childhood, her breakdown, her journey to Pasadena to begin a new life with her daughter Katharine, her poverty, her literary accomplishments (such as her European reception), and her literary and personal struggles (particularly the agonizing scandal caused by her decision to let Katharine live with her first husband Walter Stetson following his remarriage to Gilman's lifelong friend, Grace Channing). The autobiography provides ample information for the interested student, specialist, and biographer of Gilman, but a sense of reticence punctuates her work. In focusing on the onset of her depression, for instance, she paints a glowing picture of her devoted husband and does not entertain the possible social causes for her nervous breakdown following her marriage to Walter Stetson, whom her biographer Ann Lane describes as a prototype for John in "The Yellow Wallpaper."

Although her fiction may prove more personally revealing than her autobiography, these selections from *The Living of Charlotte Perkins Gilman* illuminate the truthfulness of "The Yellow Wallpaper." In "The Breakdown" Gilman frankly records that a trip west—independent of husband and child—revealed "a worse horror than before, for now I saw the stark fact—that I was well while away and sick, while at home" (62). She elected to undergo Mitchell's rest cure treatment, which she describes in these pages, noting Mitchell's cool reception, his prejudice against her famous Beecher relatives, and his opinion that Gilman's involvement in her own case history "proved self-conceit" (62).

In the selection from "Pasadena" Gilman reveals her personal reasons for writing the story of a woman's breakdown: "to reach Dr. S. Weir Mitchell, and convince him of the error of his ways" (65). These passages overlap with her 1913 *Forerunner* article although her autobiography proves more comprehensive. In this chapter she describes in more detail the secondhand nature of her discovery that Mitchell changed his treatment for nervous prostration after reading the story she sent him. Nonetheless, she triumphantly concludes, "If that is a fact, I have not lived in vain" (65). In these passages from her autobiography Gilman includes responses to the story and her rejection letter from the *Atlantic Monthly* editor, Horace Scudder, who said, "I could not forgive myself if I made others as miserable as I have made myself!" (63). These references and Gilman's personal motivations emerge as central points in biographical criticism.

Gilman worked on her autobiography at two different times—in the mid-1920s at age sixty-six and in the mid-1930s at age seventy-five, the year of her death. Before she ended her long suffering from cancer by taking chloroform, Gilman used her remaining energy to complete her autobiography. She made the final revisions of the manuscript, proofread it, and chose the cover and photographic illustrations. Her eminently readable autobiography first appeared posthumously on October 4, 1935. Reissued in 1972 (Arno Press), in 1975 (Harper & Row), and most recently in 1991 (University of Wisconsin), the autobiography is now an essential part of Gilman's literary legacy.

THE BREAKDOWN

In those days a new disease had dawned on the medical horizon. It was called "nervous prostration." No one knew much about it, and there were many who openly scoffed, saying it was only a new name for laziness. To be recognizably ill one must be confined to one's bed, and preferably in pain.

That a heretofore markedly vigorous young woman, with every comfort about her, should collapse in this lamentable manner was inexplicable. "You should use your will," said earnest friends. I had used it, hard and long, perhaps too hard and too long; at any rate it wouldn't work now.

"Force some happiness into your life," said one sympathizer. "Take an agreeable book to bed with you, occupy your mind with pleasant things." She did not realize that I was unable to read, and that my mind was exclusively occupied with unpleasant things. This disorder involved a growing melancholia, and that, as those know who have tasted it, consists of every painful mental sensation, shame, fear, remorse, a blind oppressive confusion, utter weakness, a steady brainache that fills the conscious mind with crowding images of distress.

The misery is doubtless as physical as a toothache, but a brain, of its own nature, gropes for reasons for its misery. Feeling the sensation fear, the mind suggests every possible calamity; the sensation shame— remorse—and one remembers every mistake and misdeeds of a lifetime, and grovels to the earth in abasement.

"If you would get up and do something you would feel better," said my mother. I rose drearily, and essayed to brush up the floor a little, with a dustpan and small whiskbroom, but soon dropped those implements exhausted, and wept again in helpless shame.

I, the ceaselessly industrious, could do no work of any kind. I was so weak that the knife and fork sank from my hands—too tired to eat. I could not read nor write nor paint nor sew nor talk nor listen to talking, nor anything. I lay on that lounge and wept all day. The tears ran down into my ears on either side. I went to bed crying, woke in the night crying, sat on the edge of the bed in the morning and cried—from sheer continuous pain. Not physical, the doctors examined me and found nothing the matter.

The only physical pain I ever knew, besides dentistry and one sore finger, was having the baby, and I would rather have had a baby every week than suffer as I suffered in my mind. A constant dragging weariness miles below zero. Absolute incapacity. Absolute misery. To the spirit it was as if one were an armless, legless, eyeless voiceless cripple. Prominent among the tumbling suggestions of a suffering brain was the thought, "You did it yourself! You did it yourself! You had health and strength and hope and glorious work before you—and you threw it all away. You were called to serve humanity, and you cannot serve yourself. No good as a wife, no good as a mother, no good at anything. And you did it yourself!" . . .

The baby? I nursed her for five months. I would hold her close—that lovely child!—and instead of love and happiness, feel only pain. The tears ran down on my breast. . . . Nothing was more utterly bitter than this, that even motherhood brought no joy.

The doctor said I must wean her, and go away, for a change. So she was duly weaned and throve finely on Mellins' Food, drinking eagerly from the cup—no bottle needed. With mother there and the excellent maid I was free to go.

Those always kind friends, the Channings, had gone to Pasadena to live, and invited me to spend the winter with them. Feeble and hopeless I set forth, armed with tonics and sedatives, to cross the continent. From the moment the wheels began to turn, the train to move, I felt better. A visit to my brother in Utah broke the journey.

He had gone west as a boy of nineteen, working as a surveyor in Nevada, and later, finding Utah quite a heaven after Nevada, had settled in Ogden and married there. At one time he was City Engineer. His wife knew of my coming, but it was to be a surprise to my brother, and succeeded.

He came to the door in his shirt-sleeves, as was the local custom, holding a lamp in his hand. There stood the sister he had not seen in eight years, calmly smiling.

"Good evening," said I with equanimity. This he repeated, nodding his head fatuously, "Good evening! Good evening! Good evening!" It was a complete success.

As I still bore a grudge for the teasing which had embittered my childish years, I enjoyed this little joke, already feeling so much better that I could enjoy. There was another little joke, too. He took me to ride in that vast, shining, mile-high valley, and pointing to some sharply defined little hills which looked about five or ten miles away, asked me how far I thought they were. But I had read stories of that dry, deceiving air, and solemnly replied, "Three hundred miles." They were forty, but that didn't sound like much.

Society in Ogden at that time was not exacting; the leading lady, I was told, was the wife of a railroad conductor. We went to a species of ball in a hotel. The bedrooms were all occupied by sleeping babies, as described in The Virginian. Among the dancers there was pointed out to me a man who had killed somebody—no one seemed to hold it against him; and another who had been scalped three times—the white patches were visible among the hair. I had thought scalping a more exhaustive process. At that rate a disingenuous savage could make three triumphant exhibits from one victim. As I did not dance we had a game of whist, and I was somewhat less than pleased to see each of the gentlemen playing bring a large cuspidor and set it by his side. They needed them.

From Utah to San Francisco—on which trip I first met the San Francisco flea. Long since he has been largely overcome, but then was what the newspapers call "a force to be reckoned with"—not California newspapers, of course.

My father was then at the head of the San Francisco Public Library. He met me on the Oakland side, and took me across to a room he had engaged for me for a day or two. Here he solemnly called on me, as would any acquaintance, and went with me across the ferry again when I started south.

"If you ever come to Providence again I hope you will come to see me," said I politely, as we parted, to which he courteously replied, "Thank you. I will bear your invitation in mind."

So down the great inland plain of California, over the Mojave Desert, and to heaven.

Pasadena was then but little changed from the sheep-ranch it used to be. The Channings had bought a beautiful place by the little reservoir at the corner of Walnut Street and Orange Avenue. Already their year-old trees were shooting up unbelievably, their flowers a glory.

The Arroyo Seco was then wild and clean, its steep banks a tangle of loveliness. About opposite us a point ran out where stood a huge twin live oak, still to be seen, but not to be reached by strangers. There was no house by them then, callas bloomed by the hydrant, and sweet alyssum ran wild in the grass.

Never before had my passion for beauty been satisfied. This place did not seem like earth, it was paradise. Kind and congenial friends, pleasant society, amusement, out-door sports, the blessed mountains, the long, unbroken sweep of the valley, with snow-peaks at the far eastern end—with such surroundings I recovered so fast, to outward appearance at least, that I was taken for a vigorous young girl. Hope came back, love came back, I was eager to get home to husband and child, life was bright again.

The return trip was made a little sooner than I had intended because of a railroad war of unparalleled violence which drove prices down unbelievably. It seemed foolish not to take advantage of it, and I bought my ticket from Los Angeles to Chicago, standard, for $5.00. If I had waited for a few days more it could have been bought for $1. The eastern end was unchanged, twenty dollars from Chicago to Boston, but that cut-throat competition was all over the western roads, the sleepers had every berth filled, often two in each. So many traveled that it was said the roads made quite as much money as usual.

Leaving California in March, in the warm rush of its rich spring, I found snow in Denver, and from then on hardly saw the sun for a fortnight. I reached home with a heavy bronchial cold, which hung on long, the dark fog rose again in my mind, the miserable weakness—within a month I was as low as before leaving. . . .

This was a worse horror than before, for now I saw the stark fact—that I was well while away and sick while at home—a heartening prospect! Soon ensued the same utter prostration, the unbearable inner misery, the ceaseless tears. A new tonic had been invented, Essence of Oats, which was given me, and did some good for a time. I pulled up enough to do a little painting that fall, but soon slipped down again and stayed down. An old friend of my mother's, dear Mrs. Diman, was so grieved at this condition that she gave me a hundred dollars and urged me to go away somewhere and get cured.

At that time the greatest nerve specialist in the country was Dr. S. W. Mitchell of Philadelphia. Through the kindness of a friend of Mr. Stetson's living in that city, I went to him and took "the rest cure"; went with the utmost confidence, prefacing the visit with a long letter giving "the history of the case" in a way a modern psychologist would have appreciated. Dr. Mitchell only thought it proved self-conceit. He had a prejudice against the Beechers. "I've had two women of your blood here already," he told me scornfully. This eminent physician was well versed in two kinds of nervous prostration; that of the business man exhausted from too much work, and the society woman exhausted from too much play. The kind I had was evidently beyond him. But he did reassure me on one point—there was no dementia, he said, only hysteria.

I was put to bed and kept there. I was fed, bathed, rubbed, and responded with the vigorous body of twenty-six. As far as he could see there was nothing the matter with me, so after a month of this agreeable treatment he sent me home, with this prescription:

"Live as domestic a life as possible. Have your child with you all the time." (Be it remarked that if I did but dress the baby it left me shaking and crying—certainly far from a healthy companionship for her, to say nothing of the effect on me.) "Lie down an hour after each meal. Have but two hours' intellectual life a day. And never touch pen, brush or pencil as long as you live."

I went home, followed those directions rigidly for months, and came perilously near to losing my mind. The mental agony grew so unbearable that I would sit blankly moving my head from side to side – to get out from under the pain. Not physical pain, not the least "headache" even, just mental torment, and so heavy in its nightmare gloom that it seemed real enough to dodge.

I made a rag baby, hung it on a doorknob and played with it. I would crawl into remote closets and under beds – to hide from the grinding pressure of that profound distress. . . .

Finally, in the fall of '87, in a moment of clear vision, we agreed to separate, to get a divorce. There was no quarrel, no blame for either one, never an unkind word between us, unbroken mutual affection – but it seemed plain that if I went crazy it would do my husband no good, and be a deadly injury to my child.

What this meant to the young artist, the devoted husband, the loving father, was so bitter a grief and loss that nothing would have justified breaking the marriage save this worse loss which threatened. It was not a choice between going and staying, but between going, sane, and staying, insane. If I had been of the slightest use to him or to the child, I would have "stuck it," as the English say. But this progressive weakening of the mind made a horror unnecessary to face; better for that dear child to have separated parents than a lunatic mother.

PASADENA

Besides "Similar Cases" the most outstanding piece of work of 1890 was "The Yellow Wallpaper." It is a description of a case of nervous breakdown beginning something as mine did, and treated as Dr. S. Weir Mitchell treated me with what I considered the inevitable result, progressive insanity.

This I sent to Mr. Howells, and he tried to have the *Atlantic Monthly* print it, but Mr. Scudder, then the editor, sent it back with this brief card:

DEAR MADAM,
  Mr. Howells has handed me this story.
  I could not forgive myself if I made others as miserable as I have made myself!
        Sincerely yours,
                    H. E. SCUDDER.

This was funny. The story was meant to be dreadful, and succeeded. I suppose he would have sent back one of Poe's on the same ground. Later I put it in the hands of an agent who had written me, one Henry Austin, and he placed it with the *New England Magazine*. Time passed, much time, and at length I wrote to the editor of that periodical to this effect:

> DEAR SIR
>
> A story of mine, "The Yellow Wallpaper," was printed in your issue of May, 1891. Since you do not pay on receipt of ms. nor on publication, nor within six months of publication, may I ask if you pay at all, and if so at what rates?

They replied with some heat that they had paid the agent, Mr. Austin. He, being taxed with it, denied having got the money. It was only forty dollars anyway! As a matter of fact I never got a cent for it till later publishers brought it out in book form, and very little then. But it made a tremendous impression. A protest was sent to the Boston *Transcript*, headed "Perilous Stuff"—

> TO THE EDITOR OF THE TRANSCRIPT:
>
> In a well-known magazine has recently appeared a story entitled "The Yellow Wallpaper." It is a sad story of a young wife passing the gradations from slight mental derangement to raving lunacy. It is graphically told, in a somewhat sensational style, which makes it difficult to lay aside, after the first glance, til it is finished, holding the reader in morbid fascination to the end. It certainly seems open to serious question if such literature should be permitted in print.
>
> The story can hardly, it would seem, give pleasure to any reader, and to many whose lives have been touched through the dearest ties by this dread disease, it must bring the keenest pain. To others, whose lives have become a struggle against an heredity of mental derangement, such literature contains deadly peril. Should such stories be allowed to pass without severest censure?
>
> M.D.

Another doctor, one Brummel Jones, of Kansas City, Missouri, wrote me in 1892 concerning this story, saying: "When I read 'The Yellow Wallpaper' I was very much pleased with it; when I read it again I was delighted with it, and now that I have read it again I am overwhelmed with the delicacy of your touch and the correctness of portrayal. From a doctor's standpoint, and I am a doctor, you have made a success. So far as I know, and I am fairly well up in literature, there has been no detailed account of incipient insanity." Then he tells of an opium addict who refused to be treated on the ground that physicians had no real knowledge of the disease, but who returned to Dr. Jones, bringing a paper of his on the opium habit, shook it in his face and said, "Doctor, you've been there!" To which my correspondent added, "Have you ever been—er——; but of course you haven't." I replied that I had been as far as one could go and get back.

One of the *New England Magazine's* editors wrote to me asking if the story was founded on fact, and I gave him all I decently could of my case as a foundation for the tale. Later he explained that he had a friend who was in similar trouble, even to hallucinations about her wallpaper, and whose family were treating her as in the tale, that he had not dared show them my story till he knew that it was true, in part at least, and that when he did they were so frightened by it, so impressed by the clear implication of what ought to have been done, that they changed her wallpaper and the treatment of the case—and she recovered! This was triumph indeed.

But the real purpose of the story was to reach Dr. S. Weir Mitchell, and convince him of the error of his ways. I sent him a copy as soon as it came out, but got no response. However, many years later, I met some one who knew close friends of Dr. Mitchell's who said he had told them that he had changed his treatment of nervous prostration since reading "The Yellow Wallpaper." If that is a fact, I have not lived in vain.

A few years ago Mr. Howells asked leave to include this story in a collection he was arranging—*Masterpieces of American Fiction*. I was more than willing, but assured him that it was no more "literature" than my other stuff, being definitely written "with a purpose." In my judgment it is a pretty poor thing to write, to talk, without a purpose.

All these literary efforts providing but little, it was well indeed that another avenue of work opened to me at this time.

The Psychiatric Case History of Isabella Shawe Thackeray

Stanley Cobb

THE CASE HISTORY OF the wife of William Makepeace Thackeray, Isabella Shawe Thackeray (1818–93), lends insight into Charlotte Perkins Gilman's own postpartum depression as well as her fictional treatment of a woman undergoing a three-month rest cure for a postpartum depression in "The Yellow Wallpaper." Described as an intelligent young woman with a "quick mind" (67) at the time of her marriage to Thackeray in 1836, Isabella Shawe suffered a mental breakdown in 1840 following the birth of her third daughter (the second dying soon after childbirth). Living a life of relative ease under the watchful eye of her widowed mother (like Gilman she was raised solely by her mother), Isabella experienced depression following three consecutive pregnancies. Her early symptoms resemble Gilman's — despondency, weakness, fatigue, and unworthiness. Becoming rapidly suicidal, she did not respond to a range of treatments including a strenuous month's water cure; when her condition became chronic and severe, Thackeray placed her in a French sanitarium at Chaillot. Thackeray raised his two surviving daughters, Anne and Harriet, with the aid of his mother and numerous governesses.

Dr. Stanley Cobb's psychiatric case history of Isabella Shawe Thackeray presents the facts leading up to Isabella's depression, her dramatic deterioration, and her eventual placement in a mental hospital in 1843. In his analysis of her deterioration, Cobb puts emphasis on the precise point when the onset of her depression occurred — after childbirth. In summarizing the cause of her psychosis, he concludes: "So if blame is to be placed, it may well begin with putting it on the egg, with stressful environment as secondary" (69). Cobb's clinical account of Isabella Shawe Thackeray's "post-puerperal depression" reveals the widespread belief that the uterus and the ovary determined women's

66

characteristics and that mental disorders, which plagued Isabella Shawe Thackeray and Charlotte Perkins Gilman, resulted from the ovary, or, in Cobb's terminology, "the egg."

Isabella Shawe Thackeray was eventually moved to a private home in England where she remained under the care of a nurse until her death in 1893. Whereas Isabella Shaw Thackeray lived in a permanent state of psychosis for fifty years, Gilman recovered from her nervous disorder but claimed that many of her faculties were never the same.

The data from which this psychiatric case history is assembled are to be found in the letters from Thackeray to Isabella Shawe, a few letters written by her, many letters from Thackeray to his mother, and some others. These are listed below.[1] With the patient buried 2,000 miles away in 1893 and the action taking place one hundred years ago, an accurate evaluation is, of course, impossible. Yet the description of her symptoms in the letters and the story of the development of the illness supply one with enough facts to make reasonable a tentative diagnosis.

Before her marriage, Isabella Shawe seems to have been a happy, bright girl with a quick mind and ability to turn a phrase aptly. Thackeray usually spoke of her as the "dear little woman" and once as "redpoll," so one pictures a small lady with red hair, fine manners, and much restraint in love relations. When they were engaged Thackeray seems to have been impetuous at one time and frightened her. Although they apparently could discuss being bedfellows and having children, it seems that passion shocked her. Such a reaction is to be looked on as normal in an age when girls were poorly educated and well protected. Moreover, she appears to have lived a life of ease, in a small way, lying in bed late and idling her time away under the guidance of a resentful, widowed mother to whom keeping up the appearance of gentility was all-important.

She was married at the age of eighteen, and her four years with Thackeray before her illness seem to have been happy ones, although she bore three children and had many responsibilities. The first child was born within a year (June 1837). The birth was relatively easy and she seems to have met the situation normally. The child, Anne, was healthy and caused only the usual amount of trouble. In the late autumn she was pregnant again and Jane was born in July 1838. The next months were difficult and the baby died in March 1839. There is nothing to indicate that the mother showed any unusual signs of emotional disturbance throughout this trying period. In October or November she was pregnant again and went through this in good spirits and without untoward symptoms. The child, Harriet, was born on May 27, 1840. There were no especial obstetrical difficulties mentioned, and for a few weeks all appears to have gone well.

The first hint of mental illness is found in a letter from Thackeray to his mother in which he says on July 18, 1840: "Isabella is better." Isabella says in a letter to her mother-in-law August 4: "I feel myself excited, my strength is not great and my head flies away with me as if it were a balloon. This is mere weakness and a walk will set me right but in case there should be incoherence in my letter you will know what to attribute it to." (There is no incoherence in the letter.) Later is another significant remark: "I try to think my fears imaginary and exaggerated and that I am a coward by nature." By August 21, it is obvious that she is depressed and is described by Thackeray as "very low. For the last four days I have not been able to write a line in consequence of her." She remained "low in spirits" with "fretful looks" especially in the mornings and seemed so "absent" at that time that Thackeray did not "like to trust her." She often had feelings of guilt and "worked up these charges so as to fancy herself a perfect demon of wickedness." There was a short improvement early in September, but when the family started for London on September 12 to sail for Ireland her depression deepened. On the thirteenth, when at sea off the Isle of Wight, she went to the water closet of the boat and climbed out the window, dropping into the sea. She was in the water for twenty minutes before she was found "floating on her back, paddling with her hands." "The next night she made fresh attempts at destruction." On the seventeenth they arrived at Cork and boarded near her mother's house. The experience of the voyage augmented her "melancholy" to "absolute insanity" and she landed "quite demented." During the next two weeks her mood varied, described as "low and ennuyee," lacking in "interest and devoured by gloom," "clouded and rambling." At times the feelings of unworthiness come up and she says she was "never fit to be a wife," but she made no more suicidal attempts. She "won't sit still, won't employ herself, won't do anything she is asked and vice versa."

After this the psychosis seemed to become chronic, and three months later, in writing to Edward FitzGerald on January 14, 1841, Thackeray says: "At first she was violent, then she was indifferent, now she is melancholy and silent and we are glad of it. She bemoans her condition and that is a great step to cure. She knows everybody and recollects things but in a stunned confused sort of way. She kissed me at first very warmly and with tears in her eyes, then she went away from me, as if she felt she was unworthy of having such a God of a husband."

During the next year she was in a state of "indifference, silence and sluggishness" with variation up and down, sometimes showing slight interest in her children, at other times apathy. Various treatments were tried in England and on the continent. A month's strenuous hydrotherapy at Boppart on the Rhine made her "extraordinarily better," but the improvement was short-lived. At last Thackeray put her in a mental hospital at Chaillot where she was "perfectly happy, obedient and reasonable" (March 1843). During the next year, however, she seems to have become less reasonable and to have had strange ideas or trains of thought, "if you can call it a train." In 1846 Thackeray says: "The poor little woman gets no better and plays the nastiest pranks more frequently than ever." In 1848 he remarks: "She cares for none of us now." In this state she lived on under a nurse in England until 1893, fifty-three years in psychosis!

In discussing the cause of this mental breakdown the fact that the patient's mother had periods of depression after her children were born is probably important. Although mild depressions are common enough during the nursing period, there is abundant evidence that Mrs. Shawe was unstable and difficult. So if blame is to be placed, it may well begin with putting it on the egg, with stressful environment as secondary. Life before her marriage was not easy for Isabella Shawe, and the year of engagement to Thackeray had stormy passages with the mother, who wished to break up the match, and with the lover as mentioned above. Then the four years of marriage, though happy, brought heavy physical burdens—three pregnancies in quick succession. Added to this were all the adjustments to marriage and the grief over losing a child. There is no evidence that Thackeray himself was a cause of trouble; in fact, he seems to have made a positive contribution towards happiness.

The diagnosis is schizophrenia, of a type that often begins with depression and ideas of unworthiness a few weeks after childbirth.[2] Some of these patients get well spontaneously in a few months and the diagnosis of a "post-puerperal depression" is made. Others seem to drift into a permanent state of apathy and live the rest of their lives in an unreal world of fantasy, with gradual mental deterioration. Such was the fate of Mrs. Thackeray.

NOTES

1. Letters of Thackeray to his Mother: 1840: Jan. 19, Feb. 15, May 27, July 18, Aug. 21, Sept. 1, Sept. 12, Sept. 17, Sept. 20, Sept. 24, Sept. 26, Sept. 30, Oct. 1 (?), Oct. 6; 1841: Feb. 27, April 15; 1842: June 30, Sept. 30; 1844: June 1. Letter of Isabella Shawe Thackeray to her mother-in-law, Aug. 4, 1840. Letter of Thackeray to Edward FitzGerald, Jan. 14, 1841.

2. E. A. Strecker and F. G. Ebaugh, "Psychoses Occurring during Puerperium," *Archives of Neurology and Psychiatry*, vol. 14, page 239 (1926).

From "Stereotypes of Femininity in a Theory of Sexual Evolution"

Jill Conway

VICTORIAN ENGLAND AND AMERICA possessed a rigid ideal of femininity for the upper and middle classes, yet this stereotype of the dutiful, maternal, selfless, submissive angel in the house did not match the situations of numerous women of upper- and middle-class households, including that of Charlotte Perkins Gilman. Conway's essay serves as a reminder of the theories of sex differentiation and the social position of women in the late nineteenth century when Gilman wrote "The Yellow Wallpaper." This selection focuses on the now forgotten but once influential work of Scottish biologist Patrick Geddes, *The Evolution of Sex* (1889). Jill Conway recalls the biological metaphors used to describe the innate and inherited traits and sexual temperaments of men and women, natural laws that simply determined men's superior and women's inferior social positions.

Conway's discussion of Geddes's dichotomy of sexual temperaments, particularly his belief that the "emotional, intuitive female" (77) must conserve energy for survival, provides a context for understanding two components of the rest cure treatment which Mitchell prescribed and Gilman defied in writing "The Yellow Wallpaper." Total and enforced bed rest for periods of six to eight weeks restored energy to neurasthenic women while excessive feeding increased body volume and thus provided them with new stores of energy.

An extremely influential, but now forgotten, study of sex-differentiation and its significance in social evolution was the work of the Scottish biologist Patrick Geddes, written in collaboration with his pupil, J. Arthur Thomson.[1] Published in 1889 with the title *The Evolution of Sex* the book contained expositions of the existing state of

71

knowledge on reproduction and sex-differences together with Geddes's own theories about the way in which the social position of women accorded with a vast evolutionary design. In part Geddes's argument seeks to defend Spencer and Darwin on the inheritance of acquired characteristics. In part it attempts to synthesize the growing body of knowledge on cell structure with a new concern for the mechanisms for stability and variation in forms of life. It is thus part of the convergence of several lines of biological enquiry which were to meet in the following decade in the study of heredity.

Geddes had impressive scholarly credentials for attempting a grand scheme of scientific synthesis. He had trained for four years with Huxley at the Royal School of Mines in South Kensington. As a student he had produced a minor correction of the master's work deemed worthy of publication in the *Transactions* of the London Zoological Society. After completing his studies with Huxley in 1877 he had served as senior demonstrator in practical physiology at University College, London, while doing research on the lower forms of life aimed at clarifying the boundaries between botany and zoology. The next year he began training as a field naturalist at the French marine biological station at Roscoff, followed by another two years of work in biology and histology at the Sorbonne and the École de Médecine. After a brief field trip to the zoological station at Naples in 1879 Geddes planned a major expedition to Mexico. This was undertaken to collect biological specimens for the British Association for the Advancement of Science and was to provide Geddes with the field work which he admired so intensely in the career of his intellectual model, Darwin. Shortly after his arrival in Mexico these hopes were permanently blighted by an attack of blindness attributed to lengthy periods of uninterrupted work with microscopes. Though his sight returned, Geddes was not able to use microscopes again for sustained research. The disaster brought about the reorientation of his career toward the interpretation of science for the layman and the synthesis of knowledge from a variety of scientific fields.[2]

His passion for synthesizing had already been demonstrated in his student years by a growing interest in the new science of sociology. As the child of strict Scotch Presbyterians he had been troubled by the apparent conflict between science and religion, and deeply disturbed by Huxley's dismissal of religious belief. In search of a way out of these intellectual difficulties he began to attend the Positivist church on Chapel Street and the week-night meetings of the London Positivist

Society. In Paris he followed up his interest in a synthesis of scientific knowledge by attending the lectures of the Société International des études practique de l'Economie Sociale. Founded in 1856 by the social scientist Frédéric Le Play the society was dedicated to the development of scientific methods for the study of social structures and in particular to the study of the interaction of human groups with a given regional environment. These two sources in London and Paris provided Geddes with a knowledge of the developing science of sociology which inspired him to accept Comte's idea that the science of society would bring about the synthesis of scientific knowledge. In 1880 when it became clear that he could no longer be a creative researcher in biology he saw his future in the application of biological method to the study of society.[3]

Thus, while apparently pursuing a conventional scholarly career as a demonstrator in botany and lecturer in zoology at the University of Edinburgh, Geddes was in fact bent on branching out into the science of society. His first steps in the direction of sociology took the form of adaptations of economic theory to biological principles,[4] but his long-term project during the decade of the 1880's was to synthesize what was known about sex-differences and to interpret the social and economic significance of this knowledge. Geddes was convinced that sex differences should be viewed as arising from a basic difference in cell metabolism. The physical laws concerning the conservation and dissipation of energy applied to all living things. At the level of the cell, maleness was characterized by the tendency to dissipate energy, femaleness by the capacity to store or build up energy. From this single factor Geddes was able to depict reproduction and the determination of sex as arising from the general state of nutrition of an organism at the time of fertilization. "Favorable nutritive conditions tend to produce females," he wrote (in *The Evolution of Sex*), "and unfavorable conditions males" (p. 44). Preponderance of waste over new sources of energy would produce an organism with a male or "*katabolic* habit of body." Rich nutrition and abundant supplies of energy produced organisms with an "*anabolic* habit," which were female (pp. 44–45). Many consequences flowed from this division. Male cells had the power to transmit variation along with their tendency to dissipate energy. Female cells by contrast had the power to conserve energy, support new life, and to maintain stability in new forms of life.

In this theory Geddes was addressing himself to the question which Weismann had emphasized, the problem of accounting for the stability of forms of life and their continuity. Geddes's answer was to assume an immutable order and predictability in reproduction arising from cell metabolism. By making sperm and ovum exhibit the qualities of male *katabolism* or female *anabolism* Geddes was able to deduce a dichotomy between the temperaments of the sexes which was easily accommodated to the romantic idea of male rationality and female intuition. This dichotomy of temperament duplicated the dual pattern of cell metabolism, "the hungry, active cell becomes flagellate sperm, while the quiescent, well-fed one becomes an ovum" (pp. 115–117). Male aggression arising from the male tendency to dissipate energy and female passivity flowing from the complementary tendency to conserve resources were thus not merely to be observed in animal and human societies, but were to be found in the very simplest forms of life. In fact the entire evolutionary progression from the lowest organism up to man rested upon these male and female qualities. The lesson which was to be drawn from this picture of reproduction and evolutionary development was clear. Male and female sex roles had been decided in the lowest forms of life and neither political nor technological change could alter the temperaments which had developed from these differing functions.

Cell metabolism and sex differences were of course merely the base upon which Geddes wished to erect a sound and scientifically rigorous social theory. In a chapter of *The Evolution of Sex* entitled "Psychological and Ethical Aspects" Geddes sketched out the implications for future social development of the scheme he had propounded. He was a Victorian moralist and optimist who saw both psychic and ethical growth arising from evolutionary processes. In the scientific study of sexuality he saw no evidence leading to the deflation of romantic ideas about love. On the contrary, proper study of the role of sex differences in evolution showed that mankind was journeying toward a utopia of the emotions in which all humanity would experience the transports of romantic attachment celebrated in poetry and art. A rare Eloise and Abelard merely prefigured the emotional range to be developed by the entire human race. The deepening of the capacity for passionate feelings was to be accompanied by a parallel development in the sense of moral order so that the new sexual paradise did not threaten Victorian ideas of decorum. Such a pattern of development brought together harmoniously the chivalric tradition of romantic love and the potentially disturbing idea that human sexual appetites were mere animal instincts. While the romantic hero and heroine might be subjected to critical comment in the literary culture of the closing decades of the century, Geddes was hard at work shoring up a highly idealized picture of romantic love in his study of social evolution. Neither social realism nor the revived critical current of classicism entered into his treatment of future sexual relationships.

Although he cheerfully acknowledged, as did Freud, that sexual attraction originated in "an organic hunger" he could see no reason for a reductive view of the psychic accompaniments of physical appetite (p. 246). This assertion was based upon his belief that in higher organisms all the social emotions derived from reproduction. The prolonged care of an offspring which was a characteristic of the higher forms of life was accompanied by the psychic evolution of altruism from which the entire range of social feelings was developed. Altruism arising as it did from a biological function was as deeply rooted in human nature as the egoism which drove individual organisms in their "struggle for survival." For Geddes this meant that sexuality in humans was not associated with dominance and lust, but entirely with the rise of the social emotions. In society in his own day he saw a situation in which egoism and altruism were kept in precarious balance in the human psyche. For the future, however, he predicted a great increase in altruistic feelings to be brought about by the elevation of women in a society formerly ordered by male egoism. Females, through their nurture of the young, had unrivalled opportunities to develop their capacities for social feeling, and Geddes expected that their increased participation in social and political life would result in a redirection of social change toward a cooperative society, provided that it preserved separate sex roles appropriate to male and female temperaments. By postulating an infinite human capacity for social feeling, Geddes was able to retain both the idea of romantic intensity in individual human relationships and an increasing ability for generalized social sentiments.

For the correct path to the future, however, it was necessary to follow the signs of biology. The growth of feminine altruism might be arrested if women abandoned passivity for masculine activism. To alter the profound psychic differences between the sexes it would be necessary to "have all of evolution over again on a new basis." Indeed to free women from their passivity and to open areas of social activity to them which placed them in competition with men would be socially dangerous. Certainly political agitation for female equality with men was fruitless. "What was decided among the prehistoric *Protozoa*," wrote Geddes, "can not be annulled by act of parliament" (p. 247).

Lest women should rail against a biological providence which had given them "habits of body" which could be exploited by stronger men, Geddes hastened to proclaim that the study of sexuality in human societies gave no hint that political or social factors had led to the subjection of women. The situation of women in society was not the result of acquired characteristics. It merely reflected the economy of cell metabolism and its parallel psychic differentiation between the sexes. Women were not confined within the home because of their inferior muscular strength. Nor was their domesticity a reflection of a male conspiracy to monopolize military occupations and political power. On the contrary, even in the most primitive societies there had been no male domination in the allocation of sex roles. An uninformed observer might feel that in savage society there was inequity in a situation which gave menial tasks to women while their men lazed around between hunting trips, but once metabolism was considered as a basic factor determining social structures, it became clear that the male savage rested to accumulate the energy for sudden bursts of hunting, while the female merely kept going at routine occupations. There was no injustice in the routine, since female functions and the need to conserve energy for them made hunting out of the question for women (pp. 248–249).

Beyond the stage of primitive societies, the constitutional differences between the sexes had more profound social ramifications. Male intelligence was greater than female, men had greater independence and courage than women, and men were able to expend energy in sustained bursts of physical or cerebral activity. Men were thus activists and excelled in the species-preserving capacities of egoism. Women on the other hand possessed the social talents. They were superior to men in constancy of affection and sympathetic imagination. They were patient because of their passivity and the need to store energy – not, as feminists claimed, because patience is one of the qualities of the oppressed. Here was the traditional Victorian scheme of sexual temperaments. The male temperament was characterized, said Geddes, by "greater power of maximum effort, of scientific insight or cerebral experiment with impressions." Females had "greater patience, more open-mindedness, greater appreciation of subtle details, and consequently what we call more rapid intuition" (p. 250).

This typology of biologically determined sexual temperaments expressed unaltered the romantic myth of the rational male and the emotional, intuitive female. While preserving romantic images Geddes was able to give scientific authority to views of relationships between the sexes which were being questioned in the debate over the women question. History and anthropology might suggest the possibility of matriarchy, but Geddes's sexes had known the same division of labor since the most primitive single-celled organisms. There was no human guilt to be felt over the inferior position of women. It was a function of natural laws which operated well beyond the boundaries of human society.

When he turned his attention from the *protozoa* to contemporary society the social problem which troubled Geddes most deeply was the impact of industrialization on the roles of the sexes. He was afraid that in industrial capitalist society the laws of biology were being ignored because of the peremptory demands of an unnatural economic system. Women were plunging into the industrial struggle to earn their daily bread. By entering the work force they were competing with men and sabotaging the metabolic economy already defined by nature. Woolly headed social reformers might dream about the arrival of social equality through a redistribution of wealth brought about by paying higher wages for women's work, but such fantasies neglected the hard facts of biology, "it is not for the sake of production or distribution, or self-interest or mechanism, or any other idol of the economists, that the male organism organizes the climax of his life's struggle and labour, but for his mate; as she then, he also, for their little ones. Production is for consumption; the species is its own highest, its sole essential product . . ." (p. 249). There must be an angel in the house busy with her brood of children ready to turn the commercial world of everyday economic laws into something finer. It was upon this kind of cooperation between the sexes that "all progress past or future must depend" (p. 259).

If the sexual stereotypes which Geddes enshrined in his social theory were the conventional ones of Victorian domesticity, he departed from convention on the question of family size. He saw human progress arising from such new forms of cooperation between the sexes as the control of conception to permit smaller broods of children and greater individual development for females. Drawing on Herbert Spencer's *Principles of Biology* (1866), Geddes accepted the idea that advancing evolution was associated with a decline in fertility, because the matter and energy expended in completing and maintaining an individual life could not also be made available for the creation of new generations. Thus individual human development could only be achieved at the expense of fertility. This price Geddes was quite willing to pay for the achievement of better human organisms and an improved human environment. In his discussion of the laws of multiplication in the twentieth chapter of *The Evolution of Sex* he treated in some detail the various artificial means of preventing conception (pp. 270–272). Like all Victorians he feared that the universal adoption of birth-control might open such floodgates of sexuality that the human species might in future breed only virtuosos of the senses. Nonetheless he was convinced that rational attempts to control population were the key to future progress. The risk of increased sensuality was worth taking in view of the possibility of "a conscious and rational adjustment of the struggle [for survival] into the culture of existence" (p. 269).

The control of family size was necessary for both eugenic and economic reasons. Women should not be exhausted physically by annual child-bearing. It was also clear that the exploitive character of capitalism could only be maintained while there was an expanding labour force compelled by population pressure to accept employment at subsistence wages. Eugenics and economics thus both required reduction in family size. Yet fear of sensuality made Geddes reluctant to accept universal use of contraceptive devices. He advocated instead a new psychic development which would bring about a temperance in intercourse for married couples as controlling as the obligation to pre-marital chastity. However, where such new forms of consciousness had not evolved, eugenics required contraception. These might have an evolutionary value of their own because "by the very transition from unconscious animalism to deliberate prevention of fertilization" men and women would be bringing sexuality under rational control (p. 273). From this rationality it was possible that physical appetites might be eroded and relations between the sexes limited to the stimulation of romantic emotions. Sexual intemperance in marriages was to be discouraged by ethical development, otherwise married couples might fall to the "ethical level of the harlots and profligates of the streets" (p. 273). The Victorian fear of ungovernable sexual appetites would be disposed of in Geddes's new eugenic order by changes in social attitude and social structures. Human generative powers would be brought under control, not by economic or political measures, but by the improved education and increasing civic activity of women. Linked with this social change there would be a new economy of the sexes, in which female resources formerly allocated to reproduction would be placed at the disposal of society. Nature decreed that these resources would remain intuitive and sympathetic but human reason could be relied upon to direct them to wider social goals. Naturally the principle which is not articulated in this argument is that male reason would of necessity direct the utilization of feminine capacities. Nonetheless, the new social order derived from studying the laws of evolutionary progress was to be one in which female capacities had a central importance (pp. 273–274).

The new social order would be brought about by transforming relationships between the sexes so that their sensual encounters would be minimized and their sex-linked temperaments given new social expression (here Geddes resembled Freud for he saw progress in culture taking place at the expense of sensual gratification).[5] But, unlike Freud, he concluded that women as well as men were capable of sublimation. This view was derived from his understanding of the role of sex in the evolution of the higher forms of life. "Creation's final law" was not struggle but love, because the social affections were a precondition of progress (p. 286). It followed that the development of female emotive capacities was as essential to social progress as the masculine power of rationality. Geddes differed from Freud in seeing no danger to either sex from the repression of sexual drives. These could always be given adequate expression through generalized social affections. In part this difference can be explained by the social context in which Geddes carried out his study of sexuality. His passion for the study of social structures and family life led him in 1887 to take up residence in a crowded slum quarter of Edinburgh.[6] Residence in poverty-stricken James Court meant that Geddes saw sexuality from the standpoint of the urban poor, rather than from the genteel context of the prosperous middle class. Since women were vital to the economy of the pauper household, Geddes could no more imagine them lacking in social function than he could question their biological function. Passive and emotive they must be, but never dysfunctional.

The Evolution of Sex enjoyed considerable réclame after its publication in 1889. Because of its treatment of the forbidden subject of birth-control it went through three printings and two different editions in Great Britain.[7] It came out the next year in the United States as a volume in the Humboldt Library of Science. Two years later, when a French translation was published, Geddes had become an authority of international reputation on his chosen subject. Besides the impact of his published work Geddes was an influential teacher.

In 1887 he borrowed from the American Chautauqua Society the idea of a summer series of lectures for adult education. In his Edinburgh version of the summer school, the lectures alternated between French and English and the student body was decidedly cosmopolitan. While his courses on evolutionary ethics were scantily attended during the early summer sessions, the program began to attract an average of about 120 students by 1893.[8] Among them Charles Zeublin (the Chicago sociologist) and William James have left records testifying to the impact of Geddes's teaching and to the scientific credentials of his students. When the Edinburgh summer school was abandoned it was replaced by more ambitious schemes for international education. The one which had the most transatlantic significance was the International School which Geddes supervised at the Paris Exposition of 1900.[9] Organized under the joint auspices of the British and French Associations for the Advancement of Science, the school had such distinguished lecturers as Lester Ward and Jane Addams representing American sociology, Henri Bergson teaching evolutionary science, and James Bryce outlining the stages of constitutional development. Though attended only by fellow intellectuals visiting the Exposition, the International School made a deep impression on its small student and teaching body. Geddes, as its organizer, planned the courses offered so that they provided an integrated and synthetic view of the vast array of technological and cultural displays at the Exposition. He hoped that, by pooling the intellectual resources of the United States, France, and Great Britain, new insights could be developed into the emerging character of urban, technological society, and a truly Comtean synthesis of existing knowledge in sociology could be forged. But by 1900 the wave of the future in the social sciences was no longer towards a positivist reliance on biological determinants of social structures and, therefore, the International School was one of the last gatherings of social scientists at which scholars claimed to range over the entire field of biology, cultural anthropology, and social psychology with the confidence that Geddes had exhibited in writing *The Evolution of Sex*. After 1900 the inheritance of sex and sex-linked characteristics became the province of genetics. The question of sexual behavior was illuminated by developments in endocrinology. And the whole question of cultural evolution was divorced from the single progression from primitive to civilized societies which the positivists had envisioned. Thus, with the closing of the International School in 1900, the synthesis of biological, physical, and sociological ideas which Geddes had been trying to achieve became progressively more outmoded. He was to move on to another career as an expert in regional surveys, town planning, and the study of urban civilizations. Nevertheless, his influence on social thought was far reaching; he had intellectual heirs both in Great Britain and the United States.

In the United States his most important popularizer was Jane Addams. She accepted Geddes's idea of biologically determined masculine and feminine temperaments, and based her hopes for the ethical and social improvement of American society upon the political and social activism of women. Following Geddes to the letter, she expected the collectivization of the competitive industrial order of the United States to come about through the moral insights of women, and she undertook to articulate this feminine consciousness for her fellow Americans. Two of her most widely read books took as their point of departure Geddes's sexually determined temperaments. In *Democracy and Social Ethics* (New York, 1902), she worked a familiar theme from Geddes's evolutionary thought by pointing to the need for a psychic evolution by which the domestic morality of small-town America could be generalized to create a cooperative community appropriate to a democratic society. The agents of this moral change were to be women, whose powers of intuition and empathy could be redirected from family to society. *Newer Ideals of Peace* (New York, 1907) was a further treatise on the possibility of psychic and ethical evolution. In it she examined the possibility that industrial societies had evolved beyond warfare and that heroism should consequently take on new psychic and ethical forms. In accordance with Geddes's view of the female temperament, Jane Addams was finally moved to become one of the founders of the Woman's Peace Party in the United States and to lead its campaign to join with other women's organizations in Europe in attempting mediation between the belligerent powers in World War I. This abortive effort at mediation was based on the assumption that there was a universal feminine temperament governed by the biological function of nurturing life, which could be relied on to harness male aggressions under all circumstances of nationality and international conflict. The messianic hopes of the women's peace movement, which were to prove sadly mistaken during 1915–19, derived directly from the kind of evolutionary speculation which Geddes had publicized with such vigor and effectiveness. They were particularly strong in the United States where the social role of middle-class women could most easily be approximated to Geddes's picture of the *anabolic* female.[10]

NOTES

1. Patrick Geddes (1854–1932) later Sir Patrick. Scottish biologist and sociologist. The standard biographies of Geddes are Philip Boardman, *Patrick Geddes: Maker of the Future* (University of North Carolina Press, 1944), and Philip Mairet, *Pioneer of Sociology: The Life and Letters of Patrick Geddes* (London, 1957). Patrick Geddes and J. Arthur Thomson, *The Evolution of Sex* (London, 1889). References in this paper are to the New York edition (1890). On the nature of the collaboration between Geddes and J. Arthur Thomson (later Sir Arthur) see Philip Boardman, pp. 120–121.

2. See Boardman, pp. 23–52, and Mairet, pp. 13–30, for Geddes's student career and the crisis of his blindness. On Geddes's studies with Huxley see Patrick Geddes, "Huxley as Teacher," *Nature* CXV (9 May 1925), 740–743.

3. Boardman, pp. 41–43, Mairet, pp. 27–28.

4. See his "Analysis of the Principles of Economics," *Proceedings of the Royal Society of Edinburgh*, XII (1884), 943–980.

5. See Philip Rieff, *Freud: The Mind of the Moralist* (New York, 1959), pp. 161–168, for a summary of Freud's views on culture and sensual gratification.

6. See Boardman, pp. 101–105, and Mairet, pp. 51–54.

7. Boardman, p. 125.

8. Boardman, p. 156, Mairet, pp. 62–69.

9. See Boardman, pp. 222–231, and Mairet, pp. 98–108.

10. On the woman's peace movement see Jane Addams, *Peace and Bread in Time of War* (New York, 1922). On the impact of Geddes and the International School see Jane Addams to Mary R. Smith, Paris, 10 June 1900, and same to same, Paris, 27 June 1900. Both letters in the Jane Addams Correspondence, Jane Addams Collection, Swarthmore College Peace Collection, Swarthmore, Pa.

From the Introduction to
The Oven Birds:
American Women on
Womanhood, 1820–1920

Gail Parker

GAIL PARKER'S *The Oven Birds* places Gilman's "The Yellow Wallpaper" in an important context of American feminism. The story stands alongside diary excerpts, letters, and fiction and nonfiction by leading American feminist thinkers, whose minds Gilman respected: Elizabeth Cady Stanton, Jane Addams, and Gilman's great aunts Catharine Esther Beecher and Harriet Beecher Stowe. Gilman's pride in her famous Beecher relatives infuses her autobiography. In the first chapter Gilman proclaims: "The immediate line I am really proud of is the Beecher family" (Appleton-Century, 3); she singles out Harriet Beecher Stowe (author of *Uncle Tom's Cabin* [1848]), Catharine Esther Beecher (known for promoting women's higher education), and Isabella Beecher Hooker (a leader in the Suffrage Movement). Gilman recalls in a later chapter, "I was particularly impressed by Elizabeth Cady Stanton" (Appleton-Century, 216); she describes Jane Addams as "a truly great woman. Her mind had more 'floor space' in it than any other I have known. She could set a subject down, unprejudiced, and walk all around it, allowing fairly for everyone's point of view" (Appleton-Century, 184). Addams shared Gilman's contempt for S. Weir Mitchell; as Parker explains in this selection, Mitchell had treated Addams with the rest cure in his Philadelphia sanitarium when she suffered a nervous breakdown.

The comparisons Parker makes between Gilman, Addams, Stanton, and the Beechers command more attention than Parker's brief discussion of "The Yellow Wallpaper." Her largely biographical presentation is not as thorough as that of other critics, some of whom have questioned the accuracy of her account. But in this introduction published prior to the Feminist Press edition, Parker casts the story in a feminist context by arguing that the narrator "has her moment of triumph when her horrified husband faints dead away after being forced to recognize what happens to a woman who is denied the right to be an adult" (85). Furthermore, Parker chides William Dean Howells for his response to Gilman's work, suggesting that the forefather of American Realism preferred a "genteel Realism" (89), a criticism often remarked in the 1920s and 1930s when Howells's reputation declined.

I n *Twenty Years at Hull-House*, Jane Addams recounted her collapse after a semester in medical school as "but the development of the spinal difficulty which had shadowed me from childhood."[1] Three years earlier in *Democracy and Social Ethics*, she had had a more complicated analysis of the plight of the female college graduate whose health gives way under the strain of trying to live according to her convictions. Waiting for some worthy demand to be made on her powers, the young woman collapses and "her physician invariably advises a rest. But to be put to bed and fed on milk is not what she requires."[2] This is precisely what did happen to Jane Addams when she entered S. Weir Mitchell's hospital after her own breakdown. Dr. Mitchell specialized in a drastic rest cure in which massage was substituted for exercise, visitors and letters were banned, and the patient was fed an all-milk diet to which bland and starchy foods were gradually added. His specialty was the cure of neurasthenic women, women whose complaints were believed to be largely neurotic, by reducing them to a condition of infantile dependence on their physician.

Mitchell was outspoken in his anti-feminism and was convinced, among other things, that higher education was debilitating to the female. At the same time, he was determined to reduce the pleasures of invalidism by removing the suffering woman from her home, making it impossible for her to play upon the sympathies of her relatives. It has been suggested that the great popularity of his regimen was correlated with its drastic quality—what could be more shocking in America at the end of the nineteenth century than to be told to take to your bed and do nothing? But if this explains why exhausted businessmen were drawn to Mitchell's hospital, it does not tell us why his methods attracted their wives and daughters. In prescribing the ultimate in feminist put-down, Dr. Mitchell no doubt appealed to the oppressed relatives of the never-well, yet his directives must also have had a real (if temporary) attraction for the neurasthenic woman herself. She could find relief from the gnawing sense that her life was being wasted in his assurances that what she mistook for unused potential was nothing more than diseased imagination.

Charlotte Perkins Gilman wrote a story about her experiences under S. Weir Mitchell's care, a story which William Dean Howells, despite misgivings, chose to include in his *Great Modern American Stories* (along with "The Courting of Sister Wisby"). Howells felt he had to apologize for his selection saying, in his introductory remarks, that he had "shivered" over "The Yellow Wall-Paper" and still basically agreed "with the editor of *The Atlantic* . . . that it was too terribly good to be printed."[3] Mrs. Gilman set her story in a nursery to underscore the determination of Mitchell and his disciples to reduce their female patients to the docility and dependency of childhood. Ironically, however, the former residents of Mrs. Gilman's barred playroom were more vicious and hostile than anything Mitchell ever bargained for; they had gouged off the wallpaper and gnawed at the bedstead. And it is this childish rage that Mrs. Gilman's heroine relives under the watchful eyes of her husband, brother, and serenely domestic sister-in-law. She tears the paper and bites the bed and has her moment of triumph when her horrified husband faints dead away after being forced to recognize what happens to a woman who is denied the right to be an adult.[4]

Mrs. Gilman's life story as she later told it in her autobiography suggests some of the sources of her hostility to dependence in any form. Her father deserted his family; her mother, who as a girl had been threatened by consumption and besieged by lovers, grew up to be a passionately domestic woman with a spaniel-like devotion to her absent husband. Mrs. Perkins' domestic disappointments drove her to try to protect her daughter from a similar fate by stifling every impulse to show her affection. She apparently felt, or so her daughter believed, that if Charlotte never grew accustomed to love she would never crave it. Mrs. Gilman managed to internalize her mother's stoicism, and to place even more stringent demands on herself, with the result that she achieved a kind of emotional anesthesia.

Her descriptions of her relentless self-culture sound like a more flagellatory and self-hating Benjamin Franklin. In an attempt to overcome a reputation for thoughtlessness, Charlotte Perkins methodically visited a young invalid whose infirmities repelled her. She felt certain that by sacrificing her own tastes and time to the comfort of the crippled girl she would grow to love her. "And sure enough," she wrote in her autobiography, "after a while I became quite fond of the girl." But the real climax of the tale was yet to come. "In about two years I heard through a kind cousin that some old lady had said that she did like Charlotte Perkins—she was so thoughtful of other people. 'Hurrah!' said I, 'another game won!'"[5]

How little a "game" this really was to Mrs. Gilman can be seen when she herself became an invalid after giving birth to a daughter. Her "handmade character" disintegrated when she was faced with the responsibility for a wholly dependent creature. Her "riotous virtues," like her ritual body building, represented the attempts of a severely mistrustful person to make it absolutely on her own. With a father who could never be counted on and a mother who demanded a total sacrifice of independence and individuality, Charlotte Perkins' earliest training had been in mortifying her feelings, in ignoring her deepest needs. It is not hard to understand why she was unable to cope with the demands of a husband and infant. "Motherhood means giving. . . ." she wrote in her autobiography, and then: "Here was a charming home; a loving and devoted husband; an exquisite baby, healthy, intelligent and good; a highly competent mother [Mrs. Perkins] to run things; a wholly satisfactory servant—and I lay all day on the lounge and cried."[6]

Before she visited S. Weir Mitchell, Charlotte Gilman had sent him a complete history of her case—which he interpreted as "self conceit. He had a prejudice against the Beechers. 'I've had two women of your blood here already,' he told me scornfully." Then he put her to bed and had her fed, bathed, and rubbed. His parting advice was to live as domestic a life as possible, to keep her baby with her at all times, to "have but two hours intellectual life a day, never [to] touch pen, brush or pencil" as long as she lived.[7] There is something ludicrously misogynistic about this last injunction—a total ban not only on penis envy but on its most sublimated forms. Yet what is more appalling is the fact that Dr. Mitchell gave the same advice to Jane Addams, although European travel was to take the place of a baby in her case. Of course there were similarities between the two women; both had terrific energies they were unable to find outlets for. Both were full of self-mistrust and had great difficulty expressing affection. But left to heal themselves they did so in diametrically opposed ways.

A settlement house was a nightmare to Charlotte Gilman, an institutionalization of her worst fears about invasion of privacy. A handmade character always seemed vulnerable, and she was revolted by the prying presence of servants long before she turned her attention to the "mind-meddling" of psychiatrists. Jane Addams's preservationist tendencies were anathema to her. Mrs. Gilman did not love people best for their memories; on the contrary, she was a dedicated idol smasher, who attacked orthodox religion and that holy of holies the home.

Charlotte Perkins Gilman has been called the only genuinely radical thinker in the woman's movement since Elizabeth Cady Stanton. Certainly they shared a profound anti-authoritarianism. But Mrs. Gilman lacked the self-love that characterized Elizabeth Stanton's self-reliance. Mrs. Stanton was intrigued by experiments like Brook Farm because she believed that women would never be able to explore their full potential within the confines of the nuclear family. But Charlotte Gilman, for all her "humanitarian" socialism, had a horror of co-operative housekeeping. Mrs. Perkins had been infatuated with Swedenborg, and for a time she and her two children had lived in a communal household of the like-minded. Charlotte Gilman emerged from the experience with an abiding mistrust of the occult—and a repugnance for communal living. The doctrine of correspondence in which Lydia Maria Child had found a sanction for social sympathy had no appeal for her. Nor did she seem to consider that her thwarted mother might have needed to commune with spirits, or with other adults. Charlotte Gilman preferred to go it alone, aided by specialists in food preparation, child care, and housecleaning, whose professional touch would keep each home an immaculate sanctum where the besieged individual could pull herself together.

If Jane Addams represented Sentimentalism, in a nostalgic and therefore less virulent form, come into the twentieth century, Charlotte Gilman was the heir of the anti-Romantic Catharine Beecher in temperament as well as fact. She named her daughter Katherine Beecher Stetson, and began her autobiography with a tribute to the whole Beecher family, and significantly to the New England they lived in; "a seed-bed of progressive movements, scientific, mechanical, educational, humanitarian as well as religious."[8] Mrs. Gilman was her Aunt Catharine—without this cultural background. She had the same scientism, the same compulsive interest in physical culture and fresh air, the same inability to trust her emotions, the same paranoia rooted in a repressed knowledge of her own aggressive feelings. And, not coincidentally, Mrs. Gilman and her great aunt were the foremost Jeremiahs of American feminism.

Charlotte Gilman had been one of the few young women to speak out against censure of *The Woman's Bible* at the suffrage convention in

1896, and Mrs. Stanton always meant a great deal to her—she was woman on the old and therefore larger scale. "Of the many people I met during these years lecturing on women and economics I was particularly impressed by Elizabeth Cady Stanton. To have been with her and 'Aunt Susan,' as we called the great Susan B. Anthony, seemed to establish a connection with a splendid period of real heroism."[9] Elizabeth Stanton was not a more rigorous or scientific socialist than Charlotte Gilman, but her thoughts had a genuine coherence, the result of her lifelong commitment to a Romantic ideology. Mrs. Gilman's thoughts, like those of her great aunt, were finally not quite reasonable because of her desperate valuation of self-control, her projection of her own hostile impulses on the outside world, her privatism. Yet it seems beside the point to suggest, as William O'Neill has done in his recent book on the woman's movement in America, that what Mrs. Gilman and her contemporaries really needed was the Socialist Party.[10] Although this is not the most patronizing suggestion O'Neill could have made about what the feminists needed, it completely ignores these women's own sense of what was missing in their lives.

In the next-to-last chapter of her autobiography Charlotte Perkins Gilman described her escape from polyglot New York to the New England of her visions. Yet not precisely of her visions, for she realized that the enclaves of her "own people" were doomed to extinction, and were already dominated by a species of ancestor worship. Norwich, Connecticut, was "labeled with the names of long dead residents, not merely on gravestones, but on neat white signs hung on old houses, nailed on trees, set on the ground here and there." The Gilman's "ancient mansion" was decorated with two such signs, "on either side of the front door, one a list of ancestors, the other announcing 'Lydia Huntley Sigourney born here.'"[11] Perhaps nothing is so eloquent of what had gone out of American feminism by the end of the nineteenth century as this reduction of the Sentimental poetess from an inspirer of feeling—and ultimately of action—to an embodiment of native-born-ness.

Mrs. Gilman's own lack of contact with the Romantic-Sentimental ideology may have had as much to do with her own psychology as with broad cultural revaluations. Her father had been a librarian who often sent books when his family needed financial and emotional support, and one lasting symptom of Charlotte Gilman's breakdown was an inability to do sustained reading. This, however, does not change the fact that Madame de Staël and George Eliot and Charlotte Brontë and Felicia

Hemans never let Elizabeth Cady Stanton down. Nothing, not even her father's bitter opposition could undermine her Romantic faith in self-expression. There is, of course, something pathetic about Elizabeth Stanton's dependence on fictional models, and about Stowe and Jewett and Addams' wistful memories of grandmothers and great aunts. Yet their feminist mythology kept alive a reverence for women as selves, as competent, feeling, worthy beings, that legal reforms, and even the prospect of revolution could not sustain. Women who knew what they felt and could value those feelings were the only ones capable of radical belief—or action. And when women like Mrs. Stanton sensed that William Dean Howells was really the enemy, despite his well-meaning support of female suffrage, they were right. He had ridiculed their chosen heroines and then hinted that Mr. Gilman's story was too true to have been told; a genteel Realism was the last thing American feminists needed.

NOTES

1. Jane Addams, *Twenty Years at Hull House* (New York, 1911), p. 65.

2. Jane Addams, *Democracy and Social Ethics* (New York, 1907), p. 87.

3. William Dean Howells, ed., *Great Modern American Stories*, vii.

4. Charlotte Perkins Gilman, "The Yellow Wall-Paper," *Great Modern American Stories*, pp. 320–37. As Mrs. Gilman reconstructed her motives in *The Living of Charlotte Perkins Gilman*, "The real purpose of the story was to reach Dr. S. Weir Mitchell and convince him of the error of his ways. I sent him a copy as soon as it came out, but got no response. However, many years later, I met some one who knew close friends of Dr. Mitchell's who said he had told him that he had changed his treatment of nervous prostration since reading 'The Yellow Wallpaper.' If that is a fact, I have not lived in vain." (New York, 1935), p. 399.

5. Ibid., pp. 58–59.

6. Ibid., p. 89.

7. Ibid., pp. 95–96.

8. Ibid., p. 3.

9. Ibid., p. 216.

10. "In retrospect, perhaps the best course for feminists would have been to join the Socialist party, which alone promised to change the American social order enough so that women could exercise in practice those rights they were increasingly accorded in principle." William O'Neill, *Everyone Was Brave* (Chicago, 1969), ix.

11. Gilman, *Living*, pp. 324–26.

The "Sick" Women of
the Upper Classes

Barbara Ehrenreich and
Deirdre English

THE RISE OF THE WOMEN'S MOVEMENT promoted an interest in
long-overlooked or neglected aspects of social history and literature. In the late
1960s and early 1970s, studies of women within nineteenth-century social
history emerged in areas such as women and health. These new studies sought
to "correct" traditional history, using a feminist lens to do so. Two works by
Barbara Ehrenreich and Deirdre English, *Witches, Midwives and Nurses* (1973)
and *Complaints and Disorders: The Sexual Politics of Sickness* (1973), form a part of
this "corrective" scholarship noted for its marked political emphasis. In this
selection Ehrenreich and English provide background on "the myth of female
frailty" (96) that fed the affluent turn-of-the-century practices of male
physicians, such as S. Weir Mitchell. The authors explain in lay terms the
popular beliefs that feminine complaints, both physical and emotional, were
thought to be predestined by anatomy, particularly the uterus and the ovaries.
They discuss the oppressive role of the physician in the treatment of upper-class
women, particularly the overuse of radical gynecological surgery (ovariotomies,
clitoridectomies) for hysteria and a range of personality and nervous disorders.
Ehrenreich and English argue that the rise of radical gynecological surgery and
nonradical treatments of long-term bed rest increased the number of women
who began to see themselves as "sick" and dependent on the male doctor for
their cure.

In her introduction to *Women and Health in America* (Madison, Wis.:
University of Wisconsin Press, 1984), Judith Walzer Leavitt notes that the work
of Ehrenreich and English has been criticized for presenting a "conspiracy
argument" about women as victims and men as oppressors, a contention that
women's historians, such as Regina Markell Morantz, quickly criticized (see

90

headnote on Woods). Following these early revisionist studies, the scholarship on women and health at the turn of the century identifies the role of the male physician as one of many interconnected factors influencing women's health. Although controversial, the work of Ehrenreich and English made scholars aware of the once-ignored male medical influence in shaping women's lives. Their bold indictment of the nineteenth-century male medical profession pointed to new directions in social and feminist history. It also paved the way for more complex analyses that entertain multiple factors in the historical development of women by such scholars as Carroll Smith-Rosenberg and Charles Rosenberg, whose works are included in Leavitt's collection.

Like Ann Douglas Wood, Ehrenreich and English importantly place Gilman's story and her emotional life firmly in the context of the social history of women and health in which hysteria becomes an inevitable disease of women living in a patriarchal society. In their analysis of nonradical treatment for nervous disorders (such as passivity and uninterrupted bed rest), they note Dr. S. Weir Mitchell's rest cure treatment and Gilman's fictionalization of it in "The Yellow Wallpaper." Their forceful discussion of hysteria underscores that the nervous disorder from which Gilman suffered was widespread. This selection suggests that the treatment Gilman received, though severe, was less sinister than the commonly prescribed radical cures for mental disorders.

The affluent woman normally spent a hushed and peaceful life indoors, sewing, sketching and reading romances, planning menus and supervising servants and children. Her clothes, a sort of portable prison of tight corsets and long skirts, prevented activity any more vigorous than a Sunday stroll. Society agreed that she was frail and sickly. Her delicate nervous system had to be shielded as carefully as her body, for the slightest shock could send her reeling off to bed. Elizabeth Barrett Browning, for example, although she was an extraordinarily productive woman, spent six years in bed following her brother's death in a sailboat accident.

But not even the most sheltered woman lived in a vacuum. Just outside the suffocating world of the parlor and the boudoir lay a world of industrial horror. This was the period of America's industrial revolution, a revolution based on the ruthless exploitation of working people. Women, and children as young as six, worked fourteen-hour days in factories and sweatshops for sub-subsistence wages. Labor struggles were violent bordering, at times, on civil wars. For businessmen, too, survival was a bitter struggle: you squeezed what you could out of the workers, screwed the competition, and the devil take the hindmost. Fortunes were made and destroyed overnight, and with them rode the fates of thousands of smaller businessmen.

The genteel lady of leisure was not just an anomaly in an otherwise dog-eat-dog world. She was as much a product of that world as her husband or his employees. It was the wealth extracted in that harsh outside world that enabled a man to afford a totally leisured wife. She was the social ornament that proved a man's success: her idleness, her delicacy, her childlike ignorance of "reality" gave a man the "class" that money alone could not provide. And it was the very harshness of the outside world that led men to see the home as a refuge—"a sacred place, a vestal temple," a "tent pitch'd in a world not right," presided over by a gentle, ethereal wife. Among the affluent classes, the worlds of men and women drifted further and further apart, with divergent standards of decorum, of health, of morality itself.

There were exceptional women in the upper classes—women who rebelled against the life of enforced leisure, the limitations on meaningful work—and it is these exceptional women who usually are remembered in history books. Many became women's rights activists or social reformers. A brave few struggled to make their way in the professions. And toward the end of the nineteenth century a growing number were demanding, and getting, college educations. But the majority of upper- and upper-middle-class women had little chance to make independent lives for themselves; they were financially at the mercy of husbands or fathers. They had to accept their roles—outwardly at least—and remain dutifully housebound, white-gloved and ornamental. Of course, only a small minority of urban women could afford a life of total leisure, but a great many more women in the middle class aspired to it and did their best to live like "ladies."

THE CULT OF FEMALE INVALIDISM

The boredom and confinement of affluent women fostered a morbid cult of hypochondria—"female invalidism"—that began in the mid-nineteenth century and did not completely fade until the late 1910s. Sickness pervaded upper- and upper-middle-class female culture. Health spas and female specialists sprang up everywhere and became part of the regular circuit of fashionable women. And in the 1850s a steady stream of popular home readers by doctors appeared, all on the subject of female health. Literature aimed at female readers lingered on the romantic pathos of illness and death; popular women's magazines featured such stories as "The Grave of My Friend" and "Song of Dying." Paleness and lassitude (along with filmy white gowns) came into vogue. It was acceptable, even fashionable, to retire to bed with "sick headaches," "nerves," and a host of other mysterious ailments.

In response, feminist writers and female doctors expressed their dismay at the chronic invalidism of affluent women. Dr. Mary Putnam Jacobi, an outstanding woman doctor of the late nineteenth century, wrote in 1895:

> . . . it is considered natural and almost laudable to break down under all conceivable varieties of strain—a winter dissipation, a houseful of servants, a quarrel with a female friend, not to speak of more legitimate reasons. . . . Women who expect to go to bed every menstrual period expect to collapse if by chance they find themselves on their feet for a few hours during such a crisis. Constantly considering their nerves, urged to consider them by well-intentioned but short-sighted advisors, they pretty soon became nothing but a bundle of nerves.

Charlotte Perkins Gilman, the feminist writer and economist, concluded bitterly that American men "have bred a race of women weak enough to be handed about like invalids; or mentally weak enough to pretend they are—and to like it."

It is impossible to tell, in retrospect, how sick upper-middle-class women really were. Life expectancies for women were slightly higher than for men though the difference was nowhere near as great as it is today.

It is true, however, that women—*all* women—faced certain risks that men did not share, or share to the same degree. First were the risks associated with childbearing, which were all the greater in an age of primitive obstetrical technique when little was known about the importance of prenatal nutrition. In 1915 (the first year for which national figures are available) 61 women died for every 10,000 live babies born, compared to 2 per 10,000 today, and the maternal mortality rates were doubtless higher in the nineteenth century. Without adequate, and usually without any, means of contraception, a married woman could expect to face the risk of childbirth repeatedly through her fertile years. After each childbirth a woman might suffer any number of gynecological complications, such as a prolapsed (slipped) uterus or irreparable pelvic tear, which would stay with her for the rest of her life.

Another special risk to women came with tuberculosis, the "white plague." In the mid-nineteenth century, TB raged at epidemic proportions, and it continued to be a major threat until well into the twentieth century. Everyone was affected, but women, especially young women, were particularly vulnerable, often dying at rates twice as high as those of men of their age group. For every hundred women aged twenty in 1865, more than five would be dead from TB by the age of thirty, and more than eight would be dead by the age of fifty. (It is now believed that hormonal changes associated with puberty and childbearing accounted for the greater vulnerability of young women to TB.)

The dangers of childbearing, and of TB, must have shadowed women's lives in a way we no longer know. But these dangers cannot explain the cultural phenomenon of "female invalidism" which, unlike TB and maternal mortality, was confined to women of a particular social class. The most important legitimization of this fashion came not from the actual dangers faced by women but from the medical profession.

The medical view of women's health not only acknowledged the specific risks associated with reproductivity, it went much further: it identified *all* female functions as *inherently* sick. Puberty was seen as a "crisis," throwing the entire female organism into turmoil. Menstruation—or the lack of it—was regarded as pathological throughout a woman's life. Dr. W. C. Taylor, in his book *A Physician's Counsels to Woman in Health and Disease* (1871), gave a warning typical of those found in popular health books of the time:

> We cannot too emphatically urge the importance of regarding these monthly returns as periods of ill health, as days when the ordinary occupations are to be suspended or modified. . . . Long walks, dancing, shopping, riding and parties should be avoided at this time of month invariably and under all circumstances. . . . Another reason why every woman should look upon herself as an invalid once a month, is that the monthly flow aggravates any existing affection of the womb and readily rekindles the expiring flames of disease.

Similarly, a pregnant woman was "indisposed," and doctors campaigned against the practice of midwifery on the grounds that pregnancy was a disease and demanded the care of a doctor. Menopause was the final, incurable ill, the "death of the woman in the woman."

Women's greater susceptibility to TB was seen as proof of the inherent defectiveness of female physiology. Dr. Azell Ames wrote in 1875: "It being beyond doubt that consumption . . . is itself produced by the failure of the [menstrual] function in the forming girls . . . one has been the parent of the other with interchangeable priority." Actually, as we know today, it is true that consumption may *result* in suspension of the menses. But at that time consumption was blamed on woman's nature and on her reproductive system. When men were consumptive, doctors sought some environmental factor, such as over-exposure, to explain the disease. But in popular imagery, consumption was always effeminate: novels of the time usually featured as male consumptives only such "effete" types as poets, artists, and other men "incompetent" for serious masculine pursuits.

The association of TB with innate feminine weakness was strength-ened by the fact that TB is accompanied by an erratic emotional pattern in which a person may behave sometimes frenetically, sometimes mor-bidly. The behavior characteristic for the disease fit expectations about woman's personality, and the look of the disease suited—and perhaps helped to create—the prevailing standards of female beauty. The female consumptive did not lose her feminine identity, she embodied it: the bright eyes, translucent skin, and red lips were only an extreme of traditional female beauty. A romantic myth rose up around the figure of the female consumptive and was reflected in portraiture and literature: for example, in the sweet and tragic character of Beth, in *Little Women*. Not only were women seen as sickly—sickness was seen as feminine.

The doctors' view of women as innately sick did not, of course, *make* them sick, or delicate, or idle. But it did provide a powerful rationale against allowing women to act in any other way. Medical arguments were used to explain why women should be barred from medical school (they would faint in anatomy lectures), from higher education alto-gether, and from voting. For example, a Massachusetts legislator proclaimed:

> Grant suffrage to women, and you will have to build insane asylums in every county, and establish a divorce court in every town. Women are too nervous and hysterical to enter into politics.

Medical arguments seemed to take the malice out of sexual oppression: when you prevented a woman from doing anything active or interesting, you were only doing this for her own good.

THE DOCTORS' STAKE IN WOMEN'S ILLNESS

The myth of female frailty, and the very real cult of female hypochondria that seemed to support the myth, played directly to the financial interests of the medical profession. In the late nineteenth and early twentieth centuries, the "regular" AMA doctors (members of the American Medical Association—the intellectual ancestors of today's doctors) still had no legal monopoly over medical practice and no legal control over the number of people who called themselves "doctors." Competition from lay healers of both sexes, and from what the AMA saw as an excess of formally trained male physicians, had the doctors running scared. A good part of the competition was female: women lay healers and midwives dominated the urban ghettos and the countryside in many areas; suffragists were beating on the doors of the medical schools.

For the doctors, the myth of female frailty thus served two purposes. It helped them to disqualify women as healers, and, of course, it made women highly qualified as patients.* In 1900 there were 173 doctors (engaged in primary patient care) per 100,000 population, compared to 50 per 100,000 today. So, it was in the interests of doctors to cultivate the illnesses of their patients with frequent home visits and drawn-out "treatments." A few dozen well-heeled lady customers were all that a doctor needed for a successful urban practice. Women—at least, women whose husbands could pay the bills—became a natural "client caste" to the developing medical profession.

In many ways, the upper-middle-class woman was the ideal patient: her illnesses—and her husband's bank account—seemed almost inexhaustible. Furthermore, she was usually submissive and obedient to the "doctor's orders." The famous Philadelphia doctor S. Weir Mitchell expressed his profession's deep appreciation of the female invalid in 1888:

> With all her weakness, her unstable emotionality, her tendency to morally warp when long nervously ill, she is then far easier to deal with, far more

---

*See *Witches, Midwives and Nurses* by Barbara Ehrenreich and Deirdre English. Glass Mountain Pamphlets, no. 1 (New York: The Feminist Press, 1973).

amenable to reason, far more sure to be comfortable as a patient, than the man who is relatively in a like position. The reasons for this are too obvious to delay me here, and physicians accustomed to deal with both sexes as sick people will be apt to justify my position.

In Mitchell's mind women were not only easier to relate to, but sickness was the very key to femininity: "The man who does not know sick women does not know women."

Some women were quick to place at least some of the blame for female invalidism on the doctors' interests. Dr. Elizabeth Garrett Anderson, an American woman doctor, argued that the extent of female invalidism was much exaggerated by male doctors and that women's natural functions were not really all that debilitating. In the working classes, she observed, work went on during menstruation "without intermission, and, as a rule, without ill effects." (Of course, working-class women could not have afforded the costly medical attention required for female invalidism.) Mary Livermore, a women's suffrage worker, spoke against "the monstrous assumption that woman is a natural invalid," and denounced "the unclean army of 'gynecologists' who seem desirous to convince women that they possess but one set of organs— and that these are always diseased." And Dr. Mary Putnam Jacobi put the matter most forcefully when she wrote in 1895, "I think, finally, it is in the increased attention paid to women, and especially in their new function as lucrative patients, scarcely imagined a hundred years ago, that we find explanation for much of the ill-health among women, freshly discovered today. . . ."

The "Scientific" Explanation of Female Frailty

As a businessman, the doctor had a direct interest in a social role for women that encouraged them to be sick; as a doctor, he had an obligation to find the causes of female complaints. The result was that, as a "scientist," he ended up proposing medical theories that were actually justifications of women's social role.

This was easy enough to do at the time: no one had a very clear idea of human physiology. American medical education, even at the best schools, put few constraints on the doctors' imaginations, offering only a scant introduction to what was known of physiology and anatomy and no training in rigorous scientific method. So doctors had considerable intellectual license to devise whatever theories seemed socially appropriate.

Generally, they traced female disorders either to women's inherent "defectiveness" or to any sort of activity beyond the mildest "feminine" pursuits—especially sexual, athletic, and mental activity. Thus promiscuity, dancing in hot rooms, and subjection to an overly romantic husband were given as the origins of illness, along with too much reading, too much seriousness or ambition, and worrying.

The underlying medical theory of women's weakness rested on what doctors considered the most basic physiological law: "conservation of energy." According to the first postulate of this theory, each human body contained a set quantity of energy that was directed variously from one organ or function to another. This meant that you could develop one organ or ability only at the expense of others, drawing energy away from the parts not being developed. In particular, the sexual organs competed with the other organs for the body's fixed supply of vital energy. The second postulate of this theory—that reproductivity was central to a woman's biological life—made this competition highly unequal, with the reproductive organs in almost total command of the whole woman.

The implications of the "conservation of energy" theory for male and female roles are important. Let's consider them.

Curiously, from a scientific perspective, men didn't jeopardize their reproductivity by engaging in intellectual pursuits. On the contrary, since the mission of upper- and upper-middle-class men was to be doers, not breeders, they had to be careful not to let sex drain energy away from their "higher functions." Doctors warned men not to "spend their seed" (i.e., the essence of their energy) recklessly, but to conserve themselves for the "civilizing endeavors" they were embarked upon. College youths were jealously segregated from women—except on rare sexual sprees in town—and virginity was often prized in men as well as women. Debilitated sperm would result from too much "indulgence," and this in turn could produce "runts," feeble infants, and girls.

On the other hand, because reproduction was woman's grand purpose in life, doctors agreed that women ought to concentrate their physical energy internally, toward the womb. All other activity should be slowed down or stopped during the peak periods of sexual energy use. At the onset of menstruation, women were told to take a great deal of bed rest in order to help focus their strength on regulating their periods—though this might take years. The more time a pregnant woman spent lying down quietly, the better. At menopause, women were often put to bed again.

Doctors and educators were quick to draw the obvious conclusion that, for women, higher education could be physically dangerous. Too much development of the brain, they counseled, would atrophy the uterus. Reproductive development was totally antagonistic to mental development. In a work entitled *Concerning the Physiological and Intellectual Weakness of Women*, the German scientist P. Moebius wrote:

> If we wish woman to fulfill the task of motherhood fully she cannot possess a masculine brain. If the feminine abilities were developed to the same degree as those of the male, her material organs would suffer and we should have before us a repulsive and useless hybrid.

In the United States this thesis was set forth most cogently by Dr. Edward Clarke of Harvard College. He warned, in his influential book *Sex in Education* (1873), that higher education was *already* destroying the reproductive abilities of American women.

Even if a woman should choose to devote herself to intellectual or other "unwomanly" pursuits, she could hardly hope to escape the domination of her uterus and ovaries. In *The Diseases of Women* (1849), Dr. F. Hollick wrote: "The Uterus, it must be remembered, is the *controlling* organ in the female body, being the most excitable of all, and so intimately connected, by the ramifications of its numerous nerves, with every other part." To other medical theorists, it was the ovaries that occupied center stage. This passage, written in 1870 by Dr. W. W. Bliss, is, if somewhat overwrought, nonetheless typical:

> Accepting, then, these views of the gigantic power and influence of the ovaries over the whole animal economy of woman,—that they are the most powerful agents in all the commotions of her system; that on them rest her intellectual standing in society, her physical perfection, and all that lends beauty to those fine and delicate contours which are constant objects of admiration, all that is great, noble and beautiful, all that is voluptuous, tender, and endearing; that her fidelity, her devotedness, her perpetual vigilance, forecast, and all those qualities of mind and disposition which inspire respect and love and fit her as the safest counsellor and friend of man, spring from the ovaries,—*what must be their influence and power over*

the great vocation of woman and the august purposes of her existence when these organs have become compromised through disease! Can the record of woman's mission on earth be otherwise than filled with tales of sorrow, sufferings, and manifold infirmities, all through the influence of these important organs?

This was not mere textbook rhetoric. In their actual medical practices, doctors found uterine and ovarian "disorders" behind almost every female complaint, from headaches to sore throats and indigestion. Curvature of the spine, bad posture, or pains anywhere in the lower half of the body could be the result of "displacement" of the womb, and one doctor ingeniously explained how constipation results from the pressure of the uterus on the rectum. Dr. M.E. Dirix wrote in 1869:

> Thus, women are treated for diseases of the stomach, liver, kidneys, heart, lungs, etc.; yet, in most instances, these diseases will be found, on due investigation, to be, in reality, no diseases at all, but merely the sympathetic reactions or the symptoms of one disease, namely, a disease of the womb.

THE PSYCHOLOGY OF THE OVARY

If the uterus and ovaries could dominate woman's entire body, it was only a short step to the ovarian take-over of woman's entire personality. The basic idea, in the nineteenth century, was that female psychology functioned merely as an extension of female reproductivity, and that woman's nature was determined solely by her reproductive functions. The typical medical view was that "The ovaries . . . give to woman all her characteristics of body and mind. . . ." And Dr. Bliss remarked, somewhat spitefully, "The influence of the ovaries over the mind is displayed in woman's artfulness and dissimulation." According to this "psychology of the ovary," all woman's "natural" characteristics were directed from the ovaries, and any abnormalities—from irritability to insanity—could be attributed to some ovarian disease. As one doctor wrote, "All the various and manifold derangements of the reproductive system, peculiar to females, add to the causes of insanity." Conversely, actual physical reproductive problems and diseases, including cancer, could be traced to bad habits and attitudes.

Masturbation was seen as a particularly vicious character defect that led to physical damage, and although this was believed to be true for both men and women, doctors seemed more alarmed by female masturbation. They warned that "The Vice" could lead to menstrual dysfunction, uterine disease, and lesions on the genitals. Masturbation was one form of "hypersexuality," which was said to lead to consumption; in turn, consumption might result in hypersexuality. The association between "hypersexuality" and TB was easily "demonstrated" by pointing to the high rates of TB among prostitutes. All this fueled the notion that "sexual disorders" led to disease, and conversely, that disease lay behind women's sexual desires.

The medical model of female nature, embodied in the "psychology of the ovary," drew a rigid distinction between reproductivity and sexuality. Women were urged by the health books and the doctors to indulge in deep preoccupation with themselves as "The Sex"; they were to devote themselves to developing their reproductive powers, their maternal instincts, their "femininity." Yet they were told that they had no "natural" sexual feelings whatsoever. They were believed to be completely governed by their ovaries and uteruses, but to be repelled by the sex act itself. In fact, sexual feelings were seen as unwomanly, pathological, and possibly detrimental to the supreme function of reproduction. (Men, on the other hand, *were* believed to have sexual feelings, and many doctors went so far as to condone prostitution on the grounds that the lust of upper-middle-class males should have some outlet other than their delicate wives.)

The doctors themselves never seemed entirely convinced of this view of female nature. While they denied the existence of female sexuality as vigorously as any other men of their times, they were always on the lookout for it. Medically, this vigilance was justified by the idea that female sexuality could only be pathological. So it was only natural for some doctors to test for it by stroking the breasts or the clitoris. But under the stern disapproval, there always lurked the age-old fear of and fascination with woman's "insatiable lust" that, once awakened, might be totally uncontrollable. In 1853, when he was only twenty-five years old, the British physician Robert Brudenell Carter wrote (in a work entitled *On the Pathology and Treatment of Hysteria*):

. . . no one who has realized the amount of moral evil wrought in girls . . . whose prurient desires have been increased by Indian hemp and partially gratified by medical manipulations, can deny that remedy is worse than disease. I have . . . seen young unmarried women, of the middle class of society, reduced by the constant use of the speculum to the mental and moral condition of prostitutes; seeking to give themselves the same indulgence by the practice of solitary vice; and asking every medical practitioner . . . to institute an examination of the sexual organs.

(Did Dr. Carter's patients actually smoke "Indian hemp" or beg for internal examinations? Unfortunately, we have no other authority on the subject than Dr. Carter himself.)

MEDICAL TREATMENTS

Uninformed by anything that we would recognize today as a scientific description of the way human bodies work, the actual practice of medicine at the turn of the century was largely a matter of guesswork, consisting mainly of ancient remedies and occasional daring experiments. Not until 1912, according to one medical estimate, did the average patient, seeking help from the average American doctor, have more than a fifty-fifty chance of benefiting from the encounter. In fact, the average patient ran a significant risk of actually getting worse as a result: bleeding, violent purges, heavy doses of mercury-based drugs, and even opium were standard therapeutic approaches throughout the nineteenth century, for male as well as female patients. Even well into the twentieth century, there was little that we would recognize as modern medical technology. Surgery was still a highly risky enterprise; there were no antibiotics or other "wonder drugs"; and little was understood, medically, of the relationship between nutrition and health or of the role of hormones in regulating physiological processes.

Every patient suffered from this kind of hit-or-miss treatment, but some of the treatments applied to women now seem particularly useless and bizarre. For example, a doctor confronted with what he believed was an inflammation of the reproductive organs might try to "draw away" the inflammation by creating what he thought were counter-irritations—blisters or sores on the groin or the thighs. The common medical practice of bleeding by means of leeches also took on some very peculiar forms in the hands of gynecologists. Dr. F. Hollick, speaking of methods of curing amenorrhea (chronic lack of menstrual periods), commented: "Some authors speak very highly of the good effects of leeches, applied to the external lips [of the genitals], a few days before the period is expected." Leeches on the breasts might prove effective too, he observed, because of the deep sympathy between the sexual organs. In some cases leeches were even applied to the cervix despite the danger of their occasional loss in the uterus. (So far as we know, no doctor ever considered perpetrating similar medical insults to the male organs.)

Such methods could be dismissed as well intentioned, if somewhat prurient, experimentation in an age of deep medical ignorance. But there were other "treatments" that were far more sinister—those aimed at altering female *behavior*. The least physically destructive of these was based, simply, on isolation and uninterrupted rest. This was used to treat a host of problems diagnosed as "nervous disorders."

Passivity was the main prescription, along with warm baths, cool baths, abstinence from animal foods and spices, and indulgence in milk and puddings, cereals, and "mild sub-acid fruits." Women were to have a nurse—not a relative—to care for them, to receive no visitors, and as Dr. Dirix wrote, "all sources of mental excitement should be perseveringly guarded against." Charlotte Perkins Gilman was prescribed this type of treatment by Dr. S. Weir Mitchell, who advised her to put away all her pens and books. Gilman later described the experience in the story "The Yellow Wallpaper," in which the heroine, a would-be writer, is ordered by her physician-husband to "rest":

> So I take phosphates or phosphites—whichever it is, and tonics and jour-neys, and air, and exercise, and am absolutely forbidden to "work" until I am well again.
> Personally, I disagree with their ideas.
> Personally, I believe that congenial work, with excitement and change, would do me good.
> But what is one to do?
> I did write for a while—in spite of them; but it *does* exhaust me a good deal—having to be so sly about it, . . . or else meet with heavy opposition.

Slowly Gilman's heroine begins to lose her grip ("It is getting to be a great effort for me to think straight. Just this nervous weakness, I sup-pose.") and finally she frees herself from her prison—into madness, crawling in endless circles about her room, muttering about the wallpaper.

But it was the field of gynecological surgery that provided the most brutally direct medical treatments of female "personality disorders." And the surgical approach to female psychological problems had what was considered a solid theoretical basis in the theory of the "psychology of the ovary." After all, if a woman's entire personality was dominated by her reproductive organs, then gynecological surgery was the most logical approach to any female psychological problem. Beginning in the late 1860s, doctors began to act on this principle.

At least one of their treatments probably *was* effective: surgical removal of the clitoris as a cure for sexual arousal. A medical book of this period stated: "Unnatural growth of the clitoris . . . is likely to lead to immorality as well as to serious disease . . . amputation may be necessary." Although many doctors frowned on the practice of removing the clitoris, they tended to agree that this might be necessary in cases of "nymphomania." (The last clitorectomy we know of in the United States was performed twenty-five years ago on a child of five, as a cure for masturbation.)

More widely practiced was the surgical removal of the ovaries— ovariotomy, or "female castration." Thousands of these operations were performed from 1860 to 1890. In his article "The Spermatic Economy," Ben Barker-Benfield describes the invention of the "normal ovariotomy," or removal of ovaries for non-ovarian conditions—in 1872 by Dr. Robert Battey of Rome, Georgia.

> Among the indications were a troublesomeness, eating like a ploughman, masturbation, attempted suicide, erotic tendencies, persecution mania, simple "cussedness," and dysmenorrhea. Most apparent in the enormous variety of symptoms doctors took to indicate castration was a strong current of sexual appetitiveness on the part of women.

Patients were often brought in by their husbands, who complained of their unruly behavior. When returned to their husbands, "castrated," they were "tractible, orderly, industrious and cleanly," according to Dr. Battey. (Today ovariotomy, accompanying a hysterectomy, for example, is not known to have these effects on the personality. One can only wonder what, if any, personality changes Dr. Battey's patients really went through.) Whatever the effects, some doctors claimed to have removed from fifteen hundred to two thousand ovaries; in Barker-Benfield's words, they "handed them around at medical society meetings on plates like trophies."

We could go on cataloging the ludicrous theories, the lurid cures, but the point should be clear: late nineteenth-century medical treatment of women made very little sense as *medicine*, but it was undoubtedly effective at keeping certain women—those who could afford to be patients—in their place. As we have seen, surgery was often performed with the explicit goal of "taming" a high-strung woman, and whether or not the surgery itself was effective, the very threat of surgery was probably enough to bring many women into line. Prescribed bed rest was obviously little more than a kind of benign imprisonment—and the prescriptions prohibiting intellectual activity speak for themselves!

But these are just the extreme "cures." The great majority of upper-middle-class women were never subjected to gynecological surgery or long-term bed rest, yet they too were victims of the prevailing assumptions about women's "weakness" and the necessity of frequent medical attention. The more the doctors "treated," the more they lured women into seeing themselves as sick. The entire mystique of female sickness— the house calls, the tonics and medicines, the health spas—served, above all, to keep a great many women busy at the task of doing nothing. Even among middle-class women who could not afford constant medical attention and who did not have the leisure for full-time invalidism, the myth of female frailty took its toll, with cheap (and often dangerous) patent medicines taking the place of high-priced professional "cures."

One very important effect of all this was a great increase in the upper-middle-class woman's dependence on men. To be sure, the leisured lady of the "better" classes was already financially dependent on her husband. But the cult of invalidism made her seem dependent for her very physical survival on both her doctor and her husband. She might be tired of being a kept woman, she might yearn for a life of meaning and activity, but if she was convinced that she was seriously sick or in danger of becoming so, would she dare to break away? How could she even survive on her own, without the expensive medical care paid for by her husband? Ultimately, she might even become convinced that her restlessness was itself "sick"—just further proof of her need for a confined, inactive life. And if she did overcome the paralyzing assumption of women's innate sickness and begin to act in unconventional ways, a doctor could always be found to prescribe a return to what was considered normal.

In fact, the medical attention directed at these women amounted to what may have been a very effective surveillance system. Doctors were in a position to detect the first signs of rebelliousness, and to interpret them as symptoms of a "disease" which had to be "cured."

SUBVERTING THE SICK ROLE

It would be a mistake to assume that women were merely the passive victims of a medical reign of terror. In some ways, they were able to turn the sick role to their own advantage, especially as a form of birth control. For the "well-bred" woman to whom sex really *was* repugnant, and yet a "duty," or for any woman who wanted to avoid pregnancy, "feeling sick" was a way out—and there were few others. Contraceptive methods were virtually unavailable; abortion was risky and illegal. It would never have entered a respectable doctor's head to advise a lady on contraception (if he *had* any advice to offer, which is unlikely). Or to offer to perform an abortion (at least according to AMA propaganda). In fact, doctors devoted considerable energy to "proving" that contraception and abortion were inherently unhealthy, and capable of causing such diseases as cancer. (This was before the pill!) But a doctor *could* help a woman by supporting her claims to be too sick for sex: he could recommend abstinence. So who knows how many of this period's drooping consumptives and listless invalids were actually well women, feigning illness to escape intercourse and pregnancy?

If some women resorted to sickness as a means of birth—and sex—control, others undoubtedly used it to gain attention and a limited measure of power within their families. Today, everybody is familiar with the (sexist) myth of the mother-in-law whose symptoms conveniently strike during family crises. In the nineteenth century, women developed, in epidemic numbers, an entire syndrome which even doctors sometimes interpreted as a power grab rather than a genuine illness. The new disease was hysteria, which in many ways epitomized the cult of female invalidism. It affected upper- and upper-middle-class women almost exclusively; it had no discernible organic basis; and it was totally resistant to medical treatment. For those reasons alone, it is worth considering in some detail.

A contemporary doctor described the hysterical fit this way:

The patient . . . loses the ordinary expression of countenance, which is replaced by a vacant stare; becomes agitated; falls if before standing; throws her limbs about convulsively; twists the body into all kinds of violent contortions; beats her chest; sometimes tears her hair; and attempts to bite herself and others; and, though a delicate woman, evinces a muscular strength which often requires four or five persons to restrain her effectually.

Hysteria appeared, not only as fits and fainting, but in every other form: hysterical loss of voice, loss of appetite, hysterical coughing or sneezing, and, of course, hysterical screaming, laughing, and crying. The disease spread wildly, yet almost exclusively in a select clientele of urban middle- and upper-middle-class white women between the ages of fifteen and forty-five.

Doctors became obsessed with this "most confusing, mysterious and rebellious of diseases." In some ways, it was the ideal disease for the doctors: it was never fatal, and it required an almost endless amount of medical attention. But it was not an ideal disease from the point of view of the husband and family of the afflicted woman. Gentle invalidism had been one thing; violent fits were quite another. So hysteria put the doctors on the spot. It was essential to their professional self-esteem either to find an organic basis for the disease, and cure it, or to expose it as a clever charade.

There was plenty of evidence for the latter point of view. With mounting suspicion, the medical literature began to observe that hysterics never had fits when alone, and only when there was something soft to fall on. One doctor accused them of pinning their hair in such a way that it would fall luxuriantly when they fainted. The hysterical "type" began to be characterized as a "petty tyrant" with a "taste for power" over her husband, servants, and children, and, if possible, her doctor.

In historian Carroll Smith-Rosenberg's interpretation, the doctor's accusations had some truth to them: the hysterical fit, for many women, must have been the only acceptable outburst—of rage, of despair, or simply of *energy*—possible. But as a form of revolt it was very limited. No matter how many women might adopt it, it remained completely individualized: hysterics don't unite and fight. As a power play, throwing a fit might give a brief psychological advantage over a husband or a doctor, but ultimately it played into the hands of the doctors by confirming their notion of woman as irrational, unpredictable, and diseased.

On the whole, however, doctors did continue to insist that hysteria was a real disease—a disease of the uterus, in fact. (Hysteria comes from the Greek word for uterus.) They remained unshaken in their conviction that their own house calls and high physician's fees were absolutely necessary; yet at the same time, in their treatment and in their writing, doctors assumed an increasingly angry and threatening attitude. One doctor wrote, "It will sometimes be advisable to speak in a decided tone, in the presence of the patient, of the necessity of shaving the head, or of giving her a cold shower bath, should she not be soon relieved." He then gave a "scientific" rationalization for this treatment by saying, "The sedative influence of fear may allay, as I have known it to do, the excitement of the nervous centers. . . ."

Carroll Smith-Rosenberg writes that doctors recommended suffocating hysterical women until their fits stopped, beating them across the face and body with wet towels, and embarrassing them in front of family and friends. She quotes Dr. F.C. Skey: "Ridicule to a woman of sensitive mind, is a powerful weapon . . . but there is not an emotion equal to fear and the threat of personal chastisement. . . . They will listen to the voice of authority." The more women became hysterical, the more doctors became punitive toward the disease; and at the same time, they began to see the disease everywhere themselves until they were diagnosing every independent act by a woman, especially a women's rights action, as "hysterical."

With hysteria, the cult of female invalidism was carried to its logical conclusion. Society had assigned affluent women to a life of confinement and inactivity, and medicine had justified this assignment by describing women as innately sick. In the epidemic of hysteria, women were both accepting their inherent "sickness' *and* finding a way to rebel against an intolerable social role. Sickness, having become a way of life, became a way of rebellion, and medical treatment, which had always had strong overtones of coercion, revealed itself as frankly and brutally repressive.

But hysteria is more than a bizarre twist of medical history. The nineteenth-century epidemic of hysteria had lasting significance because it ushered in a totally new "scientific" approach to the medical management of women.

While the conflict between women and their doctors in America was escalating on the issue of hysteria, Sigmund Freud, in Vienna, was beginning to work on a treatment that would remove the disease altogether from the arena of gynecology. In one stroke, he solved the problem of hysteria and marked out a new medical specialty. "Psychoanalysis," as Carroll Smith-Rosenberg has said, "is the child of the hysterical woman." Freud's cure was based on changing the rules of the game: in the first place, by eliminating the issue of whether or not the woman was faking. Psychoanalysis, as Thomas Szasz has pointed out, insists that "malingering *is* an illness—in fact, an illness 'more serious' than hysteria." Secondly, Freud established that hysteria was a mental disorder. He banished the traumatic "cures" and legitimized a doctor-patient relationship based solely on talking. His therapy urged the patient to confess her resentments and rebelliousness, and then at last to accept her role as a woman.

Under Freud's influence, the scalpel for the dissection of female nature eventually passed from the gynecologist to the psychiatrist. In some ways, psychoanalysis represented a sharp break with the past and a genuine advance for women: it was not physically injurious, and it did permit women to have sexual feelings (although only vaginal sensations were believed to be normal for adult women; clitoral sensation was "immature" and "masculine"). But in important ways, the Freudian theory of female nature was in direct continuity with the gynecological view which it replaced. It held that the female personality was inherently defective, this time due to the absence of a penis, rather than to the presence of the domineering uterus. Women were still "sick," and their sickness was still totally predestined by their anatomy.

From " 'The Fashionable Diseases': Women's Complaints and Their Treatment in Nineteenth-Century America"

Ann Douglas Wood

ANN DOUGLAS WOOD discusses "the fashionable diseases" among upper- and middle-class American Victorian women confined to the home as caretakers of husbands and children—a situation that proved problematic to intelligent, imaginative, and ambitious women such as Charlotte Perkins Gilman. Wood's presentations of the male physician and pioneering women doctors have been criticized by historians who regard her work as polemics, not history. Raising these objections in her response to Wood's article, Regina Markell Morantz argues that Wood too readily presents the woman as a victim of the patriarchal medical profession (which she deems a "caricature") and fails to explore the larger context of the treatment of diseases in nineteenth-century America or the complexities informing Victorian attitudes toward women. Wood's essay and Morantz's response, entitled "The Perils of Feminist History," are included in *Women and Health in America* (Ed. Judith Walzer Leavitt [Madison, Wis.: University of Wisconsin, 1984]).

Although historically controversial and somewhat dated in its approach to the health of Victorian women, Wood's essay—like that of Ehrenreich and English—raised the awareness of historians and literary scholars about the issues of women and health in America. It also placed Gilman's "The Yellow Wallpaper" in the larger context of nineteenth-century diagnosis of women's sexual and nervous diseases, which generated a wider readership for Gilman and her story. In this selection Wood refers to the lives of Gilman and S. Weir Mitchell to illuminate the autobiographical nature of "The Yellow Wallpaper."

Wood notes that Mitchell had a second career as a novelist.[1] Although virtually unknown today, Mitchell was one of the most popular and prolific turn-of-the-century American writers. Wood argues that in Mitchell's *Roland*

Blake (1886) and *Constance Trescott* (1905) the heroines fall prey to invalidism due to their failure to conform to the ideal woman, the angel in the house. Wood's extreme portrait of Mitchell as a physician undeniably advances her argument of the woman patient fighting against victimization by her male physician. She also compares Gilman's work to Catharine Esther Beecher's *Letters to the People in Health and Happiness*, a more veiled account of the motives of male physicians in treating women patients. Wood forcefully concludes that "Gilman and Beecher [Gilman's great aunt] simply in writing their works, are implying that the untutored common sense of two women can outdo the professionally trained brains of those male doctors who labored in vain to cure them. Both are thus in essence urging that a woman should be independent, that *she be her own physician*, so that the real business of healing can get underway" (117).

One finds an underlying logic running through popular books by physicians on women's diseases to the effect that ladies get sick *because* they are unfeminine—in other words, sexually aggressive, intellectually ambitious, and defective in proper womanly submission and selflessness. Bad health habits were often put forth by doctors and others as causes of nervous complaints. But these, consisting as they did of improper diet, light reading, late hours, tight lacing, and inadequate clothing, were in themselves a badge of the "fashionable" and flirtatious female, only a step removed in popular imagination from the infamous one. Byford believed that "the influence of lascivious books" and frequent "indulgence" in intercourse would precipitate neuralgia.[2] Significantly, in Mitchell's fiction, the sick woman is almost invariably the closest thing he has to a villainess and she is often intelligent and usually predatory to an extreme. In *Roland Blake*, published in 1886, Octapia Darnell, an invalid, is branded by her name. Octapuslike, she uses her sickness like tentacles to try to squeeze the life out of her innocent young cousin, Olivia Wynne. Although we see her in genuine nervous spasms, Mitchell never shows her seized by a convulsion where it would be inconvenient to her purposes, nor does he let us forget that when she needs physical strength to accomplish her will, she always summons it. Again, the heroine of *Constance Trescott* (1905), his last and best novel, is driven by a demonic will to possess utterly where she loves and to revenge totally where she hates. Rather predictably she turns to invalidism at the book's close to gain her ends.

It is not that Mitchell totally condemns these women. Instead, he understands them, and adopts a tone of pitying patronage toward them.

He thinks they are genuinely sick, but he believes, as did Clarke, that the root of their sickness was their failure to be women, to sacrifice themselves for others, and to perform their feminine duties. Typically, Octapia Darnell has a brief period of improvement when a "recent need to think of others had beneficently taken her outside of the slowly narrowing circle of self-care and self-contemplation, and, by relieving her of some of the morbid habits of disease, had greatly bettered her physical condition."[3] The truth is that Mitchell does not even need to blame or punish her: In his view, nature has conveniently done that job for him.

Mitchell's analysis, then, one standard with doctors in the nineteenth century, served an important psychological purpose, whatever its medical validity. The doctor, on some unacknowledged level, feared his female patient. Could he so emphasize the diseased potency of woman's unique and mysterious organ, the womb, if he did not worry that his sex, the constant companion of hers, was in some way menaced? How comfortable Mitchell must have felt, when, addressing a graduating Radcliffe class, he expressed his clearly faint hope "that no wreck from these shores will be drifted into my dockyard."[4] They might begin as his competitors, but, despite it — in fact, because of it — they would end as his patients.

Mitchell and his peers could indeed afford to pity the fair sex, even perhaps to "cure" them. Yet the consequent "cures" bore unmistakable signs of their culturally determined origin, for they made a woman's womb very much a liability. Since her disease was unconsciously viewed as a symptom of a failure in femininity, its remedy was designed both as a punishment and an agent of regeneration, for it forced her to acknowledge her womanhood and made her totally dependent on the professional prowess of her male doctor. The cauterizer, with his injections, leeches, and hot irons seems suggestive of a veiled but aggressively hostile male sexuality and superiority, and the rest-cure expert carried this spirit to a sophisticated culmination.

Mitchell's treatment depended in actuality not so much on the techniques of rest and overfeeding, as on the commanding personality and charismatic will of the physician. "A slight, pale lad of no physical strength" by his own description, he moved as a young man in the shadow of his dominating, joyous, strong doctor-father.[5] To be the strong, healing male in a world of ailing, dependent women had obvious charms for him. "Electric with fascination" for women as his granddaughter saw him, he acknowledged that he played the "despot" in the sickroom, and boasted of reducing patients to the docility of children.[6] Doctors had always preferred to keep women in ignorance, and Mitchell was no exception. In a characteristically urbane and aphoristic remark, he said, "Wise women choose their doctors and trust them. The wisest ask the fewest questions."[7] But he wanted to be more than trusted: He wished to be revered, even adored, and he succeeded. The totality of the power he could acquire is revealed in a letter he received from a sick woman who positively grovels before him as she rhapsodizes on his potency:

> Whilst laid by the heels in a country-house with an attack of grippe, also an invalid from gastric affection, the weary eyes of a sick woman fall upon your face in the *Century* of this month—a thrill passed through me—at last I saw the true physician![8]

It is clear, moreover, that Mitchell encouraged this worshiping attitude as an important element in his "cure." A doctor, in his view, if he had the proper mesmeric powers of will, could become almost god-like.[9] Women doctors would always be inferior to male physicians, he believed, precisely because they could not exercise such tyranny: They were unable to "obtain the needed control over those of their own sex."[10] Mitchell here skated on the edge of a theory of primitive healing through mesmeric sexual powers.[11] Furthermore, his treatment was designed to make his female patients take his view of the doctor's role. They were allowed to see no one but him, and to talk of their ills and problems to no one else. As doctor he became the only spot of energy, the only source of *life*, during the enforced repose of a cure process.

Undoubtedly, if Mitchell were aware of what he was doing, he would have felt it justifiable and even merciful. He was curing his patients—by restoring them to their femininity or, in other words, by subordinating them to an enlightened but dictatorial male will. His admirers delighted to tell how, when a strangely recalcitrant patient refused to rise from bed after Mitchell had decreed that her rest cure was over, Mitchell threatened to move into bed with her if she did not get up, and even started to undress. When he got to his pants, she got up. Although the story may well be apocryphal, its spirit is not. Not surprisingly, the lady in question was fleeing the fact where she embraced the shadow, for symbolically, Mitchell, like his cauterizing predecessor, played the role of possessor, even impregnator, in the cure process. Dominated, overfed often to the point of obesity, caressed and (quite literally) vibrating, were not his patients being returned to health—to womanhood?[12] The only other time that the Victorian lady took to her bed and got fat was, in fact, before delivery. J. Marion Sims had noted that his colleagues were erroneously wont to lament about a sick woman: "If she could only have a child, it would cure her."[13] Although he was a generation later, Mitchell was not so different from the doctors Sims opposed who looked to pregnancy for the cure of all feminine ills.

Here one senses a clue to the pertinacity with which doctors told women anxious to avoid pregnancy that they should sleep with their husbands only during what we now know as their most fertile period. In a sense, the practices and writings of the medical profession provide the other half of the picture of ideal womanhood presented in the sentimental literature of the day. Woman was at her holiest, according to the genteel novels and poetry of Victorian America, as a mother. Pregnancy itself, however, was avoided by the authors of such works as completely as the act of impregnation. The medical manual took on the role of frankness disowned by its more discreet companion. All the logic of contemporary medical lore adds up to the lesson that women were at their most feminine when they were pregnant. Pregnant, they were visible emblems of masculine potency.

It is impossible to determine how many nineteenth-century middle-class American women went to doctors, just as it is difficult to tell how real their much-advertised ailments were. Reluctant as American women apparently were to undergo local examination, many of them presumably stayed home and suffered with no medical aid except that provided by earlier versions of Lydia Pinkham's patent medicine. Others trusted to the hydropathic remedies provided at numerous water-cures or used homeopathic drugs, both of which represented forms of protest against current medical practices.[14] Furthermore, the majority of women suffering from uterine and/or nervous disorders who underwent a form of local treatment or, later, the rest cure, were presumably in real distress and glad of whatever help their physician could offer.[15] Some, however, were undoubtedly using prescribed treatments for their own purposes. According to numerous masculine and feminine observers, many women grew positively addicted to local treatment as others did later to the rest cure, but, not surprisingly, these women have not left any direct confessions to posterity.[16]

What we do have record of is a masked but almost hysterical paranoia among a small group of feminist hygiene experts and lady doctors, a paranoia stemming from their exaggerated but astute perception of the unconscious purposes underlying the attitudes and practices of doctors with women patients. In their excited view, current medical treatment was patently not science, for which they professed respect, but a part of their male-dominated culture, for which they had both fear and contempt. They saw it as a form of rape, designed to keep woman prostrate, a perpetual patient dependent on a doctor's supposed professional expertise.

No one expressed this attitude better than did two Beecher women, Catharine Esther Beecher, who crusaded against local treatment, and her grandniece Charlotte Perkins Gilman, who protested against Mitchell's rest cure a generation later. Each of them wrote a work dedicated to exposing what they felt were the unstated motives of physicians treating women patients. In *Letters to the People on Health and Happiness*, Beecher described with heavy-handed irony the ineffectuality of the string of "talented, highly-educated and celebrated" doctors who had tried to cure her own severe nervous ailments (115).[17] She consumed sulphur and iron, she let one doctor sever the "wounded nerves from their centres," she let another cover her spine with "tartar emetic pustules," she subjected herself to "animal magnetism" and the water cure, but all to no purpose.

Beecher does not admit to having personally undergone local treatment, but when she discusses it, her tone changes from the condescending playfulness she uses to devastate such methods as the "tartar emetic pustules" to one of outraged horror. Doctors playing professional games with pustules had kept her sick perhaps, but they had left her with her honor. Local treatment, roughly equivalent to rape according to Beecher, seldom allowed a lady to retain that valuable possession. It is "performed," she explains, "with bolted doors and curtained windows, and with no one present but patient and operator," by doctors who have all too often "freely advocated the doctrine that there was no true marriage but the union of persons who were in love." Predictably, these immoral practitioners were said to have "lost all reverence for the Bible." With his "interesting" female patients, such a physician "naturally," in Beecher's gloomy view, tries "to lead them to adopt *his views of truth and right*" on moral matters. "Then he daily has all the opportunities indicated [through local examination]. Does anyone need more than to hear these facts to know what the not unfrequent results must be?" she ominously concludes (136). By the time she is through with this subject, she is calling the female patients "victims" and lamenting their "entire helplessness" (137). She refers the reader to an appended letter from a woman doctor, Mrs. R. B. Gleason of the Elmira Water Cure in New York, who solemnly testifies that manual replacement for *prolapsus uteri* was "in most cases totally needless, and in many decidedly injurious" (6). After such evidence, Beecher can hardly avoid "the painful inquiry": "how can a woman *ever know* to whom she may safely entrust herself . . . in such painful and peculiar circumstances?" (138).

Gilman, a brilliant theorist and critic on women's role in American society, went through periods of nervous prostration strikingly similar to those of her aged relative's.[18] She sampled the fruits of medical wisdom a few decades later, undergoing Mitchell's rest cure. She expressed the result in a story entitled "The Yellow Wall Paper," published in 1890, and designed to convince Mitchell "of the error of his ways."[19]

The story concerns a married woman, the mother of a young child, suffering from "nervous" disorders, and clearly laboring under disguised but immense (and justifiable) hostility for both her spouse and her offspring. Her husband, John, who is a doctor, is ostensibly overseeing her cure, but is in reality intent with sadistic ignorance on destroying her body and soul. John, apparently modeled on Mitchell himself, confines his wife to a country house, which to her seems "haunted," remote from friends or neighbors. Presumably hoping to force her back to her feminine and maternal functions, he symbolically makes her sleep in an old nursery. With its barred windows, rings attached to the wall, bed nailed to the floor, and disturbing and torn yellow wallpaper, this nursery all too significantly and frighteningly resembles a cell for the insane. Treating her like a pet, the doctor alternates condescending tenderness ("Then he took me in his arms and called me a blessed little goose" [323]) with threats of punishment ("John says if I don't pick up faster he shall send me to Weir Mitchell in the fall' [326]). Since John "never was nervous in his life" (323), and is a doctor "of high standing" (320) to boot, he can "laugh" at her fears because he "knows there is no *reason* to suffer, and that satisfies him" (323). Complacently smug in his masculine insensitivity and his professional superiority, he is totally obtuse about the nature of her suffering and its possible cure. An early-day "mad housewife," she has been so browbeaten by his calm assumption of superiority that she can only timidly air the frightening truth:

John is a physician, and *perhaps*—(I would not say it to a living soul, of course, but this is dead paper and a great relief to my mind)—*perhaps* that is one reason I do not get well faster [320].

He has left her with only one recourse, and she takes it. Slowly but steadily, she goes mad, thus dramatically pointing up the results of his "cure." At the story's close, she is creeping on hands and knees with insane persistence around the walls of her chamber. In a symbolic moment, her husband, suspicious about her behavior, breaks down the door she has finally locked against him. His act is the essence of his "cure" and her "problem"; like Catharine Beecher, Gilman sees the doctor "treating" his patient as violating her. But this patient is finally beyond feeling. When John faints away in shock at her state, their roles have been reversed: *He* has become the woman, the nervous, susceptible, sickly patient, and she wonders with a kind of calm, self-centered vindictiveness fully equal to his former arrogance: "Now why should that man have fainted? But he did, and right across my path by the wall, so that I had to creep over him every time!" (337). She has won, because she can ignore him now as completely as he ignored her, but she has won at the cost of becoming what he subconsciously sought to make her—a creeping creature, an animal and an automaton.

Beecher's *Letters* and Gilman's story are both intended to convey a nightmare vision of sick women dependent on male doctors who use their professional superiority as a method to prolong their patients' sickness and, consequently, the supremacy of their own sex. Both writers also hint, however, at a possible escape for such feminine victims. Beecher, according to her account, was finally cured by a timely tip from a *woman* physician, Dr. Elizabeth Blackwell. Gilman's heroine knows what her cure should be—work and intellectual stimulation—although she is too cowed and powerless to insist on it. Both Gilman and Beecher simply in writing their works, are implying that the untutored common sense of two women can outdo the professionally trained brains of those male doctors who labored in vain to cure them. Both are thus in essence urging that a woman should be independent, that *she be her own physician*, so that the real business of healing can get under way.[20]

After all, Beecher and Gilman realized, there might be two possible ways of looking at the much-advertised problem of the increasingly bad health of middle-class American women. Doctors like Clarke and Mitchell liked to think that the fault lay with the women themselves, who were neglecting their homes and pursuing such an unfeminine goal as higher education. Women like Beecher and Gilman, shrewdly reversing the charge, queried whether the blame might not belong to the men who were supposed to cure them and to the professional training which was supposed to enable them to do it. Harriet Hunt, one of the most impressive of the early women doctors in America, put the challenge succinctly: "Man, man alone has had the care of *us* [women], and I would ask how *our health stands now*. Does it do credit to *his* skill?"[21] Hunt is clearly aware that what had been a condemnation of women (the charge of ill health) could be used as a powerful weapon in their defense. The women doctors who began to appear on the American scene in the 1850s saw women's diseases as a *result* of submission, and promoted independence from masculine domination, whether professional or sexual, as their cure for feminine ailments.[22]

NOTES

1. See also Jeffrey Berman, "The Unrestful Cure: Charlotte Perkins Gilman and 'The Yellow Wallpaper,'" included in this critical edition.

2. Byford, *A Treatise on the Chronic Inflammation*, 15.

3. S. Weir Mitchell, *Roland Blake* (Boston, 1886), 254.

4. Anna Robeson Burr (ed.), *Weir Mitchell: His Life and Letters* (New York, 1929), 374. Mitchell makes the same point in *Doctor and Patient*, 13.

5. Burr, *Weir Mitchell*, 37. The best recent biography is Ernest Earnest, *S. Weir Mitchell: Novelist and Physician* (Philadelphia, 1950).

6. Mitchell, *Fat and Blood*, 48.

7. Mitchell, *Doctor and Patient*, 48.

8. Quoted in Burr, *Weir Mitchell*, 290.

9. There are striking similarities between Mitchell's conception of his role, and that of Freudian psychiatrists. See Earnest, *Weir Mitchell*, 250.

10. Mitchell, *Fat and Blood*, 39.

11. He tried hypnosis in his practice, though with little success. See Earnest, *Weir Mitchell*, 229. Robert Herrick was to dramatize this aspect of the physician's role in *The Healer* (New York, 1911) and in *Together* (New York, 1909).

12. For examples of these weight gains, see Mitchell, *Fat and Blood*, 80–94. One 5'8" woman went from 118 lbs. to 169 lbs.

13. Quoted in Harris, *Woman's Surgeon*, 181.

14. Both the homeopathic school, with its distrust of drugs and violent remedies, and the hydropathic school with its reliance on the efficacy of water, advocated relatively mild treatments for women's ailments. For examples, see

John A. Tarbell, *Homeopathy Simplified: or Domestic Practice Made Easy* (Boston, 1859), 214–218; R. T. Trall, *The Hydropathic Encyclopedia: A System of Hydropathy and Hygiene* (New York, 1852), II, 285–296. It must also be added, however, that such doctors were outside the higher echelons of American medicine. Furthermore, it is striking how many women turned to such doctors as a result of bad experiences at the hands of more orthodox doctors. In other words, it seems likely that the lady at the water-cure had also sampled other forms of treatment.

15. Angelina Grimké, for instance, a famous abolitionist and speaker for women's rights, suffered terribly from *prolapsus uteri*. See Gerda Lerner, *The Grimké Sisters from South Carolina* (Boston, 1967), 288–292.

16. See Austin, *Perils of American Women*, 94–95.

17. All page references will be to the edition already cited.

18. See her own account in her autobiography, *The Living of Charlotte Perkins Gilman* (New York, 1935), 90 ff. She may have felt her similarities to Beecher since she named her daughter after her.

19. All page references will be to Charlotte Perkins Gilman, "The Yellow Wall Paper," in William Dean Howells (ed.), *The Great Modern American Short Stories* (New York, 1920), 320–337; Gilman, *Living of Charlotte Perkins Gilman*, 121.

20. The demand for women doctors could be quite explicit. See Julia Ward Howe (ed.), *A Reply to Dr. E. H. Clarke's 'Sex in Education'* (Boston, 1874), 158.

21. Harriet K. Hunt, *Glances and Glimpses; or, Fifty Years Social, Including Twenty Years Professional, Life* (Boston, 1856), p. 414.

22. For the history of women doctors in America, see Kate Campbell Hurd-Mead, *Medical Women of America: A Short History of the Pioneer Medical Women of America and a Few of Their Colleagues in England* (New York, 1933); Esther Pohl Lovejoy, *Women Doctors of the World* (New York, 1957).

Criticism

Afterword to
"The Yellow Wallpaper,"
Feminist Press Edition

Elaine R. Hedges

"The Yellow Wallpaper" is a small literary masterpiece. For almost fifty years it has been overlooked, as has its author, one of the most commanding feminists of her time. Now, with the new growth of the feminist movement, Charlotte Perkins Gilman is being rediscovered, and "The Yellow Wallpaper" should share in that rediscovery. The story of a woman's mental breakdown, narrated with superb psychological and dramatic precision, it is, as William Dean Howells said of it in 1920, a story to "freeze our . . . blood."[1]

The story was wrenched out of Gilman's own life, and is unique in the canon of her works. Although she wrote other fiction—short stories and novels—and much poetry as well, none of it ever achieved the power and directness, the imaginative authenticity of this piece. Polemical intent often made her fiction dry and clumsily didactic; and the extraordinary pressures of publishing deadlines under which she worked made careful composition almost impossible. (During one seven-year period she edited and published her own magazine, *The Forerunner*, writing almost all of the material for it—a sum total, she estimated, of twenty-one thousand words per month or the equivalent of twenty-eight books.)

Charlotte Perkins Gilman was an active feminist and primarily a nonfiction writer: the author of *Women and Economics*, a witty, bitingly satirical analysis of the situation of women in her society, which was used as a college text in the 1920s and translated into seven languages;

and the author of many other nonfiction works dealing with the socio-economic status of women. She was also an indefatigable and inspiring lecturer. Her work during the last decade of the nineteenth century and the first two of the twentieth has led one recent historian to say that she was "the leading intellectual in the women's movement in the United States" in her time.[2]

That interest in her has recently revived is satisfying, and only just. In the past few years several masters theses and doctoral dissertations have been written about her, and *Women and Economics* was reissued in 1966. The recent acquisition of her personal papers by the Schlesinger Library of Radcliffe College is bound to lead to further research and publication. Even "The Yellow Wallpaper" has resurfaced in several anthologies. However, tucked away among many other selections and frequently with only brief biographical information about its author, the story will not necessarily find in these anthologies the wide audience it deserves.[3]

Yet it does deserve the widest possible audience. For aside from the light it throws on the personal despairs, and the artistic triumph over them, of one of America's foremost feminists, the story is one of the rare pieces of literature we have by a nineteenth-century woman which directly confronts the sexual politics of the male-female, husband-wife relationship. In its time (and presumably still today, given its appearance in the anthology *Psychopathology and Literature*), the story was read essentially as a Poe-esque tale of chilling horror—and as a story of mental aberration. It is both of these. But it is more. It is a feminist document, dealing with sexual politics at a time when few writers felt free to do so, at least so candidly. Three years after Gilman published her story, Kate Chopin published *The Awakening*, a novel so frank in its treatment of the middle-class wife and her prescribed submissive role that it lost its author both reputation and income. It is symptomatic of their times that both Gilman's story and Chopin's novel end with the self-destruction of their heroines.

It wasn't easy for Charlotte Perkins Gilman to get her story published. She sent it first to William Dean Howells, and he, responding to at least some of its power and authenticity, recommended it to Horace Scudder, editor of *The Atlantic Monthly*, then the most prestigious magazine in the United States. Scudder rejected the story, according to Gilman's account in her autobiography, with a curt note:

Dear Madam,

    Mr. Howells has handed me this story.

    I could not forgive myself if I made others as miserable as I have made myself!

Sincerely yours,[4]

H.E. Scudder

In the 1890s editors, and especially Scudder, still officially adhered to a canon of "moral uplift" in literature, and Gilman's story, with its heroine reduced at the end to the level of a groveling animal, scarcely fitted the prescribed formula. One wonders, however, whether hints of the story's attack on social mores—specifically on the ideal of the sub-missive wife—came through to Scudder and unsettled him?

The story was finally published, in May 1892, in *The New England Magazine*, where it was greeted with strong but mixed feelings. Gilman was warned that such stories were "perilous stuff," which should not be printed because of the threat they posed to the relatives of such "deranged" persons as the heroine.[5] The implications of such warnings—that women should "stay in their place," that nothing could or should be done except maintain silence or conceal problems—are fairly clear. Those who praised the story, for the accuracy of its portrayal and its delicacy of touch, did so on the grounds that Gilman had captured in literature, from a medical point of view, the most "detailed account of incipient insanity."[6] Howells's admiration for the story, when he reprinted it in 1920 in the *Great Modern American Stories*, limited itself to the story's "chilling" quality. Again, however, no one seems to have made the connection between the insanity and the sex, or sexual role, of the victim, no one explored the story's implications for male-female relationships in the nineteenth century.

To appreciate fully these relationships, and hence the meaning of Gilman's story, requires biographical background. Born in 1860 in Connecticut, Charlotte Perkins grew up in Rhode Island and her childhood and youth were hard. Her mother bore three children in three years; one child died; after the birth of the third the father abandoned the family. Charlotte said of her mother that her life was "one of the most painfully thwarted I have ever known." Her mother had been idolized as a young girl, had had many suitors, and was then left with two children after a few brief years of marriage. Did the conflicting patterns imposed on women at that time (and still today)—"belle of the ball" versus housewife and producer of children—contribute to, or indeed even account for, the destruction of her marriage? Gilman suggests that the father may have left the family because the mother had been told that if she were to have another child she might die.[7] In any event, the effect of the broken marriage on Charlotte was painful. According to Gilman's autobiography, her mother sacrificed both her own and her daughter's need for love, out of an understandably desperate yet inevitably self-destructive need for protection against further betrayal; the mother seems literally to have refused so much as a light physical caress. It was her way of initiating Charlotte into the sufferings that life would hold for a woman.

Growing up without tenderness Charlotte grew up also, perhaps as a result of the treatment she received, determined to develop her will-power and refusing to be defeated. Her own description of herself at sixteen is of a person who had "My mother's profound religious tendency and implacable sense of duty; my father's intellectual appetite; a will power, well developed, from both; a passion of my own for scientific knowledge, for real laws of life; an insatiable demand for perfection in everything. . . ."[8] These traits would characterize her, and her work, throughout her life.

That, at seventeen, she could write, "Am going to try hard this winter to see if I cannot enjoy myself like other people" is both painful indication of the deprivations of her childhood and tribute to the strengths she wrested from those deprivations.[9] She had inherited the New England Puritan tradition of duty and responsibility: what she described as the development of "noble character."[10] (She was related to the famous Beecher family; Harriet Beecher Stowe was her great-aunt.) On the whole her Puritan heritage served her well; but it had its painful effects, as would be seen in her first marriage.

By the time she was in her late teens Charlotte Perkins had begun seriously to ponder "the injustices under which women suffered."[11] Although not in close touch with the suffrage movement (with which indeed she never in her later career directly associated herself, finding its objectives too limited for her own more radical views on the need for social change), she was becoming increasingly aware of such current developments as the entrance of some young women into colleges—and the ridicule they received—of the growing numbers of young women in the working population, of a few books being written that critically examined the institution of marriage, and of the somewhat more open discussion of matters of sexuality and chastity. She began to write poems—one in defense of prostitutes—and to pursue her own independent thinking. Her commitment was to change a world which she saw as unhappy and confused: she would use logic, argument, and demonstration; she would write and she would lecture.

Meanwhile she had met Charles Stetson, a Providence, Rhode Island, artist. She was drawn to him by his artistic ability, his ideals, and his loneliness—so much like her own. The story of their courtship, as she recounts it in her autobiography, is evidence of the effects on her of the life of self-denial she had led. There was, she says, "no natural response of inclination or desire, no question of, 'Do I love him?' only, 'Is it right?'" Only after reluctance and refusal, and at a time when he had met with "a keen personal disappointment," did she agree to marry him.[12] Actually, her motives in marrying, and her expectations of marriage are, until further evidence is available, difficult to sort out. Although her autobiography stresses her sense of duty and pity there seems also to be evidence, from some early notebooks and journals at the Schlesinger Library, that love and companionship were also involved. But what is clear is that Charlotte Perkins knew she was facing the crucial question so many nineteenth-century women had to face: marriage or a career. A woman "*should* be able to have marriage and motherhood, and do her work in the world also," she argued.[13] Yet she was not convinced by her own argument—what models did she have? And her fears that marriage and motherhood might incapacitate her for her "work in the world" would prove to be true, for her as for most women in our society.

Although she claims to have been happy with her husband, who was "tender" and "devoted," and helped with the housework, and toward whom she felt "the natural force of sex-attraction," she soon began to experience periods of depression: ". . . something was going wrong from the first." As she describes it, "A sort of gray fog drifted across my mind, a cloud that grew and darkened." Increasingly she felt weak, sleepless, unable to work. A year after the marriage she gave birth to a daughter and within a month of the birth she became, again in her own words, "a mental wreck." There was a constant dragging weariness. . . . Absolute incapacity. Absolute misery."[14]

It would seem that Charlotte Perkins Stetson felt trapped by the role assigned the wife within the conventional nineteenth-century marriage. If marriage meant children and too many children meant incapacity for other work; if she saw her father's abandonment and her mother's coldness as the result of this sexual-marital bind; if she saw herself as victimized by marriage, the woman playing the passive role—then she was simply seeing clearly.

It was out of this set of marital circumstances, but beyond that out of her larger social awareness of the situation of women in her century, that "The Yellow Wallpaper" emerged five years later. Witness to the personal and social anguish of its author, the story is also an indictment of the incompetent medical advice she received. Charlotte Perkins Stetson was sent to the most preeminent "nerve specialist" of her time, Dr. S. Weir Mitchell of Philadelphia, and it was his patronizing treatment of her that seems ultimately to have provoked her to write her story. Dr. Mitchell could not fit Mrs. Stetson into either of his two categories of victims of what was then called "nervous prostration": businessmen exhausted from too much work or society women exhausted from too much play. His prescription for her health was that she devote herself to domestic work and to her child, confine herself to, at most, two hours of intellectual work a day, and "never touch pen, brush or pencil as long as you live."[15]

After a month in Dr. Mitchell's sanitarium Charlotte Stetson returned home. She reports that she almost lost her mind. Like the heroine in her story, she would often "crawl into remote closets and under beds—to hide from the grinding pressure of that profound distress."[16]

In 1887, after four years of marriage, Charlotte Perkins Stetson and her husband agreed to a separation and a divorce. It was an obvious necessity. When away from him—she had made a trip to California shortly after the onset of her illness—she felt healthy and recovered. When she returned to her family she began again to experience depression and fatigue.

For the rest of her life Charlotte Perkins would suffer from the effects of this nervous breakdown. Her autobiography reveals her as a woman of iron will, but also as one who was constantly troubled by periods of severe fatigue and lethargy, against which she fought constantly. Her formidable output of writing, traveling, and lecturing, in the years after her first marriage, would seem to have been wrested from a slim budget of energy, but energy so carefully hoarded and directed that it sustained her through over thirty years as a leading feminist writer and lecturer.

In 1890 Charlotte Perkins Stetson moved to California, where, struggling for economic survival as a woman alone, she began lecturing on the status of women. The years between 1890 and 1894 were, she recalls, the hardest of her life. She was fighting against public opinion, against outright hostility, as she gave her lectures on socialism and freedom for women. She taught school, kept a boarding house, edited newspapers, all the time writing and speaking. She accepted her husband's new marriage to her best friend, to whom she relinquished her child, and this action led to even greater public hostility, of course, against which she had to fight. In the midst of this most difficult period in her life she produced "The Yellow Wallpaper."

The story is narrated with clinical precision and aesthetic tact. The curt, chopped sentences, the brevity of the paragraphs, which often consist of only one or two sentences, convey the taut, distraught mental state of the narrator. The style creates a controlled tension: everything is low key and understated. The stance of the narrator is all, and it is a very complex stance indeed, since she is ultimately mad and yet, throughout her descent into madness, in many ways more sensible than the people who surround and cripple her. As she tells her story the reader has confidence in the reasonableness of her arguments and explanations.

The narrator is a woman who has been taken to the country by her husband in an effort to cure her of some undefined illness—a kind of nervous fatigue. Although her husband, a doctor, is presented as kindly and well meaning, it is soon apparent that his treatment of his wife, guided as it is by nineteenth-century attitudes toward women, is an important source of her affliction and a perhaps inadvertent but none-theless vicious abettor of it. Here is a woman who, as she tries to explain to anyone who will listen, wants very much to *work*. Specifically, she wants to write (and the story she is narrating is her desperate and secret attempt both to engage in work that is meaningful to her and to retain her sanity). But the medical advice she receives, from her doctor/ husband, from her brother, also a doctor, and from S. Weir Mitchell, explicitly referred to in the story, is that she do nothing. The prescribed cure is total rest and total emptiness of mind. While she craves intellec-tual stimulation and activity, and at one point poignantly expresses her wish for "advice and companionship" (one can read today respect and equality) in her work, what she receives is the standard treatment meted out to women in a patriarchal society. Thus her husband sees her as a "blessed little goose."[17] She is his "little girl" and she must take care of herself for his sake. Her role is to be "a rest and comfort to him." That he often laughs at her is, she notes forlornly and almost casually at one point, only what one expects in marriage.

Despite her pleas he will not take her away from this house in the country which she hates. What he does, in fact, is choose for her a room in the house that was formerly a nursery. It is a room with barred windows originally intended to prevent small children from falling out. It is the room with the fateful yellow wallpaper. The narrator herself had preferred a room downstairs; but this is 1890 and, to use Virgina Woolf's phrase, there is no choice for this wife of "a room of one's own."

Without such choice, however, the woman has been emotionally and intellectually violated. In fact, her husband instills guilt in her. They have come to the country, he says "solely on [her] account." Yet this means that he must be away all day, and many nights, dealing with his patients.

The result in the woman is subterfuge. With her husband she cannot be her true self but must pose; and this, as she says, "makes me very tired." Finally, the fatigue and the subterfuge are unbearable. Increasingly she concentrates her attention on the wallpaper in her room—a paper of a sickly yellow that both disgusts and fascinates her. Gilman works out the symbolism of the wallpaper beautifully, without ostentation. For, despite all the elaborate descriptive detail devoted to it, the wallpaper remains mysteriously, hauntingly undefined and only vaguely visuable. But such, of course, is the situation of this wife, who identifies herself with the paper. The paper symbolizes her situation as seen by the men who control her and hence her situation as seen by herself. How can she define herself?

The wallpaper consists of "lame uncertain curves" that suddenly "commit suicide—destroy themselves in unheard-of contradictions." There are pointless patterns in the paper, which the narrator nevertheless determines to pursue to some conclusion. Fighting for her identity, for some sense of independent self, she observes the wallpaper and notes that just as she is about to find some pattern and meaning in it, it "slaps you in the face, knocks you down, and tramples upon you."

Inevitably, therefore, the narrator, imprisoned within the room, thinks she discerns the figure of a woman behind the paper. The paper is barred—that is part of what pattern it has, and the woman is trapped

behind the bars, trying to get free. Ultimately, in the narrator's distraught state, there are a great many women behind the patterned bars,
all trying to get free.

Given the morbid social situation that by now the wallpaper has
come to symbolize, it is no wonder that the narrator begins to see it as
staining everything it touches. The sickly yellow color runs off, she
imagines, on her husband's clothes as well as on her own.

But this woman, whom we have come to know so intimately in the
course of her narrative, and to admire for her heroic efforts to retain her
sanity despite all opposition, never does get free. Her insights, and her
desperate attempts to define and thus cure herself by tracing the bewil-
dering pattern of the wallpaper and deciphering its meaning, are poor
weapons against the male certainty of her husband, whose attitude
toward her is that "bless her little heart" he will *allow* her to be "as sick as
she pleases."

It is no surprise to find, therefore, that at the end of the story the
narrator both does and does not identify with the creeping women who
surround her in her hallucinations. The women creep out of the wallpaper, they creep through the arbors and lanes and along the roads
outside the house. Women must creep. The narrator knows this. She
has fought as best she could against creeping. In her perceptivity and in
her resistance lie her heroism (her heroineism). But at the end of the
story, on her last day in the house, as she peels off yards and yards of
wallpaper and creeps around the floor, she has been defeated. She is
totally mad.

But in her mad-sane way she has seen the situation of women for
what it is. She has wanted to strangle the woman behind the paper—tie
her with a rope. For that woman, the tragic product of her society, is of
course the narrator's self. By rejecting that woman she might free the
other, imprisoned woman within herself. But the only available rejection is suicidal, and hence she descends into madness. Madness is her
only freedom, as, crawling around the room, she screams at her husband
that she has finally "got out"—outside the wallpaper—and can't be put
back.[18]

Earlier in the story the heroine gnawed with her teeth at the nailed-
down bed in her room: excruciating proof of her sense of imprisonment.
Woman as prisoner; woman as child or cripple; woman, even, as a
fungus growth, when at one point in her narrative the heroine describes
the women whom she envisions behind the wallpaper as "strangled

heads and bulbous eyes and waddling fungus growths." These images permeate Gilman's story. If they are the images men had of women, and hence that women had of themselves, it is not surprising that madness and suicide bulk large in the work of late nineteenth-century women writers. "Much madness is divinest sense . . . Much sense the starkest madness," Emily Dickinson had written some decades earlier; and she had chosen spinsterhood as one way of rejecting society's "requirements" regarding woman's role as wife. One thinks, too, of Edith Wharton's *The House of Mirth*, with its heroine, Lily Bart, "manacled" by the bracelets she wears. Raised as a decorative item, with no skills or training, Lily must find a husband, if she is to have any economic security. Her bracelets, intended to entice young bachelors, are really her chains. Lily struggles against her fate, trying to retain her independence and her moral integrity. In the end, however, she commits suicide.

Such suicides as that of Lily, or of Kate Chopin's heroine mentioned earlier, as well as the madness that descends upon the heroine in "The Yellow Wallpaper," are all deliberate dramatic indictments, by women writers, of the crippling social pressures imposed on women in the nineteenth century and the sufferings they thereby endured: women who could not attend college although their brothers could; women expected to devote themselves, their lives, to aging and ailing parents; women treated as toys or as children and experiencing who is to say how much loss of self-confidence as a result. It is to this entire class of defeated, or even destroyed women, to this large body of wasted, or semi-wasted talent, that "The Yellow Wallpaper" is addressed.

The heroine in "The Yellow Wallpaper" is destroyed. She has fought her best against husband, brother, doctor, and even against women friends (her husband's sister, for example, is "a perfect and enthusiastic housekeeper, and hopes for no better profession"). She has tried, in defiance of all the social and medical codes of her time, to retain her sanity and her individuality. But the odds are against her and she fails.

Charlotte Perkins Stetson Gilman did not fail. She had been blighted, damaged, like the heroine in her story, by society's attitudes toward women. But having written the story she transcended the heroine's fate—although at what inner cost we shall never know. She went on to carve out a famous career as a feminist lecturer and writer. From the 1890s until about 1920 she was in demand as a speaker both in the United States and abroad, and her books were read on both continents.

The books, especially *Women and Economics*, attacked the social and economic system that enslaved and humiliated women. About this enslavement and humiliation she was adamant, as some of her more striking metaphors show:

That women are kept, like horses:

> The labor of women in the house, certainly, enables men to produce more wealth than they otherwise could; and in this way women are economic factors in society. But so are horses. The labor of horses enables men to produce more wealth than they otherwise could. The horse is an economic factor in society. But the horse is not economically independent, nor is the woman.[19]

That women are used like cows:

> The wild cow is a female. She has healthy calves, and milk enough for them. And that is all the femininity she needs. Otherwise than that she is bovine rather than feminine. She is a light, strong, swift, sinewy creature, able to run, jump, and fight, if necessary. We, for economic uses, have artificially developed the cow's capacity for producing milk. She has become a walking milk-machine, bred and tended to that express end, her value measured in quarts.[20]

Women's ineffectual domestic status was the target of some of Gilman's strongest attacks. As she said elsewhere in *Women and Economics*, the same world exists for women as for men,

> the same human energies and human desires and ambitions within. But all that she may wish to have, all that she may wish to do, must come through a single channel and a single choice. Wealth, power, social distinction, fame, – not only these, but home and happiness, reputation, ease and pleasure, her bread and butter, – all, must come to her through a small gold ring.[21]

The damaging effects on women of being manacled to that small gold ring she explored in detail. Women are bred for marriage, yet they cannot actively pursue it but must sit passively and wait to be chosen. The result is strain and hypocrisy, and an overemphasis on sex or "femininity." "For, in her position of economic dependence in the sex-relation, sex-distinction is with her not only a means of attracting a mate, as with all creatures, but a means of getting her livelihood, as is the case with no other creature under heaven."[22]

Gilman was not opposed to the home nor to domestic work. She believed indeed that the home tended to produce such qualities, necessary for the development of the human race, as kindness and caring. But her evolutionary approach to social change enabled her to see that the institution of the home had not developed consonant to the development of other institutions in society. Women, and children, were imprisoned within individual homes, where the women had no recognized economic independence and the children often suffocated, "noticed, studied, commented on, and incessantly interfered with. . . . How can they grow up without injury?"[23] For, she argued, in the home as presently established there can be neither freedom nor equality. Rather, there is "ownership": a dominant father, a more or less subservient mother, and an utterly dependent child. Injustice, rather than justice, was the result.

In her attack on the nuclear family Gilman thus anticipated many current complaints. Or, one should rather say, that more than half a century after she began her campaign against women's subservient status we are still struggling with the problems she diagnosed and described.

Her suggested solutions included community kitchens, whereby the work of cooking would be more efficiently and sociably performed, leaving those women free for other occupations who were not adept at this particular skill but meanwhile making that skill economically respectable; and childcare centers—even if only play space on walled-in roofs of city apartment buildings—to release the child and the mother from the tyranny of the individual family.

Work must be respected: this was one of Gilman's basic tenets. But women must be admitted into the human work world on equal terms with men. The domestic work they do must be respected, and they must be free to do other kinds of work as well. Gilman believed in continuing human progress (she wrote a utopian novel, *Moving the Mountain*, in which women had achieved true equality with men), and she saw the situation of women in the nineteenth century as thwarting this progress as well as thwarting their own development. For some human beings to be classified as horses, or cows, or sexual objects, was to impoverish not only themselves but human society as a whole.

She herself refused to be so thwarted. In 1900 she married her cousin, George Houghton Gilman and she continued to work until the day when she chose her own death. Suffering from breast cancer, she chose not to be a burden to others. She took chloroform and died. It was her final willed choice.

NOTES

1. William Dean Howells, ed., *The Great Modern American Stories* (New York: Boni and Liveright, 1920), p. vii.

2. Carl Degler, ed., *Women and Economics* (reprint ed., New York: Harper and Row, 1966), p. xiii.

3. Leslie Y. Rabkin, ed., *Psychopathology and Literature* (San Francisco: Chandler Publications, 1966); Elaine Gottlieb Hemley and Jack Matthews, eds., *The Writer's Signature: Idea in Story and Essay* (Glenview, Ill.: Scott, Foresman, Co., 1972); Gail Parker, ed., *The Oven Birds: American Women on Womanhood, 1820–1920* (Garden City, N.Y.: Anchor Books, 1972). The last of these anthologies is the only one that puts "The Yellow Wallpaper" into the context of the struggle of American women for self-, social, and political expression. However, Dr. Parker's treatment of Gilman in her introduction is negative and sometimes factually shaky. Nor does she discuss the story itself in any detail.

4. Charlotte Perkins Gilman, *The Living of Charlotte Perkins Gilman. An Autobiography* (New York: D. Appleton-Century Co., 1935), p. 119.

5. Ibid., p. 120. It is interesting to note that the writer of this letter, a doctor, ascribed the heroine's problem to "an *heredity* of mental derangement." (My italics.)

6. Ibid., p. 120.

7. Ibid., p. 5. "Whether the doctor's dictum was the reason [for the father's abandoning the family] or merely a reason I do not know," Gilman writes in her autobiography.

8. Ibid., p. 44.

9. Ibid.

10. Ibid., p. 45.

11. Ibid., p. 61.

12. Ibid., pp. 82, 83.

13. Ibid., p. 83 (My italics.)

14. Ibid., pp. 83, 87–8, 89, 91.

15. Ibid., p. 96.

16. Ibid.

17. "The Yellow Wall-Paper," *The New England Magazine*, May 1892, p. 649. (Since the reader has the text in this present edition, subsequent page references to the original printing seem unnecessary.)

18. At this point, at the end of her story, Gilman has the narrator say to

her husband, "I've got out at last, . . . in spite of you and Jane." There has been no previous reference to a "Jane" in the story, and so one must speculate as to the reference. It could conceivably be a printer's error, since there are both a Julia and a Jennie in the story (Jennie is the housekeeper and functions as a guardian/imprisoner for the heroine, and Julia is an ineffectual female relative). On the other hand, it could be that Gilman is referring here to the narrator herself, to the narrator's sense that she has gotten free of both her husband and her "Jane" self: free, that is, of herself as defined by marriage and society.

19. *Women and Economics*, p. 13.

20. Ibid., pp. 43–44.

21. Ibid., p. 71.

22. Ibid., p. 38.

23. *The Home: Its Work and Influence* (New York: Charlton Co., 1910), pp. 40–41.

Environment as Psychopathological Symbolism in "The Yellow Wallpaper"

Loralee MacPike

Charlotte Perkins Gilman's short story "The Yellow Wallpaper," first published in 1892, is a study of social degeneration into madness. As such it may seem an unlikely focus of American literary realism; yet it is a very fine illustration of realist symbolism. The furnishings of the narrator's room become a microcosm of the world that squeezes her into the little cell of her own mind, and the wallpaper represents the state of that mind.

The story line is deceptively simple. The narrator, a writer, finds herself increasingly depressed and indefinably ill. Her husband John (a physician), her brother, and her doctor all concur that she needs complete rest and a cessation of her work if she is to "recover," by which they mean "appear as a normal female in a world created by and for men." Gilman is not speaking in any militant feminist terms; she merely shows how her narrator needs to work in order to feel at ease with herself and the self's potential. Instead, she is hustled off to the country into a life of enforced idleness of body and mind. Although she would have preferred a room opening on the garden, her husband consigns her to the upstairs room, a former nursery, whose major features are ancient yellow wallpaper, bars on the windows, and a huge bedstead nailed to the floor.

The fact that the narrator's prison-room is a nursery indicates her status in society. The woman is legally a child; socially, economically, and philosophically she must be led by an adult—her husband; and therefore the nursery is an appropriate place to house her. The narrator's work threatens to destroy her status as a mere child by gaining her recognition in the adult world; this is reason enough for her husband to forbid her to work. Her work is, as he suggests, dangerous; but its danger is for him, not her, because it removes her from his control. The nursery, then, is an appropriate symbol for the desired state of childlikeness vis-à-vis the adult world that her husband wishes to enforce.

The nursery's windows are barred, making the setting not only a retreat into childhood but a prison. The narrator is to be forever imprisoned in childhood, forbidden to "escape" into adulthood. She instinctively feels that, just as only her work can transport her out of the world of childhood, so too can it alone free her from her dependence upon her husband in particular and the male-created world in general. Emergence from the chrysalis of childhood would also free her in the larger sense, making her a responsible member of society rather than merely a cloistered woman. It could provide for her a physical movement out into an active life, but the bars in the unchosen room of her existence effectively prevent such an emergence.

The bedstead is the third symbol of the narrator's situation. A representation of her sexuality, it is nailed to the floor, ostensibly to prevent the former youthful occupants of the room from pushing it about. As the nursery imprisons her in a state of childhood, so the bedstead prevents her from moving "off center" sensually—not merely sexually—in any sort of physical contact with another human being. Her inability to care for her own child is but another fixity in her life, and the immovable bedstead symbolizes the static nature of both the expression and the product of her sexuality, thus denying her this outlet for her energies just as the bars deny her physical movement and the nursery her adult abilities.

These three items—the nursery, the bars on the windows, and the bedstead—show not only the narrator's mind but the state of the world that formed that mind. Her dilemma is not strictly personal, for the forces that shaped her, cutting off all possibility of personal realization, movement, or sexuality, are the processes that shape many women's lives. Gilman shows, through the normality of the narrator's life, the sources of her frustrations. The apparently unusual circumstances of bars, a nailed-down bed, a nursery for a bedroom are all explained as possible occurrences in a normal household. Although unusual perhaps, they are not extraordinary in the way Hawthorne's settings or Wilkie Collins' plots can be said to be extraordinary. It is not necessary for

Gilman to give any background whatever, neither social comment nor history; for her use of the stuff of the narrator's life as symbolic of her state of mind and its causes suffices.

The three symbols of the narrator's existence coalesce in the yellow wallpaper, which is the primary symbol of the story which not only represents the narrator's state of mind but *becomes* that state of mind. As she grows increasingly fond of the wallpaper, the narrator realizes that it may well be the only part of her life she can control. She learns to use it on an intellectual level to replace the adult intellectual activity forbidden her. Seeking a human with whom to interact, she finds heads in the wallpaper, sees them move as if behind undulating, almost-imperceptible bars. At first she becomes angry with the heads' "impertinence" and "everlastingness," not recognizing that these are the two qualities she herself exhibits: the impertinence of trying to achieve humanness against all restrictions and the everlastingness of her own stubborn core of self which can never fully yield to outside expectations. Her refusal to accept the wallpaper as either ugly or meaningless is a representation of the tenacity of her own character, which can yield to such outside constraints as a prison nursery but will never surrender its right to remain outside interpretation, as does the wallpaper. In relation to the "principle of design" imposed by the masculine universe, both the wallpaper and her mind refuse to follow any logic other than their own.

Slowly, the wallpaper becomes something more than an object for the narrator. She begins to see in it a movement and a purpose she has been unable to realize in her own life. As her madness develops, she shifts her own desire for escape from the limitations of her husband's expectations onto the figure behind the undulating bars of the wallpaper, the figure of a woman, "stooping down and creeping about" behind the pattern as she herself creeps behind her restricted life. The rescue of that woman becomes her one object, and the wallpaper becomes at once the symbol of her confinement and of her freedom. The disparate symbols of Gilman's story coalesce in the symbol of the wallpaper, itself imprisoned in the nursery, with the humanoid heads, behind their intangible bars, denied the sexuality of bodies.

If realism is to be defined, as Wellek has defined it, as "the objective representation of contemporary social reality," Gilman's story is indeed realism; but her realism, like Henry James's, is a representation of what is real *to the author*. There can be no "objective reality" as such because it is always seen by subjective observers. Gilman was such a subjective observer insofar as she was a member of a group (women) viewed as external to integral (male) society. Her reality she presented not directly, but through the objects comprising the backdrop of her narrator's life — objects which symbolize her assigned status in the world but which, paradoxically, also give her the opportunity to achieve complete freedom. In a world where half the human race must be rendered nonentities in the most radical sense of the word, insanity is the only creative act available to those doomed to be defined as subhuman by submission to society's standards. In this sense Gilman anticipates R. D. Laing, who says that in an insane world only the mad are sane.

"The Yellow Wallpaper": A Rediscovered "Realistic" Story

Beate Schöpp-Schilling

Most of Charlotte Perkins Gilman's rather didactic literary productions were written between 1890 and 1916 and can be characterized as "realistic" in the sense defined by literary critics of that period. "The Yellow Wallpaper,"[1] however, a short story written in a highly expressionistic manner, can be seen within the framework of a specific kind of "psychological realism"[2] that so far has not been sufficiently appreciated. With the help of an interdisciplinary combination of Adlerian depth psychology and literary criticism, I want first to give an interpretation that explores the relationship between Gilman's life and this specific literary work from a psychological point of view. In a second step, I will evaluate the story as a psychologically realistic account of the causes and the progressive stages of mental illness.

Published in 1892 and read by contemporary readers and reviewers as an effective tale of incipient insanity, the story is seen today by feminist scholars primarily in the light of Gilman's own life. Ann Douglas Wood[3] and Gail Parker[4] accept Gilman's motives for writing the story as expressed in her autobiography, where she speaks of her desire to convince Dr. S. Weir Mitchell, famous for his rest-cures, of the errors of his medical treatment, which she herself had to undergo.[5] In their attempt to analyze the various causes and consequences of women's psychic and somatic illnesses within the framework of the patriarchal attitudes of the nineteenth century, Wood and Parker point to the story as a truthful depiction of the consciously and unconsciously designed male chauvinist medical practices to which women were exposed.

Elaine Hedges, who has written the most detailed critical discussion of the story so far,[6] also sees it partly as an indictment of the medical advice Gilman received from Mitchell. But beyond that she praises it as a feminist document "which directly confronts the sexual politics of the male-female, husband-wife relationship."[7] She, too, has recourse to Gilman's autobiography. In closely following Gilman's own arguments concerning her difficulties in accepting her first husband's proposal as well as the causes and consequences of her psychic breakdown, she comes to the conclusion that the story, having emerged both from Gilman's personal experience and her general awareness of women's victimization through marriage, dramatizes the "connection between the insanity and the sex, or sexual role, of the victim."[8]

While all of these analyses are illuminating, they certainly do not cover all the aspects of the story. Furthermore, these critics do not avoid two pitfalls of literary criticism, i.e., the intentional and the biographical fallacy. Especially in the case of Hedges[9] the method of reading Gilman's life into her story is particularly deceptive since she relies exclusively on Gilman's own interpretation of her life. This sort of information can never be taken at face value for autobiographical statements combine fact *and* fiction,[10] the latter being an expression of the individual's unconscious need to justify his life-style.

After having decoded the autobiography with the tools of Adlerian depth psychology, one has to disqualify Gilman's own interpretation of her breakdown as just this sort of rationalization. Beneath the self-sacrificing attitude which places her work, "the elevation of the race,"[11] above her "more intimate personal happiness,"[12] one senses an extreme fear of entering into close personal relationships due to her utter lack of confidence in her ability to succeed in them. When confronted with the demands of marriage and motherhood, she helplessly escaped into a serious depression, using the role-conflict as a convenient cover. Seeing her breakdown in these terms allowed her to ask for the freedom to realize herself in the realm of work, where she felt more secure, though even there she was plagued by feelings of inferiority.[13] Viewed in the light of these psychic processes, a more complex connection between author and work than the usual *l'homme et l'oeuvre* approach achieves is established: Gilman's gruesome relentlessness in depicting the sado-masochistic relationship between husband and wife can be explained as her unconscious attempt to cope with her fears and to justify her decision to leave her husband.

If looked at aside from Gilman's life and interpreted with the help of Adlerian depth psychology, the story itself reveals an intuitive grasp of psychological processes which so far has not been sufficiently acknowledged by the critics. The story's heroine, after having been forbidden by her husband to exercise her creative powers in writing, defies him by turning to a different kind of paper, the hideous wallpaper with which he forces her to live. Through her exclusive preoccupation with its design, she descends into madness, which ultimately enables her to creep triumphantly over her husband. Here Gilman reveals a fundamental truth about interpersonal relationships, hinting at the active, protest-like characteristics of mental illness, which represents the continual though completely perverted attempt of a human being to overcome his feelings of inferiority.

Beyond this, Gilman succeeds with high artistic perfection in the realistic depiction of the progressive stages of her heroine's psychic disintegration, which starts with depression and feelings of guilt and aggression, then develops into increasing withdrawal from reality, a persecution complex, odor hallucinations, synaesthesia, and ends in the complete breakdown of her ego. She objectifies this through her ingenious use of the image of the wallpaper with its multiple function as part of the setting, as objective correlative to the heroine's repressed emotions, and finally as the symbol of her life.

NOTES

1. Charlotte Perkins Stetson [Gilman], "The Yellow Wall-Paper," *New England Magazine*, NS 5 (Jan 1892), 647–656. Published in book form in 1899, it was later included in *The Great Modern American Stories / An Anthology*, ed. William Dean Howells (NY: Boni and Liveright, 1920), pp. 320–337.

2. I define "psychological realism" as a truthful depiction of a mental condition, which corresponds to the empirical research as well as to the theoretical formulations of psychologists.

3. Ann Douglas Wood, " 'The Fashionable Diseases': Women's Complaints and Their Treatment in Nineteenth-Century America," *Journal of Interdisciplinary History*, 6 (1973), 25–52, esp. 41–44.

4. Gail Parker, "Introduction," in *The Ovenbirds / American Women on Womanhood*, 1820–1920, ed. Gail Parker (Garden City, N.Y.: Doubleday, 1972), pp. 37–63.

5. Charlotte Perkins Gilman, *The Living of Charlotte Perkins Gilman / An Autobiography* (NY: Appleton, 1935), p. 121.

6. Elaine Hedges, "Afterword," in Charlotte Perkins Gilman, *The Yellow Wallpaper*, ed. Elaine Hedges (New York: Feminist Press, 1973), pp. 37–63.

7. Ibid., p. 39.

8. Ibid., p. 41.

9. Parker does attempt a psychoanalytical interpretation of Gilman's autobiography in pointing to Gilman's fears of dependency. However, she does not make sufficient use of it for the interpretation of the story.

10. Even this "life-style" is based on a "fiction," an "as-if condition," according to Adler. Adler sees human personality as an organic entity that continually strives towards ideals of perfection. In the early periods of his life every human being unconsciously *interprets* the physical, emotional, and social conditions that surround him within the framework of this striving. As a result of these interpretations he builds up a "life-style" that determines his responses to the demands life makes on him and that is neurotic to the degree that his fictive goal lacks what Adler calls "social feeling."

11. Gilman, *Living*, p. 80.

12. Ibid., p. 83.

13. This can be deduced from the grand scale of her self-chosen task as well as from her constant apologetic references to the incapacitating effects of her breakdown on her mental energy. Therefore, it can be said that the breakdown served her both to escape from her marriage and to find an excuse for possible failures in her work.

From *The Madwoman in the Attic:* The Woman Writer and the Nineteenth-Century Literary Imagination

Sandra Gilbert and Susan Gubar

As if to comment on the unity of all these points—on, that is, the anxiety-inducing connections between what women writers tend to see as their parallel confinements in texts, houses, and maternal female bodies—Charlotte Perkins Gilman brought them all together in 1890 in a striking story of female confinement and escape, a paradigmatic tale which (like *Jane Eyre*) seems to tell *the* story that all literary women would tell if they could speak their "speechless woe." "The Yellow Wallpaper," which Gilman herself called "a description of a case of nervous breakdown," recounts in the first person the experiences of a woman who is evidently suffering from a severe postpartum psychosis.[1] Her husband, a censorious and paternalistic physician, is treating her according to methods by which S. Weir Mitchell, a famous "nerve specialist," treated Gilman herself for a similar problem. He has confined her to a large garret room in an "ancestral hall" he has rented, and he has forbidden her to touch pen to paper until she is well again, for he feels, says the narrator, "that with my imaginative power and habit of story-making, a nervous weakness like mine is sure to lead to all manner of excited fancies, and that I ought to use my will and good sense to check the tendency" (15–16).

The cure, of course, is worse than the disease, for the sick woman's mental condition deteriorates rapidly. "I think sometimes that if I were only well enough to write a little it would relieve the press of ideas and rest me," she remarks, but literally confined in a room she thinks is a

one-time nursery because it has "rings and things" in the walls, she is
literally locked away from creativity. The "rings and things," although
reminiscent of children's gymnastic equipment, are really the parapher-
nalia of confinement, like the gate at the head of the stairs, instruments
that definitively indicate her imprisonment. Even more tormenting,
however, is the room's wallpaper: a sulphurous yellow paper, torn off in
spots, and patterned with "lame uncertain curves" that "plunge off at
outrageous angles" and "destroy themselves in unheard of contradictions." Ancient, smoldering, "unclean" as the oppressive structures of the
society in which she finds herself, this paper surrounds the narrator like
an inexplicable text, censorious and overwhelming as her physician
husband, haunting as the "hereditary estate" in which she is trying to
survive. Inevitably she studies its suicidal implications—and inevitably,
because of her "imaginative power and habit of story-making," she
revises it, projecting her own passion for escape into its otherwise incomprehensible hieroglyphics. "This wall-paper," she decides, at a key point
in her story,

> has a kind of sub-pattern in a different shade, a particularly irritating one,
> for you can only see it in certain lights, and not clearly then.
> But in the places where it isn't faded and where the sun is just so—I can
> see a strange, provoking, formless sort of figure, that seems to skulk about
> behind that silly and conspicuous front design. [18]

As time passes, this figure concealed behind what corresponds (in
terms of what we have been discussing) to the facade of the patriarchal
text becomes clearer and clearer. By moonlight the pattern of the wallpaper "becomes bars! The outside pattern I mean, and the woman
behind it is as plain as can be." And eventually, as the narrator sinks
more deeply into what the world calls madness, the terrifying implications of both the paper and the figure imprisoned behind the paper
begin to permeate—that is, to *haunt*—the rented ancestral mansion in
which she and her husband are immured. The "yellow smell" of the
paper "creeps all over the house," drenching every room in its subtle
aroma of decay. And the woman creeps too—through the house, in the
house, and out of the house, in the garden and "on that long road under
the trees." Sometimes, indeed, the narrator confesses, "I think there are a
great many women" both behind the paper and creeping in the garden,

and sometimes only one, and she crawls around fast, and her crawling shakes [the paper] all over. . . . And she is all the time trying to climb through. But nobody could climb through that pattern—it strangles so; I think that is why it has so many heads. [30]

Eventually it becomes obvious to both reader and narrator that the figure creeping through and behind the wallpaper is both the narrator and the narrator's double. By the end of the story, moreover, the narrator has enabled this double to escape from her textual/architectural confinement: "I pulled and she shook, I shook and she pulled, and before morning we had peeled off yards of that paper." Is the message of the tale's conclusion mere madness? Certainly the righteous Doctor John—whose name links him to the anti-hero of Charlotte Brontë's *Villette*—has been temporarily defeated, or at least momentarily stunned. "Now why should that man have fainted?" the narrator ironically asks as she creeps around her attic. But John's unmasculine swoon of surprise is the least of the triumphs Gilman imagines for her madwoman. More significant are the madwoman's own imaginings and creations, mirages of health and freedom with which her author endows her like a fairy godmother showering gold on a sleeping heroine. The woman from behind the wallpaper creeps away, for instance, creeps fast and far on the long road, in broad daylight. "I have watched her sometimes away off in the open country," says the narrator, "creeping as fast as a cloud shadow in a high wind."

Indistinct and yet rapid, barely perceptible but inexorable, the progress of that cloud shadow is not unlike the progress of nineteenth-century literary women out of the texts defined by patriarchal poetics into the open spaces of their own authority. That such an escape from the numb world behind the patterned walls of the text was a flight from dis-ease into health was quite clear to Gilman herself. When "The Yellow Wallpaper" was published she sent it to Weir Mitchell, whose strictures had kept her from attempting the pen during her own breakdown, thereby aggravating her illness, and she was delighted to learn, years later, that "he had changed his treatment of nervous prostration since reading" her story. "If that is a fact," she declared, "I have not lived in vain."[2] Because she was a rebellious feminist besides being a medical iconoclast, we can be sure that Gilman did not think of this triumph of hers in narrowly therapeutic terms. Because she knew, with Emily Dickinson, that "Infection in the sentence breeds," she knew that the cure for female despair must be spiritual as well as physical, aesthetic as well as social. What "The Yellow Wallpaper" shows she knew, too, is that even when a supposedly "mad" woman has been sentenced to imprisonment in the "infected" house of her own body, she may discover that, as Sylvia Plath was to put it seventy years later, she has "a self to recover, a queen."[3]

Notes

1. Charlotte Perkins Gilman, *The Yellow Wallpaper* (New York: The Feminist Press, 1973). All references in the text will be to page numbers in this edition.

2. *The Living of Charlotte Perkins Gilman*, p. 121.

3. "Stings," *Ariel*, p. 62.

A Map for Rereading:
Or, Gender and the Interpretation
of Literary Texts

Annette Kolodny

Appealing particularly to a generation still in the process of divorcing itself from the New Critics' habit of bracketing off any text as an entity in itself, as though "it could be read, understood, and criticized entirely in its own terms,"[1] Harold Bloom has proposed a dialectical theory of influence between poets and poets, as well as between poems and poems which, in essence, does away with the static notion of a fixed or knowable text. As he argued in *A Map of Misreading* in 1975, "a poem is a response to a poem, as a poet is a response to a poet, or a person to his parent." Thus, for Bloom, "poems . . . are neither about 'subjects' nor about 'themselves.' They are necessarily about *other poems*."[2]

To read or to know a poem, according to Bloom, engages the reader in an attempt to map the psychodynamic relations by which the poet at hand has willfully misunderstood the work of some precursor (either single or composite) in order to correct, rewrite, or appropriate the prior poetic vision as his own. As first introduced in *The Anxiety of Influence* in 1973, the resultant "wholly different practical criticism . . . give[s] up the failed enterprise of seeking to 'understand' any single poem as an entity in itself" and "pursue[s] instead the quest of learning to read any poem as its poet's deliberate misinterpretation, *as a poet*, of a precursor poem or of poetry in general."[3] What one deciphers in the process of reading, then, is not any discrete entity but, rather, a complex relational event, "itself a synecdoche for a larger whole including other texts."[4] "Reading a text is necessarily the reading of a whole system of texts,"

Bloom explains in *Kabbalah and Criticism*, "and meaning is always wandering around between texts" (*KC*, pp. 107–8).

To help purchase assent for this "wholly different practical criticism,"
Bloom asserted an identity between critics and poets as coequal participants in the same "belated and all-but-impossible act" of reading (which,
as he hastens to explain in *A Map of Misreading*, "if strong is always a
misreading"–p. 3). As it is a drama of epic proportions, in Bloom's
terms, when the ephebe poet attempts to appropriate and then correct a
precursor's meaning, so, too, for the critic, his own inevitable misreadings or *misprisions* are no less heroic–nor any the less creative. "Poets'
misinterpretations or poems" may be "more drastic than critics' misinterpretations or criticism," Bloom admits, but since he recognizes no such
thing as "interpretations but only misinterpretations . . . all criticism" is
necessarily elevated to a species of "prose poetry" (*Al*, pp. 94–95). The
critic's performance, thereby, takes place as one more "act of misprision
[which] displaces an earlier act of misprision"–presumably the poet's or
perhaps that of a prior critic; and, in this sense, the critic participates in
that same act of "defensive warfare" before his own critical forebears, or
even before the poet himself, as the poet presumably enacted before his
poetic father/precursor (*KC*, pp. 125, 104, 108). Their legacy, whether as
poetry or as "prose poetry" criticism, consequently establishes the strong
survivors of these psychic battles as figures whom others, in the future,
will need to overcome in their turn: "A poet is strong because poets after
him must work to evade him. A critic is strong if his readings similarly
provoke other readings."[5] It is unquestionably Bloom's most brilliant
rhetorical stroke, persuading not so much by virtue of the logic of his
argument as by the pleasure his (intended and mostly male) readership
will take in the discovery that their own activity replicates the psychic
adventures of The Poet, every critic's *figura* of heroism.[6]

What is left out of account, however, is the fact that whether we
speak of poets and critics "reading" texts or writers "reading" (and
thereby recording for us) the world, we are calling attention to interpretive strategies that are learned, historically determined, and thereby
necessarily gender-inflected. As others have elsewhere questioned the
adequacy of Bloom's paradigm of poetic influence to explain the production of poetry by women,[7] so now I propose to examine analogous
limitations in his model for the reading–and hence critical–process
(since both, after all, derive from his revisionist rendering of the Freudian family romance). To begin with, to locate that "meaning" which "is

always wandering around between texts" (KC, pp. 107–8), Bloom assumes a community of readers (and, thereby, critics) who know that same "whole system of texts" within which the specific poet at hand has enacted his *misprision*. The canonical sense of a shared and coherent literary tradition is thereby essential to the utility of Bloom's paradigm of literary influence as well as to his notions of reading (and misreading). "What happens if one tries to write, or to teach, or to think or even to read without the sense of a tradition?" Bloom asks in *A Map of Misreading*. "Why," as he himself well understands, "nothing at all happens, just nothing. You cannot write or teach or think or even read without imitation, and what you imitate is what another person has done, that person's writing or teaching or thinking or reading. Your relation to what informs that person *is* tradition, for tradition is influence that extends past one generation, a carrying-over of influence" (MM, p. 32).

So long as the poems and poets he chooses for scrutiny participate in the "continuity that began in the sixth century B.C. when Homer first became a schoolbook for the Greeks" (MM, pp. 33–34), Bloom has a great deal to tell us about the carrying over of literary influence; where he must remain silent is where carrying over takes place among readers and writers who in fact have been, or at least have experienced themselves as, cut off and alien from that dominant tradition. Virginia Woolf made the distinction vividly over a half-century ago, in *A Room of One's Own*, when she described being barred entrance, because of her sex, to a "famous library" in which was housed, among others, a Milton manuscript. Cursing the "Oxbridge" edifice, "venerable and calm, with all its treasures safe locked within its breast," she returns to her room at the inn later that night, still pondering "how unpleasant it is to be locked out; and I thought how it is worse perhaps to be locked in; and, thinking of the safety and prosperity of the one sex and of the poverty and insecurity of the other and of the effect of tradition and of the lack of tradition upon the mind of a writer."[8] And, she might have added, on the mind of a reader as well. For while my main concern here is with reading (albeit largely and perhaps imperfectly defined), I think it worth noting that there exists an intimate interaction between readers and writers in and through which each defines for the other what s/he is about. "The effect . . . of the lack of tradition upon the mind of a writer" will communicate itself, in one way or another, to her readers; and, indeed, may respond to her readers' sense of exclusion from high (or highbrow) culture.

An American instance provides perhaps the best example. Delim-ited by the lack of formal or classical education, and constrained by the social and aesthetic norms of their day to conceptualizing "authorship as a profession rather than a calling, as work and not art,"[9] the vastly popular women novelists of the so-called feminine fifties often enough, and somewhat defensively, made a virtue of their sad necessities by invoking an audience of readers for whom aspirations to "literature" were as inappropriate as they were for the writer. As Nina Baym remarks in her recent study *Woman's Fiction*, "often the women deliberately and even proudly disavowed membership in an artistic fraternity." " 'Mine is a story for the table and arm-chair under the reading lamp in the livingroom, and not for the library shelves,' " Baym quotes Marion Harland from the introduction to Harland's autobiography; and then, at greater length, Baym cites Fanny Fern's dedicatory pages to her novel *Rose Clark*:

> When the frost curtains the windows, when the wind whistles fiercely at the key-hole, when the bright fire glows, and the tea-tray is removed, and father in his slippered feet lolls in his arm-chair; and mother with her nimble needle "makes auld claes look amaist as weel as new," and grand-mamma draws closer to the chimney-corner, and Tommy with his plate of chestnuts nestles contentedly at her feet; then let my unpretending story be read. For such an hour, for such an audience, was it written.
>
> Should any *dictionary on legs* rap inopportunely at the door for admit-tance, send him away to the groaning shelves of some musty library, where "literature" lies embalmed, with its stony eyes, fleshless joints, and ossified heart, in faultless preservation.[10]

If a bit overdone, prefaces like these nonetheless point up the self-consciousness with which writers like Fern and Harland perceived them-selves as excluded from the dominant literary tradition and as writing for an audience of readers similarly excluded. To quote Baym again, these "women were expected to write specifically for their own sex and within the tradition of their woman's culture rather than within the Great Tradition. They never presented themselves as followers in the footsteps of Milton or Spenser."[11]

On the one hand, of course, increased literacy (if not substantially improved conditions of education) marked the generation of American women at midcentury, opening a vast market for a literature which would treat the contexts of their lives—the sewing circle rather than the whaling ship, the nursery instead of the lawyer's office—as functional symbols of the human condition.[12] On the other hand, while this vast new audience must certainly be credited with shaping the features of what then became popular women's fiction, it is also the case that the writers in their turn both responded to and helped to formulate their readers' tastes and habits. And both together, I would suggest, found this a means of accepting (or at least coping with) the barred entryway that was to distress Virginia Woolf so in the next century. But these facts of our literary history also suggest that from the 1850s on, in America at least, the meanings "wandering around between texts" were wandering around somewhat different groups of texts where male and female readers were concerned.[13] So that with the advent of women "who wished to be regarded as artists rather than careerists,"[14] toward the end of the nineteenth century, there arose the critical problem with which we are still plagued and which Bloom so determinedly ignores: the problem of reading any text as "a synecdoche for a larger whole including other texts" when that necessarily assumed "whole system of texts" in which it is embedded is foreign to one's reading knowledge.

The appearance of Kate Chopin's novel *The Awakening* in 1899, for example, perplexed readers familiar with her earlier (and intentionally "regional") short stories not so much because it turned away from themes or subject matter implicit in her earlier work, nor even less because it dealt with female sensuality and extramarital sexuality, but because her elaboration of those materials deviated radically from the accepted norms of women's fiction out of which her audience so largely derived its expectations. The nuances and consequences of passion and individual temperament, after all, fairly define the focus of most of her preceding fictions. "That the book is strong and that Miss Chopin has a keen knowledge of certain phases of feminine character will not be denied," wrote the anonymous reviewer for the Chicago *Times-Herald*. What marked an unacceptable "new departure" for this critic, then, was the impropriety of Chopin's focus on material previously edited out of the popular genteel novels by and about women which, somewhat inarticulately, s/he translated into the accusation that Chopin had "enter[ed] the overworked field of sex fiction."[15]

Charlotte Perkins Gilman's initial difficulty in seeing "The Yellow Wallpaper" into print repeated the problem, albeit in a somewhat different context: for her story located itself not as any deviation from a previous tradition of women's fiction but, instead, as a continuation of a genre popularized by Poe. And insofar as Americans had earlier learned to follow the fictive processes of aberrant perception and mental break-down in *his* work, they should have provided Gilman, one would imag-ine, with a ready-made audience for *her* protagonist's progressively debil-itating fantasies of entrapment and liberation. As they had entered popular fiction by the end of the nineteenth century, however, the linguistic markers for those processes were at once heavily male-gendered and highly idiosyncratic, having more to do with individual temperament than with social or cultural situations per se. As a result, it would appear that the reading strategies by which cracks in ancestral walls and suggestions of unchecked masculine willfulness were immedi-ately noted as both symbolically and semantically relevant did not, for some reason, necessarily *carry over* to "the nursery at the top of the house" with its windows barred, nor even less to the forced submission of the woman who must "take great pains to control myself before" her physician husband.[16]

A reader today seeking meaning in the way Harold Bloom outlines that process might note, of course, a fleeting resemblance between the upstairs chamber in Gilman—with its bed nailed to the floor, its win-dows barred, and metal rings fixed to the walls—and Poe's evocation of the dungeon chambers of Toledo; in fact, a credible argument might be made for reading "The Yellow Wallpaper" as Gilman's willful and pur-poseful misprision of "The Pit and the Pendulum." Both stories, after all, involve a sane mind entrapped in an insanity-inducing situation. Gilman's "message" might then be that the equivalent revolution by which the speaking voice of the Poe tale is released to both sanity and freedom is unavailable to her heroine. No *deus ex machina*, no General Lasalle triumphantly entering the city, no "outstretched arm" to prevent Gilman's protagonist from falling into her own internal "abyss" is con-ceivable, given the rules of the social context in which Gilman's narra-tive is embedded. When gender is taken into account, then, so this interpretation would run, Gilman is saying that the nature of the trap envisioned must be understood as qualitatively different, and so too the possible escape routes.

Contemporary readers of "The Yellow Wallpaper," however, were apparently unprepared to make such connections. Those fond of Poe could not easily transfer their sense of mental derangement to the mind of a comfortable middle-class wife and mother; and those for whom the woman in the home was a familiar literary character were hard-pressed to comprehend so extreme an anatomy of the psychic price she paid. Horace Scudder, the editor of *The Atlantic Monthly* who first rejected the story, wrote only that "I could not forgive myself if I made others as miserable as I have made myself!" (Hedges, p. 40). And even William Dean Howells, who found the story "chilling" and admired it sufficiently to reprint it in 1920, some twenty-eight years after its first publication (in *The New England Magazine* of May 1892), like most readers, either failed to notice or neglected to report "the connection between the insanity and the sex, or sexual role, of the victim" (Hedges, p. 41). For readers at the turn of the century, then, that "meaning" which "is always wandering around between texts" had as yet failed to find connective pathways linking the fanciers of Poe to the devotees of popular women's fiction, or the shortcut between Gilman's short story and the myriad published feminist analyses of the ills of society (some of them written by Gilman herself). Without such connective contexts, Poe continued as a well-traveled road, while Gilman's story, lacking the possibility of further influence, became a literary dead-end.

In one sense, by hinting at an audience of male readers as ill-equipped to follow the symbolic significance of the narrator's progressive breakdown as was her doctor-husband to diagnose properly the significance of his wife's fascination with the wallpaper's patternings; and by predicating a female readership as yet unprepared for texts which mirrored back, with symbolic exemplariness, certain patterns underlying their empirical reality, "The Yellow Wallpaper" anticipated its own reception. For insofar as writing and reading represent linguistically-based interpretive strategies—the first for the recording of a reality (that has, obviously, in a sense, already been "read") and the second for the deciphering of that recording (and thus also the further decoding of a prior imputed reality)—the wife's progressive descent into madness provides a kind of commentary upon, indeed is revealed in terms of, the sexual politics inherent in the manipulation of those strategies. We are presented at the outset with a protagonist who, ostensibly for her own good, is denied both activities and who, in the course of accommodating herself to that deprivation, comes more and more to experience her self as a text which can neither get read nor recorded.

In his doubly authoritative role as both husband and doctor, John not only appropriates the interpretive processes of reading—diagnosing his wife's illness and thereby selecting what may be understood of her "meaning"; reading to her, rather than allowing her to read for herself—

but, as well, he determines what may get written and hence communicated. For her part, the protagonist avers, she does not agree with her husband's ideas: "Personally, I believe that congenial work, with excitement and change, would do me good." But given the fact of her marriage to "a physician of high standing" who "assures friends and relatives that there is really nothing the matter with one but temporary nervous depression—a slight hysterical tendency—what is one to do?" she asks. Since her husband (and by extension the rest of the world) will not heed what she says of herself, she attempts instead to communicate it to "this . . . dead paper . . . a great relief to my mind." But John's insistent opposition gradually erodes even this outlet for her since, as she admits, "it *does* exhaust me a good deal—having to be so sly about it, or else meet with heavy opposition" (p. 10). At the sound of his approach, following upon her first attempt to describe "those sprawling flamboyant patterns" in the wallpaper, she declares, "There comes John, and I must put this away,—he hates to have me write a word" (p. 13).

Successively isolated from conversational exchanges, prohibited free access to pen and paper, and thus increasingly denied what Jean Ricardou has called "the local exercise of syntax and vocabulary,"[17] the protagonist of "The Yellow Wallpaper" experiences the extreme extrapolation of those linguistic tools to the processes of perception and response. In fact, it follows directly upon a sequence in which: (1) she acknowledges that John's opposition to her writing has begun to make "the effort . . . greater than the relief"; (2) John refuses to let her "go and make a visit to Cousin Henry and Julia"; and (3) as a kind of punctuation mark to that denial, John carries her "upstairs and laid me on the bed, and sat by me and read to me till it tired my head." It is after these events, I repeat, that the narrator first makes out the dim shape lurking "behind the outside pattern" in the wallpaper: "it is like a woman stooping down and creeping" (pp. 21–22).

From that point on, the narrator progressively gives up the attempt to *record* her reality and instead begins to *read* it—as symbolically adumbrated in her compulsion to discover a consistent and coherent pattern amid "the sprawling outlines" of the wallpaper's apparently "pointless pattern" (pp. 20, 19). Selectively emphasizing one section of the pattern while repressing others, reorganizing and regrouping past impressions into newer, more fully realized configurations—as one might with any complex formal text—the speaking voice becomes obsessed with her quest for meaning, jealous even of her husband's or his sister's momentary interest in the paper. Having caught her sister-in-law "with her hand on it once," the narrator declares, "I know she was studying that pattern, and I am determined that nobody shall find it out but myself!" (p. 27). As the pattern changes with the changing light in the room, so too do her interpretations of it. And what is not quite so apparent by daylight becomes glaringly so at night: "At night in any kind of light, in twilight, candle light, lamplight, and worst of all by moonlight, it becomes bars! The outside pattern I mean, and the woman behind it is as plain as can be." "By daylight," in contrast (like the protagonist herself), "she is subdued, quiet" (p. 26).

As she becomes wholly taken up with the exercise of these interpretive strategies, so, too, she claims, her "life is very much more exciting now than it used to be. You see I have something more to expect, to look forward to, to watch" (p. 27). What she is watching, of course, is her own psyche writ large; and the closer she comes to "reading" in the wallpaper the underlying if unacknowledged patterns of her real-life experience, the less frequent becomes that delicate oscillation between surrender to or involvement in and the more distanced observation of developing meaning. Slowly but surely the narrative voice ceases to distinguish itself from the woman in the wallpaper pattern, finally asserting that "I don't want anybody to get that woman out at night but myself" (p. 31), and concluding with a confusion of pronouns that merges into a grammatical statement of identity:

> As soon as it was moonlight and that poor thing began to crawl and shake the pattern, I got up and ran to help her.
> *I* pulled and *she* shook, and *I* shook and *she* pulled, and before morning *we* had peeled off yards of that paper.
>
> [P. 32, my italics]

She is, in a sense, now totally surrendered to what is quite literally her own text—or, rather, her self as text. But in decoding its (or her) meaning, what she has succeeded in doing is discovering the symbolization of her own untenable and unacceptable reality. To escape that reality she attempts the destruction of the paper which seemingly encodes it: the pattern of bars entrapping the creeping woman. " 'I've got out at last,' said I, 'in spite of you and Jane. I've pulled off most of the paper, so you can't put me back!' " (p. 36). Their paper pages may be torn and moldy (as is, in fact, the smelly wallpaper), but the meaning of texts is not so easily destroyed. Liberation here is liberation only into madness: for in decoding her own projections onto the paper, the protagonist had managed merely to reencode them once more, and now more firmly than ever, within.

With the last paragraphs of the story, John faints away — presumably in shock at his wife's now totally delusional state. He has repeatedly misdiagnosed, or misread, the heavily edited behavior with which his wife has presented herself to him; and never once has he divined what his wife sees in the wallpaper. But given his freedom to read (or, in this case, misread) books, people, and the world as he chooses, he is hardly forced to discover for himself so extreme a text. To exploit Bloom's often useful terminology once again, then, Gilman's story represents not so much an object for the recurrent misreadings, or misprisions, of readers and critics (though this, of course, continues to occur) as an exploration, within itself, of the gender-inflected interpretive strategies responsible for our mutual misreadings, and even horrific misprisions, across sex lines. If neither male nor female reading audiences were prepared to decode properly "The Yellow Wallpaper," even less, Gilman understood, were they prepared to comprehend one another.

It is unfortunate that Gilman's story was so quickly relegated to the backwaters of our literary landscape because, coming as it did at the end of the nineteenth century, it spoke to a growing concern among American women who would be serious writers: it spoke, that is, to their strong sense of writing out of nondominant or subcultural traditions (both literary and otherwise), coupled with an acute sensitivity to the fact that since women and men learn to read different worlds, different groups of texts are available to their reading and writing strategies. Had "The Yellow Wallpaper" been able to stand as a potential precursor for the generation of subsequent corrections and revisions, then, as in Bloom's paradigm, it might have made possible a form of fiction by women capable not only of commenting upon but even of overcoming that impasse. That it did not — nor did any other woman's fiction become canonical in the United States[18] — meant that, again and again, each woman who took up the pen had to confront anew her bleak premonition that, both as writers and as readers, women too easily became isolated islands of symbolic significance, available only to, and decipherable only by, one another.[19] If any Bloomian "meaning" wanders around between women's texts, therefore, it must be precisely this shared apprehension.

On the face of it such statements should appear nothing less than commonsensical, especially to those most recent theorists of reading who combine an increased attentiveness to the meaning-making role of the reader in the deciphering of texts with a recognition of the links between our "reading" of texts and our "reading" of the world and one another. Among them, Bloom himself seems quite clearly to understand this when, in *Kabbalah and Criticism*, he declares: "That which you are, that only can you read" (*KC*, p. 96). Extrapolating from his description of the processes involved in the reading of literary texts to a larger comment on our ability to take in or decipher those around us, Wolfgang Iser has lately theorized that "we can only make someone else's thought into an absorbing theme for ourselves, provided the virtual background of our own personality can adapt to it."[20] Anticipating such pronouncements in almost everything they have been composing for over a hundred years now, the women who wrote fiction, most especially, translated these observations into the structures of their stories by invoking that single feature which critics like Iser and Bloom still manage so resolutely to ignore: and that is, the crucial importance of the *sex* of the "interpreter" in that process which Nelly Furman has called "the active attribution of significance to formal signifiers."[21] Antedating both Bloom and Iser by over fifty years, for example, Susan Keating Glaspell's 1917 short story "A Jury of Her Peers" explores the necessary (but generally ignored) gender marking which *must* constitute any definition of "peers" in the complex process of unraveling truth or meaning.[22]

The opening paragraph of Glaspell's story serves, essentially, to alert the reader to the significations to follow: Martha Hale, interrupted at her kitchen chores, must drop "everything right where it was" in order to hurry off with her husband and the others. In so doing, "her eye made a scandalized sweep of her kitchen," noting with distress "that her kitchen was in no shape for leaving: her bread all ready for mixing, half the flour sifted and half unsifted." The point, of course, is that highly unusual circumstances demand this of her, and "it was no ordinary thing that called her away." When she seats herself "in the big two-seated buggy" alongside her impatient farmer husband, the sheriff and his wife, and the county attorney, the story proper begins.

All five drive to a neighboring farm where a murder has been committed — the farmer strangled, his wife already arrested. The men intend to seek clues to the motive for the crime, while the women are, ostensibly, simply to gather together the few necessities required by the wife incarcerated in the town jail. Immediately upon approaching the place, however, the very act of perception becomes sex-coded: the men look at the house only to talk "about what had happened," while the women note the geographical topography which makes it, repeatedly in the narrative, "a lonesome-looking place." Once inside, the men " 'go upstairs first—then out to the barn and around there' " in their search for clues (even though the actual crime took place in the upstairs master bedroom), while the women are left to the kitchen and parlor. Convinced as they are of "the insignificance of kitchen things," the men cannot properly attend to what these might reveal and, instead, seek elsewhere for " 'a clue to the motive,' " so necessary if the county attorney is to make his case. Indeed, it is the peculiar irony of the story that although the men never question their attribution of guilt to Minnie Foster, they nonetheless cannot meaningfully interpret this farm wife's world—her kitchen and parlor. And, arrogantly certain that the women would not even " 'know a clue if they did come upon it,' " they thereby leave the discovery of the clues, and the consequent unraveling of the motive, to those who do, in fact, command the proper interpretive strategies.

Exploiting the information sketched into the opening, Glaspell has the neighbor, Mrs. Hale, and the sheriff's wife, Mrs. Peters, note, among the supposedly insignificant kitchen things, the unusual, and on a farm unlikely, remnants of kitchen chores left "half done," denoting an interruption of some serious nature. Additionally, where the men could discern no signs of " 'anger—or sudden feeling' " to substantiate a motive, the women comprehend the implications of some "fine, even sewing" gone suddenly awry, " 'as if she didn't know what she was about!' " Finally, of course, the very drabness of the house, the miserliness of the husband to which it attests, the old and broken stove, the patchwork that has become Minnie Foster's wardrobe—all these make the women uncomfortably aware that to acknowledge fully the meaning of what they are seeing is " 'to get her own house to turn against her!' " Discovery by discovery, they destroy the mounting evidence—evidence which the men, at any rate, cannot recognize as such; and, sealing the bond between them as conspirators in saving Minnie Foster, they hide from the men the canary with its neck broken, the penultimate clue to the strangling of a husband who had so systematically destroyed all life, beauty, and music in his wife's environment.

Opposing against one another male and female realms of meaning and activity—the barn and the kitchen—Glaspell's narrative not only invites a semiotic analysis but, indeed, performs that analysis for us. If the absent Minnie Foster is the "transmitter" or "sender" in this schema, then only the women are competent "receivers" or "readers" of her "message," since they alone share not only her context (the supposed insignificance of kitchen things) but, as a result, the conceptual patterns which make up her world. To those outside the shared systems of quilting and knotting, roller towels and bad stoves, with all their symbolic significations, these may appear trivial, even irrelevant to meaning; but to those within the system, they comprise the totality of the message: in this case, a reordering of who in fact has been murdered and, with that, what has constituted the real crime in the story.

For while the two women who visit Minnie Foster's house slowly but surely decipher the symbolic significance of her action—causing her husband's neck to be broken because he had earlier broken her canary's neck—the narrative itself functions, for the reader, as a further decoding of what that symbolic action says about itself. The essential crime in the story, we come to realize, has been the husband's inexorable strangulation, over the years, of Minnie Foster's spirit and personality; and the culpable criminality is the complicity of the women who had permitted the isolation and the loneliness to dominate Minnie Foster's existence: " 'I wish I had come over to see Minnie Foster sometimes,' " declares her neighbor guiltily. " 'I can see now—' She did not put it into words."

> "I wish you'd seen Minnie Foster," [says Mrs. Hale to the sheriff's wife] "when she wore a white dress with blue ribbons, and stood up there in the choir and sang."
>
> The picture of that girl, the fact that she had lived neighbor to that girl for twenty years, and had let her die for lack of life, was suddenly more than she could bear.
>
> "Oh, I *wish* I'd come over here once in a while!" she cried. "That was a crime! That was a crime! Who's going to punish that?"

The recognition is itself, of course, a kind of punishment. With it comes, as well, another recognition, as Mrs. Peters reveals experiences in her own life of analogous isolation, desperate loneliness, and brutality at the hands of a male. Finally they conclude: " 'We all go through the same things—it's all just a different kind of the same thing! If it weren't—why do you and I *understand?* Why do we *know*—what we know this minute?'" By this point the narrative emphasis has shifted: To understand why it is that they know what they now know is for these women to recognize the profoundly sex-linked world of meaning which they inhabit; to discover how specialized is their ability to read that world is to discover anew their own shared isolation within it.

While neither the Gilman nor the Glaspell story necessarily excludes the male as reader—indeed, both in a way are directed specifically at educating him to become a better reader—they do, nonetheless, insist that, however inadvertently, he is a *different kind* of reader and that, where women are concerned, he is often an inadequate reader. In the first instance, because the husband cannot properly diagnose his wife or attend to her reality, the result is horrific: the wife descends into madness. In the second, because the men cannot even recognize as such the very clues for which they search, the ending is a happy one: Minnie Foster is to be set free, no motive having been discovered by which to prosecute her. In both, however, the same point is being made: lacking familiarity with the women's imaginative universe, that universe within which their acts are signs,[23] the men in these stories can neither read nor comprehend the meanings of the women closest to them—and this in spite of the apparent sharing of a common language. It is, in short, a fictive rendering of the dilemma of the woman writer. For while we may all agree that in our daily conversational exchanges men and women speak more or less meaningfully and effectively with one another, thus fostering the illusion of a wholly shared common language, it is also the case that where figurative usage is invoked—that usage which often enough marks the highly specialized language of literature—it "can be inaccessible to all but those who share information about one another's knowledge, beliefs, intentions, and attitudes."[24] Symbolic representations, in other words, depend on a fund of shared recognitions and potential inference. For their intended impact to *take hold* in the reader's imagination, the author simply must, like Minnie Foster, be able to call upon a shared context with her audience; where she cannot, or dare not, she may revert to silence, to the imitation of male forms, or, like the narrator in "The Yellow Wallpaper," to total withdrawal and isolation into madness.

It may be objected, of course, that I have somewhat stretched my argument so as to conflate (or perhaps confuse?) *all* interpretive strategies with language processes, specifically *reading*. But in each instance, it is the survival of the *woman as text*—Gilman's narrator and Glaspell's Minnie Foster—that is at stake; and the competence of her reading audience alone determines the outcome. Thus, in my view, both stories intentionally function as highly specialized language acts (called "literature") which examine the difficulty inherent in deciphering other highly specialized realms of meaning—in this case, women's conceptual and symbolic worlds. And further, the intended emphasis in each is the inaccessibility of female meaning to make interpretation.[25] The fact that in recent years each story has increasingly found its way into easily available textbooks, and hence into the Women's Studies and American Literature classroom, to be read and enjoyed by teachers and students of both sexes happily suggests that their fictive premises are attributable not so much to necessity as to contingency.[26] Men can, after all, learn to apprehend the meanings encoded in texts by and about women—just as women have learned to become sensitive readers of Shakespeare and Milton, Hemingway and Mailer.[27] Both stories function, in effect, as a prod to that very process by alerting the reader to the fundamental problem of "reading" correctly within cohabiting but differently structured conceptual worlds.

To take seriously the implications of such relearned reading strategies is to acknowledge that we are embarking upon a revisionist rereading of our entire literary inheritance and, in that process, demonstrating the full applicability of Bloom's second formula for canon-formation, "You are or become what you read" (KC, p. 96). To set ourselves the task of learning to read a wholly different set of texts will make of us different kinds of readers (and perhaps different kinds of people as well). But to set ourselves the task of doing this in a public way, on behalf of women's texts specifically, engages us—as the feminists among us have learned—in a challenge to the inevitable issue of "*authority* . . . in all questions of canon-formation" (KC, p. 100). It places us, in a sense, in a position analogous to that of the narrator of "The Yellow Wallpaper," bound, if we are to survive, to challenge the (accepted and generally male) authority who has traditionally wielded the power to determine what may be written and how it shall be read. It challenges fundamentally not only the shape of our canon of major American authors but, indeed, that very "continuity that began in the sixth century B.C. when Homer first became a schoolbook for the Greeks" (MM, pp. 33–34).

It is no mere coincidence, therefore, that readers as diverse as

Adrienne Rich and Harold Bloom have arrived by various routes at the conclusion that *re-vision* constitutes the key to an ongoing literary history. Whether functioning as ephebe/poet or would-be critic, Bloom's reader, as "revisionist," "strives to *see* again, so as to esteem and *estimate* differently, so as then to *aim* 'correctively'" (MM, p. 4). For Rich, "re-vision" entails "the act of looking back, of seeing with fresh eyes, of entering an old text from a new critical direction."[28] And each, as a result—though from different motives—strives to make the "literary tradition . . . the captive of the revisionary impulse" (MM, p. 36). What Rich and other feminist critics intended by that "re-visionism" has been the subject of this essay: not only would such revisionary rereading open new avenues for comprehending male texts but, as I have argued here, it would, as well, allow us to appreciate the variety of women's literary expression, enabling us to take it into serious account for perhaps the first time rather than, as we do now, writing it off as caprice or exception, the irregularity in an otherwise regular design. Looked at this way, feminist appeals to revisionary rereading, as opposed to Bloom's, offer us all a potential enhancing of our capacity to read the world, our literary texts, and even one another, anew.

To end where I began, then, Bloom's paradigm of poetic history, when applied to women, proves useful only in a negative sense: for by omitting the possibility of poet/mothers from his psychodynamic of literary influence (allowing the feminine only the role of Muse—as composite whore and mother), Bloom effectively masks the fact of an *other* tradition entirely—that in which women taught one another how to read and write about and out of their own unique (and sometimes isolated) contexts. In so doing, however, he points up not only the ignorance informing our literary history as it is currently taught in the schools, but, as well, he pinpoints (however unwittingly) what must be done to change our skewed perceptions: all readers, male and female alike, must be taught first to recognize the existence of a significant body of writing by women in America and, second, they must be encouraged to learn how to read it within its own unique and informing contexts of meaning and symbol. *Re-visionary rereading*, if you will. No more must we impose on future generations of readers the inevitability of Norman Mailer's "terrible confession . . .—I have nothing to say about any of the talented women who write today. . . . I do not seem able to read them."[29] Nor should Bloom himself continue to suffer an inability to express useful "judgment upon . . . the 'literature of Women's Liberation.'"[30]

NOTES

1. Albert William Levi, "*De Interpretatione*: Cognition and Context in the History of Ideas," *Critical Inquiry*, 3, No. 1 (Autumn 1976), 164.

2. Harold Bloom, *A Map of Misreading* (New York, 1975), p. 18 (hereafter cited as MM).

3. Bloom, *The Anxiety of Influence: A Theory of Poetry* (New York, 1973), p. 43 (hereafter cited as AI).

4. Bloom, *Kabbalah and Criticism* (New York, 1975), p. 106 (hereafter cited as KC). The concept is further refined in his *Poetry and Repression: Revisionism from Blake to Stevens* (New Haven, 1976), p. 26, where Bloom describes poems as "defensive processes in constant change, which is to say that poems themselves are *acts of reading*. A poem is a fierce, proleptic debate *with itself*, as well as with precursor poems."

5. *KC*, p. 125; by way of example, and with a kind of Apollonian modesty, Bloom demonstrates his own propensities for misreading, placing himself amid the excellent company of those other Super Misreaders, Blake, Shelley, C. S. Lewis, Charles Williams, and T. S. Eliot (all of whom misread Milton's Satan), and only regrets the fact "that the misreading of Blake and Shelley by Yeats is a lot stronger than the misreading of Blake and Shelley by Bloom" (pp. 125–26).

6. In *Poetry and Repression*, p. 18, Bloom explains that "by 'reading' I intend to mean the work both of poet and of critic, who themselves move from dialectic irony to synecdochal representation as they confront the text before them."

7. See, for example, Joanne Feit Diehl's attempt to adapt the Bloomian model to the psychodynamics of women's poetic production in " 'Come Slowly – Eden': An Exploration of Women Poets and Their Muse," *Signs*, 3, No. 3 (Spring 1978), 572–87; and the objections to that adaptation raised by Lillian Faderman and Louise Bernikow in their Comments, *Signs*, 4, No. 1 (Autumn 1978), 188–91 and 191–95, respectively. More recently, Sandra M. Gilbert and Susan Gubar have tried to correct the omission of women writers from Bloom's male-centered literary history in *The Madwoman in the Attic: The Woman Writer and the Nineteenth-Century Literary Imagination* (New Haven, 1979).

8. Virginia Woolf, *A Room of One's Own* (1928; rpt. Harmondsworth, 1972), pp. 9–10, 25–26.

9. Nina Baym, *Woman's Fiction: A Guide to Novels By and About Women in America 1820–1870* (Ithaca, 1978), p. 32.

10. See Baym, *Woman's Fiction*, pp. 32–33.

11. Ibid., p. 178.

12. I paraphrase rather freely here from some of Baym's acutely perceptive and highly suggestive remarks, p. 14.

13. The problem of audience is compiicated by the fact that in nineteenth-

century America distinct classes of so-called highbrow and lowbrow readers were emerging cutting across sex and class lines; and, for each sex, distinctly separate "serious" and "popular" reading materials were also being marketed. Full discussion, however, is beyond the scope of this essay. In its stead, I direct the reader to Henry Nash Smith's clear and concise summation in the introductory chapter to his *Democracy and the Novel: Popular Resistance to Classic American Writers* (New York, 1978), pp. 1–15.

14. Baym, p. 178.

15. From "Books of the Day," Chicago *Times-Herald* (1 June 1899), p. 9; excerpted in Kate Chopin, *The Awakening*, ed. Margaret Culley (New York, 1976), p. 149.

16. Charlotte Perkins Gilman, *The Yellow Wallpaper*, with Afterword by Elaine R. Hedges (New York, 1973), pp. 12, 11. Page references to this edition will henceforth be cited parenthetically in the text, with references to Hedges's excellent Afterword preceded by her name.

17. Jean Ricardou, "Composition Discomposed," tr. Erica Freiberg, *Critical Inquiry*, 3, No. 1 (Autumn 1976), 90.

18. The possible exception here is Harriet Beecher Stowe's *Uncle Tom's Cabin; or, Life Among the Lowly* (1852).

19. If, to some of the separatist advocates in our current wave of New Feminism, this sounds like a wholly acceptable, even happy circumstance, we must nonetheless understand that, for earlier generations of women artists, acceptance within male precincts conferred the mutually understood marks of success and, in some quarters, vitally needed access to publishing houses, serious critical attention, and even financial independence. That this was *not* the case for the writers of domestic fictions around the middle of the nineteenth century was a fortunate but anomalous circumstance. Insofar as our artist-mothers were separatist, therefore, it was the result of impinging cultural contexts and not (often) of their own choosing.

20. Wolfgang Iser, *The Implied Reader: Patterns of Communication in Prose Fiction from Bunyan to Beckett* (Baltimore, 1974), p. 293.

21. Nelly Furman, "The Study of Women and Language: Comment on Vol. 3, No. 3," *Signs*, 4, No. 1 (Autumn 1978), 184.

22. First published in *Every Week* (15 March 1917), the story was then collected in *Best Short Stories of 1917*, ed. Edward O'Brien (London, 1917). My source for the text is Mary Anne Ferguson's *Images of Women in Literature* (Boston, 1973), pp. 370–85; for some reason the story was dropped from Ferguson's 1975 revised edition but, as will be indicated below, it is elsewhere collected. Since there are no textual difficulties involved, I have omitted page references to any specific reprinting.

23. I here paraphrase Clifford Geertz, *The Interpretation of Cultures* (New

York, 1973), p. 13, and specifically direct the reader to the parable from Wittgenstein quoted on that same page.

24. Ted Cohen, "Metaphor and the Cultivation of Intimacy," *Critical Inquiry*, 5, No. 1 (Autumn 1978), 78.

25. It is significant, I think, that the stories do not suggest any difficulty for the women in apprehending the men's meanings. On the one hand this simply is not relevant to either plot; and on the other, since in each narrative the men clearly control the public realms of discourse, it would, of course, have been incumbent upon the women to learn to understand them. Though masters need not learn the language of their slaves, the reverse is never the case: for survival's sake, oppressed or subdominant groups always study the nuances of meaning and gesture in those who control them.

26. For example, Gilman's "The Yellow Wallpaper" may be found, in addition to the Feminist Press reprinting previously cited, in *The Oven Birds: American Women on Womanhood, 1820–1920*, ed. Gail Parker (Garden City, 1972), pp. 317–34; and Glaspell's "A Jury of Her Peers" is reprinted in *American Voices, American Women*, ed. Lee R. Edwards and Arlyn Diamond (New York, 1973), pp. 359–81.

27. That women may have paid a high psychological and emotional price for their ability to read men's texts is beyond the scope of this essay, but I enthusiastically direct the reader to Judith Fetterley's provocative study of the problem in her *The Resisting Reader: A Feminist Approach to American Fiction* (Bloomington, 1978).

28. Adrienne Rich, "When We Dead Awaken: Writing as Re-Vision," *College English*, 34, No. 1 (October 1972), 18; rpt. in *Adrienne Rich's Poetry*, ed. Barbara Charlesworth Gelpi and Albert Gelpi (New York, 1975), p. 90.

29. Norman Mailer, "Evaluations—Quick and Expensive Comments on the Talent in the Room," collected in his *Advertisements for Myself* (New York, 1966), pp. 434–35.

30. MM, p. 36. What precisely Bloom intends by the phrase is nowhere made clear; for the purposes of this essay, I have assumed that he is referring to the recently increased publication of new titles by women writers.

Convention Coverage or How to Read Your Own Life

Jean E. Kennard

I must have reread Northrop Frye's *Anatomy of Criticism*—or at least many parts of it—several times since the first reading fifteen years ago. Yet despite this familiarity, when I looked at it again this spring, I found myself uncomfortable with a couple of sentences which had never troubled me before: "All humor demands agreement that certain things, such as a picture of a wife beating her husband in a comic strip, are conventionally funny. To introduce a comic strip in which a husband beats his wife would distress the reader, because it would mean learning a new convention."[1]

My objection had nothing to do with Frye's basic concept of a convention as an agreement which allows art to communicate. I agreed with this definition which he had developed more fully earlier: "The contract agreed on by the reader before he can start reading is the same thing as a convention."[2] I was also in sympathy with a critical approach based upon the response of the reader. Nor did my objection concern the question of humor, which, it is perhaps worth noting, I was quite able to ignore even though it was Frye's primary focus.

My distress as a reader was with his example. I was uncomfortable with a discussion of wife beating as an even potentially acceptable source of humor. To talk about it as a new convention seemed insensitive. My discomfort extended, though more diffusely, to the idea of considering any form of violence amusing. I had a strong feeling that the picture of a wife beating her husband was no longer funny; in other words, that other people (that is, people I knew) would no longer find it funny. I granted, however, that it was at one time "conventionally funny" and realized that I had probably accepted it as such when I first read Frye. The indication of that acceptance was a failure to notice or remember the example.

For me, obviously, a convention had changed, and some of the reasons at least seemed apparent. Such extraliterary experiences as talking with friends who worked with battered women, an increased awareness of violence in every city I visited, together with reading feminist scholarship, had led me to formulate values which resisted the convention Frye named. I no longer agreed to find it funny.

I start with this quotation from Frye and my response to it as a reader because, while providing a useful definition of convention (that is, one that I agree with), it raises some interesting questions (that is, the ones I want to consider here): How and when do literary conventions change? To what extent can the sources of these changes be other than literary?

These questions are, of course, part of the broader issue of the relationship between literary conventions and life. I am using the term *life* to mean any experience other than that of reading literature, realizing that the peculiarity of this exclusion is part of the question. As my discussion of Frye's quotation suggests, I believe the questions can be most usefully addressed through an approach which has been rather loosely defined as reader-response criticism. Since I am a feminist critic, my interest in these issues is to understand their usefulness, if any, to feminist literary criticism and to feminist concerns generally. In saying this I believe I am admitting to as much but to no more bias than that of any other critic.

It is against a naive equation of literature with life that Frye is arguing when he emphasizes the importance of the literary tradition: "Poetry can only be made out of other poems; novels out of other novels. Literature shapes itself, and is not shaped externally. . . . it is possible for a story of the sea to be archetypal, to make a profound imaginative impact on a reader who has never been out of Saskatchewan."[3] While some contemporary critics might point out that the impact would no doubt be different on a reader who lived in Maine, many would agree with Frye's basic assumption that reading and writing involve an understanding of literary conventions and that in order to read (or write) one has to have read. This assumption lies behind Harold

Bloom's work on influences,[4] for example, and behind Roland Barthes's discussion of the "intertextual."[5] Geoffrey Hartman points out that "we must read the writer as a reader";[6] Nelly Furman that "the writer's work can also be construed as the product of a prior reading."[7]

For Jonathan Culler the literary conventions we learn from reading are a set of expectations—of significance, of metaphorical coherence, of thematic unity—which we impose on the text; the ability to apply these conventional procedures in reading other works constitutes a reader's "literary competence": "To read a text as literature is not to make one's mind a *tabula rasa* and approach it without preconceptions; one must bring to it an implicit understanding of the operations of literary discourse which tells one what to look for."[8] But Culler does not account for why readers who have learned the same literary strategies will read the same texts differently nor why the same readers will read the same texts differently at different times.

In an attempt to answer these questions, Stanley Fish introduces the notion of "interpretive communities," groups of readers who share certain interpretive strategies (who agree to apply particular literary conventions).[9] He gives as his examples psychoanalytic critics, Robertsonians, and numerologists. According to Fish, readers may move from one "interpretive community" to another and may belong to more than one at any one time. Fish believes that interpretive communities create the texts they read—write rather than read them[10]—by selectively applying certain conventional procedures, a position more radical than that of many other reader-response critics. He allows for the possibility of an endless series of interpretations of any one work.

Fish does not, however, examine the process of or the reasons for "ways of interpreting" being "forgotten or supplanted, or complicated or dropped from favor";[11] and although he certainly allows for extraliterary influences on changing conventions, he does not claim to be primarily interested in discussing them. His emphasis is on the lack of a fixed text: "When any of these things happens," he continues, "there is a corresponding change in texts, not because they are being read differently but because they are being written differently."[12] He does not examine what conditions are necessary to make "these things happen" nor what results from texts changing.

I suggest that any account of changes in literary conventions will have to consider nonliterary as well as literary influences. The fact that the word *convention* has meaning in both literary and nonliterary contexts alone suggests this connection. Raymond Williams, while agreeing with the definition of convention I have been employing so far,[13] begins his discussion of the term with a reminder of its origins in a nonliterary context: "The meaning of convention was originally an assembly and then, by derivation, an agreement. Later the sense of agreement was extended to tacit agreement and thence to custom. An adverse sense developed, in which a convention was seen as no more than as old rule, or somebody else's rule, which it was proper and often necessary to disregard."[14]

The interrelation of literary conventions and life is suggested also in the parallels between the history of the word in this nonliterary sense and the process of growth and decline literary conventions undergo. In 1899 readers of Kate Chopin's *The Awakening* reacted with bewilderment expressed as anger when Edna Pontellier rejected her husband, took a lover, and left the family house because they had at that point no agreement that (1) leaving her house and husband and taking a lover can indicate a woman is searching for self-fulfillment, and (2) this search for self-fulfillment should be approved. By the time Sue Kaufman published *Diary of a Mad Housewife* (1967), Joyce Carol Oates *Do With Me What You Will* (1973), Erica Jong *Fear of Flying* (1974), and Doris Lessing *The Summer Before the Dark* (1974), agreement on these interpretations had taken place among a sufficient number of readers to make the novels readily understood. A convention had been established. Yet by 1977 when Marilyn French published *The Women's Room*, she talked of this convention as "an old rule," "a convention of the women's novel" which she intended to break.[15] When does bewilderment become boredom? When did we begin to talk of "just another mad housewife novel"? By what process does the convention become too conventional?

As my example suggests, when a convention is an agreement on the meaning of a symbolic gesture in a literary context rather than agreement to use a specific interpretive strategy, to seek metaphorical coherence, for example, the question of value is made more obvious. This is not to say that interpretive strategies are neutral and do not in themselves imply certain moral values, only that these values become clearer when we are considering what Frye has called "associative clusters" or archetypes. His example is a good illustration of this: "When we speak of 'symbolism' in ordinary life we usually think of such learned cultural archetypes as the cross or the crown, or of conventional associations, as of white with purity or green with jealousy."[16] When we consider changes in literary conventions, we are considering changes in our agreements on both how we shall interpret and how we shall evaluate that interpretation. These changes are certainly influenced, then, by aspects of our cultural context which are not specifically literary.

Norman Holland claims readers imprint every text with their own "identity themes";[17] and, although there may be limitations to his definition of identity,[18] in any consideration of changes in reading conventions some attention must be paid to the subjective judgment of the individual reader. Nelly Furman recognizes the reader as "a carrier of perceptual prejudices";[19] Annette Kolodny argues convincingly that gender often affects the ability to read specific texts.[20] "That which you are, that only can you read," claims Bloom.[21] And here we come full circle since "what we are" is compounded of our experiences, literary and nonliterary.

Let me sum up the assumptions I have been discussing so far and from which I shall be arguing in the latter part of this article. An interpretation/reading of any text (whether or not the text is to any extent fixed) is dependent on two things: one, the literary conventions known to the reader at the time—these conventions include both reading strategies and associative clusters of meaning; two, the choices the reader makes to apply or not any one of these conventions—these choices are dependent on what the reader is at the time. It is a question, then, of what the individual reader chooses to notice or to ignore at the time of reading, and this idea raises the specter of a multiplicity of unchallengeable readings and the end of our discipline as we have known it. I shall attempt to exorcise the specter later.

If a convention is that which allows literature to be read, then readings of the same texts separated by many years should be instructive on the question of changes in conventions. It is here that the work of feminist scholars can be extremely helpful. This is partly because we see as one of our major tasks the rereading of earlier works, both those well established in the traditional literary canon and those previously excluded from it.[22] In the past ten years feminist scholarship has provided us with a large number of new readings which have resurrected such neglected works as Charlotte Perkins Gilman's *The Yellow Wallpaper* (1892) and Kate Chopin's *The Awakening* (1899) and radically changed our view of entire centuries. Sandra Gilbert and Susan Gubar's *The Madwoman in the Attic*, for example, has completely reinterpreted the women writers of the nineteenth century.[23] Feminist rereadings are also helpful in understanding changes in conventions for two other reasons: one, they are often unusually radical in their divergence from earlier readings;[24] two, they represent the views of a clearly defined "interpretive community."

Though feminist critics have successfully employed many different methodologies, the alliance between feminist criticism and reader-response criticism seems to have been particularly fruitful. In the past three years Judith Fetterley's *The Resisting Reader*,[25] Annette Kolodny's "A Map for Rereading: Or, Gender and the Interpretation of Literary Texts"[26] and "Dancing Through the Minefield: Some Observations on the Theory, Practice and Politics of Feminist Criticism," Gilbert and Gubar's *The Madwoman in the Attic*, and Nelly Furman's "Textual Feminism" have all demonstrated the usefulness of reader-response criticism to feminists.[27] In my own footnotes to this article I have already found reason to refer to four of these texts. This connection is not surprising, of course, since rereading is to such a large extent our enterprise, and we might be expected therefore to be concerned with many of the same questions about the process of reading and the nature of audiences.

Despite radical reinterpretations, feminist critics have on the whole remained on the conservative side with regard to the question of the "fixed text." If the implication is not always that a feminist rereading reveals the only "correct" meaning of a text, it is usually assumed that it reveals what has always been there but not previously seen. Elaine Showalter claims feminist criticism "has allowed us to see meaning in what has previously been empty space. The orthodox plot recedes, and another plot, hitherto submerged in the anonymity of the background, stands out in bold relief like a thumbprint."[28] Sandra Gilbert and Susan Gubar talk of "literary works that are in some sense palimpsestic, works whose surface designs conceal or obscure deeper, less accessible (and less socially acceptable) levels of meaning" (p. 91). Annette Kolodny, in an article which discusses and allows for a plurality of interpretations, talks of a male critic's possible inability when reading women's writing "to completely decipher its intended meaning" (p. 456).

It is perhaps because feminist critics have usually held to the notions of a fixed text and of discovering rather than of creating meaning that we have not examined the question of why our rereadings, our discoveries, took place when they did. I suggest that when we look at why it was possible for Elaine Hedges to read *The Yellow Wallpaper* as a feminist work in 1973, for this reading to become accepted, for Gilman's novella to find a place in a revised canon of American literature, we are looking at a series of conventions available to readers of the 1970s which were not available to those of 1892. It is an examination of these conventions that I intend to undertake here in order to see whether it allows us to hypothesize in any way about how literary conventions change.

My suggestion that it is the literary conventions of the 1970s that allowed feminist readings of *The Yellow Wallpaper* does not necessarily imply anything about Gilman's intention. It is essentially irrelevant to my concern here—though in other contexts important—whether or not this meaning was, as Gilbert and Gubar claim, "quite clear to Gilman herself" (p. 91). I am using *The Yellow Wallpaper* as an example, realizing that other works would perhaps be equally fruitful,[29] because of the similarity in the readings which have taken place since 1973 and because of the vast discrepancy between these readings and previous ones. I shall draw on four feminist readings: Elaine Hedges' "Afterword" to the Feminist Press edition of the text; Annette Kolodny's in "A Map for Rereading"; Sandra Gilbert and Susan Gubar's in *The Madwoman in the Attic*; and my own. Although these interpretations emphasize different aspects of the text, they do not conflict with each other.

In its time and until the last eight years, *The Yellow Wallpaper* was read, when it was read at all, "as a Poesque tale of chilling horror,"[30] designed "to freeze our blood,"[31] praised, when it was praised, for the detail with which it recorded developing insanity. Even as late as 1971 Seon Manley and Gogo Lewis included it in a collection entitled *Ladies of Horror: Two Centuries of Supernatural Stories by the Gentle Sex* and introduced it with the following words: "There were new ideas afloat: perhaps some of the horrors were in our own minds, not in the outside world at all. This idea gave birth to the psychological horror story and *The Yellow Wallpaper* by Charlotte Perkins Gilman shows she was a mistress of the art."[32]

No earlier reader saw the story as in any way positive. When Horace Scudder rejected it for publication in *The Atlantic Monthly*, he explained that he did not wish to make his readers as miserable as the story had made him. As Elaine Hedges points out, "No one seems to have made the connection between insanity and the sex, or sexual role of the victim, no one explored the story's implications for male-female relationships in the nineteenth century" (p. 41).

Feminist critics approach *The Yellow Wallpaper* from the point of view of the narrator. "As she tells her story," says Hedges, "the reader has confidence in the reasonableness of her arguments and explanations" (p. 49). The narrator is seen as the victim of an oppressive patriarchal social system which restricts women and prevents their functioning as full human beings. The restrictions on women are symbolized by the narrator's imprisonment in a room with bars on the window, an image the narrator sees echoed in the patterns of the room's yellow wallpaper. "The wallpaper," claims Hedges, symbolizes "the morbid social situation" (p. 52). Gilbert and Gubar talk of "the anxiety-inducing connections between what women writers tend to see as their parallel confinements in texts, houses and maternal female bodies" and describe the wallpaper as "ancient, smoldering, 'unclean' as the oppressive structures of the society in which she finds herself" (p. 90). The women the narrator "sees" in the wallpaper and wants to liberate are perceived to be "creeping." "Women must creep," says Hedges, "the narrator knows this" (p. 53). I see the indoor images of imprisonment echoed in the natural world of the garden with its "walls and gates that lock, and lots of separate little houses for the gardeners and people" (p. 11). Like so many other women in literature, the only access to nature the narrator has is to a carefully cultivated and confined garden. Gilbert and Gubar point out that in contrast the idea of "open country" is the place of freedom (p. 91).

The representative of the repressive patriarchal society is the narrator's husband John, "a censorious and paternalistic physician" (p. 89), as Gilbert and Gubar call him. John has "a doubly authoritative role as both husband and doctor" (p. 457), Kolodny points out. The description of John as rational rather than emotional, as a man who laughs at what cannot be put down in figures, emphasizes his position as representative of a male power which excludes feeling and imagination. Indeed, the first sentence in the story which suggests a feminist reading to me is a comment on John's character: "John laughs at me, of course, but one expects that in marriage" (p. 9).

John's treatment of his wife's mental illness is isolation and the removal of all intellectual stimulation, "a cure worse than the disease" (p. 89), as Gilbert and Gubar call it. Feminist critics see the narrator's being deprived of an opportunity to write, the opportunity for self-expression, as particularly significant. Kolodny (p. 457) and Gilbert and Gubar (p. 89) remind us that the narrator thinks of writing as a relief. Hedges sees the narrator as someone who "wants very much to work" (p. 49). By keeping her underemployed and isolated, John effectively ensures his wife's dependence on him. She must remain the child he treats her as.

Hedges draws attention to the fact that he calls her "blessed little goose" and his "little girl" and that the room she stays in was once a nursery (p. 50). For Hedges, John is "an important source of her afflictions" (p. 49).

The narrator experiences her victimization as a conflict between her own personal feelings, perceived by feminist critics as healthy and positive, and the patriarchal society's view of what is proper behavior for women. Since, like so many women up to the present day, she has internalized society's expectations of women, this conflict is felt as a split within herself. Early in the story the words "Personally, I" (p. 10) are twice set against the views of John and her brother. Nevertheless, she also continues to judge her own behavior as John does. "I get unreasonably angry with John sometimes" (p. 11), she explains; "I cry at nothing, and cry most of the time" (p. 19). As Hedges points out, this split is symbolized by the woman behind the wallpaper: "By rejecting that woman, she might free the other imprisoned woman within herself" (p. 53). The narrator's madness is perceived by Hedges and others as a direct result of societally induced confusion over personal identity. If the images of women as child or cripple, as prisoner, even as fungus growth in Gilman's story are "the images men had of women, and hence that women had of themselves," Hedges writes, "it is not surprising that madness and suicide bulk large in the work of late nineteenth-century women writers" (p. 54).

The most radical aspect of the feminist reading of *The Yellow Wallpaper* lies in the interpretation of the narrator's descent into madness as a way to health, as a rejection of and escape from an insane society. Gilbert and Gubar describe her as sinking "more and more deeply into what the world calls madness" (p. 90). They see her "imaginings and creations" as "mirages of health and freedom" (p. 91). Hedges stresses this aspect of the story. She describes the narrator as "ultimately mad and yet, throughout her descent into madness, in many ways more sensible than the people who surround and cripple her" (p. 49). "In her mad-sane way she has seen the situation of women for what it is," Hedges continues, and so "madness is her only freedom" (p. 53).

It is the interpretation of madness as a higher form of sanity that allows feminist critics finally to read this story as a woman's quest for her own identity. Deprived of reading material, she begins to read the wallpaper. "Fighting for her identity, for some sense of independent self, she observes the wallpaper" (pp. 50–51), writes Hedges. More sophisticatedly, Kolodny claims the narrator "comes more and more to experience herself as a text which can neither get read nor recorded" (p. 457). Both Kolodny and Gilbert and Gubar emphasize that the narrator creates meaning in the wallpaper in her need to find an image of herself which will affirm the truth of her own situation and hence her identity. Kolodny writes: "Selectively emphasizing one section of the pattern while repressing others, reorganizing and regrouping past impressions into newer, more fully realized configurations—as one might with any formal text—the speaking voice becomes obsessed with her quest for meaning" (p. 458). Gilbert and Gubar describe the narrator's creation of meaning as a reversal of the wallpaper's implications: "Inevitably she studies its suicidal implications—and inevitably, because of her 'imaginative power and habit of story-making,' she revises it, projecting her own passion for escape into its otherwise incomprehensible hieroglyphics" (p. 90). Although the narrator is not seen to emerge either from madness or marriage at the end of the novella, her understanding of her own situation and, by extension, the situation of all women can be read as a sort of triumph. This triumph is symbolized by the overcoming of John, who is last seen fainting on the floor as his wife creeps over him.

In order to read the novel this way, much must be assumed that is not directly stated, much must be ignored that is. There is no overt statement, for example, that invites us to find a socially induced cause for the narrator's madness, to assume that her situation is that of all women. There is perhaps even a certain perversity in claiming that a mentally deranged woman crawling around an attic floor is experiencing some sort of victory. It is also true that if the narrator claims she thinks writing would relieve her mind, she also says it tires her when she tries (p. 16). Since she so often contradicts herself, we are free to believe her only when her comments support our reading. Much is made in the novella of the color yellow; feminist readings do little with this. Despite all these objections, which could probably be continued indefinitely, it is the feminist reading I teach my students and which I believe is the most fruitful. In pointing out the "weaknesses" in my own reading, I am only providing the sort of evidence that could be used to counter any interpretation of the story. I am interested in why we read it as we do, not whether we are correct in doing so.

In order to read/write the story or any story in a feminist or in any other way, we are, of course, dependent on some interpretive strategies, some reading conventions which, if not fixed, have remained relatively so for a long period of time. The ability to see the narrator's confinement in a room as symbolic, for example, comes from other reading; we have learned to symbolize. We have come to the text as to any text, as Culler says, with certain expectations based on our previous literary experience.

But the ability to read the narrator's confinement in a room as symbolic of the situation of women in a patriarchal society depends on an agreement, on a literary convention, which, I suggest, was formed from contemporary experience—both literary and extraliterary. The feminist reading of *The Yellow Wallpaper* depends on the knowledge of a series of "associative clusters" of meaning which have been employed sufficiently frequently in contemporary literature for us to accept them as conventions. The existence of these conventions in the 1970s accounts both for the new reading and for its widespread acceptance. In saying this I am not claiming that any one reader had read any particular works or been exposed to specific experiences.

The conventions I refer to overlap each other but are associated with four basic concepts: patriarchy, madness, space, quest. The concept of patriarchy or of male power appears most frequently in contemporary fiction in the characters of men, often husbands, who are unimaginative, compartmentalized, obsessively rational and unable to express their feelings. The prototype for these figures—like so much else in contemporary feminist thought—comes from Virginia Woolf, from the character of Mr. Ramsay in *To The Lighthouse* (1927). These men are to be found everywhere in contemporary fiction by women, particularly in the fiction of the seventies. Norm in French's *The Women's Room*, Brooke Skelton in Margaret Laurence's *The Diviners* (1974), and the narrator's father in *Surfacing* are three examples of the type. As husbands they are unquestioning representatives of the status quo. As a result their wives, usually the protagonists of the novels, begin to feel they are being treated as children or as dolls. Ibsen's image of a wife as doll is conventional in this fiction—for example, Joyce Carol Oates's *Do With Me What You Will*—and occurs also in poetry. In Margaret Atwood's "After I Fell Apart" the speaker talks of herself as a broken doll gradually being mended;[33] in Sylvia Plath's "The Applicant" the speaker, as doll, applies for a position as wife.[34]

In fiction the female protagonist gradually learns to recognize the universality of her experience, conceives in some fashion of the notion of patriarchy, and "slams the door" on her past. In such "early" feminist works as Erica Jong's *Fear of Flying* or Doris Lessing's *The Summer Before the Dark*, the agent of her freedom is another man, a lover. This is the contemporary version of the nineteenth-century convention of the two suitors which I explored in my book *Victims of Convention*.[35] In the older convention the maturity of the female protagonist is measured by her choice of a "right" suitor, one who represents the novelist's views, over a "wrong" suitor, one whose views parallel the heroine's own initial weaknesses. She marries the right suitor and the novel ends. In the contemporary version the husband has become the "wrong" suitor, the representative of patriarchal restrictions; the lover represents freedom. It was the contemporary version of the convention that Marilyn French described herself as breaking when she set out to explore in *The Women's Room* what really happens after the heroine walks out.

John in *The Yellow Wallpaper* can easily be read as an example of the husband as patriarch; his well-meaning but misguided efforts to help his wife as the result of a view of women as less than adult. He is also a doctor and that compounds the situation. Recent nonfiction, both popular magazines and books, has challenged the conventional notion of the good doctor and emphasized the fact that the traditional treatment of women, particularly in childbirth, exists for the convenience of the medical profession, not for the health of their patients. Two highly influential feminist studies, Adrienne Rich's *Of Woman Born* (1976) and Mary Daly's *Gyn/Ecology* (1978), make this point. Traditional medicine is indicted for treating women as objects, for committing the basic sin of patriarchy. Just as the antidote for the compartmentalization of traditional medicine is seen to be holistic medicine, the values implied by the indictment of patriarchy are those considered implicit in matriarchy: nurturance, collaboration, emotion, unity. It is here that feminist values and those of the sixties counterculture overlap.

The concept of madness is related to patriarchy since female madness is read as a result of patriarchal oppression. Gilbert and Gubar point out that "recently, in fact, social historians like Jessie Bernard, Phyllis Chesler, Naomi Weisstein, and Pauline Bart have begun to study the ways in which patriarchal socialization literally makes women sick, both physically and mentally" (p. 53). The observation that many women novelists and poets experienced mental breakdowns, that many of those who did committed suicide, is made frequently in feminist scholarship since 1970. "Suicides and spinsters-/ all our kind!" writes Erica Jong in "Dear Colette," "Even decorous Jane Austen / never marrying, / & Sappho leaping, / & Sylvia in the oven, / & Anna Wickham,

Tsvetaeva, Sara Teasdale, / & pale Virginia floating like Ophelia, / & Emily alone, alone, alone."[36]

In seventies' fiction by women, madness or some form of mental disturbance became a conventional representation of the situation of women in a patriarchal society. Kate Brown, in Lessing's *The Summer Before the Dark*, looks back on her married life and decides she has acquired not virtues but a form of dementia. In Sue Kaufman's *Diary of a Mad Housewife*, Tina Balser subscribes to the notion that her failure to perform as the perfect wife means she is going mad. In Joyce Carol Oates's *Do With Me What You Will*, Elena's total passivity so well fulfills the desires of her husband that he does not consider her, as the reader (this reader at least) does, mentally ill. Again, the same convention occurs in the poetry—for example, Jong's "Why I Died"[37] or Carol Cox's "From the Direction of the Mental Institution."[38]

The appropriateness of this convention (our willingness to agree to it) is probably a coalescence of two aspects of experience. First, women frequently feel mad because their own reality/feeling is in conflict with society's expectations. This is often expressed in literature as the sense of being "split." The protagonists of Sylvia Plath's *The Bell Jar* (1963), Margaret Laurence's *The Diviners*, Margaret Atwood's *Surfacing*, and Rita Mae Brown's *Rubyfruit Jungle* (1973) are among many who describe this sensation. The nameless narrator of *Surfacing* says, "I'd allowed myself to be cut in two";[39] her head (her rationality) is no longer attached to her body (her emotions). Morag Gunn in *The Diviners* experiences an increased sense of "being separated from herself."[40] So feminist critics can readily identify the narrator of *The Yellow Wallpaper's* division of herself in two as an example of this split. The need to assert the female personal voice as a way to reestablish wholeness or health results from an awareness of the split. When Gilman's narrator asserts "Personally, I," I personally read it with this knowledge in mind.[41]

Second, women who try to express difference (do not submit to patriarchal expectations) are frequently called "crazy." Alice Munro's short story "The Office," in which a woman who rents an office to write in is considered mad, is a good illustration of this,[42] as is Ellen Goodman's column in the *Boston Globe* on the occasion of Martha Mitchell's death, "Here's To All the Crazy Ladies."

Another aspect of this "associated cluster" of meanings is the Laingian notion of madness as a form of higher sanity, as an indication of a capacity to see truths other than those available to the logical mind. An extension of the tradition of the wise fool, this concept was reinforced by a vision-seeking drug culture in the sixties and occurs frequently in literature by both women and men. Such novels as Ken Kesey's *One Flew Over the Cuckoo's Nest* (1962), in which inhabitants of a mental institution are seen to be saner than their doctors, and Doris Lessing's *Briefing For a Descent into Hell* (1971), in which the reader must choose between the reality of the institutionalized protagonist and that of his doctors, are typical examples. The work of Doris Lessing is perhaps the best illustration of the use of this concept, which is first fully developed in her novel *The Four-Gated City* (1969). Here Martha Quest identifies herself with the apparently mad wife of her lover Mark and comes to hear voices from a world validated as superior at the end of the novel. Carol P. Christ describes Lynda, the wife, as being "destroyed by psychologists who called her powers madness."[43] Especially useful to feminist writers since it defines the established society as less perceptive than she who is called deviant, the concept is conventional enough by 1973 for Elaine Hedges to talk of "her mad-sane way" and speak volumes (particularly those of Doris Lessing) to her readers.

It is significant that the central experience of *The Four-Gated City* takes place during two weeks in which Martha and Lynda remain enclosed in Lynda's room and, like the narrator of *The Yellow Wallpaper*, crawl around its perimeter. The conventions associated with space, particularly with rooms, are central to a feminist reading of *The Yellow Wallpaper*. Although still indicative in contemporary fiction by women of the limitations of women's sphere, a convention French employs in the first—the toilet—scene of *The Women's Room*, rooms are also claimed as independent space (with or without the five hundred pounds a year Woolf told us was also necessary). "You keep me in" has become "I keep you out." This dual use of the conventions associated with rooms, which as Gilbert and Gubar remind us are also representative of female bodies, can be seen in two short stories: Doris Lessing's "To Room 19"[44] and the Munro story "The Office" I referred to earlier. In the former a woman rents a hotel room in which to be alone and is forced to invent a lover to protect her space; in the latter a woman is accused of sexual promiscuity when she rents an office in which to work. The association between independent space and women's creative work—a connection we make in reading *The Yellow Wallpaper*—is, of course, established clearly by Woolf in *A Room of One's Own* (1929).

The concept of space also includes the question of women in relationship to nature, too large a subject to fully explore here, and which only peripherally affects the reading of *The Yellow Wallpaper*. It is interesting to note, though, that Gilbert and Gubar read the narrator's double's escape into open country as "not unlike the progress of nineteenth-century women out of the texts defined by patriarchal poetics into the open spaces of their own authority" (p. 91). Traditionally women have been identified with nature, a convention which has effectively precluded, in American literature at least, the possibility of female protagonists interacting with nature in the way male protagonists have. This applies to the wilderness rather than to such tamed natural environments as gardens, and to the American wilderness rather than, for example, to the Canadian where female protagonists do not find the space already occupied by the heroes of Hemingway, Faulkner, and Steinbeck. The possibilities for the boy in Faulkner's "The Bear," who sees the woods as both mistress and wife, to find himself in nature by confronting a bear are simply not open to women. No American woman novelist has written a novel like Marian Engel's *Bear* (1976) in which a female character has her version of the same experience.

For this reason, perhaps, women on spiritual quests—I come to my final concept—do not journey horizontally in contemporary American literature, do not cross wildernesses like frontier heroes, despite the actualities of frontier history. We appear to quest vertically: we dive and surface or we fly. Carol P. Christ's recent book, *Diving Deep and Surfacing*, examines some of these motifs in the novels of Doris Lessing and Margaret Atwood and in Adrienne Rich's *Diving into the Wreck* (1973) and *The Dream of a Common Language* (1978). *Surfacing* is a particularly interesting example since the protagonist begins by searching for her father horizontally, which involves a long journey by road and an exploration of the woods, but she only finds him when she dives. Christ does not examine the flying metaphor, which is obvious in the titles of Erica Jong's *Fear of Flying* and Kate Millett's *Flying* (1974).

The aspect of the quest concept which we need to reread *The Yellow Wallpaper*, however, has more to do with a different convention. To see the narrator as a quester for self-fulfillment is to agree to grant her our trust (to see her as the accurate perceiver of reality), which we do partly because she is female, partly because she speaks to us directly (though we have the choice here of opting for the unreliable narrator convention), and partly because we agree to read madness as sanity. Both Gilbert and Gubar and Kolodny see her as searching for her identity, her place, in the wallpaper and call this "reading." The convention we are using here is that suggested by Adrienne Rich in "Diving into the Wreck." We are aware of the "book of myths / in which our names do not appear," recognize the need for a literary past which reflects "the thing itself and not the myth,"[45] and examine our literary history with this in mind. Again, the convention has two aspects: one, literature is seen as lying about women, and our truths remain unwritten or suppressed, as Tillie Olsen explains in *Silences* (1978); two, the literature we have been given is seen as a quarry which must be mined to produce the truths we need. So Jane Clifford in Gail Godwin's *The Odd Woman* (1974) hunts fiction to find the character she most resembles; so Maxine Hong Kingston's narrator in *The Woman Warrior* (1976) translates the legends of her Chinese past into workable myths for her American present and learns to say "I" and "Here"; so Morag Gunn learns that whether or not her adopted father Christie's tales of her Scottish ancestors were true is unimportant since they have given her the "strength of conviction." So the narrator of *The Yellow Wallpaper* can be read as reading her own text in (into) the patterns of the wallpaper.

What does this examination of the contemporary conventions necessary for rereading *The Yellow Wallpaper* demonstrate about the way literary conventions change? I suggest that these conventions can all be seen as responses to, changes in, conventions which had become oppressive to the feminist "interpretive community." By oppressive I mean both dishonest, suggesting an idea contrary to the view of experience called reality by the interpretive community, and inadequate, not able to provide a form in which to express that view of experience. If a conventional view is seen as dishonest, then the convention is often reversed. So a gothic treatment of female madness which exploits the reader's sadistic impulses (pleasure in another's pain) and sees women as basically unstable (hysterical) is reversed in two ways in the contemporary conventions associated with madness: the woman's mental dis-ease is seen to be the fault of society (patriarchy) rather than her own; madness is read as sanity. The conventional associations of space function in the same way. Reversal here takes the form of changing a negative evaluation to a positive one. In other literature by women we have seen women writers adopt the supposedly negative slurs directed at them: they have written poems which celebrate themselves as witches, lesbians, Amazons;[46] they have deliberately exploited the confessional mode for which their writing had been condemned;[47] they have emphasized the "insignificant" kitchen imagery of their own lives.[48] This is a tactic also used by other victims of discrimination: "Black is beautiful"; "gay is good."

Reversal may take the form of exposing the implications of an old convention by changing the point of view, often by changing the gender of the participants. Erica Jong's *Fear of Flying*, for example, was considered original at the time of publication because it made men rather than women sex objects. Similarly, in a recent film *Nine to Five*, a male is held captive by his female employees. Poems in which male poets are rewritten from the female point of view employ this same procedure. See, for example, Mona Van Duyn's "Leda" and "Leda Reconsidered,"[49] Julie Randall's "To William Wordsworth from Virginia,"[50] Judith Rechter's "From Faye Wray to the King."[51]

When experience cannot be expressed in the available literary conventions, new conventions appear to develop. I say "appear" because these new conventions could perhaps be described as occupying the gaps left by the old. At all events they are not totally unrelated to what has gone before. So the conventions associated with diving, surfacing, and flying as forms of quest may seem to be new until they are recognized as vertical alternatives to a traffic jam on the horizontal. Woman's search for her own story, which ends in its creation, is a response to the absence of that story in literary history.

To fully test my hypothesis that literary conventions change when their implications conflict with the vision of experience of a new "interpretive community" would require going beyond the feminist rereading I have examined here, and more space than I have. It can certainly be demonstrated, though, that changes in literary conventions are frequently justified in the name of a greater truth to present reality, to "life." "Is life like this? Must novels be like this?" asks Virginia Woolf as she builds her case against the fictional conventions of "realistic" novels in favor of a truth to the reality of the mind, to the stream of consciousness: "If he [a writer] could write what he chose and not what he must, if he could base his work upon his own feeling and not upon convention, there would be no plot, no comedy, no tragedy, no love interest or catastrophe in the accepted sense. . . . Life is not a series of gig lamps symmetrically arranged."[52] In Lessing's *A Proper Marriage* Martha Quest complains: "In the books, the young and idealistic girl gets married, has a baby—she at once turns into something quite different; and she is perfectly happy to spend her whole life bringing up children with a tedious husband."[53] This convention no longer represents life as Martha knows it; it has clearly become "someone else's rule" which it is now "necessary to disregard."

The appeal to "real life" is not limited to the twentieth century. In the sixteenth century Marguerite de Navarre is already concerned that the "flowers of rhetoric" not hide "the truth of history."[54] Nor is it limited to female writers. Ford Madox Ford appeals in the same way as Virginia Woolf to perceived experience as he explains why he and Conrad began changing a fictional convention: "It became very early evident to us that what was the matter with the Novel, and the British novel in particular, was that it went straight forward, whereas in your gradual making acquaintanceship with your fellows you never do go straight forward. . . . We agreed that the general effect of a novel must be the general effect that life makes on mankind."[55]

The problem with appealing to the "general effect life makes" is that we do not all agree on what is lifelike. When we talk about "reality," we are really talking about a writer's or a reader's vision of experience, the way s/he needs to see it. Conventions change according to our needs as readers or, if we accept Fish's views, as groups of readers, as "interpretive communities." It follows, then, that conventions are always to some extent outmoded, always "old rules," lagging necessarily behind the vision they are designed to express. Once we can identify "a mad housewife novel," it is already too late to write another one successfully.

This view of literary conventions can prove useful to feminist critics. The fact that the conventions we use to reread the literary past are already dying should remind us that the remaking of the literary canon is a process and must remain ongoing; it is not a goal to be achieved. New texts will appear hidden in the old in answer to new needs, in response to new conventions. These texts in turn will affect that "real life" experience which forces changes in conventions.[56]

Like the narrators of *The Yellow Wallpaper* and *The Woman Warrior*, like Morag Gunn, we project ourselves into the text's "otherwise incomprehensible hieroglyphics." The value of our rereadings lies not in their "correctness" nor in our ability to demonstrate their intentionality but, like Christie's tales, in their ability to enrich our present by providing us with that book of myths in which our names do appear. To do this they do not need to be "true," merely satisfying. As Morag Gunn says to her daughter Pique when she asks whether the stories she was told as a child really happened. " 'Some did and some didn't, I guess. It doesn't matter a damn, don't you see?' "[57]

The idea that we invent rather than discover new meanings does not lessen the importance of the rereading enterprise.[58] To remind ourselves that we all create the conventions that allow us to read the text is to grant our readings as much authority—or as little—as any other. Indeed, it provides us with an answer to those frequent accusations of bias. Feminists and other clearly defined interpretive communities are no more biased than any other readers; our biases are simply more readily identifiable and often more acknowledged.

Nor should this notion raise what Walter Benn Michaels has called "the fear of subjectivity" among Anglo-American literary critics, the fear that "if there were no determinate meanings, the interpreter's freedom could make a text anything it wanted."[59] In theory (some theories) we as individual readers can choose to make of the text anything we wish, but in practice we do not do so. This is not only because we read by means of the conventions shared by our interpretive communities and are, as Fish has pointed out, programmed by our experience: "To the list of made or constructed objects we must add ourselves, for we no less than the poems and assignments we see are the product of social and cultural patterns of thought."[60] It is equally, or perhaps alternatively, because we always surrender some part of the individual freedom we do have in order to seek affirmation for our reading from our interpretive community. If our reading is not accepted, it will not satisfy us, that is, comfort us by providing that sense of community we read for in the first place. In reading we seek a coming together, a convention.

NOTES

1. Northrop Frye, *Anatomy of Critcism: Four Essays* (1957; rpt. Princeton, 1971), p. 225.

2. Frye, p. 76. Cf. p. 99: "The problem of convention is the problem of how art can be communicable."

3. Frye, pp. 97 and 99.

4. See, e.g., Harold Bloom, "The Breaking of Form," in *Deconstruction and Criticism*, ed. Geoffrey Hartman (New York, 1979), p. 3: "The truest sources, again necessarily, are in the powers of poems *already written*, or rather, *already read.*"

5. See, e.g., Roland Barthes, "From Work to Text," in *Image-Music-Text*, ed. and tr. Stephen Heath (New York, 1977), p. 160: "The citations which go to make up a text are anonymous, untraceable, and yet *already read*: they are quotations without inverted commas."

6. Geoffrey Hartman, "Words, Wish, Worth: Wordsworth," in *Deconstruction and Criticism*, p. 187.

7. Nelly Furman, "Textual Feminism," in *Woman and Language in Literature and Society*, ed. Sally McConnell-Ginet, Ruth Borker, and Nelly Furman (New York, 1980), p. 49.

8. Jonathan Culler, "Literary Competence," in *Structuralist Poetics* (Ithaca, 1975). Rpt. in *Reader-Response Criticism: From Formalism to Post-Structuralism*, ed. Jane P. Tompkins (Baltimore, 1980), p. 102. Cf. Annette Kolodny, "Dancing Through the Minefield: Some Observations on the Theory, Practice and Politics of A Feminist Literary Criticism," *Feminist Studies*, 6, No. 1 (Spring 1980), 10: "What we have really come to mean when we speak of competence in reading historical texts, therefore, is the ability to recognize literary conventions which have survived through time."

9. Stanley E. Fish, "Interpreting the *Variorum*," *Critical Inquiry*, 2 (Spring 1976), 465–85.

10. Fish, p. 483: "In other words these strategies exist prior to the act of reading and therefore determine the shape of what is read." Cf. Furman, p. 52: "Furthermore the reader is not a passive consumer, but an active producer of a new text."

11. Fish, p. 484.

12. Fish, p. 484.

13. Raymond Williams, *Marxism and Literature* (Oxford, 1977), p. 179: "For it is of the essence of a convention that it ratifies an assumption or a point of view so that the work can be made and received."

14. Williams, p. 173.

15. Quoted in "Breaking the Conventions of the Women's Novel," *Boston Globe*, 28 Nov. 1977, p. 15.

16. Frye, p. 102.

17. Norman Holland, "Unity Identity Text Self," *PMLA*, 90, No. 5 (October 1975), 818: "All readers create from the fantasy seemingly 'in' the work fantasies to suit their several character structures. Each reader in effect, recreates the work in terms of his own identity theme."

18. Jonathan Culler points out that Holland is working with a simplified notion of personal identity, that people "are not harmonious wholes whose every action expresses their essence or is determined by their ruling 'identity theme.'" "Prolegomena to a Theory of Reading," in *The Reader in the Text: Essays on Audience and Interpretation*, ed. Susan R. Suleiman and Inge Crosman (Princeton, 1980), p. 53.

19. Furman, p. 52.

20. Kolodny, p. 12.

21. Harold Bloom, *Kabbalah and Criticism* (New York, 1975), p. 76.

22. All feminist critics agree on the importance of this enterprise. The most

frequently cited reference on the subject is Adrienne Rich's call for "re-visioning" our literary past in "When We Dead Awaken: Writing as Re-Vision," *College English*, 34, No. 1 (October 1978), 18.

23. Sandra Gilbert and Susan Gubar, *The Madwoman in the Attic: The Woman Writer and the Nineteenth-Century Literary Imagination* (New Haven, 1979). Since this work will be cited frequently, all subsequent page references will be indicated in the text.

24. Hélène Cixous's comments provide the strongest explanation for this. See "The Laugh of the Medusa," tr. Keith Cohen and Paula Cohen, *Signs*, 1, No. 4 (Summer 1976), 875–93: "A feminine text cannot fail to be more than subversive. It is volcanic; as it is written it brings about an upheaval of the old property crust, carrier of masculine investments; there's no other way."

25. Judith Fetterley, *The Resisting Reader: A Feminist Approach to American Fiction* (Bloomington, 1978).

26. Annette Kolodny, "A Map for Rereading: Or, Gender and the Interpretation of Literary Texts," *New Literary History*, 11, No. 3 (Spring 1980), 451–67. Since this article will be cited frequently, all subsequent page references will be indicated in the text.

27. What is surprising and annoying is that reader-response critics so rarely recognize the similarities or refer to the work of feminist critics. Even two recent collections, both with extensive bibliographies and both edited by women, make no mention of feminist criticism: Tompkins, ed., *Reader-Response Criticism*, and Suleiman and Crosman, eds., *The Reader of the Text*.

28. Elaine Showalter, "Review Essay," *Signs*, 1, No. 2 (Winter 1975), 435.

29. Kate Chopin's *The Awakening* is the obvious second choice. Conventions available to readers differ for other reasons than time, of course. An interesting illustration of the influence of geography is Margaret Atwood's novel *Surfacing* (New York, 1972), which was read in the United States as a feminist statement and in Canada as a statement about Canadian nationalism.

30. Elaine R. Hedges, "Afterword," in Charlotte Perkins Gilman's *The Yellow Wallpaper* (New York, 1973), p. 39. Since this work will be cited frequently, all subsequent page references will be indicated in the text.

31. William Dean Howells, ed., *The Great Modern American Stories* (New York, 1920), p. vii.

32. Interestingly, the work is classified as "Juvenile Literature" under the Library of Congress classification system.

33. Atwood, "After I Fell Apart," in *The Animals in That Country* (Boston, 1968).

34. Sylvia Plath, *Ariel* (New York, 1966).

35. Jean E. Kennard, *Victims of Convention* (Hamden, Conn., 1978).

36. Erica Jong, *Loveroot* (New York, 1968).

37. Jong, *Half-Lives* (New York, 1973).

38. In *Mountain Moving Day*, ed. Elaine Gill (New York, 1973).

39. *Surfacing*, p. 129.

40. *The Diviners* (Toronto, 1974), p. 263.

41. The use of the first person in feminist criticism is related to this notion. See Suzanne Juhasz, "The Critic as Feminist: Reflections on Women's Poetry, Feminism and the Art of Criticism," *Women's Studies*, 5 (1977), 113–27; Sandra Gilbert, "Life Studies, or, Speech After Long Silence: Feminist Critics Today," *College English*, 40 (1979), 849–63; Jean E. Kennard, "Personally Speaking: Feminist Critics and the Community of Readers," *College English*, 43 (1981), 140–45.

42. Alice Munro, *Dance of the Happy Shades* (Toronto, 1968).

43. Carol P. Christ, *Diving Deep and Surfacing: Women Writers on Spiritual Quest* (Boston, 1980), p. 64.

44. Doris Lessing, *A Man and Two Women and Other Stories* (New York, 1963).

45. Adrienne Rich, *Diving into the Wreck* (New York, 1973), p. 24.

46. See, e.g., Susan Sutheim, "For Witches," and Jean Tepperman, "Witch," in *No More Masks*, ed. Florence Howe and Ellen Bass (New York, 1973), pp. 297 and 333. *Amazon Poetry*, ed. Elly Bulkin and Joan Larkin (New York, 1975).

47. See, e.g., Kate Millett's *Flying* (New York, 1974) and Kolodny's article on critical responses to it, "The Lady's Not for Spurning: Kate Millett and the Critics," *Contemporary Literature*, 17, No. 4 (1976), 541–62.

48. See, e.g., Tillie Olsen's "I Stand Here Ironing," in *Tell Me A Riddle* (New York, 1961). Also Jong's "The Woman Who Loved to Cook," in *Half-Lives*; Nikki Giovanni's "Woman Poem," in *Black Feeling, Black Talk/Black Judgement* (New York, 1970).

49. Mona Van Duyn, *To See, To Take* (New York, 1970).

50. In *No More Masks*, p. 158.

51. *No More Masks*, p. 257.

52. Virginia Woolf, "Modern Fiction," in *The Common Reader* (London, 1951).

53. Doris Lessing, *A Proper Marriage* (1952; rpt. New York, 1970), p. 206.

54. Marguerite de Navarre, *The Heptameron*, tr. Walter K. Kelly (London, n.d.), p. 9.

55. Quoted in Jocelyn Baines, *Joseph Conrad: A Critical Biography* (London, 1960), pp. 136–37.

56. Cf. Christ, pp. 4–5: "In a very real sense, there is no experience without stories. There is a dialectic between stories and experience. Stories give shape to experience, experience gives rise to stories."

57. *The Diviners*, p. 350.

58. Cf. Nelly Furman's discussion of textual criticism in "Textual Feminism."

59. Walter Benn Michaels, "The Interpreter's Self: Peirce on the Cartesian Subject," *Georgia Review*, 31 (1977), 383–402.

60. Fish, *Is There A Text in This Class? The Authority of Interpretive Communities* (Cambridge, Mass., 1980), p. 332.

Escaping the Sentence: Diagnosis and Discourse in "The Yellow Wallpaper"

Paula A. Treichler

Almost immediately in Charlotte Perkins Gilman's story "The Yellow Wallpaper," the female narrator tells us she is "sick." Her husband, "a physician of high standing," has diagnosed her as having a "temporary nervous depression—a slight hysterical tendency."[1] Yet her journal—in whose words the story unfolds—records her own resistance to this diagnosis and, tentatively, her suspicion that the medical treatment it dictates—treatment that confines her to a room in an isolated country estate—will not cure her. She suggests that the diagnosis itself, by undermining her own conviction that her "condition" is serious and real, may indeed be one reason why she does not get well.

A medical diagnosis is a verbal formula representing a constellation of physical symptoms and observable behaviors. Once formulated, it dictates a series of therapeutic actions. In "The Yellow Wallpaper," the diagnosis of hysteria or depression, conventional "women's diseases" of the nineteenth century, sets in motion a therapeutic regimen which involves language in several ways. The narrator is forbidden to engage in normal social conversation; her physical isolation is in part designed to remove her from the possibility of overstimulating intellectual discussion. She is further encouraged to exercise "self-control" and avoid expressing negative thoughts and fears about her illness; she is also urged to keep her fancies and superstitions in check. Above all, she is forbidden to "work"—to write. Learning to monitor her own speech, she develops an artificial feminine self who reinforces the terms of her hus-

191

band's expert diagnosis: this self attempts to speak reasonably and in "a very quiet voice," refrains from crying in his presence, and hides the fact that she is keeping a journal. This male-identified self disguises the true underground narrative: a confrontation with language.

Because she does not feel free to speak truthfully "to a living soul," she confides her thoughts to a journal—"dead paper"—instead. The only safe language is dead language. But even the journal is not altogether safe. The opening passages are fragmented as the narrator retreats from topic after topic (the first journal entry consists of 39 separate paragraphs). The three points at which her language becomes more discursive carry more weight by contrast. These passages seem at first to involve seemingly unobjectionable, safe topics: the house, her room, and the room's yellow wallpaper. Indeed, the very first mention of the wallpaper expresses conventional hyperbole: "I never saw worse paper in my life." But the language at once grows unexpected and intense:

> One of those sprawling flamboyant patterns committing every artistic sin. It is dull enough to confuse the eye in following, pronounced enough to constantly irritate and provoke study, and when you follow the lame uncertain curves for a little distance they suddenly commit suicide—plunge off at outrageous angles, destroy themselves in unheard of contradictions. (13)

Disguised as an acceptable feminine topic (interest in decor), the yellow wallpaper comes to occupy the narrator's entire reality. Finally, she rips it from the walls to reveal its real meaning. Unveiled, the yellow wallpaper is a metaphor for women's discourse. From a conventional perspective, it first seems strange, flamboyant, confusing, outrageous: the very act of women's writing produces discourse which embodies "unheard of contradictions." Once freed, it expresses what is elsewhere kept hidden and embodies patterns that the patriarchal order ignores, suppresses, fears as grotesque, or fails to perceive at all. Like all good metaphors, the yellow wallpaper is variously interpreted by readers to represent (among other things) the "pattern" which underlies sexual inequality, the external manifestation of neurasthenia, the narrator's unconscious, the narrator's situation within patriarchy.[2] But an emphasis on discourse—writing, the act of speaking, language—draws us to the central issue in this particular story: the narrator's alienation from work, writing, and intellectual life. Thus the story is inevitably concerned with the complicated and charged relationship between women and language: analysis then illuminates particular points of conflict between patriarchal language and women's discourse. This conflict in turn raises a number of questions relevant for both literary and feminist scholarship: In what senses can language be said to be oppressive to women? How do feminist linguistic innovations seek to escape this oppression? What is the relationship of innovation to material conditions? And what does it mean, theoretically, to escape the sentence that the structure of patriarchal language imposes?

THE YELLOW WALLPAPER

The narrator of "The Yellow Wallpaper" has come with her husband to an isolated country estate for the summer. The house, a "colonial mansion," has been untenanted for years through some problem with inheritance. It is "the most beautiful place!" The grounds contain "hedges and walls and gates that lock, and lots of separate little houses for the gardeners and people" (11). Despite this palatial potential to accommodate many people, the estate is virtually deserted with nothing growing in its greenhouses. The narrator perceives "something queer about it" and believes it may be haunted.

She is discouraged in this and other fancies by her sensible physician-husband who credits only what is observable, scientific, or demonstrable through facts and figures. He has scientifically diagnosed his wife's condition as merely "a temporary nervous depression"; her brother, also a noted physician, concurs in this opinion. Hence husband and wife have come as physician and patient to this solitary summer mansion in quest of cure. The narrator reports her medical regimen to her journal, together with her own view of the problem:

> So I take phosphates or phosphites—whichever is it, and tonics, and journeys, and air, and exercise, and am absolutely forbidden to "work" until I am well again.
> Personally, I disagree with their ideas.
> Personally, I believe that congenial work, with excitement and change, would do me good.
> But what is one to do? (10)

Her room at the top of the house seems once to have been a nursery or a playroom with bars on the windows and "rings and things on the walls." The room contains not much more than a mammoth metal bed. The ugly yellow wallpaper has been stripped off in patches—perhaps by the children who formerly inhabited the room. In this "atrocious nursery" the narrator increasingly spends her time. Her husband is often away on medical cases, her baby makes her nervous, and no other company is permitted her. Disturbed by the wallpaper, she asks for another room or for different paper; her husband urges her not to give way to her "fancies." Further, he claims that any change would lead to more change: "after the wall-paper was changed it would be the heavy bedstead, and then the barred windows, and then that gate at the head of the stairs, and so on" (14). So no changes are made, and the narrator is left alone with her "imaginative power and habit of story-making" (15). In this stimulus-deprived environment, the "pattern" of the wallpaper becomes increasingly compelling: the narrator gradually becomes intimate with its "principle of design" and unconventional connections. The figure of a woman begins to take shape behind the superficial pattern of the paper. The more the wallpaper comes alive, the less inclined is the narrator to write in her journal—"dead paper." Now with three weeks left of the summer and her relationship with the wallpaper more and more intense, she asks once more to be allowed to leave. Her husband refuses: "I cannot possibly leave town just now. Of course if you were in any danger, I could and would, but you really are better, dear, whether you can see it or not. I am a doctor, dear, and I know" (23). She expresses the fear that she is not getting well. "Bless her little heart!" he responds, "She shall be as sick as she pleases" (24). When she hesitantly voices the belief that she may be losing her mind, he reproaches her so vehemently that she says no more. Instead, in the final weeks of the summer, she gives herself up to the wallpaper. "Life is very much more exciting now than it used to be," she tells her journal. "You see I have something more to expect, to look forward to, to watch. I really do eat better, and am more quiet than I was" (27). She reports that her husband judges her "to be flourishing in spite of my wall-paper."

She begins to strip off the wallpaper at every opportunity in order to free the woman she perceives is trapped inside. She becomes increasingly aware of this woman and other female figures creeping behind the surface pattern of the wallpaper: there is a hint that the room's previous female occupant has left behind the marks of her struggle for freedom. Paranoid by now, the narrator attempts to disguise her obsession with the wallpaper. On the last day, she locks herself in the room and succeeds in stripping off most of the remaining paper. When her husband comes home and finally unlocks the door, he is horrified to find her creeping along the walls of the room. "I've got out at last," she tells him triumphantly, "And I've pulled off most of the paper, so you can't put me back" (36). Her husband faints, and she is obliged to step over him each time she circles the room.

"The Yellow Wallpaper" was read by nineteenth-century readers as a harrowing case study of neurasthenia. Even recent readings have treated the narrator's madness as a function of her individual psychological situation. A feminist reading emphasizes the social and economic conditions which drive the narrator — and potentially all women — to madness. In these readings, the yellow wallpaper represents (1) the narrator's own mind, (2) the narrator's unconscious, (3) the "pattern" of social and economic dependence which reduces women to domestic slavery. The woman in the wallpaper represents (1) the narrator herself, gone mad, (2) the narrator's unconscious, (3) all women. While these interpretations are plausible and fruitful, I interpret the wallpaper to be women's writing or women's discourse, and the woman in the wallpaper to be the representation of women that becomes possible only after women obtain the right to speak. In this reading, the yellow wallpaper stands for a new vision of women — one which is constructed differently from the representation of women in patriarchal language. The story is thus in part about the clash between two modes of discourse: one powerful, "ancestral," and dominant; the other new, "impertinent," and visionary. The story's outcome makes a statement about the relationship of a visionary feminist project to material reality.

DIAGNOSIS AND DISCOURSE

It is significant that the narrator of "The Yellow Wallpaper" is keeping a journal, confiding to "dead paper" the unorthodox thoughts and perceptions she is reluctant to tell to a "living soul." Challenging and subverting the expert prescription that forbids her to write, the journal evokes a sense of urgency and danger. "There comes John," she tells us at the end of her first entry, "and I must put this away, — he hates to have me write a word" (13). We, her readers, are thus from the beginning her confidantes, implicated in forbidden discourse.

Contributing to our suspense and sense of urgency is the ambiguity of the narrator's "condition," whose etiology is left unstated in the story.

For her physician-husband, it is a medical condition of unknown origin to be medically managed. Certain imagery (the "ghostliness" of the estate, the "trouble" with the heirs) suggests hereditary disease. Other evidence points toward psychological causes (e.g., postpartum depression, failure to adjust to marriage and motherhood). A feminist analysis moves beyond such localized causes to implicate the economic and social conditions which, under patriarchy, make women domestic slaves. In any case, the fact that the origin of the narrator's condition is never made explicit intensifies the role of diagnosis in putting a name to her "condition."

Symptoms are crucial for the diagnostic process. The narrator reports, among other things, exhaustion, crying, nervousness, synesthesia, anger, paranoia, and hallucination. "Temporary nervous depression" (coupled with a "slight hysterical tendency") is the medical term that serves to diagnose or define these symptoms. Once pronounced, and reinforced by the second opinion of the narrator's brother, this diagnosis not only names reality but also has considerable power over what that reality is now to be: it dictates the narrator's removal to the "ancestral halls" where the story is set and generates a medical therapeutic regimen that includes physical isolation, "phosphates and phosphites," air, and rest. Above all, it forbids her to "work." The quotation marks, registering her husband's perspective, discredit the equation of writing with true work. The diagnostic language of the physician is coupled with the paternalistic language of the husband to create a formidable array of controls over her behavior.

I use "diagnosis," then, as a metaphor for the voice of medicine or science that speaks to define women's condition. Diagnosis is powerful and public; representing institutional authority, it dictates that money, resources, and space are to be expended as consequences in the "real world." It is a male voice that privileges the rational, the practical, and the observable. It is the voice of male logic and male judgment which dismisses superstition and refuses to see the house as haunted or the narrator's condition as serious. It imposes controls on the female narrator and dictates how she is to perceive and talk about the world. It is enforced by the "ancestral halls" themselves: the rules are followed even when the physician-husband is absent. In fact, the opening imagery—"ancestral halls," "a colonial mansion," "a haunted house"—legitimizes the diagnostic process by placing it firmly within an institutional frame: medicine, marriage, patriarchy. All function in the story to define and prescribe.

In contrast, the narrator in her nursery room speaks privately to her journal. At first she expresses her views hesitantly, "personally." Her language includes a number of stereotypical features of "women's language": not only are its topics limited, it is marked formally by exclamation marks, italics, intensifiers, and repetition of the impotent refrain, "What is one to do?"[3] The journal entries at this early stage are very tentative and clearly shaped under the stern eye of male judgment. Oblique references only hint at an alternative reality. The narrator writes, for example, that the wallpaper has been "torn off" and "stripped away," yet she does not say by whom. Her qualms about her medical diagnosis and treatment remain unspoken except in her journal, which functions only as a private respite, a temporary relief. "Dead paper," it is not truly subversive.

Nevertheless, the narrator's language almost from the first does serve to call into question both the diagnosis of her condition and the rules established to treat it. As readers, therefore, we are not permitted wholehearted confidence in the medical assessment of the problem. It is not that we doubt the existence of her "condition," for it obviously causes genuine suffering; but we come to doubt that the diagnosis names the real problem—the narrator seems to place her own inverted commas around the words "temporary nervous depression" and "slight hysterical tendency"—and perceive that whatever its nature it is exacerbated by the rules established for its cure.

For this reason, we are alert to the possibility of an alternative vision. The yellow wallpaper provides it. Representing a different reality, it is "living paper," aggressively alive: "You think you have mastered it, but just as you get well underway in following, it turns a back-somersault and there you are. It slaps you in the face, knocks you down, and tramples upon you. It is like a bad dream" (25). The narrator's husband refuses to replace the wallpaper, "white-wash" the room, or let her change rooms altogether on the grounds that other changes will then be demanded. The wallpaper is to remain: acknowledgment of its reality is the first step toward freedom. Confronting it at first through male eyes, the narrator is repelled and speculates that the children who inhabited the room before her attacked it for its ugliness. There is thus considerable resistance to the wallpaper and an implied rejection of what it represents, even by young children.

But the wallpaper exerts its power and, at the same time, the narrator's journal entries falter; "I don't know why I should write this" (21), she says, about halfway through the story. She makes a final effort to be allowed to leave the room; when this fails, she becomes increasingly absorbed by the wallpaper and by the figure of a woman that exists behind its confusing surface pattern. This figure grows clearer to her, to the point where she can join her behind the paper and literally act within it. At this point, her language becomes bolder: she completes the predicates that were earlier left passively hanging. Describing joint action with the woman in the wallpaper, she tells us that the room has come to be damaged at the hands of women: "I pulled and she shook, I shook and she pulled, and before morning we had peeled off yards of that paper" (32); "I am getting angry enough to do something desperate" (34). From an increasingly distinctive perspective, she sees an alternative reality beneath the repellent surface pattern in which the figures of women are emerging. Her original perception is confirmed: the patriarchal house is indeed "haunted" by figures of women. The room is revealed as a prison inhabited by its former inmates, whose struggles have nearly destroyed it. Absorbed almost physically by "living paper"—writing—she strives to liberate the women trapped within the ancestral halls, women with whom she increasingly identifies. Once begun, liberation and identification are irreversible: "I've got out at last . . . cries the narrator, "And I've pulled off most of the paper, so you can't put me back!" (36).

This ending of "The Yellow Wallpaper" is ambiguous and complex. Because the narrator's final proclamation is both triumphant and horrifying, madness in the story is both positive and negative. On the one hand, it testifies to an alternative reality and challenges patriarchy head on. The fact that her unflappable husband faints when he finds her establishes the dramatic power of her new freedom. Defying the judgment that she suffers from a "temporary nervous depression," she has followed her own logic, her own perceptions, her own projects to this final scene in which madness is seen as a kind of transcendent sanity. This engagement with the yellow wallpaper constitutes a form of the "work" which has been forbidden—women's writing. As she steps over the patriarchal body, she leaves the authoritative voice of diagnosis in shambles at her feet. Forsaking "women's language" forever, her new mode of speaking—an unlawful language—escapes "the sentence" imposed by patriarchy.

On the other hand, there are consequences to be paid for this escape. As the ending of the narrative, her madness will no doubt commit her to more intense medical treatment, perhaps to the dreaded Weir Mitchell of whom her husband has spoken. The surrender of patriarchy is only temporary: her husband has merely fainted, after all, not died, and will no doubt move swiftly and severely to deal with her. Her individual escape is temporary and compromised.

But there is yet another sense in which "The Yellow Wallpaper" enacts a clash between diagnosis and women's discourse. Asked once whether the story was based on fact, Gilman replied "I had been as far as one could go and get back."[4] Gilman based the story on her own experience of depression and treatment. For her first visit to the noted neurologist S. Weir Mitchell, she prepared a detailed case history of her own illness, constructed in part from her journal entries. Mitchell was not impressed: he "only thought it proved conceit" (*The Living*, 95). He wanted obedience from patients, not information. "Wise women," he wrote elsewhere, "choose their doctors and trust them. The wisest ask the fewest questions."[5] Gilman reproduced in her journal Mitchell's prescription for her:

> Live as domestic a life as possible. Have your child with you all the time (Be it remarked that if I did but dress the baby it left me shaking and crying—certainly far from a healthy companionship for her, to say nothing of the effect on me.) Lie down an hour after every meal. Have but two hours intellectual life a day. And never touch pen, brush or pencil as long as you live. (*The Living*, 96)

Gilman spent several months trying to follow Mitchell's prescription, a period of intense suffering for her:

> I could not read nor write nor paint nor sew nor talk nor listen to talking, nor anything. I lay on that lounge and wept all day. The tears ran down into my ears on either side. I went to bed crying, woke in the night crying, sat on the edge of the bed in the morning and cried—from sheer continuous pain. (*The Living*, 121).

At last in a "moment of clear vision," Gilman realized that for her the traditional domestic role was at least in part the cause of her distress. She left her husband and with her baby went to California to be a writer and a feminist activist. Three years later she wrote "The Yellow Wallpaper." After the story was published, she sent a copy to Mitchell. If it in any way influenced his treatment of women in the future, she wrote, "I have not lived in vain" (*The Living*, 121).

There are several points to note here with respect to women's discourse. Gilman's use of her own journal to create a fictional journal which in turn becomes a published short story problematizes and calls our attention to the journal form. The terms "depression" and "hysteria" signal a non-textual as well as a textual conundrum: contemporary readers could (and some did) read the story as a realistic account of madness; for feminist readers (then and now) who bring to the text some comprehension of medical attitudes toward women in the nineteenth century, such a non-ironic reading is not possible. Lest we miss Gilman's point, her use of a real proper name in her story, Weir Mitchell's, draws explicit attention to the world outside the text.[6]

Thus "The Yellow Wallpaper" is not merely a fictional challenge to the patriarchal diagnosis of women's condition. It is also a public critique of a real medical treatment. Publication of the story added power and status to Gilman's words and transformed the journal form from a private to a public setting. Her published challenge to diagnosis has now been read by thousands of readers. By living to tell the tale, the woman who writes escapes the sentence that condemns her to silence.

ESCAPING THE SENTENCE

To call "The Yellow Wallpaper" a struggle between diagnosis and discourse is to characterize the story in terms of language. More precisely, it is to contrast the signification procedures of patriarchal medicine with discursive disruptions that call those procedures into question. A major problem in "The Yellow Wallpaper" involves the relationship of the linguistic sign to the signified, of language to "reality." Diagnosis, highlighted from the beginning by the implicit inverted commas around diagnostic phrases ("a slight hysterical tendency"), stands in the middle of an equation which translates a phenomenological perception of the human body into a finite set of signs called "symptoms"—fever, exhaustion, nervousness, pallor, and so on—which are in turn assembled to produce a "diagnosis"; this sign generates treatment, a set of prescriptions that impinge once more upon the "real" human body. Part of the power of diagnosis as a scientific process depends upon a notion of language as transparent, as *not* the issue. Rather the issue is the precision, efficiency, and plausibility with which a correct diagnostic sign is generated by a particular state of affairs that is assumed to exist in reality. In turn, the diagnostic sign is not complete until its clinical implications have been elaborated as a set of concrete therapeutic practices designed not merely to refer to but actually to change the original physical reality. Chary with its diagnostic categories (as specialized lexicons go), medicine's rich and intricate descriptive vocabulary testifies to the history of its mission: to translate the realities of the human body into human language and back again. As such, it is a perfect example of language which "reflects" reality and simultaneously "produces" it.[7]

Why is this interesting? And why is this process important in "The Yellow Wallpaper"? Medical diagnosis stands as a prime example of an authorized linguistic process (distilled, respected, high-paying) whose representational claims are strongly supported by social, cultural, and economic practices. Even more than most forms of male discourse, the diagnostic process is multiply-sanctioned.[8] "The Yellow Wallpaper" challenges both the particular "sentence" passed on the narrator and the elaborate sentencing process whose presumed representational power can sentence women to isolation, deprivation, and alienation from their own sentencing possibilities. The right to author or originate sentences is at the heart of the story and what the yellow wallpaper represents: a figure for women's discourse, it seeks to escape the sentence passed by medicine and patriarchy. Before looking more closely at what the story suggests about the nature of women's discourse, we need to place somewhat more precisely this notion of "the sentence."

Diagnosis is a "sentence" in that it is simultaneously a linguistic entity, a declaration or judgment, and a plan for action in the real world whose clinical consequences may spell dullness, drama, or doom for the diagnosed. Diagnosis may be, then, not merely a sentence but a death sentence. This doubling of the word "sentence" is not mere playfulness. "I sat down and began to speak," wrote Anna Kavan in *Asylum Piece*, describing the beginning of a woman's mental breakdown, "driving my sluggish tongue to frame words that seemed useless even before they were uttered." This physically exhausting process of producing sentences is generalized: "Sometimes I think that some secret court must have tried and condemned me, unheard, to this heavy sentence."[9] The word "sentence" is both sign and signified, word and act, declaration and discursive consequence. Its duality emphasizes the difficulty of an analysis which privileges purely semiotic relationships on the one hand or the representational nature of language on the other. In "The Yellow Wallpaper," the diagnosis of hysteria may be a sham: it may be socially constituted or merely individually expedient quite apart from even a conventional representational relationship. But it dictates a rearrangement of material reality nevertheless. The sentence may be unjust, inaccurate, or irrelevant, but the sentence is served anyway.[10]

The sentence is of particular importance in modern linguistics, where it has dominated inquiry for twenty-five years and for more than seventy years has been the upper cut-off point for the study of language: consideration of word sequences and meaning beyond the sentence has been typically dismissed as too untidy and speculative for linguistic science. The word "sentence" also emphasizes the technical concentration, initiated by structuralism but powerfully developed by transformational grammar, on syntax (formal grammatical structure at the sentence level). The formulaic sentence $S \rightarrow NP + VP$ which initiates the familiar tree diagram of linguistic analysis could well be said to exemplify the tyranny of syntax over the study of semantics (meaning) and pragmatics (usage). As a result, as Sally McConnell-Ginet has argued, linguistics has often failed to address those aspects of language with which women have been most concerned: on the one hand, the semantic or non-linguistic conditions underlying given grammatical structures, and on the other, the contextual circumstances in which linguistic structures are actually used.[11] One can generalize and say that signs alone are of less interest to women than are the processes of signification which link signs to semantic and pragmatic aspects of speaking. To "escape the sentence" is to move beyond the boundaries of formal syntax.

But is it to move beyond language? In writing about language over the last fifteen years, most feminist scholars in the United States have argued that language creates as well as reflects reality and hence that feminist linguistic innovation helps foster more enlightened social conditions for women. A more conservative position holds that language merely reflects social reality and that linguistic reform is hollow unless accompanied by changes in attitudes and socioeconomic conditions that also favor women's equality. Though different, particularly in their support for innovation, both positions more or less embody a view that there *is* a non-linguistic reality to which language is related in systematic ways.[12] Recent European writing challenges the transparency of such a division, arguing that at some level reality is inescapably linguistic. The account of female development within this framework emphasizes the point at which the female child comes into language (and becomes a being now called female); because she is female, she is from the first alienated from the processes of symbolic representation. Within this symbolic order, a phallocentric order, she is frozen, confined, curtailed, limited, and represented as "lack," as "other." To make a long story short, there is as yet no escaping the sentence of male-determining discourse.[13]

According to this account, "the sentence," for women, is inescapably bound up with the symbolic order. Within language, says Luce Irigaray for example, women's fate is a "death sentence."[14] Irigaray's linguistic innovations attempt to disrupt this "law of the father" and exemplify the possibilities for a female language which "has nothing to do with the syntax which we have used for centuries, namely, that constructed according to the following organization: subject, predicate, or, subject, verb, object."[15] Whatever the realities of that particular claim, at the moment there are persuasive theoretical, professional, and political reasons for feminists to pay attention to what I will now more officially call discourse, which encompasses linguistic and formalistic considerations, yet goes beyond strict formalism to include both semantics and pragmatics. It is thus concerned not merely with speech, but with the conditions of speaking. With this notion of "sentencing," I have tried to suggest a process of language production in which an individual word, speech, or text is linked to the conditions under which it was (and could have been) produced as well as to those under which it is (and could be) read and interpreted. Thus the examination of diagnosis and discourse in a text is at once a study of a set of representational practices, of mechanisms for control and opportunities for resistance, and of communicational possibilities in fiction and elsewhere.[16]

In "The Yellow Wallpaper" we see consequences of the "death sentence." Woman is represented as childlike and dysfunctional. Her complaints are wholly circular, merely confirming the already-spoken patriarchal diagnosis. She is constituted and defined within the patriarchal order of language and destined, like Athena in Irigaray's analysis, to repeat her father's discourse "without much understanding."[17] "Personally," she says, and "I sometimes fancy": this is acceptable language in the ancestral halls. Her attempts to engage in different, serious language — self-authored — are given up; to write in the absence of patriarchal sanction requires "having to be so sly about it, or else meet with heavy opposition" (10) and is too exhausting. Therefore, the narrator speaks the law of the father in the form of a "women's language" which is prescribed by patriarchy and exacts its sentence upon her: not to author sentences of her own.

The yellow wallpaper challenges this sentence. In contrast to the orderly, evacuated patriarchal estate, the female lineage that the wall-paper represents is thick with life, expression, and suffering. Masquerad-ing as a symptom of "madness," language animates what had been merely an irritating and distracting pattern:

> This paper looks to me as if it *knew* what a vicious influence it had!
> There is a recurrent spot where the pattern lolls like a broken neck and two bulbous eyes stare at you upside down.
> I get positively angry with the impertinence of it and the everlasting-ness. Up and down and sideways they crawl, and those absurd, unblinking eyes are everywhere. (16)

The silly and grotesque surface pattern reflects women's conventional representation; one juxtaposition identifies "that silly and conspicuous front design" with "sister on the stairs!" (18). In the middle section of the story, where the narrator attempts to convey her belief that she is seriously ill, the husband-physician is quoted verbatim (23–25), enabling us to see the operation of male judgment at first hand. He notes an improvement in her symptoms: "You are gaining flesh and color, your appetite is better, I feel really much easier about you." The narrator disputes these statements: "I don't weigh a bit more, nor as much; and my appetite may be better in the evening when you are here, but it is worse in the morning when you are away!" His response not only pre-empts further talk of facts, it reinforces the certainty of his original diagnosis and confirms his view of her illness as non-serious: " 'Bless her little heart!' said he with a big hug, 'she shall be as sick as she pleases!' " (24).

His failure to let her leave the estate initiates a new relationship to the wallpaper. She begins to see women in the pattern. Until now, we as readers have acquiesced in the fiction that the protagonist is keeping a journal, a fiction initially supported by journal-like textual references. This now becomes difficult to sustain: how can the narrator keep a journal when, as she tells us, she is sleeping, creeping, or watching the wallpaper the whole time? In her growing paranoia, would she confide in a journal she could not lock up? How did the journal get into our hands? Because we are nevertheless reading this "journal," we are forced to experience a contradiction: the narrative is unfolding in an impossible form. This embeds our experience of the story in self-conscious attention to its construction. A new tone enters as she reports that she defies orders to take naps by not actually sleeping: "And that cultivates deceit, for I don't tell them I'm awake—O no!" (26). This crowing tone announces a decisive break from the patriarchal order. She mocks her husband's diagnosis by diagnosing for herself why he "seems very queer sometimes": "It strikes me occasionally, just as a scientific hypothesis,— that perhaps it is the paper!" (26–27).

The wallpaper never becomes attractive. It remains indeterminate, complex, unresolved, disturbing; it continues to embody, like the form of the story we are reading, "unheard of contradictions." By now the narrator is fully engrossed by it and determined to find out its meaning. During the day—by "normal" standards—it remains "tiresome and perplexing" (28). But at night she sees a woman, or many women, shaking the pattern and trying to climb through it. Women "get through," she perceives, "and then the pattern strangles them off and turns them upside down, and makes their eyes white!" (30). The death sentence imposed by patriarchy is violent and relentless. No one escapes.

The story is now at its final turning point: "I have found out another funny thing," reports the narrator, "but I shan't tell it this time! It does not do to trust people too much" (31). This is a break with patriarchy— and a break with us. What she has discovered, which she does not state, is that she and the woman behind the paper are the same. This is communicated syntactically by contrasting sentences: "This bedstead is fairly gnawed!" she tells us, and then: "I bit off a little piece (of the bedstead) at one corner" (34). "If that woman does get out, and tries to get away, I can tie her!" and "But I am securely fastened now by my well-hidden rope" (34–35). The final passages are filled with crowing, "impertinent" language: "Hurrah!" "The sly thing!" "No person touches this paper but me,—not *alive!*" (32–33). Locked in the room, she addresses her husband in a dramatically different way: "It is no use, young man, you can't open it!"

She does not make this declaration aloud. In fact, she appears to have difficulty even making herself understood and must repeat several times the instructions to her husband for finding the key to the room. At first we think she may be too mad to speak proper English. But then we realize that he simply is unable to accept a statement of fact from her, his little goose, until she has "said it so often that he had to go and see"

(36). Her final triumph is her public proclamation, "I've got out at last . . . you can't put me back!" (36).

There is a dramatic shift here both in *what* is said and in *who* is speaking. Not only has a new "impertinent" self emerged, but this final voice is collective, representing the narrator, the woman behind the wallpaper, and women elsewhere and everywhere. The final vision itself is one of physical enslavement, not liberation: the woman, bound by a rope, circles the room like an animal in a yoke. Yet that this vision has come to exist and to be expressed changes the terms of the representational process. That the husband-physician must at last listen to a woman speaking—no matter what she says—significantly changes conditions for speaking. Though patriarchy may be only temporarily unconscious, its ancestral halls will never be precisely the same again.

We can return now to the questions raised at the outset. Language in "The Yellow Wallpaper" is oppressive to women in the particular form of a medical diagnosis, a set of linguistic signs whose representational claims are authorized by society and whose power to control women's fate, whether or not those claims are valid, is real. Representation has real, material consequences. In contrast, women's power to originate signs is monitored; and, once produced, no legitimating social apparatus is available to give those signs substance in the real world.

Linguistic innovation, then, has a dual fate. The narrator in "The Yellow Wallpaper" initially speaks a language authorized by patriarchy, with genuine language ("work") forbidden her. But as the wallpaper comes alive she devises a different, "impertinent" language which defies patriarchal control and confounds the predictions of male judgment (diagnosis). The fact that she becomes a creative and involved language user, producing sentences which break established rules, *in and of itself* changes the terms in which women are represented in language and extends the conditions under which women will speak.

Yet language is intimately connected to material reality, despite the fact that no direct correspondence exists. The word is theory to the deed: but the deed's existence will depend upon a complicated set of material conditions. The narrator of "The Yellow Wallpaper" is not free at the end of the story because she has temporarily escaped her sentence: though she has "got out at last," her triumph is to have sharpened and articulated the nature of women's condition; she remains physically bound by a rope and locked in a room. The conditions she has diagnosed must change before she and other women will be free. Thus women's control of language is left metaphorical and evocative: the story only hints at possibilities for change. Woman is both passive and active, subject and object, sane and mad. Contradictions remain, for they are inherent in women's current "condition."

Thus to "escape the sentence" involves both linguistic innovation and change in material conditions: both change in what is said and change in the conditions of speaking. The escape of individual women may constitute a kind of linguistic self-help which has intrinsic value as a contribution to language but which functions socially and politically to isolate deviance rather than to introduce change. Representation is not without consequences. The study of women and language must involve the study of discourse, which encompasses both form and function as well as the representational uncertainty their relationship entails. As a metaphor, the yellow wallpaper is never fully resolved: it can be described, but its meaning cannot be fixed. It remains trivial and dramatic, vivid and dowdy, compelling and repulsive: these multiple meanings run throughout the story in contrast to the one certain meaning of patriarchal diagnosis. If diagnosis is the middle of an equation that freezes material flux in a certain sign, the wallpaper is a disruptive center that chaotically fragments any attempt to fix on it a single meaning. It offers a lesson in language, whose sentence is perhaps not always destined to escape us.

NOTES

1. Charlotte Perkins Gilman, *The Yellow Wallpaper* (New York: The Feminist Press, 1973), p. 13. Subsequent references are cited parenthetically in the text.

2. Umberto Eco describes a "good metaphor" as one which, like a good joke, offers a shortcut through the labyrinth of limitless semiosis. "Metaphor, Dictionary, and Encyclopedia," *New Literary History*, 15 (Winter 1984), 255–71. Though there is relatively little criticism on "The Yellow Wallpaper" to date, the wallpaper seems to be a fruitful metaphor for discussions of madness, women's relationship to medicine, sexual inequality, marriage, economic dependence, and sexuality. An introduction to these issues is provided by Elaine R. Hedges in her "Afterword," *The Yellow Wallpaper*, pp. 37–63. Hedges also cites a number of nineteenth-century responses to the story. A useful though condescending discussion of the story in the light of Gilman's own life is Mary A. Hill, "Charlotte Perkins Gilman: A Feminist's Struggle with Womanhood," *Massachusetts Review*, 21 (Fall 1980), 503–26. A Bachelardian critical reading is Mary

Beth Pringle, " 'La Poétique de l'Espace' in Charlotte Perkins Gilman's 'The Yellow Wallpaper,' " *The French-American Review*, 3 (Winter 1978/Spring 1979), 15–22. See also Loralee MacPike, "Environment as Psychopathological Symbolism in "The Yellow Wallpaper,' " *American Literary Realism 1870–1910*, 8 (Summer 1975), 286–88, and Beate Schöpp-Schilling, " 'The Yellow Wallpaper': A Rediscovered 'Realistic' Story," *American Literary Realism 1870–1910*, 8 (Summer 1975), 284–86.

3. "Women's language" is discussed in Robin Lakoff, *Language and Woman's Place* (New York: Harper and Row, 1975); Casey Miller and Kate Swift, *Words and Women* (New York: Anchor/Doubleday, 1976); Barrie Thorne, Cheris Kramarae, and Nancy Henley, eds., "Introduction," *Language, Gender and Society* (Rowley, Mass.: Newbury House, 1983); Cheris Kramarae, *Women and Men Speaking* (Rowley, Mass.: Newbury House, 1981); Sally McConnell-Ginet, Ruth Borker, and Nelly Furman, eds., *Women and Language in Literature and Society* (New York: Praeger, 1980); Mary Ritchie Key, *Male/Female Language* (Metuchen, New Jersey: Scarecrow Press, 1975); and Paula A. Treichler, "Verbal Subversions in Dorothy Parker: 'Trapped like a Trap in a Trap,' " *Language and Style*, 13 (Fall 1980), 46–61.

4. Charlotte Perkins Gilman, *The Living of Charlotte Perkins Gilman: An Autobiography* (New York: Appleton-Century, 1935), p. 121. Subsequent references are cited parenthetically in the text.

5. S. Weir Mitchell, *Doctor and Patient* (Philadelphia: Lippincott, 1888), p. 48.

6. A feminist understanding of medical treatment of women in the nineteenth century is, however, by no means uncomplicated. An analysis frequently quoted is that by Barbara Ehrenreich and Deirdre English, *For Her Own Good: 150 Years of the Experts' Advice to Women* (Garden City, N.Y.: Anchor/Doubleday, 1979). Their analysis is critiqued by Regina Morantz, "The Lady and Her Physician," in *Clio's Consciousness Raised: New Perspectives on the History of Women*, eds. Mary S. Hartman and Lois Banner (New York: Harper Colophon, 1974), pp. 38–53; as well as by Ludi Jordanova, "Conceptualizing Power Over Women," *Radical Science Journal*, 12 (1982), 124–28. Attention to the progressive aspects of Weir Mitchell's treatment of women is given by Morantz and by Suzanne Poirier, "The Weir Mitchell Rest Cure: Four Women Who 'Took Charge,' " paper presented at the conference Women's Health: Taking Care and Taking Charge, Morgantown, West Virginia, 1982 [Author's affiliation: Humanistic Studies Program, Health Sciences Center, University of Illinois at Chicago.] See also Barbara Sicherman, "The Uses of Diagnosis: Doctors, Patients, and Neurasthenia," *Journal of the History of Medicine and Allied Sciences*, 32 (January 1977), 33–54; Carroll Smith-Rosenberg and Charles Rosenberg, "The Female Animal: Medical and Biological Views of Woman and Her Role in Nineteenth-Century America," rpt. in *Concepts of Health and Disease; Interdisci-*

plinary Perspectives, eds. Arthur Caplan, H. Tristram Engelhardt, Jr. and James J. McCartney (Reading, Mass.: Addison-Wesley, 1981), pp. 281–303; and Ann Douglas Wood, " 'The Fashionable Diseases': Women's Complaints and Their Treatment in Nineteenth-Century America," in *Clio's Consciousness Raised: New Perspectives on the History of Women*, pp. 1–22.

7. The notion that diagnosis is socially constituted through doctor-patient interaction is discussed by Marianne A. Paget, "On the Work of Talk: Studies in Misunderstanding," in *The Social Organization of Doctor-Patient Communication*, eds. Sue Fisher and Alexandra Dundas Todd (Washington, D.C.: Center for Applied Linguistics, 1983), pp. 55–74. See also Barbara Sicherman, "The Uses of Diagnosis."

8. Discussions of the multiple sanctions for medicine and science include Shelley Day, "Is Obstetric Technology Depressing?" *Radical Science Journal*, 12 (1982), 17–45; Donna J. Haraway, "In the Beginning was the Word: The Genesis of Biological Theory," *Signs*, 6 (Spring 1981), 469–81; Bruno Latour and Steve Woolgar, *Laboratory Life: Social Contruction of Scientific Facts* (Beverly Hills: Sage, 1979); Evan Stark, "What is Medicine?" *Radical Science Journal*, 12 (1982), 46–89; and P. Wright and A. Treacher, eds., *The Problem of Medical Knowledge* (Edinburgh: Edinburgh University Press, 1982).

9. Anna Kavan, *Asylum Piece* (1940; rpt. New York: Michael Kesend, 1981), pp. 63, 65.

10. Reviewing medical evidence in "The Yellow Wallpaper," Suzanne Poirier suggests that a diagnosis of "neurasthenia" would have been more precise but that in any case, given the narrator's symptoms, the treatment was inappropriate and probably harmful. " 'The Yellow Wallpaper' as Medical Case History," paper presented to the Faculty Seminar in Medicine and Society, University of Illinois College of Medicine at Urbana-Champaign, April 13, 1983. On the more general point, two recent contrasting analyses are offered by Umberto Eco, "Metaphor, Dictionary, and Encyclopedia," who poses a world of language resonant with purely semiotic, intertextual relationships, and John Haiman, "Dictionaries and Encyclopedias," *Lingua*, 50 (1980), 329–57, who argues for the total interrelatedness of linguistic and cultural knowledge.

11. Sally McConnell-Ginet, "Linguistics and the Feminist Challenge," in *Women and Language in Literature and Society*, pp. 3–25. The linguistic formula $S \rightarrow NP + VP$ means that Sentence is rewritten from this formula. Sentences are "generated" as tree diagrams that move downward from the abstract entity S to individual components of actual sentences. It could be said that linguistics misses the forest for the trees. But the fact that the study of women and language *has* concentrated on meaning and usage does not mean that syntax might not be relevant for feminist analysis. Potentially fruitful areas might include analysis of passive versus active voice (for example, see my "The Construction of Ambiguity in *The Awakening*: A Linguistic Analysis," in *Women and*

Language in Literature and Society, pp. 239–57), of nominalization (a linguistic process particularly characteristic of male bureaucracies and technologies), of cases (showing underlying agency and other relationships, of negation and interrogation (two grammatical processes implicated by "women's language," Note 3), and of the relationship between deep and surface structure. Julia Penelope Stanley has addressed a number of these areas; see, for example, "Passive Motivation," *Foundations of Language*, 13 (1975), 25–39. Pronominalization, of course, has been a focus for feminist analysis for some time.

12. See, for example, Maija Blaubergs, "An Analysis of Classic Arguments Against Changing Sexist Language," in *The Voices and Words of Women and Men*, ed. Cheris Kramarae (Oxford: Pergamon Press, 1980), pp. 135–47; Francine Frank, "Women's Language in America: Myth and Reality," in *Women's Language and Style*, eds. Douglas Butturff and Edmund L. Epstein (Akron, Ohio: L&S Books, 1978), pp. 47–61; Mary Daly, *Gyn/Ecology* (Boston: Beacon, 1978); and Wendy Martyna, "The Psychology of the Generic Masculine," in *Women and Language in Literature and Society*, pp. 69–78. A general source is Barrie Thorne, Cheris Kramarae, and Nancy Henley, eds., *Language, Gender and Society* (Rowley, Mass.: Newbury House, 1983).

13. See, for example, Juliet Mitchell and Jacqueline Rose, eds., *Feminine Sexuality: Jacques Lacan and the école freudienne* (New York: W.W. Norton, 1982), pp. 1–57.

14. Luce Irigaray, "Veiled Lips," trans. Sara Speidel, *Mississippi Review*, 33 (Winter/Spring 1983), 99. See also Luce Irigaray, "Women's Exile: Interview with Luce Irigaray," trans. Couze Venn, *Ideology and Consciousness*, 1 (1977), 62–76; and Cary Nelson, "Envoys of Otherness: Difference and Continuity in Feminist Criticism," in *For Alma Mater: Theory and Practice in Feminist Scholarship*, eds. Paula A. Treichler, Cheris Kramarae, and Beth Stafford (Urbana: University of Illinois Press, 1985), pp. 91–118.

15. Luce Irigaray, "Women's Exile," 64.

16. See the discussion of discourse in Meaghan Morris, "A-Mazing Grace: Notes on Mary Daly's Poetics," *Intervention*, 16 (1982), 70–92.

17. Luce Irigaray, "Veiled Lips," 99–101. According to Irigaray's account, Apollo, "the always-already-speaking," drives away the chorus of women (the Furies) who want revenge for Clytemnestra's murder. His words convey his repulsion for the chaotic, non-hierarchical female voice: "Heave in torment, black froth erupting from your lungs"; "Never touch my halls, you have no right"; "Out you flock without a herdsman—out!" Calling for the forgetting of bloodshed, Athena, embodying the father's voice and the father's law, pronounces the patriarchal sentence on the matriarchal chorus: the women will withdraw to a subterranean cavern where they will be permitted to establish a cult, perform religious rites and sacrifices, and remain "loyal and propitious to the land." They are removed from positions of influence, their words destined to have only subterranean meaning.

The Unrestful Cure:
Charlotte Perkins Gilman
and "The Yellow Wallpaper"

Jeffrey Berman

I f Charlotte Perkins Gilman's name does not command the instant recognition of an Elizabeth Cady Stanton, Jane Addams, or Susan B. Anthony, it is not because her achievement was less. Social historians agree on the brilliance of her ideas and the extent to which her influential books helped to transform the condition of women in early twentieth-century America. The following judgments are representative. "The only systematic theory linking the demand for suffrage with the long sweep of history was that of Charlotte Perkins Gilman, the most influential woman thinker in the pre–World War I generation in the United States."[1] "Of all the great feminist writers, she made the finest analysis of the relation between domesticity and women's rights, perhaps the most troubling question for liberated women and sympathetic men today."[2] "Charlotte Gilman was the greatest writer that the feminists ever produced on sociology and economics, the Marx and the Veblen of the movement."[3] "It is hardly an exaggeration to speak of her as the major intellectual leader of the struggle for women's rights, in the broadest sense, during the first two decades of the twentieth century."[4] Two of her books, *Women and Economics* and *The Home: Its Work and Influence*, became immediate classics. The *Nation* called *Women and Economics* "the most significant utterance" on the women's question since John Stuart Mill.[5] She has been called the "most original and challenging mind" produced by the women's movement.[6] Not long before her death, she was placed first on a list of 12 great American women by Carrie Chapman Catt.[7]

The major source of the details of her life is *The Living of Charlotte Perkins Gilman: An Autobiography*, an absorbing book that raises more questions than it answers. In its wealth of information about the author's troubled childhood experiences, especially her relationship to a mother who refused to show affection to her and to a father who abandoned his young family, the autobiography casts much light on "The Yellow Wallpaper." The book also eloquently describes her lifelong battle with acute depression exacerbated by what can only be euphemistically called "psychiatry." Born on July 3, 1860, Charlotte Perkins was a great granddaughter of Lyman Beecher, the progenitor of the distinguished American family. Little else about her early life seemed auspicious. Although her parents appear to have been in love when they married in 1957, the marriage was short lived. In quick succession Mary Perkins gave birth to four children, two of whom died in early infancy. The first baby died "from some malpractice at birth" in 1858, a son was born in 1859, Charlotte in the next year, and a fourth child died in 1866. When the doctor forbade another child, the father deserted the family:

> There now follows a long-drawn, triple tragedy, quadruple perhaps, for my father may have suffered too; but mother's life was one of the most painfully thwarted I have ever known. After her idolized youth, she was left neglected. After her flood of lovers, she became a deserted wife. The most passionately domestic of home-worshiping housewives, she was forced to move nineteen times in eighteen years, fourteen of them from one city to another.[8]

Charlotte's father never did return. Her mother delayed 13 years before divorcing him, and even after the divorce she continued to wait for him until the end of her life. The daughter's account captures the pathos of the mother's story. "Divorced or not she loved him till her death, at sixty-three. She was with me in Oakland, California, at the time, and father was then a librarian in San Francisco, just across the bay. She longed, she asked, to see him before she died. As long as she was able to be up, she sat always at the window watching for that beloved face. He never came." To which the daughter parenthetically adds, "That's where I get my implacable temper" (*The Living*, p. 9).

The theme of a child waiting for a man who will never return, and the attendant bewilderment and rage, characterizes Charlotte Perkins Gilman's feeling toward her father in particular and men in general. "The word Father, in the sense of love, care, one to go to in trouble, means nothing to me, save indeed in advice about books and the care of them—which seems more the librarian than the father" (*The Living*, pp. 5–6). But it is not only the absent father who is responsible for the daughter's traumatized youth. Equally ominous is the impact of an embittered mother who denies her child the parental love and attention she herself had been denied by her husband's desertion. Mother becomes both victim and victimizer. Despite the fact that the mother is described as a "baby-worshiper" who devoted her entire life to the children, she also inflicted upon them the pain and lovelessness from which she herself suffered. The most poignant moment in Gilman's autobiography occurs when she writes about a recurring childhood experience which, like a bad dream or Dickensian scene, permanently haunted her imagination. What makes the passage more astonishing is the daughter's absence of criticism, even years later, of the rejecting mother:

> There is a complicated pathos in it, totally unnecessary. Having suffered so deeply in her own list of early love affairs, and still suffering for lack of a husband's love, she heroically determined that her baby daughter should not so suffer if she could help it. Her method was to deny the child all expression of affection as far as possible, so that she should not be used to it or long for it. "I used to put away your little hand from my cheek when you were a nursing baby," she told me in later years; "I did not want you to suffer as I had suffered." She would not let me caress her, and would not caress me, unless I was asleep. This I discovered at last, and then did my best to keep awake till she came to bed, even using pins to prevent dropping off, and sometimes succeeding. Then how carefully I pretended to be sound asleep, and how rapturously I enjoyed being gathered into her arms, held close and kissed (*The Living*, pp. 10–11).

Deprived of paternal protection and maternal tenderness, forced to adopt both subterfuge and self-punishment to secure the little affection the mother reluctantly offered, and reared in an environment where the image of a baby must have symbolized the mother's entrapment, the child turned inward to fabricate a fairy-tale world that would supplant grim reality. In this inner world dwelled an all-loving mother and father who rescued rather than abandoned the children of the world. The element of wish fulfillment is unmistakable here as well as a rescue fantasy in which the dreamer becomes her own idealized parent, transmuting an anguished childhood into paradise. In this fantasy world lived a "Prince and Princess of magical powers, who went about the world collecting unhappy children and taking them to a guarded Paradise in the South Seas. I had a boundless sympathy for children, feeling them to be suppressed, misunderstood."

The comforting fantasy soon collapsed, however, destroyed by a Victorian mother who under the influence of a "pre-Freudian" friend forbade her child to indulge in the pleasures of the imagination. "My dream world was no secret. I was but too ready to share it, but there were no sympathetic listeners. It was my life, but lived entirely alone. Then, influenced by a friend with a pre-Freudian mind, alarmed at what she was led to suppose this inner life might become, mother called on me to give it up. This was a command. According to all the ethics I knew I must obey, and I did . . ." (*The Living*, p. 23). And so at the tender age of 13 she was forced to give up the "inner fortress" that had been her chief happiness for five years. "But obedience was Right, the thing had to be done, and I did it. Night after night to shut the door on happiness, and hold it shut. Never, when dear, bright, glittering dreams pushed hard, to let them in. Just thirteen . . ." (*The Living*, p. 24).

In later life, Charlotte Perkins Gilman held Freud responsible for the loss of her dream world. Of the many references to Freud in her autobiography and other writings, all are pejorative. She indicts Freud for offenses ranging from the violation of the human spirit to an unnatural emphasis upon sex. In a lecture called "The Falsity of Freud," she equates the psychoanalyst with evil and oppression. Her description of a friendship with another woman links Freud with psychopathology: "In our perfect concord there was no Freudian taint, but peace of mind, understanding, comfort, deep affection" (*The Living*, p. 80). In an essay called "Parasitism and Civilised Vice," she argues that a major obstacle to the advancement of women's rights is the "resurgence of phallic worship set before us in the solemn phraseology of psychoanalysis."[9] Toward the end of her autobiography, she recalls in amazement how "apparently intelligent persons would permit these mind-meddlers, having no claims to fitness except that of having read certain utterly unproven books, to paddle among their thoughts and feelings, and extract the confessions of the last intimacy." One of these "mind-meddlers" gratuitously attempted to psychoanalyze her in an effect to render her into the psychiatric case study she had fictionalized in "The Yellow Wallpaper":

One of these men, becoming displeased with my views and their advancement, since I would not come to be "psyched," as they call it, had the impudence to write a long psychoanalysis of my case, and send it to me. My husband and I, going out in the morning, found this long, fat envelop with our mail. I looked at it, saw who it was from, and gave it to Houghton. "I don't want to read his stuff," I said. "You look it over and tell me what it is about." This he did, to my utter disgust. "Burn it up, do," I urged. "I haven't the least curiosity to know what this person thinks is the matter with me" (*The Living*, p. 314).

Whoever this anonymous "psychoanalyst" was, he only confirmed her hatred of Freud and her belief that the Viennese doctor and his unholy disciples were antithetical to the women's cause and to the imagination itself. Who can blame her anger over this violation of privacy, a violation that may have reminded her, as we shall see, of her experience with S. Weir Mitchell? Yet Gilman also condemned Freud for other, less valid, reasons. She insisted that Freud was responsible for the widespread promiscuity of the age and the lowering of standards in sexual relations. She was, of course, Victorian in her horror of sex and glorification of chastity. The deemphasis of chastity, she was convinced, had debased human nature. She accused the Freudians of a "sex-uopathic philosophy" that advocated as " 'natural' a degree of indulgence utterly without parallel in nature" (*The Living*, p. 323). Elsewhere in her writings she attacks the "present degree of sex impulse" as pathological, arguing instead for the suppression or redirection of the sexual instinct. In her female utopia, *Herland*, women conceive through parthenogenesis, virgin-birth. Men are no longer necessary and procreation is independent of the sex act. Like her exact contemporary Bertha Pappenheim, Gilman could see only the horror of sexuality.

Given these feelings, it is no wonder that the two subjects she was to spend most of her life writing about and trying to reform—marriage and motherhood—figured conspicuously in her mental breakdown. Her autobiography reveals the confusion and misgivings surrounding her decision to marry Charles Walter Stetson, whom she had met in 1882. Although she considered him "quite the greatest man, near my own age, that I had ever known," she knew intuitively that she should not marry the good-looking painter. Her experience with deprivation and denial prepared her for a life of continued abstinence. Unwilling to hurt his feelings, she postponed a decision for as long as she could. She defined her marital dilemma as a choice between love and work, the classic conflict of a woman. Only after Stetson had met with a keen personal disappointment did she consent to marry him. Her gloom deepened. A diary written during this time reflects depression and self-contempt. There is also a thinly veiled death wish. "Let me recognize fully that I do not look forward to happiness, that I have no decided hope of success. So long must I live. One does not die young who so desires it" (*The Living*, p. 84). The thought of a future filled with failure and guilt compels her to break off her narration: "Children sick and unhappy. Husband miserable because of my distress, and I—" Against this fearful backdrop Charlotte Perkins Gilman married Stetson in May 1884. A daughter Katherine was born in March 1885. Her breakdown followed immediately.

What seems so perplexing—and yet so characteristic—about the swift series of events leading to Gilman's collapse is the praise she bestows on her husband and child and her refusal to utter a word of reproach toward either of them. She insists that she and her husband were happy together both before and after the arrival of their child. From her descriptions, Walter Stetson seemed a woman's dream. "A lover more tender, a husband more devoted, woman could not ask. He helped in the housework more and more as my strength began to fail, for something was going wrong from the first" (*The Living*, pp. 87–88). The idealized description contrasts the bleakness of her diary. She uses a metaphor similar to Sylvia Plath's bell jar. "A sort of gray fog drifted across my mind, a cloud that grew and darkened." At first she attributes her growing nervousness to pregnancy, but when the baby is born the mother's health worsens. She tries repeatedly to convince us that her sickness was not due to the baby she mythologizes. "Of all angelic babies that darling was the best, a heavenly baby." The nurse's departure deepens the mother's grief, and neither the arrival of her own mother nor the move to a better house improves the situation. The chapter on "Love and Marriage" in the autobiography closes with these chilling words. "Here was a charming home; a loving and devoted husband; an exquisite baby, healthy, intelligent and good; a highly competent mother to run things; a wholly satisfactory servant—and I lay all day on the lounge and cried" (*The Living*, p. 89).

What caused the breakdown? The meaning of the illness mystified her even 50 years later. Although she could not define what it was, she knew what it was not. Angered by the accusation that her "nervous prostration" was merely a fanciful term for laziness, she insisted that it was not caused by a deficiency of will. Nor could she force happiness into her life, as one sympathizer urged. She was unable to read or write, get out of bed, or stop crying. The doctors ruled out a physical cause, for which she would have been grateful. An accusing voice within her kept shouting: "You did it yourself! You did it yourself! You had health and strength and hope and glorious work before you—and you threw it all away. You were called to serve humanity, and you cannot serve yourself. No good as a wife, no good as a mother, no good at anything. And you did it yourself!" . . . (*The Living*, p. 91).

She knew that marriage and motherhood were the problem although she did not know why. The evidence could not be more striking. From the moment she left her baby and husband to travel across the continent for a rest and change, she felt immediately better. "I recovered so fast, to outward appearance at least, that I was taken for a vigorous young girl. Hope came back, love came back, I was eager to get home to husband and child, life was bright again." But, within a month of returning home, she was depressed as before. The truth was inescapable. To preserve her sanity she had to leave her family and to repudiate society's most cherished values. It was at this time that she sought psychiatric help from S. Weir Mitchell. After a one-month rest cure she returned home, following his orders to "live as domestic a life as possible." She came perilously close to losing her mind. She made a rag doll at home, hung it on a doorknob, and played with it. "I would crawl into remote closets and under beds—to hide from the grinding pressure of that profound distress . . ." (*The Living*, p. 96). Again one is reminded of Sylvia Plath and her efforts to bury herself beneath the subbasement of her mother's house. In a moment of clear vision, Charlotte and her husband finally agreed on a divorce. "There was no quarrel, no blame for either one, never an unkind word between us, unbroken mutual affection—but it seemed plain that if I went crazy it would do my husband no good, and be a deadly injury to my child" (*The Living*, p. 96).

The fear of committing a deadly injury to her child would seem to be in light of psychoanalytic theory an unconscious repetition of the traumatic wound inflicted upon Charlotte Perkins Gilman when she was a child herself. The irony is stunning. The little girl's identification with the absent father, along with the aspiration for the glorious work that was a male privilege in a sexist society, was so intense as to compel her against her will to become her own father and, like him, to abandon spouse and baby. She could not express rage toward her husband because, as her biographer records, she had never been honest and open with him about her feelings.[10] The silent aggression she felt toward the father who abandoned her was now directed against herself. She fell desperately ill, overcome with confusion and guilt. Only by rejecting her own family, as her father had rejected his family 20 years earlier, could she free herself from the weakness and passivity that symbolized to her the condition of motherhood.

In her imagination babies came to be associated with death, bereavement, and abandonment. The deaths in infancy of two of Mary Perkins' four children indicated that, not only were the odds poor to have a healthy child, but the mother's life was also imperiled. Sex must have seemed irresponsible, procreation deadly. The act of childbirth probably evoked the fear of mutilation. The emotions Charlotte felt when she gave birth were appropriate for a funeral. Instead of rejoicing, she went into a period of mourning. The child drained her and threw her into a "black helplessness" with its "deadness of heart, its aching emptiness of mind." In becoming pregnant she was repeating her mother's dreadful mistake. Pregnancy implied maternal sacrifice bordering on suicide. "The surrender of the mother to the child is often flatly injurious, if carried to excess," she acknowledges in *Concerning Children*, and indicts motherhood as the ultimate human sacrifice:

> To put it in the last extreme, suppose the mother so utterly sacrifices herself to the child as to break down and die. She then robs the child of its mother, which is an injury. Suppose she so sacrifices herself to the child as to cut off her own proper rest, recreation, and development. She thus gives the child an exhausted and inferior mother, which is an injury to him. There are cases, perhaps, where it might be a mother's duty to die for her child; but, in general, it is more advantageous to live for him. The "unselfish devotion" of the mother we laud to the skies, without stopping to consider its effect on the child. This error is connected with our primitive religious belief in the doctrine of sacrifice,—one of those early misconceptions of a great truth.[11]

In contrast to mother's world, which symbolized death and martyrdom, father's world promised work, achievement, power. Charlotte's mother had placed two prohibitions upon her: She was to read no novels and to have no close friends. The first prohibition must have seemed incongruous in that Charlotte's father was a distinguished librarian, rising to be head of the San Francisco and Boston Public Library. Frederick Perkins, who "took to books as a duck to water," founded several influential newspapers and journals, introduced the decimal system of classification, and wrote a reference book called *The Best Reading* that became a standard work. Not only did his daughter carry on the father's achievements, she far exceeded them. She was an enormously prolific and successful writer, authoring the equivalent of 25 volumes of stories, plays, and verse. Her greatest single achievement was the writing, editing, and publishing of the *Forerunner*, a monthly magazine that lasted for seven years. *Women and Economics*, published in 1898, was translated into seven languages and went through seven English language editions. She wrote the first draft in 17 days, the second draft in 58 days. "To write was always as easy to me as to talk," she remarks, and her astonishing productivity would seem to indicate that she wrote and read effortlessly.

Nothing could be further from the truth. There were long periods of time when the act of writing or reading would throw her into black despair. To the end of her life she suffered from what she could diagnose only as a "weak mind." Often she could not read the easiest book or write the simplest letter. "When I am forced to refuse invitations, to back out of work that seems easy, to own that I cannot read a heavy book, apologetically alleging this weakness of mind, friends gibber amiably, 'I wish I had your mind!' I wish they had, for a while, as a punishment for doubting my word" (*The Living*, p. 98). No one could believe her mental distress nor the inexplicable nervous exhaustion that would cripple her mind and paralyze her will. "The natural faculties are there, as my books and lectures show. But there remains this humiliating weakness, and if I try to drive, to compel effort, the resulting exhaustion is pitiful" (*The Living*, p. 100). Nor did the self-torture long abate. She describes the landscape of her mind as a depleted library, bereft of the books so vital to its well-being:

> To step so suddenly from proud strength to contemptible feebleness, from cheerful stoicism to a whimpering avoidance of any strain or irritation for fear of the collapse ensuing, is not pleasant, at twenty-four. To spend forty years and more in the patient effort of learning how to carry such infirmity so as to accomplish something in spite of it is a wearing process, full of mortification and deprivation. To lose books out of one's life, cer-

tainly more than ninety per cent of one's normal reading capacity, is no light misfortune (*The Living*, p. 100).

"What is the psychology of it?" she asks mournfully. The answer, we suspect, lies in the library.

It is significant that twice in the autobiography she refers to the library as a symbol or symptom of the crippling psychological illness to which she was prone. "I say my mind is weak. It is precisely that, weak. It cannot hold attention, cannot study, cannot listen long to anything, is always backing out of things because it is tired. A library, which was once to me as a confectioner's shop to a child, became an appalling weariness just to look at" (*The Living*, p. 100). One page later she elaborates on the peculiar symptomatology of her illness. "For nearly all these broken years I could not look down an index. To do this one must form the matrix of a thought or word and look down the list until it fits. I could not hold that matrix at all, could not remember what I was looking for. To this day I'd rather turn the pages than look at the index." The autobiography reads like a Gothic horror story here; for the library, which had once enticed her as a confectioner's shop lures a hungry child, came to represent the feelings of betrayal and abandonment associated with her father's flight from the family into the world of the library and publishing. The price she paid for imitating her father's glorious male achievements was a lifetime of neurotic suffering, part of her paternal legacy. The father's distinguished professional career had included the introduction of the decimal system of classification. Years later his brilliant daughter found herself unable to read the index of a book.

Another symptom of her lifelong struggle against mental illness appears to be related to a childhood incident—the pain of correspondence. As a child she had pleaded with her absent father to write her letters. In the only letter from which she quotes in the autobiography, Charlotte implores him to write. First there is a request for money, then for personal news. "Please write a real long letter to me," the 12-year-old asks, repeating the request two sentences later. "I wish you would write to me often" (*The Living*, p. 22). In the same letter she complains that, whereas other people write to her brother, no one writes to her. She encloses two pictures in the hope that her father will reciprocate. Years later she found herself in the opposite position, dreading the letters sent to her by friends and admirers. She could not answer them. "Perhaps the difficulty of answering letters will serve as an illustration of the weakness of mind so jocosely denied by would-be complimenters":

> Here are a handful of letters—I dread to read them, especially if they are long—I pass them over to my husband—ask him to give me only those I must answer personally. These pile up and accumulate while I wait for a day when I feel able to attack them. A secretary does not help in the least, it is not the manual labor of writing which exhausts me, it is the effort to understand the letter, and make intelligent reply. I answer one, two, the next is harder, three—increasingly foggy, four—it's no use, I read it in vain, *I don't know what it says*. Literally, I can no longer understand what I read, and have to stop, with my mind like a piece of boiled spinach (*The Living*, p. 99).

The humiliating inability to answer her correspondence reflects a deep ambivalence toward a father who rejected his family to live quite literally in the library. The pattern of Charlotte's life consisted of escape from the woman's sanctuary of home and hearth into the father's exciting world of letters; but, no sooner did she achieve the success she had envisioned through dedication and hard work, than her neurotic suffering would return, driving her back to the mother's sickroom. She could not achieve success without imagining failure; to emulate father she had to abandon mother. The world of books and ideas remained antithetical to the world of people and emotions, and she could never integrate her paternal and maternal identifications. Her father remained impossibly aloof and uncaring. To recover from her breakdown, she left her husband and daughter to travel across the country to California, where she visited her father. He engaged a room for her and solemnly called upon her as if she were a distant acquaintance. She stayed for a few days and upon leaving politely extended an invitation to him. "If you ever come to Providence again I hope you will come to see me"; he replied: "Thank you, I will bear your invitation in mind" (*The Living*, p. 93). The offenses to which she confesses during her periods of mental illness were the identical crimes of which her father was guilty. "My forgetfulness of people, so cruel a return for kindness; an absentmindedness often working harm; many a broken engagement; unanswered letters and neglected invitations; much, very much of repeated failure of many kinds is due wholly to that continuing weakness of mind" (*The Living*, p. 102). Her father achieved success, fame, and independence but at the expense of love, responsibility, and loyalty. In fathering herself, she was tortured by the fear that she had to make the same sacrifice, with her husband and daughter as victims.

And her feelings toward mother? Filial loyalty prevented her from criticism, except when she describes the mother's rejection of the child's caresses. But even during this moment, when any other writer would have expressed righteous indignation and anger, she holds back, content to mythologize the mother's "heroic" determination to spare her child from future suffering. She could never admit that her mother was responsible for her own depression. As Patricia Meyer Spacks observes in *The Female Imagination*, "The force destroying beauty, hope, and love for her is in fact her mother, whose energy, as her daughter describes her, directs itself entirely toward rejection, suppression, denial."[12] Although she could not criticize her own mother, she could attack other mothers, as an amusing passage in the autobiography makes clear. Once, when she was feeling so ill that she should have been placed in a sanitarium, a brisk young woman greeted her with the words: "You don't remember me, do you?" Looking at her emptily, Charlotte "groped slowly about in that flaccid vacant brain of mine for some association." A memory arose. Speaking like a four-year-old child, she answers: "Why yes, I remember you. I don't like your mother." To the reader she adds: "It was true enough, but never in the world would I have said such a thing if I had been 'all there'" (*The Living*, pp. 101–102). She characterizes her behavior as "feeble-mindedness" bordering on "an almost infantile responsibility." Nevertheless, her rage toward mothers could not be totally repressed.

In fact, Charlotte Perkins Gilman spent a lifetime in critiquing motherhood. The attack was relentless. She condemned the cult of home and domesticity with a power that none of her contemporaries could rival. Many of the ideas that seemed so radical at the turn of the century are now taken for granted. She exposed the perniciousness of sex roles which confined women to housecleaning and babysitting, and she spoke out against the disastrous social and political consequences of the suppression of women's rights. At the heart of her attack was the worship of motherhood, "Matriolatry," as she bitterly called it. "Of all the myths which befog the popular mind," she writes in *The Home*, "of all false worship which prevents us from recognising the truth, this matriolatry is one most dangerous. Blindly we bow to the word 'mother'—worshipping the recreative processes of nature as did forgotten nations of old time in their great phallic religions."[13] Implicit in the last sentence is the aversion to sexuality that inevitably accompanies her attack. A more ferocious indictment of motherhood appears in *Women and Economics*. The shrillness of her language alerts us to the painful autobiographical elements she could not quite exorcise from the otherwise carefully reasoned argument:

> Human motherhood is more pathological than any other, more morbid, defective, irregular, diseased. Human childhood is similarly pathological. We, as animals, are very inferior animals in this particular. When we take credit to ourselves for the sublime devotion with which we face 'the perils of maternity,' and boast of 'going down to the gates of death' for our children, we should rather take shame to ourselves for bringing these perils upon both mother and child.[14]

To suggest that Charlotte Perkins Gilman's assault on home and motherhood originated from her own unhappy childhood, and that in attacking all mothers she was condemning her own mother, does not invalidate the prophetic truth of her ideas or the extent to which she reflected and shaped the growing women's movement. Nevertheless, we may question whether she was consciously aware of the early childhood events that influenced her writings. Carl Degler has noted the two central theses of *The Home*—that the "home crushed women" and that it was "dirty, inefficient, uninteresting and retrogressive." Yet, when he praises Gilman's book as a "model of the completely rationalistic analysis of an ancient human institution," he is underestimating the decisive role played by unconscious forces in shaping the tone and imagery of her attack.[15] Her opposition to the traditional family structure cannot be appreciated fully without an awareness of her own family matrix of maternal martyrdom and paternal abandonment. Nor can her account of madness in "The Yellow Wallpaper" be adequately understood without a recognition of her own struggle against mental illness and the obstacles she had to confront both in her personal and professional life. In exposing the "pathological" nature of human childhood, she was confessing both to her mother's failure and her own.[16] Poor mothering opened the gates of death to her, first as the innocent victim of her parents' union, then as the involuntary victimizer of her own daughter's childhood. Her final estimate of motherhood may be gleaned from the end of her book *Women and Economics*. Under the heading "Mother" and "Motherhood" appear her various indictments, with the appropriate page numbers: "criminal failure of," "a bad baby-educator," "result of servitude of," "not an exchangeable commodity," "disadvantages of," "deficiencies of," "the pathology of human," "unpreparedness for," "professions unsuitable to," "old methods of," "open to improvement," and "false perspective taught by primitive." These accusations are neatly arranged in a list appearing in—where else?—the Index. She was, finally, her father's daughter.

We are now almost ready to explore the details of Charlotte Perkins Gilman's breakdown, her experience with S. Weir Mitchell's "rest cure," and her fictional treatment of madness in "The Yellow Wallpaper." Her encounter with Mitchell takes on additional interest in light of the psychiatrist's fame as a novelist. Indeed, Mitchell's reputation as a psychiatrist and novelist was unsurpassed in his lifetime. Had he realized the implications of the therapeutic advice he gave to his then unknown patient—". . . never touch pen, brush or pencil as long as you live"—he might have understood the personal and national calamity his psychiatry nearly wrought.

"Silas Weir Mitchell was almost a genius," E. Earnest begins in the Foreword to his book, "His contemporaries believed that he was one, an opinion Mitchell came to share."[17] Medical historians agree that he was the foremost American neurologist of his time. In 1874 he was unanimously elected as the first president of the American Neurological Association. For decades his medical treatises remained the standard textbooks on the subject: *Gunshot Wounds and Other Injuries of the Nerves* (1864), *Wear and Tear* (1871), *Injuries of Nerves and Their Consequences* (1872), *Fat and Blood* (1877), and *Doctor and Patient* (1888). His discovery of the nature of rattlesnake venom laid the foundation for important toxicological and immunological research. He was less a psychiatrist in the modern sense of the word than a neurologist, a "nerve doctor" to whom patients were referred suffering from mysterious motor and sensory disorders. "It was the neurologists rather than the psychiatrists who reintroduced 'physical' methods of treatment of psychiatric disorders; whereas the psychiatrists became more and more the explorers of personality reactions and the developers of methods of restoring patients to useful existence when the neurologists threw in the sponge."[18]

Mitchell's main contribution to neurology was the introduction into the United States of the "rest cure," also called the "Weir Mitchell Treatment." The rest cure consisted of prolonged rest in bed and isolation, overfeeding, and daily body massage. *Fat and Blood* contains a graphic description of the rest cure. "As a rule," notes Mitchell, "no harm is done by rest, even in such people as give us doubts about whether it is or is not well for them to exert themselves." His notion of rest contains little that a hypochondriacal patient would find attractive:

> To lie abed half the day, and sew a little and read a little, and be interesting as invalids and excite sympathy, is all very well, but when they are bidden to stay in bed a month, and neither to read, write, nor sew, and to have one nurse,—who is not a relative,—then repose becomes for some women a rather bitter medicine, and they are glad enough to accept the order to rise and go about when the doctor issues a mandate which has become pleasantly welcome and eagerly looked for.[19]

Normally the psychiatrist required the patient to remain in bed for six to eight weeks. During the first month, Mitchell did not allow her (he generally uses the female pronoun) to sit up, sew, write, or read. She cannot even use her hands except to brush her teeth. Although Mitchell does not use the word, the regimen is designed to "baby" the patient, to facilitate a total physical and emotional regression to the condition of infancy. ". . . the sense of comfort which is apt to come about the fifth or sixth day,—the feeling of ease, and the ready capacity to digest food, and the growing hope of final cure, fed as it is by present relief,—all conspire to make patients contented and tractable."[20]

The rest cure obviously worked on the symptoms of mental illness, not on the sources. At best, it could lead to a patient's temporary improvement. It was not psychotherapy: No effort was made to probe the dynamics of mental illness. Though Mitchell's rest cure coincided exactly with Anna O.'s talking cure, Freud's major discoveries were still several years away.[21] What seems most offensive about Mitchell's rest cure was its aim to make patients tractable. Most of the people he treated were women; those who did not passively submit to him provoked his ire. To his colleagues his treatment of women appeared protective and kind; to us his methods seem paternalistic and degrading. "Wise women choose their doctors and trust them," he writes in *Doctor and Patient*. "The wisest ask the fewest questions. The terrible patients are nervous women with long memories, who question much where answers are difficult, and who put together one's answers from time to time and torment themselves and the physician with the apparent inconsistencies they detect."[22] A nervous woman, he adds, "should be made to comprehend at the onset that the physician means to have his way unhampered by the subtle distinctions with which bedridden women are apt to trouble those who most desire to help them."[23] His portrait of the neurasthenic woman evokes an image of bitchy evil:

> I do not want to do more than is needed of this ungracious talk: suffice it to say that multitudes of our young girls are merely pretty to look at, or not that; that their destiny is the shawl and the sofa, neuralgia, weak backs, and the varied forms of hysteria, — that domestic demon which has produced untold discomfort in many a household, and, I am almost ready to say, as much unhappiness as the husband's dram. My phrase may seem outrageously strong, but only the doctor knows what one of these self-made invalids can do to make a household wretched. Mrs. Gradgrind is, in fiction, the only successful portrait of this type of misery, of the woman who wears out and destroys generations of nursing relatives, and who, as Wendell Holmes has said, is like a vampire, sucking slowly the blood of every healthy, helpful creature within reach of her demands.[24]

Ironically, both Mitchell and Charlotte Perkins Gilman agreed on the horror of this type of woman, and they even used similar metaphors of the "vampire" and "parasite" to describe her. But their agreement ended here. Mitchell aligned himself with the most conservative political and social positions in the country. He believed that women should not compete with men, intellectually or economically, and he maintained that women could not equal men in persistent energy or capacity for "unbroken brain-work." It would be better, he said, not to educate girls at all between the ages of 14 and 18 unless they were in unusually good health. ". . . our growing girls are endowed with organizations so highly sensitive and impressionable that we expose them to needless dangers when we attempt to overtax them mentally."[25] He did not worry about the dangers of undertaxing women.

Mitchell's other career was as a novelist. Although his fiction is almost entirely forgotten today, he was one of the most popular American novelists between 1885 and 1905. His Renaissance versatility prompted his contemporaries to view him as a Benjamin Franklin. A biographer notes that Mitchell's *Hugh Wynne* was compared to Thackeray's *Henry Esmond*, while his *Ode on a Lycian Tomb* was ranked with Milton's *Lycidas*. He translated the fourteenth-century poem *The Pearl* into modern verse, wrote a lively and controversial biography of George Washington, and created a children's story that went through 12 editions. Only after he established his medical reputation in the mid-1880s did he begin to write and publish fiction. He was 55 years old when his first novel, *In War Time*, was published in 1884. Other novels soon followed: *Roland Blake* (1886), *Characteristics* (1891), *Hugh Wynne* (1896), the immensely popular *Dr. North and His Friends* (1900), and *Westways* (1913), published one year before his death at the age of 85. In all there were 19 novels, several volumes of short stories, and three volumes of poetry. The bulk of Mitchell's art covers 6500 pages in the *Definitive Edition.*

Although Mitchell was obviously interested in psychiatric themes, he was not, oddly enough, a psychological novelist. Whether it was due to aristocratic restraint, neurological training, or simple incuriosity, he did not search very deeply for the psychological origins of his protagonist's conflicts and breakdowns. David Rein observes in *S. Weir Mitchell as a Psychiatric Novelist* that "in pursuing a psychological cause he was inclined to take a physiological direction."[26] Rein also remarks that, if one reads Mitchell's fiction in light of his psychiatric case studies, he is bound to be surprised and disappointed by what the novelist fails to include. "He created no characters exhibiting the more spectacular forms of hysterical illness such as he described in his medical writing."[27] Curiously, Mitchell makes a statement in *Doctor and Patient* that any psychoanalyst would endorse. "The cause of breakdowns and nervous disaster, and consequent emotional disturbances and their bitter fruit, are often to be sought in the remote past. He may dislike the quest, but he cannot avoid it."[28] This statement is untypical, however, of Mitchell's approach to character. Contrary to his own advice, he disliked the investigation into his patients' remote past and therefore avoided it. He remains silent on what we would consider today the root causes of mental illness—unempathic parents, identity problems, sexual conflicts, unconscious aggression.

Mitchell's aesthetic theory may be seen from this passage in *Doctor and Patient*: "The man who desires to write in a popular way of nervous women and of her who is to be taught how not to become that sorrowful thing, a nervous woman, must acknowledge, like the Anglo-Saxon novelist, certain reputable limitations. The best readers are, however, in a measure co-operative authors, and may be left to interpolate the unsaid."[29] Discretion and respectful vagueness should be the novelist's guiding principle. The psychiatrist had no desire to evoke medical realism in his fiction. "In older times the sickness of a novel was merely a feint to gain time in the story or account for a non-appearance, and the doctor made very brief show upon the stage. Since, however, the growth of realism in literary art, the temptation to delineate exactly the absolute facts of disease has led authors to dwell freely on the details of sickness."[30] Mitchell disapproved of those novelists interested in depicting illness and symptomatology. "Depend upon it," he exclaims, the modern novelist "had best fight shy of these chronic illnesses: they make queer reading to a doctor who knows what sick people are; and above all does this advice apply to death-beds."[31] Fortunately, not all novelists followed the doctor's orders here.

The basic facts of Charlotte Perkins Gilman's treatment with Mitchell come from two sources: a one-page article called "Why I Wrote the Yellow Wallpaper" published in a 1913 issue of *The Forerunner* and the chapter in her autobiography entitled "The Breakdown." Mitchell apparently never wrote about her in his psychiatric or fictional works. After suffering for about three years from a "severe and continuous nervous breakdown tending to melancholia—and beyond," she decided to visit Mitchell, "at that time the greatest nerve specialist in the country." She took the rest cure with the utmost confidence, prefacing the visit with a long letter in which she gave the history of the case in a way that a "modern psychologist would have appreciated." Mitchell thought the letter proved only self-conceit, perhaps because of what she called his prejudice against the Beechers. " 'I've had two women of your blood here already,' he told me scornfully." The psychiatrist seemed familiar with only two types of nervous prostration—that of the businessman exhausted from too much work and the society woman exhausted from too much play. He had difficulty in diagnosing her case although he did assure her there was no "dementia," only "hysteria." He ordered her to bed where she was fed, bathed, and rubbed. After about a month of the treatment he judged her cured and sent her home. She records his prescription along with her feelings at that time:

> "Live as domestic a life as possible. Have your child with you all the time." (Be it remarked that if I did but dress the baby it left me shaking and crying—certainly far from a healthy companionship for her, to say nothing of the effect on me.) "Lie down an hour after each meal. Have but two hours' intellectual life a day. And never touch pen, brush or pencil as long as you live" (*The Living*, p. 96).

She went home, followed his directions faithfully for three months, and nearly lost her mind. The mental agony was so unbearable that she would sit blankly, moving her head from side to side, to escape the pain. No physical pain was involved, not even a headache, "just mental torment, and so heavy in its nightmare gloom that it seemed real enough to dodge." Rejecting the psychiatrist's advice, she finally committed herself to work, work which is "joy and growth and service, without which one is a pauper and a parasite," thereby recovering a degree of her former health.[32]

Why did Mitchell's rest cure fail so miserably? The psychiatrist deified the worship of matriolatry which Charlotte Perkins Gilman feared and grew to despise. She was attempting to flee from the domestic prison of the mother's world—the parasitic world of abject dependency upon men, the depressing routine of endless drudgery, screaming babies, intellectual impoverishment, and helpless resignation. Mitchell's paternalistic therapy locked her into the mother's role, first by breaking her spirit and making her a baby again through the rest cure, then by imprisoning her with her own helpless baby. The rest cure could only deepen her psychic unrest; instead of helping her to accept the responsibilities of an adult or at least to understand her morbid fear of babies, Mitchell infantilized her further. His therapy deprived her of the opportunity to pursue her father's achievements and thus blocked her life-saving identification with the man who had fled from the home in quest of the magical world of ideas and books. Charlotte's health required neither childlike submission nor maternal self-sacrifice but the heroic challenge of Mitchell's own manly world. Two of the books she later wrote symbolize the direction of the therapy she needed: an escape from *The Home* in pursuit of *The Man-Made World*.

In contrast to Mitchell's dictum to return to her husband and presumably expand her family, Gilman chose the only form of pregnancy she could imagine—literary creation. From her agonizing labor with psychiatry was born "The Yellow Wallpaper." "It is a description of a case of nervous breakdown beginning something as mine did, and treated as Dr. S. Weir Mitchell treated me with what I considered the inevitable result, progressive insanity" (*The Living*, pp. 118–119). Midway through "The Yellow Wallpaper" the unnamed narrator refers to the psychiatrist to whom her physician-husband is threatening to send her. "John says if I don't pick up faster he shall send me to Weir Mitchell in the fall."[33] Clearly it is a threat. "But I don't want to go there at all. I had a friend who was in his hands once, and she says he is just like John and my brother, only more so!" ("The Yellow Wallpaper," p. 19). Gilman does not actually describe in detail her own encounters with her therapist, as later writers were to do—Doris Lessing, Joanne Greenberg, Philip Roth. There is little attempt to characterize the psychiatrist apart from naming him (though implicitly he is linked to the sinister husband). "The Yellow Wallpaper" represents an early and shadowy attempt to describe a psychiatrist in a work of fiction. As the therapist's role in the patient's healing process is expanded in later works, so, too, will be the depth of his or her characterization. Moreover, a therapy that involves no talking, as was the case with Mitchell's rest cure, can produce little characterization and dialogue.

Why, then, does Gilman name her psychiatrist at all? Probably for several reasons: the effort to establish medical authenticity, the willingness to acknowledge the autobiographical roots of the story, and the desire to recompense the doctor for his costly therapy. Far from suggesting the writer's flight from reality, or what Freud might call the neurotic's escape into fantasy, "The Yellow Wallpaper" prophesied the frightening outcome of Mitchell's psychiatry had the patient dutifully followed his advice. Gilman boldly reversed art and life: The eerie realism of "The Yellow Wallpaper" exposed the psychiatrist's rest cure as an evil fiction having nothing to do with reality.

It is interesting to compare the two accounts of mental illness in the autobiographical *The Living of Charlotte Perkins Gilman* and the fictional "The Yellow Wallpaper." There is no doubt about the greater truthfulness of art. The achievement of "The Yellow Wallpaper" lies in its ruthless honesty, accuracy, and power. Free from the constraints of hurting people in real life, the artist is free to imagine the unnerving details of her protagonist's story. In the autobiography, Gilman describes her husband as a patient and long-suffering man, the ideal spouse. She refers to his "unbroken devotion, his manifold cares and labors in tending a sick wife, his adoring pride in the best of babies . . ." (*The Living*, p. 97). Stetson becomes a husband less human than saintly, a heroic portrait like the one of Charlotte's mother. The following sentence is typical of her characterization of him. "He has worked for me and for us both, waited on me in every tenderest way, played to me, read to me, done all for me as he always does. God be thanked for my husband" (*The Living*, p. 88).

Gilman projects these qualities onto the narrator's husband in "The

Yellow Wallpaper" but with a different emphasis. The husband displays solicitude but also incomprehension and insensitivity. Baffled by his wife's mysterious illness, he seems to aggravate the situation—indeed, she hints that he is responsible for her illness. "John is a physician, and *perhaps*—(I would not say it to a living soul, of course, but this is dead paper, and a great relief to my mind)—*perhaps* that is one reason I do not get well faster" ("The Yellow Wallpaper," pp. 9–10). The narrator's unconscious resentment of the husband momentarily surfaces here, allowing us to glimpse the truth. Nowhere in the autobiography is Gilman emboldened to voice a similar criticism, although that is the only inference a reader can draw. John's disbelief in the narrator's illness intensifies her suffering. "If a physician of high standing, and one's own husband, assures friends and relatives that there is really nothing the matter with one but temporary nervous depression—a slight hysterical tendency—what is one to do?" ("The Yellow Wallpaper," p. 10). He can urge only the platitudes of increased willpower and self-restraint. Whereas in her autobiography Gilman feels obligated to remain silent over her husband's role in her illness, in her art she can admit through the narrator to becoming "unreasonably angry" with him.

"The Yellow Wallpaper" also dramatizes the husband's prohibition against writing. "He says that with my imaginative power and habit of story-making, a nervous weakness like mine is sure to lead to all manner of excited fantasies, and that I ought to use my will and good sense to check the tendency. So I try" (pp. 15–16). Mitchell, we recall, had similarly prohibited his patient from writing. It is thus ironic that both the narrator's husband and Gilman's psychiatrist forbid their patients from the one life-saving activity, artistic creation. What proves therapeutic in Gilman's world is neither marriage nor psychiatry but art, and, when the narrator's husband deprives her of this activity in "The Yellow Wallpaper," her fate is sealed.

Opposed to the liberating world of art is the enslaving domesticity of the home. The woman remains isolated in the nursery of an old ancestral house, a "hereditary estate," that is part of an obscure national heritage. "The Yellow Wallpaper" foreshadows Gilman's more extensive assault on domesticity culminating several years later in *The Home*. Filled with "hedges and walls and gates that lock," the house reflects the alienation of nineteenth-century America, with its cult of domesticity and worship of children. The husband and wife live in the nursery at the top of the house, with barred windows for little children. The narrator's perception of the nursery slowly changes. In the beginning it seems like a big airy room to her, but after two weeks it becomes claustrophobic in its heavy bedstead, barred windows, and gate at the head of the stairs. The imagery identifies the home as a prison without escape. The woman rarely leaves the nursery, not even to look at her baby who is housed on a lower floor.

The most horrifying feature of the house, and the source of the story's great power, is the yellow wallpaper in the nursery. "It is dull enough to confuse the eye in following, pronounced enough to constantly irritate and provoke study, and when you follow the lame uncertain curves for a little distance they suddenly commit suicide—plunge off at outrageous angles, destroy themselves in unheard of contradictions" (p. 13). The wallpaper becomes a projection screen or Rorschach test of the narrator's growing fright. The chaotic pattern symbolizes her own unheard emotional contradictions: her need for security yet fear of dependency and entrapment; her acceptance of the American Dream (marriage, family, house) amidst the nightmare of reality; her passive acceptance of duty but rising protest. The narrator's perception of the wallpaper's suicide foreshadows her own self-destructive behavior. Indeed, the wallpaper functions as a Poesque black cat or telltale heart, the object upon which her madness is focused. There is a difference, however, between Poe's stories and Gilman's. The reader of "The Black Cat" or "The Tell-Tale Heart" soon learns that the first person narrator is crazy and can thus distance himself from the homicidal character. The reader of "The Yellow Wallpaper," by contrast, is far more sympathetic to the heroine and is almost seduced into sharing her increasingly psychotic point of view. The old ancestral house and its vision of America are enough to drive almost anyone mad. Yet, what we see in "The Yellow Wallpaper" is not simply an oppressive environment or a deranged woman but an organic connection between setting and character. Madness does not spring from nowhere. The story's richness lies in its ability to yield multiple meanings and points of view—psychological, sociological, historical. The house has rich symbolic meaning in "The Yellow Wallpaper": the domestic imprisonment of nineteenth-century women, the madness of the Mitchell rest cure, the isolation of rural America, the repression of the body. ("The human body as a whole is pictured by the dream-imagination as a house and the separate organs of the body by portions of a house," Freud tells us in *The Interpretation of Dreams*.[34])

Although critics have admired the complex symbolism of the yellow wallpaper, they have not sufficiently explored the relationship between the inanimate pattern and the narrator's mind, in particular, her fear of children. The violence of her imagery is striking. "There is a recurrent spot where the pattern lolls like a broken neck and two bulbous eyes stare at you upside down" (p. 16). Many of the images she uses to describe the wallpaper appear to be related to the "dear baby" whom she cannot bear to be with. Her only reference to the baby implies relief that "it" does not occupy the upstairs nursery where she and her husband live. "If we had not used it, the blessed child would have! What a fortunate escape! Why, I wouldn't have a child of mine, an impressionable little thing, live in such a room for worlds" (p. 22). True, she expresses love and concern for the baby, yet she is also solicitous toward her husband, and we know that behind this surface calm lies unconscious aggression. Is she similarly hostile toward her baby?

If so, we suspect this was not part of the author's conscious intentions. There is too much evidence, however, to ignore. The new mother's description of the wallpaper evokes an image of an insatiable child who seems to be crawling everywhere, even into the nursery which remains her only sanctuary. The unblinking eyes stare at her as if the baby demands to be nursed or held. "I get positively angry with the impertinence of it and the everlastingness. Up and down and sideways they crawl, and those absurd, unblinking eyes are everywhere" (p. 16). Her next free association is revealing. "I never saw so much expression in an inanimate thing before, and we all know how much expression they have! I used to lie awake as a child and get more entertainment and terror out of blank walls and plain furniture than most children could find in a toy-store" (pp. 16–17). Even as she renders the child into an inanimate object and consequently distances herself from its needs, the lifeless wallpaper assumes the characteristics of an angry child who grows increasingly demonic. She literally cannot escape from the baby because her imagination has projected it onto the landscape of her bedroom. Inanimate one moment and human the next, the baby evokes contradictory emotions within her—both tenderness and resentment. The baby also reminds the anxious mother of her own infancy. She tells us significantly that, when she was a child, the love and attention she craved were met with blank walls— just as her virtually motherless child meets with blank walls downstairs. The implication is that her present illness originates from an early childhood abandonment similar to the one her own child is encountering.

Tight-lipped about her own child, she speaks harshly about other children. The furniture in her bedroom had been scarred by the children of the previous owners: "I never saw such ravages as the children have made here" (p. 17). The room itself has been the victim of the children's vicious attack. The floor is "scratched and gouged and splintered," the plaster "is dug out here and there," and the great heavy bed "looks as if it had been through the wars" (p. 17). Later she returns to the oral imagery: "How those children did tear about here! This bedstead is fairly gnawed!" (p. 34).

The narrator's dilemma, then, is to escape from the voracious children who threaten to devour her body, just as they have gnawed upon the room. And indeed the other sub-pattern in the wallpaper reveals the figure of a strange woman skulking about the room. There is no doubt about her identity. "And it is like a woman stooping down and creeping about behind that pattern" (p. 22). By daylight the figure appears subdued, but at night she begins to crawl around. In the narrator's words, "You think you have mastered it, but just as you get well underway in following, it turns a back-somersault and there you are. It slaps you in the face, knocks you down, and tramples upon you. It is like a bad dream" (p. 25).

Interpreted according to dream logic, the wallpaper recreates the mother's inescapable horror of children and her regression to infancy. The pattern and sub-pattern mirror her terrified identification with the abandoned child and abandoning mother. The roles of victim and victimizer become hopelessly blurred. Who is escaping from whom? In fleeing from the image of the baby, the mother confronts its presence in the wallpaper located, appropriately enough, in the nursery of the old ancestral home. Here, the mysteries of birth, marriage, procreation, and death are played out in her imagination. The decision to isolate herself from her baby betrays the contradictory wish to protect and harm it. The child's identity remains ambiguous, both innocent and evil. The wallpaper imagery evokes an appalling eruption of subhuman life, uncontrolled reproduction. It is not just one organism but an endless stream of growth. "If you can imagine a toadstool in joints, an interminable string of toadstools, budding and sprouting in endless convolutions—why, that is something like it" (p. 25). From the psychoanalytic point of view of object relations, the narrator cannot separate her identity from the baby's: She is both the hysterical mother searching for freedom and the insatiable child demanding attention. The angry child within the adult seems responsible for the mother's illness. Nor is escape possible from the sickening yellow substance that oozes from the wall. Its mysteriousness contributes to the indefinable sexual menace lurking throughout the house and penetrating the woman's body. The movement of "The Yellow Wallpaper" is suggestive of the wife's efforts to avoid sexual defilement, beginning with her abortive attempt to sleep in the room downstairs, with its single bed, and ending with the outraged husband's cry for an ax to break into the room where she has barricaded herself.

Despite the pre-Freudian world of "The Yellow Wallpaper" and Charlotte Perkins Gilman's subsequent condemnation of psychoanalysis, the story is startlingly modern in its vision of mental illness.[35] Anticipating Freudian discoveries, the story suggests that psychological illness worsens when it is not acknowledged as real and that the rest cure is antithetical both to the talking cure and to the therapeutic value of artistic creation. Moreover, "The Yellow Wallpaper" portrays mental illness as originating from childhood experiences. Unlike Breuer's "Fräulein Anna O.," "The Yellow Wallpaper" shows the social and political as well as psychological implications of madness. Gilman rejects not psychotherapy, which Freud was introducing, but pseudotherapy, which has always been with us. Gilman's narrator is one of the first in a long line of benumbed and bedeviled patients in American literature who search desperately for understanding but who, following the accepted medical advice of the time, lose their mind.

Gilman's achievement is that she is able to transform her narrator's bad dream into superb art. And here is where the literary brilliance of "The Yellow Wallpaper" comes into play. Although the narrator in the fictional story recalls the author's self-portrait in the autobiographical *The Living of Charlotte Perkins Gilman*, "The Yellow Wallpaper" contains a shape and unity consistent with the demands of art. The difference between fiction and life lies in the greater narrative distance and formal control of art. In her autobiography, Gilman remains mystified by the origin and meaning of her breakdown; she eloquently describes the pain and confusion of a lifetime of neurotic suffering, but she is finally baffled by its significance. She depicts her illness as a digression to a life of struggle and work, rather than as a continuing conflict that compelled her to invent constructive solutions to the problems of her age.

Fiction empowered her to rework sickness into art. Dr. Mitchell had diagnosed her illness as hysteria not dementia; "I never had hallucinations or objections to my mural decorations," Gilman parenthetically adds in "Why I Wrote The Yellow Wallpaper."[36] But, for artistic reasons, she decided to confer deadly psychosis on her narrator. Although the woman begins with what her husband calls "temporary nervous depression—a slight hysterical tendency" (p. 10), she grows steadily insane until her situation is hopeless. In the beginning of the story, the narrator and the author are indistinguishable, but as the former becomes terminally insane, the latter remains firmly in control of the narrative, allowing the symbolic power of the wallpaper rather than authorial intrusions to expose the full horror. At the end, the narrator and author are worlds apart. Indeed, the technique of narrative distance and point of view is handled more confidently in "The Yellow Wallpaper" than in *The Bell Jar*, where Plath seems unable to imagine a character who is neither menacing nor locked into the bell-jar vision. We may continue to search for a full explanation of the bizarre events in "The Yellow Wallpaper," but this is secondary to witnessing a mind in the process of self-extinction. Moreover, there is no specific moment in the story when we can say that the narrator has suddenly become mad. It happens mysteriously, imperceptibly. The crackup is frighteningly appealing because it allows her to defy and mock a husband who has taken on the role of a jailor. Gilman succeeds admirably in sketching a man whose dialogue sounds well meaning but whose actions assume a diabolical quality. He prowls around the house in an effort to thwart his wife's escape. At the end he gains entry into his wife's bedroom, but then, in a cunning reversal of roles, he faints at her feet while she creeps over him.

The early readers of "The Yellow Wallpaper" keenly felt the story's horror, but not all of them were favorably impressed. William Dean Howells (who was a friend of both Gilman and Mitchell) admired the story.[37] However, when he submitted it to *Atlantic Monthly* for publication, Gilman received a rejection from the editor with an indignant note: "I could not forgive myself if I made others as miserable as I have made myself!" (*The Living*, p. 119). When it was published, the story provoked anger and ill will. A physician sent a protest to the Boston *Transcript* complaining of the "morbid fascination" of "The Yellow Wallpaper" and questioning whether stories of such "deadly peril" should be published at all. On the positive side, another physician wrote to

Gilman to praise "The Yellow Wallpaper" for its delicacy of touch and correctness of portrayal. "From a doctor's standpoint, and I am a doctor, you have made a success. So far as I know, and I am fairly well up in literature, there has been no detailed account of incipient insanity." Thus began the claims and counterclaims for the story's psychiatric authenticity. In the same letter to Gilman, the physician wondered about her experience with mental illness. "Have you ever been—er—; but of course you haven't." Her reply was that she had gone as far as one could go and still return (*The Living*, pp. 120–121).

The real purpose of writing "The Yellow Wallpaper," she admits in her autobiography, was to reach S. Weir Mitchell and "to convince him of the error of his ways." Without denying the genuineness of her didactic aim, we can also speculate on the motive of revenge toward the psychiatrist who forbade her to touch pen, brush or pencil again for as long as she lived—which might not have been very long. "The Yellow Wallpaper" thus came into existence against the orders of a psychiatrist who almost blocked the development of a major American thinker and writer.[38] In writing "The Yellow Wallpaper" Gilman became a psychiatrist herself in the advice she offered to the nervous women who might be reading her story. She was not only shrinking her former psychiatrist to his proper size but also offering her readers the sympathy and understanding that the medical establishment could not give to women. There is justifiable pride in Gilman's voice when she speaks about the story's impact upon patients and doctors alike. "The little book is valued by alienists and as a good specimen of one kind of literature. It has to my knowledge saved one woman from a similar fate—so terrifying her family that they let her out into normal activity and she recovered."[39] Best of all was the story's effect on Mitchell. Although she had sent him a copy of "The Yellow Wallpaper" and received no acknowledgment, many years later she discovered that the famous specialist had indeed read the story and, as a result of it, altered his treatment of nervous illness. "If that is a fact," she boasts, "I have not lived in vain" (*The Living*, p. 121). As she concludes in "Why I Wrote the Yellow Wallpaper," "It was not intended to drive people crazy, but to save people from being crazy, and it worked."[40] No work of literature can accomplish more than this.

NOTES

1. Aileen S. Kraditor, *The Ideas of the Woman Suffrage Movement, 1890–1920* (New York: Columbia University Press, 1965), p. 97.

2. William L. O'Neill, "Introduction" to Charlotte Perkins Gilman, *The Home: Its Work and Influence* (1903; rpt. Urbana: University of Illinois Press, 1972), p. vii.

3. Andrew Sinclair, *The Better Half: The Emancipation of the American Woman* (New York: Harper & Row, 1965), p. 272.

4. Carl N. Degler, "Charlotte Perkins Gilman on the Theory and Practice of Feminism," *American Quarterly*, Vol. 8, No. 1 (Spring 1956), p. 22.

5. *The Nation*, June 8, 1899, p. 443. Quoted by Degler, op. cit., p. 21.

6. Mary Gray Peck, *Carrie Chapman Catt: A Biography* (New York: H. W. Wilson, 1954), p. 454.

7. Ibid., p. 455.

8. Charlotte Perkins Gilman, *The Living of Charlotte Perkins Gilman: An Autobiography* (1935; rpt. New York: Harper and Row, 1975), p. 8. All references are to this edition. Born Charlotte Perkins in 1860, she married Walter Stetson in 1884, gave birth to her daughter Katherine in 1885, and immediately suffered a breakdown. She divorced Stetson a few years later. In 1900 she married her cousin, Houghton Gilman. Curiously, in the 335-page autobiography she devotes only two sentences to her second husband. This is only one of many conspicuous omissions in her autobiography. The reader interested in learning more about Gilman's life should consult Mary A. Hill, *Charlotte Perkins Gilman: The Making of a Radical Feminist 1860–1896* (Philadelphia: Temple University Press, 1980). Although not psychoanalytic, the biography confirms Gilman's intense ambivalence toward her parents and also discusses her marital difficulties with Stetson and her tension toward her daughter Katherine.

9. Charlotte Perkins Gilman, "Parasitism and Civilised Vice," in Samuel D. Schmalhausen and V. F. Calverton, eds., *Woman's Coming of Age* (New York: Liveright, 1931), p. 123. Many of the feminists who have written on Gilman share her feelings toward Freud. Witness this judgment by her friend Zona Gale in the "Foreword" to *The Living*: ". . . after all her prophetic thinking, it comes about that to-day Mrs. Gilman is regarded by many of the new generation as reactionary, because of her impatience at the useful bunglings of Freud, that husky bull in the Venetian-glass shop of certain still veiled equilibriums" (p. xxv).

10. Hill, op. cit., p. 130.

11. Charlotte Perkins [Stetson] Gilman, *Concerning Children* (Boston: Small, Maynard and Company, 1901), pp. 193–194.

12. Patricia Meyer Spacks, *The Female Imagination* (New York: Avon, 1976), p. 270.

13. Gilman, *The Home*, op cit., p. 60.

14. Charlotte Perkins Stetson, *Women and Economics* (Boston: Small, Maynard and Company, 1899), p. 181.

15. Degler, op. cit., p. 36.

16. Not surprisingly, Gilman's biographer provides abundant evidence of the daughter's severe criticisms of her feminist mother. In interviewing Katherine Beecher Stetson Chamberlin in 1975, when Charlotte's daughter was 90-years-old, Mary Hill concluded that "Katherine's recollections of Charlotte suggest a repetition of themes of mother-daughter history Charlotte described with Mary. So often, as mothers, both Mary and Charlotte had been exhausted by economic and emotional responsibilities, and both Katherine and Charlotte criticized their mothers for being churlish and mean." (Hill, op. cit., p. 232.)

17. Ernest Earnest, *S. Weir Mitchell: Novelist and Physician* (Philadelphia: University of Pennsylvania Press, 1950), p. v.

18. Walter Freeman, *The Psychiatrist: Personalities and Patterns* (New York: Grune and Stratton, 1968), p. 6.

19. S. Weir Mitchell, *Fat and Blood* (Philadelphia: Lippincott, 1884), pp. 57–58.

20. Ibid., pp. 60–61.

21. Interestingly, Freud was well aware of Mitchell's work and surprisingly sympathetic toward it. He wrote a review of *Fat and Blood* in 1887 in which he praised Mitchell as the "highly original nerve specialist in Philadelphia" and endorsed the rest cure as a means to overcome severe and long established states of nervous exhaustion. See Freud, "Review of Weir Mitchell's *The Treatment of Certain Forms of Neurasthenia and Hysteria [Fat and Blood]*," *Standard Edition* (London: The Hogarth Press, 1966), Vol. I, p. 36. In the short essay "Hysteria" (1888), Freud elaborates on his praise for Mitchell:

> In recent years the so-called "rest-cure" of Weir Mitchell (also known as Plairfair's treatment) has gained a high reputation as a method of treating hysteria in institutions, and deservedly so. . . . This treatment is of extraordinary value for hysteria, as a happy combination of *"traitement moral"* with an improvement in the patient's general nutritional state. It is not to be regarded, however, as something systematically complete in itself; the isolation, rather, and the physician's influence remain the principal agents, and, along with massage and electricity, the other therapeutic methods are not to be neglected (*Standard Edition*, Vol. I, p. 55).

In *Studies on Hysteria* (1895), Freud again praises Mitchell and observes that the rest cure in combination with cathartic psychotherapy yields excellent results, better results indeed than either method alone. Curiously, Freud makes a statement that a few years later he would have repudiated—that a danger of the rest cure is that patients "not infrequently fall into the habit of harmful day-dreaming" (*Standard Edition* [London: The Hogarth Press, 1955] Vol. II, p. 267). Freud later constructed a psychology that would make accessible for the first time the inner world of daydreaming which, when deciphered, offers clues into the causes of mental illness.

Incidentally, Freud's praise of Mitchell was never reciprocated. Like most of his colleagues, Mitchell was shocked and horrified by Freud's emphasis on sex. (This is one of the few sources of agreement between Mitchell and Gilman.) David Rein points out that "There are few references to sex in his books and articles on nervous diseases in women, nor is there much appreciation of the role of sex in normal behavior." See David M. Rein, *S. Weir Mitchell as a Psychiatric Novelist* (New York: International Universities Press, 1952), p. 44. Earnest comments that late in life Mitchell "attacked the psychoanalytic theories on the basis that they held 'that neurasthenia is always a disease of the mind alone—a psychogenesis.' His own belief was that 'a goodly proportion of neurasthenia . . . has no more psychic origin than has a colic.'" Mitchell's biographer adds that "Today, of course, even the source of a colic would be sought in the mind." See Earnest, op. cit., pp. 228–229. According to Earnest, Mitchell was so incensed with psychoanalytic theory that when he began to read a book on Freud that he had borrowed from the medical library, he sputtered: "Where did this filthy thing come from?" and threw the book in the fire.

22. S. Weir Mitchell, *Doctor and Patient* (New York: Arno Press, 1972 [Reprint of 1888 edition]), p. 48.

23. Ibid., p. 49.

24. S. Weir Mitchell, *Wear and Tear* (New York: Arno Press, 1973 [Reprint of 1887 edition]), p. 32.

25. Ibid., p. 57.

26. Rein, op. cit., p. 46.

27. Ibid., p. 50.

28. Mitchell, *Doctor and Patient*, op. cit., p. 10.

29. Ibid., p. 12.

30. Ibid., p. 72.

31. Ibid., p. 73.

32. The preceding account comes from Gilman, *The Living*, op. cit., pp. 95–96, and Gilman, "Why I Wrote the Yellow Wallpaper," *The Forerunner*, Vol. 4 (1913), p. 271.

33. Charlotte Perkins Gilman, *The Yellow Wallpaper* (1899; rpt. New York: The Feminist Press, 1973), p. 18. All references are to this edition.

34. Freud, *Standard Edition*, (London: The Hogarth Press, 1953), Vol. IV, p. 225.

35. William O'Neill has observed that "Mrs. Gilman's personal difficulties, and her distrust of sexual relations, prevented her from seeing that while popular Freudianism and the new sex ethic were certainly masculine in character, their purpose was not to divert women from marriage and motherhood but to repopularize these institutions, to make them intellectually respectable, as it were." See *Everyone Was Brave* (Chicago: Quadrangle Books, 1971), p. 319.

36. "Why I Wrote The Yellow Wallpaper," p. 271.

37. For a discussion of Howells' relationship to Mitchell, see Edwin H. Cady, *The Realist at War* (New York: Syracuse University Press, 1958), pp. 97–98. When Winifred Howells suffered what appeared to be a nervous breakdown in 1888, Howells called in Mitchell, an old friend and correspondent, to care for his daughter. In the words of Howells' biographer, "Mitchell agreed that Winifred's case was psycho-neurotic; he proposed to disregard her delusions of pain and forcefeed her from her shocking state of starvation back to the place where he could safely treat her for hysteria." After the daughter's unexpected death, an autopsy was performed and revealed that her terminal illness was organic, not psychological. Howells was flooded with guilt and remorse, though he did not blame Mitchell for the incorrect diagnosis.

38. Mitchell seems to have played a more positive therapeutic role with another woman of letters, Edith Wharton. Edmund Wilson reports that Mitchell was instrumental in encouraging Wharton to write fiction during her nervous breakdown. See Wilson, *The Wound and the Bow* (New York: Oxford University Press, 1965), p. 160. Cynthia Wolff confirms the story in her biography, *A Feast of Words: The Triumph of Edith Wharton* (New York: Oxford University Press, 1977), p. 89. Joseph Lovering remarks, however, in *S. Weir Mitchell* (New York: Twayne, 1971), p. 26, that he is unable to corroborate this idea in any of the sources he has seen. There is no mention of Mitchell's relationship to Edith Wharton in another biographical study, Richard Walter, *S. Weir Mitchell, M.D. — Neurologist: A Medical Biography* (Springfield, Illinois: Charles C. Thomas, 1970).

39. Gilman, "Why I Wrote The Yellow Wallpaper," op. cit., p. 271.

40. Ibid., p. 271.

"Too Terribly Good
To Be Printed":
Charlotte Gilman's
"The Yellow Wallpaper"

Conrad Shumaker

In 1890 William Dean Howells sent a copy of "The Yellow Wallpaper" to Horace Scudder, editor of the *Atlantic Monthly*. Scudder gave his reason for not publishing the story in a short letter to its author, Charlotte Perkins Stetson (later to become Charlotte Perkins Gilman): "Dear Madam, Mr. Howells has handed me this story. I could not forgive myself if I made others as miserable as I have made myself!"[1] Gilman persevered, however, and eventually the story, which depicts the mental collapse of a woman undergoing a "rest cure" at the hands of her physician husband, was printed in the *New England Magazine* and then later in Howells' own collection, *Great Modern American Stories*, where he introduces it as "terrible and too wholly dire," and "too terribly good to be printed."[2] Despite (or perhaps because of) such praise, the story was virtually ignored for over fifty years until Elaine Hedges called attention to its virtues, praising it as "a small literary masterpiece."[3] Today the work is highly spoken of by those who have read it, but it is not widely known and has been slow to appear in anthologies of American literature.

Some of the best criticism attempts to explain this neglect as a case of misinterpretation by audiences used to "traditional" literature. Annette Kolodny, for example, points out that though nineteenth-century readers had learned to "follow the fictive processes of aberrant perception and mental breakdown" by reading Poe's tales, they were not prepared to understand a tale of mental degeneration in a middle-class mother and wife. It took twentieth-century feminism to place the story in a "nondominant or subcultural" tradition which those steeped in the dominant tradition could not understand.[4] Jean F. Kennard suggests that the recent appearance of feminist novels has changed literary conventions and led us to find in the story an exploration of women's role instead of the tale of horror or depiction of mental breakdown its original audience found.[5] Both arguments are persuasive, and the feminist readings of the story that accompany them are instructive. With its images of barred windows and sinister bedsteads, creeping women and domineering men, the story does indeed raise the issue of sex roles in an effective way, and thus anticipates later feminist literature.

Ultimately, however, both approaches tend to make the story seem more isolated from the concerns of the nineteenth-century "dominant tradition" than it really is, and since they focus most of our attention on the story's polemical aspect, they invite a further exploration of Gilman's artistry—the way in which she molds her reformer concerns into a strikingly effective work of literature. To be sure, the polemics are important. Gilman, an avowed feminist and a relative of Harriet Beecher Stowe, told Howells that she didn't consider the work to be "literature" at all, that everything she wrote was for a purpose, in this case that of pointing out the dangers of a particular medical treatment. Unlike Gilman's other purposeful fictions, however, "The Yellow Wallpaper" transcends its author's immediate intent, and my experience teaching it suggests that it favorably impresses both male and female students, even before they learn of its feminist context or of the patriarchal biases of nineteenth-century medicine. I think the story has this effect for two reasons. First, the question of women's role in the nineteenth century is inextricably bound up with the more general question of how one perceives the world. Woman is often seen as representing an imaginative or "poetic" view of things that conflicts with (or sometimes complements) the American male's "common sense" approach to reality. Through the characters of the "rational" doctor and the "imaginative" wife, Gilman explores a question that was—and in many ways still is—central both to American literature and to the place of women in American culture: What happens to the imagination when it's defined as feminine (and thus weak) and has to face a society that values the useful and the practical and rejects anything else as nonsense? Second, this conflict and the related feminist message both arise naturally and effectively out of the action of the story because of the author's skillful handling of the narrative voice.

One of the most striking passages in Gilman's autobiography describes her development and abandonment of a dream world, a fantasy land to which she could escape from the rather harsh realities of her early life. When she was thirteen, a friend of her mother warned that such escape could be dangerous, and Charlotte, a good New England girl who considered absolute obedience a duty, "shut the door" on her "dear, bright, glittering dreams."[6] The narrator of "The Yellow Wallpaper" has a similar problem: from the beginning of the story she displays a vivid imagination. She wants to imagine that the house they have rented is haunted, and as she looks at the wallpaper, she is reminded of her childhood fancies about rooms, her ability to "get more entertainment and terror out of blank walls and plain furniture than most children could find in a toy store."[7] Her husband has to keep reminding her that she "must not give way to fancy in the least" as she comments on her new surroundings. Along with her vivid imagination she has the mind and eye of an artist. She begins to study the wallpaper in an attempt to make sense of its artistic design, and she objects to it for aesthetic reasons: it is "one of those sprawling, flamboyant patterns committing every artistic sin" (p. 13). When her ability to express her artistic impulses is limited by her husband's prescription of complete rest, her mind turns to the wallpaper, and she begins to find in its tangled pattern the emotions and experiences she is forbidden to record. By trying to ignore and repress her imagination, in short, John eventually brings about the very circumstance he wants to prevent.

Though he is clearly a domineering husband who wants to have absolute control over his wife, John also has other reasons for forbidding her to write or paint. As Gilman points out in her autobiography, the "rest cure" was designed for "the business man exhausted from too much work, and the society woman exhausted from too much play."[8] The treatment is intended, in other words, to deal with physical symptoms of overwork and fatigue, and so is unsuited to the narrator's more complex case. But as a doctor and an empiricist who "scoffs openly at things not to be felt and seen and put down in figures," John wants to deal only with physical causes and effects: if his wife's symptoms are nervousness and weight loss, the treatment must be undisturbed tranquility and good nutrition. The very idea that her "work" might be beneficial to her disturbs him; indeed, he is both fearful and contemptuous of her imaginative and artistic powers, largely because he fails to understand them or the view of the world they lead her to.

Two conversations in particular demonstrate his way of dealing with her imagination and his fear of it. The first occurs when the narrator asks him to change the wallpaper. He replies that to do so would be dangerous, for "nothing was worse for a nervous patient than to give way to such fancies." At this point, her "fancy" is simply an objection to the paper's ugliness, a point she makes clear when she suggests that they move to the "pretty rooms" downstairs. John replies by calling her a "little goose" and saying "he would go down to the cellar if she wished and have it whitewashed into the bargain" (p. 15). Besides showing his obviously patriarchal stance, his reply is designed to make her aesthetic objections seem nonsense by fastening on concrete details—color and elevation—and ignoring the real basis of her request. If she wants to go downstairs away from yellow walls, he will take her to the cellar and have it whitewashed. The effect is precisely what he intends: he makes her see her objection to the paper's ugliness as "just a whim." The second conversation occurs after the narrator has begun to see a woman behind the surface pattern of the wallpaper. When John catches her getting out of bed to examine the paper more closely, she decides to ask him to take her away. He refuses, referring again to concrete details: "You are gaining flesh and color, your appetite is better, I feel really much better about you." When she implies that her physical condition isn't the real problem, he cuts her off in midsentence: "I beg of you, for my sake and for our child's sake, as well as for your own, that you will never for one instant let that idea enter your mind! There is nothing so dangerous, so fascinating, to a temperament like yours. It is a false and foolish fancy" (p. 24). For John, mental illness is the inevitable result of using one's imagination, the creation of an attractive "fancy" which the mind then fails to distinguish from reality. He fears that because of her imaginative "temperament" she will create the fiction that she is mad and come to accept it despite the evidence—color, weight, appetite—that she is well. Imagination and art are subversive because they threaten to undermine his materialistic universe.

Ironically, despite his abhorrence of faith and superstition, John fails because of his own dogmatic faith in materialism and empiricism, a faith that will not allow him even to consider the possibility that his wife's imagination could be a positive force. In a way John is like Aylmer in Hawthorne's "The Birthmark": each man chooses to interpret a characteristic of his wife as a defect because of his own failure of imagination, and each attempts to "cure" her through purely physical means, only to find he has destroyed her in the process. He also resembles the implied villain in many of Emerson's and Thoreau's lectures and essays, the man of convention who is so taken with "common sense" and traditional wisdom that he is blind to truth. Indeed, the narrator's lament that she might get well faster if John were not a doctor and her assertion that he can't understand her "because he is so wise" remind one of Thoreau's question in the first chapter of *Walden*: "How can he remember his ignorance—which his growth requires—who has so often to use his knowledge?" John's role as a doctor and an American male requires that he use his "knowledge" continuously and doggedly, and he would abhor the appearance of imagination in his own mind even more vehemently than in his wife's.

The relationship between them also offers an insight into how and why this fear of the imagination has been institutionalized through assigned gender roles. By defining his wife's artistic impulse as a potentially dangerous part of her feminine "temperament," John can control both his wife and a facet of human experience which threatens his comfortably materialistic view of the world. Fear can masquerade as calm authority when the thing feared is embodied in the "weaker sex." Quite fittingly, the story suggests that America is full of Johns: the narrator's brother is a doctor, and S. Weir Mitchell—"like John and my brother only more so!"—looms on the horizon if she doesn't recover.

As her comments suggest, the narrator understands John's problem yet is unable to call it his problem, and in many ways it is this combination of insight and naiveté, of resistance and resignation, that makes her such a memorable character and gives such power to her narrative. The story is in the form of a journal which the writer knows no one will read—she says she would not criticize John to "a living soul, of course, but this is dead paper"—yet at the same time her occasional use of "you," her questions ("What is one to do?" she asks three times in the first two pages), and her confidential tone all suggest that she is attempting to reach or create the listener she cannot otherwise find. Her remarks reveal that her relationship with her husband is filled with deception on her part, not so much because she wants to hide things from him but because it is impossible to tell him things he does not want to acknowledge. She reveals to the "dead paper" that she must pretend to sleep and have an appetite because that is what John assumes will happen as a result of his treatment, and if she tells him that she isn't sleeping or eating he will simply contradict her. Thus the journal provides an opportunity not only to confess her deceit and explain its necessity but also to say the things she really wants to say to John and would say if his insistence on "truthfulness," i.e., saying what he wants to hear, didn't prevent her. As both her greatest deception and her attempt to be honest, the journal embodies in its very form the absurd contradictions inherent in her role as wife.

At the same time, however, she cannot quite stop deceiving herself about her husband's treatment of her, and her descriptions create a powerful dramatic irony as the reader gradually puts together details the meaning of which she doesn't quite understand. She says, for instance, that there is "something strange" about the house they have rented, but her description reveals bit by bit a room that has apparently been used to confine violent mental cases, with bars on the windows, a gate at the top of the stairs, steel rings on the walls, a nailed-down bedstead, and a floor that has been scratched and gouged. When she tries to explain her feelings about the house to John early in the story, her report of the conversation reveals her tendency to assume that he is always right despite her own reservations:

> . . . there is something strange about the house—I can feel it.
>
> I even said so to John one moonlight evening, but he said what I felt was a *draught*, and shut the window.
>
> I get unreasonably angry with John sometimes. I'm sure I never used to be so sensitive. I think it is due to this nervous condition. (p. 11)

As usual, John refuses to consider anything but physical details, but the narrator's reaction is particularly revealing here. Her anger, perfectly understandable to us, must be characterized, even privately, as "unreasonable," a sign of her condition. Whatever doubts she may have about John's methods, he represents reason, and it is her own sensitivity that must be at fault. Comments such as these reveal more powerfully than any direct statement could the way she is trapped by the conception of herself which she has accepted from John and the society whose values he represents. As Paula A. Treichler has pointed out, John's diagnosis is a "sentence," a "set of linguistic signs whose representational claims are authorized by society," and thus it can "control women's fate, whether or not those claims are valid." The narrator can object to the terms of the sentence, but she cannot question its authority, even in her own private discourse.[9]

To a great extent, the narrator's view of her husband is colored by the belief that he really does love her, a belief that provides some of the most striking and complex ironies in the story. When she says, "it is hard to talk to John about my case because he is so wise, and because he loves me so," it is tempting to take the whole sentence as an example of her naiveté. Obviously he is not wise, and his actions are not what we would call loving. Nevertheless, the sentence is in its way powerfully insightful. If John were not so wise—so sure of his own empirical knowledge and his expertise as a doctor—and so loving—so determined to make her better in the only way he knows—then he might be able to set aside his fear of her imagination and listen to her. The passage suggests strikingly the way both characters are doomed to act out their respective parts of loving husband and obedient wife right to the inevitably disastrous end.

Gilman's depiction of the narrator's decline into madness has been praised for the accuracy with which it captures the symptoms of mental breakdown and for its use of symbolism.[10] What hasn't been pointed out is the masterly use of association, foreshadowing, and even humor. Once the narrator starts attempting to read the pattern of the wallpaper, the reader must become a kind of psychological detective in order to follow and appreciate the narrative. In a sense, he too is viewing a tangled pattern with a woman behind it, and he must learn to revise his interpretation of the pattern as he goes along if he is to make sense of it. For one thing, the narrator tells us from time to time about new details in the room. She notices a "smooch" on the wall "low down, near the mopboard," and later we learn that the bedstead is "fairly gnawed." It is only afterwards that we find out that she is herself the source of these new marks as she bites the bedstead and crawls around the room, shoulder to the wallpaper. If the reader has not caught on already, these details show clearly that the narrator is not always aware of her own actions or in control of her thoughts and so is not always reliable in reporting them. They also foreshadow her final separation from her wifely self, her belief that she is the woman who has escaped from behind the barred pattern of the wallpaper.

But the details also invite us to reread earlier passages, to see if the voice which we have taken to be a fairly reliable though naive reporter has not been giving us unsuspected hints of another reality all along. If we do backtrack we find foreshadowing everywhere, not only in the way the narrator reads the pattern on the wall but in the pattern of her own narrative, the way in which one thought leads to another. One striking example occurs when she describes John's sister, Jennie, who is "a dear girl and so careful of me," and who therefore must not find out about the journal.

> She is a perfect and enthusiastic housekeeper, and hopes for no better profession. I verily believe she thinks it is the writing which made me sick!
>
> But I can write when she is out, and see her a long way off from these windows.
>
> There is one that commands the road, a lovely shaded winding road, and one that just looks off over the country. A lovely country too, full of great elms and velvet meadows.
>
> This wallpaper has a kind of sub-pattern in a different shade, a particularly irritating one, for you can only see it in certain lights, and not clearly then.
>
> But in the places where it isn't faded and where the sun is just so—I can see a strange, provoking, formless sort of figure, that seems to skulk about behind that silly and conspicuous front design.
>
> There's sister on the stairs! (pp. 17–18)

The "perfect and enthusiastic housekeeper" is, of course, the ideal sister for John, whose view of the imagination she shares. Thoughts of Jennie lead to the narrator's assertion that she can "see her a long way off from these windows," foreshadowing later passages in which the narrator will see a creeping woman, and then eventually many creeping women from the same windows, and the association suggests a connection between the "enthusiastic housekeeper" and those imaginary women. The thought of the windows leads to a description of the open country and suggests the freedom that the narrator lacks in her barred room. This, in turn, leads her back to the wallpaper, and now she mentions for the first time the "sub-pattern," a pattern which will eventually become a woman creeping behind bars, a projection of her feelings about herself as she looks through the actual bars of the window. The train of associations ends when John's sister returns, but this time she's just "sister," as if now she's the narrator's sister as well, suggesting a subconscious recognition that they both share the same role, despite Jennie's apparent freedom and contentment. Taken in context, this passage prepares us to see the connection between the pattern of the wallpaper, the actual bars on the narrator's windows, and the "silly and conspicuous" surface pattern of the wifely role behind which both women lurk.

We can see just how Gilman develops the narrator's mental collapse if we compare the passage quoted above to a later one in which the narrator once again discusses the "sub-pattern," which by now has become a woman who manages to escape in the daytime.

> I think that woman gets out in the daytime!
> And I'll tell you why—privately—I've seen her!
> I can see her out of every one of my windows!
> It is the same woman, I know, for she is always creeping, and most women do not creep by daylight.
> I see her on that long road under the trees, creeping along, and when a carriage comes she hides under the blackberry vines.
> I don't blame her a bit. It must be very humiliating to be caught creeping by daylight!
> I always lock the door when I creep by daylight! (pp. 30–31)

Here again the view outside the window suggests a kind of freedom, but now it is only a freedom to creep outside the pattern, a freedom that humiliates and must be hidden. The dark humor that punctuates the last part of the story appears in the narrator's remark that she can recognize the woman because "most women do not creep by daylight," and the sense that the journal is an attempt to reach a listener becomes clear through her emphasis on "privately." Finally, the identification between the narrator and the woman is taken a step further and becomes more nearly conscious when the narrator reveals that she too creeps, but only behind a locked door. If we read the two passages in sequence, we can see just how masterfully Gilman uses her central images—the window, the barred pattern of the paper, and the woman—to create a pattern of associations which reveals the source of the narrator's malady yet allows the narrator herself to remain essentially unable to verbalize her problem. At some level, we see, she understands what has rendered her so thoroughly powerless and confused, yet she is so completely trapped in her role that she can express that knowledge only indirectly in a way that hides it from her conscious mind.

In the terribly comic ending, she has destroyed both the wallpaper and her own identity: now she is the woman from behind the barred pattern, and not even Jane—the wife she once was—can put her back. Still unable to express her feelings directly, she acts out both her triumph and her humiliation symbolically, creeping around the room with her shoulder in the "smooch," passing over her fainting husband on every lap. Loralee MacPike suggests that the narrator has finally gained her freedom,[11] but that is true only in a very limited sense. She is still creeping, still inside the room with a rope around her waist. She has destroyed only the front pattern, the "silly and conspicuous" design that covers the real wife, the creeping one hidden behind the facade. As Treichler suggests, "her triumph is to have sharpened and articulated the nature of women's condition,"[12] but she is free only from the need to deceive herself and others about the true nature of her role. In a sense, she has discovered, bit by bit, and finally revealed to John, the wife he is attempting to create—the woman without illusions or imagination who spends all her time creeping.

The story, then, is a complex work of art as well as an effective indictment of the nineteenth-century view of the sexes and the materialism that underlies that view. It is hard to believe that readers familiar with the materialistic despots created by such writers as Hawthorne, Dickens, and Browning could fail to see the implications. Indeed, though Howells' comment that the story makes him "shiver" has been offered as evidence that he saw it as a more or less conventional horror story, I would assert that he understood quite clearly the source of the story's effect. He originally wrote to Gilman to congratulate her on her poem "Women of Today," a scathing indictment of women who fear changing sexual roles and fail to realize that their view of themselves as mothers, wives, and housekeepers is a self-deception. In fact, he praises that poem in terms that anticipate his praise of the story, calling it "dreadfully true."[13] Perhaps the story was unpopular because it was, at least on some level, understood all too clearly, because it struck too deeply and effectively at traditional ways of seeing the world and woman's place in it. That, in any case, seems to be precisely what Howells implies in his comment that it is "too terribly good to be printed."

The clearest evidence that John's view of the imagination and art was all but sacred in Gilman's America comes, ironically, from the author's own pen. When she replied to Howells's request to reprint the story by saying that she did not write "literature," she was, of course, denying that she was a mere imaginative artist, defending herself from the charge that Hawthorne imagines his Puritan ancestors would lay at his doorstep: "A writer of story-books!—what mode of glorifying God, or being serviceable to mankind in his day and generation—may that be?

Why, the degenerate fellow might as well have been a fiddler!"[14] One wonders what this later female scion of good New England stock might have done had she been able to set aside such objections. In any case, one hopes that this one work of imagination and art, at least, will be restored to the place that Howells so astutely assigned it, alongside stories by contemporaries such as Mark Twain, Henry James, and Edith Wharton.

NOTES

1. Quoted in Charlotte Perkins Gilman, *The Living of Charlotte Perkins Gilman: An Autobiography* (1935; rpt. New York: Arno, 1972), p. 119.

2. *The Great Modern American Stories: An Anthology* (New York: Boni and Liveright, 1920), p. vii.

3. Afterword, *The Yellow Wallpaper* (New York: Feminist Press, 1973) p. 37.

4. "A Map for Rereading: Or, Gender and the Interpretation of Literary Texts," *New Literary History*, 11 (1980), 455–56.

5. "Convention Coverage or How to Read Your Own Life," *New Literary History*, 13 (1981), 73–74.

6. Gilman, *Living*, p. 24.

7. *The Yellow Wallpaper* (New York: Feminist Press, 1973), p. 17. Page numbers in the text refer to this edition.

8. Gilman, *Living*, p. 95.

9. "Escaping the Sentence: Diagnosis and Discourse in 'The Yellow Wallpaper,'" *Tulsa Studies in Women's Literature*, 3 (1984), 74.

10. See Beate Schöpp-Schilling, " 'The Yellow Wallpaper': A Rediscovered 'Realistic' Story," *American Literary Realism*, 8 (1975), 284–86; Loralee MacPike, "Environment as Psychopathological Symbolism in 'The Yellow Wallpaper' " *American Literary Realism*, 8 (1975), 286–88.

11. MacPike, p. 288.

12. Treichler, p. 74.

13. Quoted in Gilman, *Living*, p. 113.

14. *The Scarlet Letter* (Columbus: Ohio State Univ. Press, 1962), p. 10.

From "Reading about Reading: 'A Jury of Her Peers,' 'The Murders in the Rue Morgue,' and 'The Yellow Wallpaper'"

Judith Fetterley

In her "Afterword" to the 1973 Feminist Press Edition of Charlotte Perkins Gilman's "The Yellow Wallpaper," Elaine Hedges claims that until recently "no one seems to have made the connection between the insanity and the sex, or sexual role, of the victim." Nevertheless, it seems likely, as she also suggests, that the content of the story has provided the reason for its negative reception, outright rejection, and eventual obliteration by a male-dominated literary establishment. Though not, I would argue, as determinedly instructive as "A Jury of Her Peers," neither, I would equally propose, is "The Yellow Wallpaper" susceptible of a masculinist reading as, for example, is "The Murders in the Rue Morgue." That it has taken a generation of feminist critics to make Gilman's story a "classic" bears out the truth of Glaspell's thesis.

Gilman opens her story with language evocative of Poe: "It is very seldom that mere ordinary people like John and myself secure ancestral halls for the summer." Here we have echoes of the "scenes of mere household events" which the narrator of "The Black Cat" wishes "to place before the world, plainly, succinctly, and without comment." Poe's ancestral halls serve as image and symbol of the mind of his narrator, and they serve as analogue for the texts men write and read. These halls/texts are haunted by the ghosts of women buried alive within them, hacked to death to produce their effect, killed by and in the service of the necessities of male art: "The death, then, of a beautiful woman is, unquestionably, the most poetical topic in the world—and

253

equally is it beyond doubt that the lips best suited for such topic are those of a bereaved lover." Die, then, women must so that men may sing. If such self-knowledge ultimately drives Roderick Usher mad, nevertheless as he goes down he takes self and text and sister with him; no other voice is heard, no alternate text remains. No doubt the madness of Poe's narrators reflects that masculine anxiety mentioned earlier, the fear that solipsism, annihilation, nothingness, will be the inevitable result of habitually silencing the other. Yet apparently such anxiety is preferable to the loss of power and control which would accompany giving voice to that other.

Gilman's narrator recognizes that she is in a haunted house, despite the protestations of her John, who is far less up-front than Poe's Roderick. Writing from the point of view of a character trapped in that male text—as if the black cat or Madeline Usher should actually find words and speak—Gilman's narrator shifts the center of attention away from the male mind that has produced the text and directs it instead to the consequences for women's lives of men's control of textuality. For it is precisely at this point that "The Yellow Wallpaper" enters this discussion of the connections between gender and reading. In this text we find the analysis of why who gets to tell the story and what story one is required, allowed, or encouraged to read matter so much, and therefore why in a sexist culture the practice of reading follows the theory proposed by Glaspell. Gilman's story makes clear the connection between male control of textuality and male dominance in other areas, and in it we feel the fact of force behind what is usually passed off as a casual accident of personal preference or justified by invoking "absolute" standards of "universal" value: these are just books I happen to like and I want to share them with you; these are our great texts and you must read them if you want to be literate. As man, husband, and doctor, John controls the narrator's life. That he chooses to make such an issue out of what and how she reads tells us what we need to know about the politics of reading.

In "The Yellow Wallpaper," Gilman argues that male control of textuality constitutes one of the primary causes of women's madness in a patriarchal culture. Forced to read men's texts, women are forced to become characters in those texts. And since the stories men tell assert as fact what women know to be fiction, not only do women lose the power that comes from authoring; more significantly, they are forced to deny their own reality and to commit in effect a kind of psychic suicide. For

Gilman works out in considerable detail the position implicit in "A Jury of Her Peers"—namely, that in a sexist culture the interests of men and women are antithetical, and, thus, the stories each has to tell are not simply alternate versions of reality, they are, rather, radically incompatible. The two stories cannot coexist; if one is accepted as true, then the other must be false, and vice versa. Thus, the struggle for control of textuality is nothing less than the struggle for control over the definition of reality and hence over the definition of sanity and madness. The nameless narrator of Gilman's story has two choices. She can accept her husband's definition of reality, the prime component of which is the proposition that for her to write her own text is "madness" and for her to read his text is "sanity"; that is, she can agree to become a character in his text, accept his definition of sanity, which is madness for her, and thus commit psychic suicide, killing herself into his text to serve his interests. Or she can refuse to read his text, refuse to become a character in it, and insist on writing her own, behavior for which John will define and treat her as mad. Though Gilman herself was able to choose a third alternative, that of writing "The Yellow Wallpaper," she implicitly recognizes that her escape from this dilemma is the exception, not the rule. Though the narrator chooses the second alternative, she does as a result go literally mad and, thus, ironically fulfills the script John has written for her. Nevertheless, in the process she manages to expose the fact of John's fiction and the implications of his insistence on asserting his fiction as fact. And she does, however briefly, force him to become a character in her text.

An appropriate title for the story the narrator writes, as distinct from the story Gilman writes, could well be "John Says." Though the narrator attempts to confide to "dead" paper her alternate view of reality, she is, at least initially, careful to present John's text as well. Thoroughly subject to his control, she writes with the distinct possibility of his discovering her text and consequently escalating her punishment for refusing to accept his text—punishment that includes, among other things, solitary confinement in an attic nursery. She rightly suspects that the treason of a resisting author is more serious than that of a resisting reader; for this reason, in part, she turns the wallpaper into her primary text: what she writes on this paper can not be read by John.

Gilman, however, structures the narrator's reporting of John's text so as to expose its madness. John's definition of sanity requires that his wife neither have nor tell her own story. Presumably the narrator would be released from her prison and even allowed to write again were John sure that she would tell only "true" stories and not "fancies"; "John has cautioned me not to give way to fancy in the least. He says that with my imaginative power and habit of story-making, a nervous weakness like mine is sure to lead to all manner of excited fancies, and that I ought to use my will and good sense to check the tendency. So I try." But, of course, what John labels "fancies" are the narrator's facts: "Still I will proudly declare that there is something queer about it. Else, why should it be let so cheaply? And why have stood so long untenanted? John laughs at me, of course, but one expects that in marriage. John is practical in the extreme"; "that spoils my ghostliness, I am afraid, but I don't care—there is something strange about the house—I can feel it." John's laughter, like that of the husbands in "A Jury of Her Peers," is designed to undermine the narrator's belief in the validity of her own perceptions and to prevent her from writing them down and thus claiming them as true. Indeed, John is "practical in the extreme."

Conversely, John's facts appear rather fanciful. In John's story, he "loves" his wife and everything he does is for her benefit: "He said we came here solely on my account, that I was to have perfect rest and all the air I could get." Yet he denies her request for a room on the first floor with access to the air outside, and confines her instead to the attic, where she can neither sleep nor rest. Later, when she asks to have the attic wallpaper changed, he "took me in his arms and called me a blessed little goose, and said he would go down to the cellar, if I wished, and have it whitewashed into the bargain." Yet while he may be willing to whitewash the cellar, he won't change the attic because "I don't care to renovate the house for a three months' rental." For a three months' confinement, though, John has been willing to rearrange the furniture so as to make her prison ugly: "The furniture in this room is no worse than inharmonious, however, for we had to bring it all from downstairs." Though the narrator is under steady pressure to validate the fiction of John's concern for her—"He is very careful and loving . . . he takes all care from me, and so I feel basely ungrateful not to value it more"—she nevertheless intuits that his "love" is part of her problem: "It is so hard to talk with John about my case, because he is so wise, and because he loves me so." And, in fact, her narrative reveals John to be her enemy whose "love" will destroy her.

John's definition of sanity for the narrator, however, includes more than the requirement that she accept his fiction as fact and reject her facts as fancy. In effect, it requires nothing less than that she eliminate from herself the subjectivity capable of generating an alternate reality from his. Thus, "John says that the very worst thing I can do is think about my condition," and he designs a treatment calculated to pressure the narrator into concluding that her self not him is the enemy, and calculated also to force her to give her self up. She is denied activity, work, conversation, society, even the opportunity to observe the activity of others. She is to receive no stimulus that might lead to the development of subjectivity. Indeed, one might argue that the narrator over-interprets the wallpaper, the one stimulus in her immediate environment, as a reaction against this sensory deprivation. Nor is the narrator allowed access to her feelings: "I get unreasonably angry with John sometimes. . . . But John says if I feel so, I shall neglect proper self-control, so I take pains to control myself." By "proper self-control," John means control to the point of eliminating the self that tells a different story from his. If the narrator learns the exercise of this kind of self-control, John need no longer fear her writing.

The more the narrator "rests," the more exhausted she becomes. Her exhaustion testifies to the energy she devotes to repressing her subjectivity and to the resistance she offers to that effort. In this struggle, "dead" paper provides her with her only vital sign. It constitutes her sole link with her embattled self. Yet because she is imprisoned in John's house and text and because his text has infected her mind, she experiences anxiety, contradiction, and ambivalence in the act of writing. Forced to view her work from the perspective of his text, to see it not as *work* but "work"—the denigrating quotation marks reflecting John's point of view—she finds it increasingly difficult to put pen to paper. Blocked from expressing herself *on* paper, she seeks to express herself *through* paper. Literally, she converts the wall*paper* into her text. Initially the narrator identifies the wallpaper with her prison and reads the text as enemy. The wallpaper represents the condition she is not to think about as she is being driven into it. It is ugly, "one of those sprawling flamboyant patterns committing every artistic sin," disorderly, confusing, and full of contradictions. In struggling to organize the paper into a coherent text, the narrator establishes her artistic self and maintains her link with subjectivity and sanity. Yet the narrator at some level identifies with the wallpaper, as well. Just as she recognizes that John's definition of madness is her idea of sanity, so she recognizes in the wallpaper elements of her own resisting self. Sprawling, flamboyant, sinful, irritating, provoking, outrageous, unheard of—not only do these adjectives describe a female self intolerable to the patriarchy, they are also code words that reflect the masculinist response to the perception of female subjectivity per se. In identifying with the wallpaper and in seeing herself in it, the narrator lets herself out; increasingly, her behavior becomes flamboyant and outrageous. Getting out through the text of the wallpaper, she not surprisingly gets in to the subtext within the text that presents the story of a woman trying to get out.

Possessed by the need to impose order on the "impertinence" of row after row of unmatched breadths and to retain, thus, a sense of the self as orderly and ordering, and at the same time identifying with the monstrously disruptive self implicit in the broken necks and bulbous eyes, the narrator continues to elaborate and revise her text. Her descriptions of the wallpaper become increasingly detailed and increasingly feminine, reflecting the intuition that her disintegration derives from the "condition" of being female: "Looked at in one way each breadth stands alone, the bloated curves and flourishes—a kind of 'debased Romanesque' with *delirium tremens*—go waddling up and down in isolated columns of fatuity." Yet the "delirium tremens" of "isolated columns of fatuity" can serve as a metaphor for the patterns conventionally assigned to women's lives and for the "sanity" conventionally prescribed for women. In the "pointless pattern," the narrator senses the patriarchal point. Thus, the narrator concentrates on her subtext, "a thing nobody seems to notice but myself," on the pattern behind the pattern, the woman who wants out.

At the end of "The Yellow Wallpaper," we witness a war between texts. The patriarchal text is a formidable foe; it has an enormous capacity for maintaining itself: "there are always new shoots on the fungus"; and its influence is pervasive: "I find it hovering in the dining-room, skulking in the parlor, hiding in the hall, lying in wait for me on the stairs. It gets into my hair. . . . I thought seriously of burning the house—to reach the smell." Its repressive power is equally large: "But nobody could climb through that pattern—it strangles so." Nevertheless, the narrator is sure that her woman "gets out in the daytime." And she is prepared to help her: "I pulled and she shook, I shook and she pulled, and before morning we had peeled off yards of that paper."

Despite the narrator's final claim that she has, like the woman in the paper, "got out at last," she does not in fact escape the patriarchal text. Her choice of literal madness may be as good as or better than the "sanity" prescribed for her by John, but in going mad she fulfills his script and becomes a character in his text. Still, going mad gives the narrator temporary sanity. It enables her to articulate her perception of reality and, in particular, to cut through the fiction of John's love: "He asked me all sorts of questions, too, and pretended to be very loving and kind. As if I couldn't see through him!" It also enables her to contact her feelings, the heart of the subjectivity that John seeks to eliminate. She no longer needs to project her rage onto the imaginary children who occupied her prison before her, gouging the floor, ripping the paper, gnawing the bedstead, for she is now herself "angry enough to do something desperate." Angry, she is energized; she has gotten through to and found her work. If the effort to be sane has made her sick, her madness makes her feel "ever so much better."

This relief, however, is only temporary, for the narrator's solution finally validates John's fiction. In his text, female madness results from work that engages the mind and will; from the recognition and expression of feelings, and particularly of anger; in a word, from the existence of a subjectivity capable of generating a different version of reality from his own. And, indeed, the onset of the narrator's literal madness coincides precisely with her expression of these behaviors. More insidious still, through her madness the narrator does not simply become the character John already imagines her to be as part of his definition of feminine nature; she becomes a version of John himself. Mad, the narrator is manipulative, secretive, dishonest; she learns to lie, obscure, and distort. Further, she masters the art of sinister definition; she claims normalcy for herself, labels John "queer," and determines that he needs watching. This desire to duplicate John's text but with the roles reversed determines the narrator's choice of an ending. Wishing to drive John mad, she selects a denouement that will reduce him to a woman seized by a hysterical fainting fit. Temporary success, however, exacts an enormous price, for when John recovers from his faint, he will put her in a prison from which there will be no escape. John has now got his story, the story, embedded in a text like *Jane Eyre*, of the victimized and suffering husband with a mad wife in the attic. John will tell his story, and there will be no alternate text to expose him.

Gilman, however, has exposed John. And in analyzing how men drive women mad through the control of textuality, Gilman has escaped the fate of her narrator and created a text that can help the woman reader to effect a similar escape. The struggle recorded in the text has its analogue in the struggle around and about the text, for nothing less than our sanity and survival is at stake in the issue of what we read.

NOTE

In conceptualizing this essay, I have been enormously helped by the work of Annette Kolodny, in particular her "A Map for Rereading: Or, Gender and the Interpretation of Literary Texts" (*New Literary History* 11 [1980]: 451–67), and of Jean E. Kennard in "Convention Coverage, or How to Read Your Own Life" (*New Literary History* 8 [1981]: 69–88). In writing, revising, and rewriting, I owe a large debt to the following readers and writers: Judith Barlow, Susan Kress, Margorie Pryse, Joan Schulz, Patsy Schweickart.

Monumental Feminism and Literature's Ancestral House: Another Look at "The Yellow Wallpaper"

Janice Haney-Peritz

In 1973, The Feminist Press brought forth a single volume edition of Charlotte Perkins Gilman's "The Yellow Wallpaper," a short story which had originally appeared in the May 1892 issue of *New England Magazine*. Since William Dean Howells included Gilman's story in his 1920 collection of *Great Modern American Stories*, it can not be said that between 1892 and 1973 "The Yellow Wallpaper" was completely ignored. What can be said, however, is that until 1973, the story's feminist thrust had gone unremarked; even Howells, who was well aware not only of Gilman's involvement in the women's movement but also of her preference for writing "with a purpose," had nothing to say about the provocative feminism of Gilman's text.[1] In the introduction to his 1920 collection, Howells notes the story's chilling horror and then falls silent.[2]

Although brief, Howells's response does place him in a long line of male readers, a line that includes the following: M.D., the anonymous doctor who in an 1892 letter to the Boston *Transcript* complained about the story's morbidity and called for its censure; Horace Scudder, the editor of *The Atlantic Monthly* who in a letter to Gilman claimed to have been made so miserable by the story that he had no other choice than to reject it for publication; Walter Stetson, Gilman's first husband who informed her that he found the story utterly ghastly, more horrifying than even Poe's tales of terror;[3] John, the physician-husband of "The Yellow Wallpaper's" narrator who in coming face to face with his mad wife is so astonished that he faints; and last but not least, Milton's

261

Adam, the 'first' man who is represented as being both chilled and horrified by a woman's story-telling:

Thus *Eve* with Count'nance blithe her story told;
But in her Cheek distemper flushing glow'd.
On th'other side, *Adam*, soon as he heard
The fatal Trespass done by *Eve*, amaz'd,
Astonied stood and Blank, while horror chill
Ran through his veins, and all his joints relax'd.[4]

It is this male line of response that the 1973 edition of "The Yellow Wallpaper" seeks to disrupt and displace, implicitly by affixing to the text the imprint of The Feminist Press and explicitly by appending to the text an afterword in which Elaine Hedges reads the story as a "feminist document," as "one of the rare pieces of literature we have by a nineteenth-century woman which directly confronts the sexual politics of the male-female, husband-wife relationship."[5] So effective has this disruption and displacement been that it is not much of an exaggeration to say that during the last ten years, Gilman's short story has assumed monumental proportions, serving at one and the same time the purposes of a memorial and a boundary marker. As a memorial, "The Yellow Wallpaper" is used to remind contemporary readers of the enduring import of the feminist struggle against patriarchical domination; while as a boundary marker, it is used to demarcate the territory appropriate to a feminist literary criticism.[6] Although I am interested in pointing out some of the more troubling implications of a literary criticism in which Gilman's story functions as a feminist monument, before doing so, it is necessary to take another look at "The Yellow Wallpaper" itself.

From beginning to end, "The Yellow Wallpaper" presents itself as the writing of a woman who along with her physician-husband John and her sister-in-law Jennie is spending the summer in what she calls an "ancestral hall," a home away from home which has been secured in the hope that it will prove beneficial to the narrator's health and well-being. In ten diary-like entries that span her three month stay in this ancestral hall, the narrator not only recounts her interactions with John and Jennie but also describes in detail the yellow wallpaper that covers the walls of a large upstairs room, a room which at one time seems to have been a nursery and, at another, a gymnasium; this summer, however, it has become the master bedroom, a place where the narrator spends much of her time, drawn in, it seems, by the very yellow wallpaper which so repels her.

However, before her attention becomes focused on the wallpaper, the narrator attempts to grasp her situation by naming the kind of place in which she finds herself as well as the kind of place she would like it to be. In the opening lines of her text, she refers to the place as both a "colonial mansion" and an "hereditary estate"; however what she would like to believe is that the place is really a "haunted house."[7] According to the narrator, a haunted house would be "the height of romantic felicity," a place more promising that that which "fate" normally assigns to "mere ordinary people like John and [herself]" (p. 9). Since haunted houses are a peculiarly literary kind of architecture, the narrator's desire for such a place may be associated not only with her desire for writing but also with her interest in the wallpaper; in all cases, what is at issue is the displacement of a colonial inheritance that fate seems to have decreed as her lot.

But even though a haunted house may be desired, the possibility of realizing that desire is seriously in doubt. Not only does John find his wife's desire laughable but in the beginning, the narrator also demurs, afraid that at this point, she is demanding too much too soon of either fate or John. As the narrator sees it, the problem is that John scoffs at "talk of things not to be felt and seen and put down in figures" (p. 9). To John, the narrator's haunted house is nothing; however, so too is her feeling that she is not well. Nevertheless, at the same time that he assures his wife that there is really nothing the matter with her, John also prescribes a regimen which will help her get well; she is not to think about haunted houses or her condition; nor, given her habit of fanciful story-making, is she to write. Instead, she is to eat well, exercise in moderation, and rest as much as she can in the airy upstairs room, the master bedroom.

Ironically, it is precisely because the narrator is patient enough to follow some of the doctor's orders that she finds it necessary to deal with the yellow wallpaper which covers the walls of the master bedroom. At first glance, that wallpaper appears to be nothing more than an error in taste—"one of those sprawling, flamboyant patterns committing every artistic sin" (p. 13); at second glance, however, more troubling possibilities emerge, for as the narrator notes, the wallpaper's pattern "is dull enough to confuse the eye in following, *pronounced* enough to constantly irritate and provoke study, and when you follow the lame uncertain curves for a little distance they suddenly commit suicide—plunge off at outrageous angles, destroy themselves in *unheard of contradictions*" (p. 13, emphasis added). Although commentators have seen in this description of the wallpaper a general representation of "the oppressive structures of the society in which [the narrator] finds herself" (*Madwoman*, p. 90), the word "pronounced" as well as the phrase "unheard of contradictions" suggest that the specific oppressive structure at issue is discourse. Furthermore, since we have just been treated to an account of John's discourse on his wife's condition, a discourse based on the unspoken and therefore "unheard of contradiction" that somehow she is both well and ill, we may want to be even more specific and say that the oppressive structure at issue is a man's prescriptive discourse about a woman.

However, as it is described by the narrator, the yellow wallpaper also resembles the text we are reading—that is, it resembles the narrator's own writing. In part, this resemblance can be attributed to the fact that the narrator's writing not only recounts John's prescriptive discourse but also relies on the very binary oppositions which structure that discourse—oppositions like sick and well, the real and the fanciful, order and anarchy, self and other, male and female. Thus, it is not surprising to find that the narrator's reflections produce a text in which one line of thinking after another "suddenly commits suicide—plung[ing] off at outrageous angles, [and] destroy[ing itself] in unheard of contradictions." For example, although the narrator claims that writing would do her good, she also says that it tires her out (p. 21). Worse yet, at the very moment that she is writing, she expresses a wish that she were well enough to write (p. 16). Such contradictions not only betray the narrator's dependence on the oppressive discursive structure we associate with John but also help us to understand why she jumps from one thing to another, producing paragraphs that are usually no more than a few lines in length. Since a discursive line of reasoning based on binary oppositions like sick and well is bound to "destroy" itself in "unheard-of contradictions",[8] one way the narrator can continue to produce a text that has some pretence to being reasonable is quickly to change the subject, say from her condition to the house or from the wallpaper to John.

If the resemblance between the narrator's writing and John's discourse is disturbing—so much so that it often goes unremarked—it may be because what we want of a woman's writing is something different, a realization of that *écriture féminine* which figures so significantly in many contemporary attempts to specify what makes a woman's writing distinctive.[9] However, if we repress this resemblance, we may forget to pose what Luce Irigaray calls "the first question": that is, "how can women analyze their exploitation, [and] inscribe their claims, within an order prescribed by the masculine?" Having posed this first question, Irigaray suggests that one answer might be for a woman "to play with mimesis," to deliberately "resubmit herself to 'ideas', notably about her, elaborated in/by a masculine logic." Although such miming runs the risk of reproducing a discursive system in which woman as Other is repressed, according to Irigaray, it may also have the uncanny effect of making " 'visible' . . . what should have remained hidden: the recovery of a possible operation of the feminine in language."[10]

In "The Yellow Wallpaper," the narrator's labor of miming does seem to produce just some such uncanny effect, for not only does her writing expose the "unheard of contradictions" in a man's prescriptive logic but in dealing with those contradictory impasses by jumping from one thing to another, it also makes the reader aware of gaps in that discursive structure. Furthermore, since the narrator occasionally notes what she might have said but didn't, those gaps can also be read as "unheard of contradictions"; that is, they can be read as the places where the narrator might have contradicted John's prescriptions, if only the woman had a voice to do so. Lacking such a voice, the narrator partially recoups her loss in a writing that is punctuated by the "unsaid," by what remains muted in a discourse which at this point seems to be what matters most.

To the extent that the narrator's writing does indeed display discourse to be what is really the matter, then we can not presume that the text's "hereditary estate" is built on or out of the bedrock of a real anatomical difference between the sexes. However, if the ancestral hall is not to be considered a real "hereditary estate," neither is it to be considered a real "colonial mansion," a place defined by the non-discursive social relations between masters and slaves. Instead the ancestral house must be thought of as in and of what Lacan has called the symbolic order, the order of Language.[11] By committing herself to a writing about discourse and by focusing her attention on the yellow wallpaper as a discursive structure, the narrator has turned what seemed to be a real hereditary and colonial estate into an uncanny place in which no-body is or can be at home—no matter what s/he might say to the contrary.

If "The Yellow Wallpaper" ended at this point, we might consider it a Poesque text, for as Joseph Riddel has convincingly argued, what Poe introduces into American literature is the theme of "de-constructed architecture," a theme which later American writers obsessively repeat.[12] By locating man's ancestral house within the symbolic order, Poe produces a writing that disrupts all non-textual origins which might once have made the house of man seem sufficient to have stood its ground. "The Yellow Wallpaper," however, does not end at this point—the point of deconstructed architecture—for in the text's crucial third section, the narrator discerns something "like a woman stooping down and creeping about behind [the wallpaper's] pattern" (p. 22) and with this vision, the register of the narrator's reading and writing begins to shift from the symbolic to the imaginary.

The possibility of such a shift was foreshadowed in the text's second movement wherein the narrator counterpointed her description of Jennie as the perfect housekeeper with a remark that the wallpaper had some kind of sub-pattern—a "formless sort of figure that seems to skulk about behind that silly and conspicuous front design" (p. 18). However, at this point no explicit splitting of the subject occurred, for the narrator still appeared to be both willing and able to comprehend this nascent imaginary figure within the symbolic order. Instead of apprehending the formless figure as a really different body, the narrator merely noted that from one perspective, the paper's design seemed to be composed of "bloated curves and flourishes . . . [which] go waddling up and down in isolated columns of fatuity" (p. 20).

By the end of the third movement, however, the imaginary does emerge as a distinctly different way of seeing and an explicit splitting of the subject does indeed take place. This crisis of sorts seems to be precipitated by a failure of intercourse; first, there is the narrator's unsuccessful attempt to have a "real earnest reasonable talk" with John; then, there is a prohibition—John's refusal to countenance his wife's proposed visit to Henry and Julia; and finally, there is a breakdown in the master bedroom itself as John reads to his wife until her head tires. The scene is now set for the emergence of something different; as the moonlight creeps into the darkened bedroom, something "*like* a woman" is seen "creeping about" behind the wallpaper's outer pattern. Although this vision initiates the shift in register from the symbolic to the imaginary, the explicit splitting of the subject only takes place after the awakened John resolutely dismisses his wife's apprehensions by reminding her that as a doctor, he is the one who really knows. From this point on, the narrator sees things otherwise; now the wallpaper's "outside pattern" is perceived to be bars, while its sub-pattern is perceived to *be* a woman rather than something "*like* a woman" (p. 26).

With the emergence of the imaginary over the symbolic, the narrator's writing takes a different tack than that of a Poe text in which a haunted house is revealed to be nothing more nor less mysterious than a house of fiction. Unable to rest secure in the no-place of such a deconstructed architecture, the narrator of "The Yellow Wallpaper" turns a symbolic house into the haunted house she initially feared might be too much to demand of fate. But even though this haunted house may seem to promise "the height of romantic felicity"—that is, the realization of a self—we should not forget that it is located within and constituted by what Lacan calls the Imaginary.[13]

In Lacanian psychoanalysis, the Imaginary is specified not only by its assimilation to a dual relation between on the one hand, a subject and an image and on the other, a subject and an other but also by the absence or repression of a symbolic mediation between the subject and its doubles. Without mediation, a subject has no access to the symbolic dimension of his or her experience and is therefore driven to establish the imaginary in the real. As a result of this realization, a complicated interplay between the eroticism and aggression characteristic of unmediated dual relations surfaces, as does a child-like transitivism.

In "The Yellow Wallpaper," the emergence of the imaginary as well as its assimilation to an unmediated dual relation first produces a clarity of perception and purpose which temporarily obscures the transitivism the story's ending exposes. As the shadow-woman becomes as "plain as can be," the narrator finds that it is possible to distinguish clearly day from night, sleep from waking, and most importantly, "me" from them. Now the woman who had earlier wondered what one was to do when caught in a contradictory situation (p. 10) knows exactly what she must do: she must free the shadow-woman from the paper-pattern that bars her full self-realization and through identification, bind that woman to herself. However, since this process of identification necessitates the alienation of the subject by and in an image, it engenders not only an implicitly ambivalent relation between the narrator and her imaginary double but also an explicit rivalry between the narrator and John. Perceiving John to be her other, the narrator acts as though she could only win a place for herself at his expense; hence, when she undertakes the realization of her imaginary double, she does so with the express intention of "astonish[ing]" John (p. 34). Apparently, the narrator wants to amaze John as Eve did Adam and as the Medusa did many a man.

If at one level this desire seems aggressive, then at another it appears erotic, for what is involved is a transitivism in which it is unclear exactly who is doing what to whom. Indeed, if it can be said that by becoming another woman, the narrator realizes herself in spite of John, then it can also be said that the self she realizes is not "her" self but a self engendered by John's demands and desires. On the one hand, the narrator seems to have become the child John has always demanded she be, for like a child, she crawls around the perimeter of the master bedroom, bound by an umbilical cord that keeps her firmly in place. On the other hand, however, the narrator's identification with the wallpaper's shadow-woman seems to have turned her into the woman of John's dreams, for not only did the shadow woman first appear while John was sleeping, but the narrator also suspects that when all is said and done, she is what John really desires, the secret he would reveal if he were given the opportunity to do so.

In the final words of "The Yellow Wallpaper," the narrator describes how she must crawl over John's astonished body. Like the transitivism of the narrator's 'self-realization,' this closing image displays a conjunction of erotic and aggressive impulses, a conjunction which once again suggests that by identifying herself with the wallpaper's shadow-woman, the narrator has firmly installed herself in the realm of the imaginary, the realm of haunted houses.

Although the text of "The Yellow Wallpaper" ends at this point, the story does not, for it has been repeated by a number of important feminist critics who have seen in "The Yellow Wallpaper" not only an accurate representation of the situation of woman in patriarchical culture but also a model for their own reading and writing practices. While Elaine Hedges can be said to have begun this repetition in her influential afterword to The Feminist Press's edition of the text, it is Sandra Gilbert and Susan Gubar who turn repetition into monumentalism. In their magesterial work, The Madwoman in the Attic, Gilbert and Gubar not only repeat the story but also present it as a paradigm, as "the story that all literary women would tell if they could speak their 'speechless woe'" (p. 89). According to Gilbert and Gubar, that woe begins when like the narrator of "The Yellow Wallpaper," a woman writer senses her "parallel confinements" in patriarchical texts, paternal houses, and maternal bodies (p. 89); and, it ends when like the narrator of "The

Yellow Wallpaper," the woman writer "escape[s] from her textual/ architectural confinement" (p. 91). The way to this end, however, is fraught with difficulty for like the narrator of "The Yellow Wallpaper," the woman writer must engage in a revisionary reading of the hand-writing on the wall; only then will she discover her double, the other woman whose passion for escape demands recognition. By identifying with this other woman, the writer effects her liberation from disease into health and thereby finds that she has entered a new space, "the open space of [her] own authority" (p. 91).

Although my reading of "The Yellow Wallpaper" makes me doubt that an imaginary revision and identification can indeed free women from either textual or architectural confinement, at this point I am less interested in questioning the specifics of Gilbert and Gubar's interpretation and more interested in pointing out some of the side-effects such a monumental reading may have on feminist literary criticism. These side effects are particularly evident in two recently published essays that attempt to delineate the nature and function of contemporary Anglo-American feminist literary criticism.

In her 1980 essay entitled "A Map for Rereading: Or, Gender and the Interpretation of Literary Texts," Annette Kolodny continues the story of "The Yellow Wallpaper" more or less along the feminist lines set down by Hedges, Gilbert and Gubar. However, since Kolodny is interested in explaining why this feminist story was not recognized as such in its own time, her essay can also help us towards an understanding of what is involved when "The Yellow Wallpaper" is turned into a feminist monument. According to Kolodny, "The Yellow Wallpaper" was unreadable in its own time because neither men nor women readers had access to a tradition or shared context which would have made the "female meaning" of the text clear. Men readers may have been familiar with Poe but Poe would not have prepared them for a woman narrator whose problems are socio-cultural rather than idiosyncratic. On the other hand, women readers may have been familiar with domestic fiction but such fiction would not have prepared them for a narrator whose home life is psychologically disturbing. Although Kolodny contends that Gilman uses the breakdown in communication between the narrator and John to prefigure her story's unreadability, she also declares this unreadability to be historically contingent. Nowadays, it seems, we have the wherewithal to read the story "correctly," for nowadays we have the shared context, if not the tradition we need to identify what she calls the story's "female meaning."

In an attempt to be more precise about how we know what we now know about female meaning, Jean Kennard takes up the story of "The Yellow Wallpaper" once again in her 1981 essay entitled "Convention Coverage or How to Read Your Own Life." Linking the feminism of the 1970s and 1980s with a massive reversal of both literary and non-literary conventions, Kennard claims that a new and explicitly feminist set of interpretive conventions has made it possible to agree on the following ideas: that the oppressive use of power by a male is an instance of patriarchy; that a patriarchical culture's socialization of women makes them ill; that a woman's discomfort in ancestral halls indicates a healthy desire for a room of her own; and that both a revisionary reading of texts and a descent into madness are creditable ways for a woman to find and therefore free herself. Although Kennard shows how all these ideas engender a reading of "The Yellow Wallpaper" as the story of woman's quest for identity within an oppressive patriarchical culture, what I find particularly valuable about her essay is its explicit linking of a certain kind of feminism, a certain kind of feminist literary criticism, and a certain reading of "The Yellow Wallpaper."

But what, we might wonder, accounts for this linking? Here too Kennard may be of assistance, for to some extent she realizes that even before new conventions can be used to engender this feminist reading of "The Yellow Wallpaper," the contemporary critic must recognize and accept the narrator as a double with whom she can identify. However, in so doing, the contemporary critic can be said to repeat the move the narrator of "The Yellow Wallpaper" makes when she discovers and identifies herself with an imaginary woman, the woman behind the wallpaper's pattern. As I see it, this repetition accounts for a number of similarities between the narrator's imaginary mode of conceiving and representing her situation and the seemingly 'new' conventions that support a certain kind of modern feminist literary criticism which might also be called imaginary. Like the narrator of "The Yellow Wallpaper," some contemporary feminist critics see in literature a really distinctive body which they seek to liberate through identification. Although this body goes by many names, including the woman's story, female meaning, *écriture féminine*, and the maternal subtext, it is usually presented as essential to a viable feminist literary criticism and celebrated as something so distinctive that it shakes, if it does not destroy, the very foundations of patriarchical literature's ancestral house.[14]

However, if it is at all accurate to say that in repeating the story of "The Yellow Wallpaper," this kind of modern feminist criticism displays itself as imaginary, then it seems to me that it behooves us to be more skeptical about what appears to be "the height of romantic felicity."[15] Although inspiring, imaginary feminism is locked into a rivalry with an other, a rivalry that is both erotic and aggressive. As I see it, the transitivism of this dual relation belies not only claims to having identified the woman's story or female meaning but perhaps more importantly, assurances that identification is liberating. Just as we can't be sure who engenders the shadow-woman of "The Yellow Wallpaper," neither can we be sure that the story we're reading is the woman's story; indeed, it may be the case that in reading "The Yellow Wallpaper," we are reading the story of John's demands and desires rather than something distinctively female. If so, then the assurance that identification is liberating becomes highly problematic, for it too appears to be an assurance generated and sanctioned by the very ancestral structure that feminists have found so confining.[16]

In "The Yellow Wallpaper," the narrator does not move out into open country; instead, she turns an ancestral hall into a haunted house and then encrypts herself therein as a fantasy figure.[17] If we wish to consider the result of this turn to be a feminist monument, then perhaps it would be better to read such a monument as a *memento mori* that signifies the death of (a) woman rather than as a memorial that encloses the body essential to a viable feminist literary criticism. Unlike a memorial, a *memento mori* would provoke sympathy rather than identification and in so doing, would encourage us to apprehend the turn to the imaginary not as a model of liberation but as a sign of what may happen when a possible operation of the feminine in *language* is repressed.

If such an apprehension seems an uninspiring alternative for those of us committed to feminism, then I suggest that we look to Gilman rather than to the narrator of "The Yellow Wallpaper" for the inspiration we seek. By representing the narrator as in some sense mad, Gilman can be said to have preferred sympathy to identification, a preference which becomes all the more significant once we recall that much of "The Yellow Wallpaper" is based on Gilman's personal experience. However, Gilman did more than sympathize, for as Dolores Hayden has documented, she also involved herself in efforts to change the material conditions of social existence through the construction of kitchenless houses and feminist apartment hotels – new architectural spaces in which alternative social and discursive relations might emerge.[18] Although those of us interested in literature may find Gilman's concern for the material conditions of social life a troubling defection,[19] it is also quite possible to consider that concern a thoughtful deferral based on a recognition that the prevailing social structure made it idealistic, if not dangerously presumptuous to lay claim to having identified either the woman's story or female meaning. Indeed, it may just be that what Gilman learned in writing and reading "The Yellow Wallpaper" was that as yet, a woman could only *imagine* that she had found herself, for until the material conditions of social life were radically changed, there would be no 'real' way out of mankind's ancestral mansion of many apartments.

NOTES

1. When Howells requested permission to include "The Yellow Wallpaper" in his collection, Gilman responded that the story "was no more 'literature' than [her] other stuff, being definitely written with a purpose." See *The Living of Charlotte Perkins Gilman: An Autobiography* (New York: D. Appleton-Century Company, 1935), p. 121. For evidence of Howells's familiarity with Gilman's interest in the 'woman question,' see p. 113.

2. William Dean Howells, ed. *The Great Modern American Stories* (New York: Boni & Liveright, 1920), p. vii.

3. For the letters by M.D. and Horace Scudder, see *The Living of Charlotte Perkins Gilman*, cited above, pp. 119–120. For Gilman's account of Walter Stetson's response, see Mary A. Hill, *Charlotte Perkins Gilman: The Making of a Radical Feminist 1860–1896* (Philadelphia: Temple University Press, 1980), p. 186.

4. John Milton, *Paradise Lost*, ed. Merrit Y. Hughes (Indianapolis: Odyssey Press, 1962), p. 226. To my knowledge, no critic has yet noted in print the connection between *Paradise Lost* and the ending of "The Yellow Wallpaper." That connection rests not only on John's response to his 'mad' wife but also on the narrator's statement to John that the "key" to the room is to be found in the garden under a "plantain leaf." In *Paradise Lost*, Eve tells Adam that she first "espi'd" him, "fair indeed and tall/Under a Plantan" (Book IV, 11.477–8). Although a plantain leaf is not exactly the same as a Plantan or plane tree, there is a sound resemblance between the two words as well as an etymological connection by way of *plátano, plátano*, the Spanish words for plane tree. Since I am interested in other matters, I do not deal at length with the connection

between "The Yellow Wallpaper" and *Paradise Lost*, nevertheless, I trust that the reader will keep the connection in mind, for it does have a bearing on both my interpretation of the story and my response to critics who read the story as a feminist monument.

5. Elaine Hedges, "Afterword" to Charlotte Perkins Gilman's *The Yellow Wallpaper* (New York: The Feminist Press, 1973), p. 39.

6. Although much of this monumentalizing occurs within classes devoted to women's studies or women's literature, at least three influential publications treat the story as both a memorial and a boundary marker: Sandra Gilbert and Susan Gubar, *The Madwoman in the Attic: The Woman Writer and the Nineteenth-Century Literary Imagination* (New Haven: Yale University Press, 1979), pp. 89–92; Annette Kolodny, "A Map for Rereading: Or, Gender and the Interpretation of Literary Texts," *NLH*, 11 (1980), 451–467; and Jean Kennard, "Convention Coverage or How to Read Your Own Life," *NLH* 13 (1981), 69–88. Hereafter, Gilbert and Gubar's book will be cited as *Madwoman*.

7. Charlotte Perkins Gilman, *The Yellow Wallpaper* (New York: The Feminist Press, 1973), p. 9. Subsequent references to "The Yellow Wallpaper" will be to this edition.

8. For a more theoretical explanation of why and how a discourse based on binary oppositions is bound to destroy itself in unheard of contradictions, see the work of Jacques Derrida, especially *Of Grammatology*, trans. Gayatri Spivak (Baltimore: Johns Hopkins University Press, 1976).

9. The term *écriture féminine* names the desired or hypothetical specificity of woman's writing; as a concept, it underwrites the work of certain French feminists, most importantly Helene Cixous's "The Laugh of the Medusa," trans. Ketih and Paula Cohen, *Signs* 1 (1976), 875–893 and Luce Irigaray's *Ce sexe qui n' en est pas un* (Paris: Minuit, 1977). Portions of Irigaray's text have been translated and printed in *New French Feminisms*, ed. Elaine Marks and Isabelle de Courtivron (Amherst: University of Massachusetts Press, 1980). In both France and America, the concept of *écriture féminine* has occasioned much debate; for a French questioning of the appeal to *écriture féminine*, see "Variations sur des themes communs" in *Questions feministes*, 1 (1977), translated by Yvonne Rochette-Ozzello as "Variations on Common Themes" in *New French Feminisms*, pp. 212–230; for Anglo-American responses to the postulate of *écriture féminine*, see the following: Ann Rosalind Jones, "Writing the Body: Toward an Understanding of L'Ecriture Feminine," *Feminist Studies*, 7 (1981), 247–263; Helene Vivienne Wenzel, "The Text as Body/Politics: An Appreciation of Monique Wittig's Writings in Context," *Feminist Studies*, 7 (1981), 264–287; Carolyn Burke, "Irigaray Through the Looking Glass," *Feminist Studies*, 7 (1981), 288–306; Elaine Showalter, "Feminist Criticism in the Wilderness," in *Writing and Sexual Difference*, ed. Elizabeth Abel (Chicago: University of Chicago Press, 1982), pp. 9–35; Mary Jacobus, "The Question of Language:

Men of Maxims and *The Mill on the Floss*," in *Writing and Sexual Difference*, pp. 37–52; and *The Future of Difference*, ed. Hester Eisenstein and Alice Jardine (Boston: G.J. Hall & Co., 1980). As this essay indicates, I am both sympathetic to the utopian political impulse that underwrites appeals to *écriture féminine* and wary of various and sundry claims to having produced or identified a demonstrably feminine writing. Like Mary Jacobus, I think such claims too often "founder on the rock of essentialism (the text as boy) [or] gesture towards an avant-garde practice which turns out not to be specific to women;" see Jacobus's essay cited above, p. 37.

10. Luce Irigaray, *Ce sexe qui n' en est pas un*, p. 78 and p. 74 respectively; I am using Mary Jacobus's translation of these passages in her essay "The Question of Language: Men and Maxims and *The Mill on the Floss*," p. 37 and p. 40 respectively.

11. Although the significance of the Symbolic order is best apprehended in terms of its relationship to what Lacan calls the Imaginary and the Real, it is possible to describe the Symbolic as if it were a determinate space in which the relations between subject and sign as well as subject and other are mediated by the law of the signifier or the structure of Language. This triadic relation in which the subject is alienated in and by the symbolic mediations of language rests on a necessary separation of the paternal role from the biological father, a separation effected by the subject's awakening not only to the "Name-of-the-Father" but also to the general naming function of language. It is this separation which allows me to claim that discourse is a structure in which no-body is or can be at-home; by (dis)placing the subject in a chain of signifiers, the symbolic institutes a double disruption between on the one hand, biological need and articulate demand and on the other, articulate demand and unconscious desire. For a more detailed exposition of the Symbolic order, see the following texts: Jacques Lacan, *The Language of the Self*, translated by Anthony Wilden (New York: Dell Publishing Co., 1968); Jacques Lacan *Ecrits* (Paris: Editions du Sueil, 1966); Jacques Lacan, *Ecrits: A Selection*, translated by Alan Sheridan (New York: W.W. Norton, 1982); Jacques Lacan, *The Four Fundamental Concepts of Psycho-analysis*, ed. Jacques-Alain Miller, trans. by Alan Sheridan (New York: W.W. Norton, 1978); Anika Lemaire, *Jacques Lacan*, translated by David Macey (London: Routledge & Kegan Paul, 1977); Samuel Ysseling, "Structuralism and Psychoanalysis in the Work of Jacques Lacan," *International Philosophical Quarterly*, 10 (1970), 102–117; Martin Thom, "The Unconscious structured like a language" in *Economy and Society*, 5 (1976), 435–469; Frederic Jameson, "Imaginary and Symbolic in Lacan: Marxism, Psychoanalytic Criticism, and the Problem of the Subject," *YFS*, 55–56 (1977), 338–395; Richard Wolheim, "The Cabinet of Dr. Lacan," *NYRB*, 25 (Jan., 1979), 36–45; Juliet Mitchell, *Psychoanalysis and Feminism* (New York: Random House, 1975), pp. 382–398; Jane Gallop, *The Daughter's Seduction: Feminism and Psychoanalysis* (Ithaca: Cornell University

Press, 1982), pp. 1–55; and Juliet Mitchell and Jacqueline Rose, eds. *Feminine Sexuality: Jacques Lacan and the Ecole Freudienne*, trans. Jacqueline Rose (New York: W.W. Norton, 1982).

12. Joseph Riddel, "The Crypt of Edgar Poe" *Boundary 2*, 7 (1979) 117–144; the reference to 'de-constructed architecture' appears on p. 125.

13. Although the significance of the Imaginary is best apprehended in terms of its relationship to what Lacan calls the Symbolic and the Real, it is possible to describe the Imaginary as if it were a specific kind of psychic space wherein bodies or forms are related to one another by means of such basic oppositions as inside-outside and container/contained. Developmentally speaking, the Imaginary originates in what Lacan calls the "mirror stage," that period between six and eighteen months during which the infant becomes aware of its image in the mirror, thereby fixing the self in a line of fiction, a line of imaginary doubles. Although this doubling is the precondition of primary narcissism, it is also the source of human aggression, for in both cases there is a transitivistic substitution of images, an indifferentiation of subject and object which leads the child who hits to imagine that s/he is being hit. For more on the Imaginary, see the works cited in note 11.

14. For the appeal to "the woman's story," see Gilbert and Gubar, *Madwoman*; for the appeal to "female meaning," see not only Annette Kolodny's "A Map for Rereading: Or, Gender and the Interpretation of Literary Texts" but also her more controversial essay, "Dancing Through the Minefield: Some Observations on the Theory, Practice and Politics of a Feminist Literary Criticism," *Feminist Studies*, 6 (1980), 1–25; for the appeal to *écriture féminine* as a body, see Helene Cixous's "The Laugh of the Medusa;" for the appeal to a maternal subtext, see Judith Kegan Gardiner's "On Female Identity and Writing by Women," in *Writing and Sexual Difference*, ed. Elizabeth Abel (Chicago: University of Chicago Press, 1982), pp. 177–191. In "Feminist Criticism in the Wilderness," Elaine Showalter distinguishes between feminist critics who appeal to the difference of the woman's body and feminist critics who appeal to the difference of a woman's language, psychology, or culture; in practice, however, much feminist criticism belies the theoretical distinction Showalter makes, for the identification of a woman's language, psychology, or culture is often presented as though it were the discovery of a distinctly feminine body, even though that body may now be defined structurally rather than biologically.

15. Since the imaginary is associated with pre-oedipal relations with the mother, the thrust of Lacanian psychoanalysis is to value the symbolic over the imaginary. Like many other feminists, I do not accept wholeheartedly this value judgment; however, I also do not believe that a simple reversal wherein the imaginary is valued over the symbolic suffices. Thus, I ask for skepticism rather than either denigration or celebration of the imaginary. For a more detailed exploration of the claims of the imaginary and the symbolic as well as an

account of Julia Kristeva's attempt to effect a semiotic displacement of the Lacanian Imaginary, see Jane Gallop's *The Daughter's Seduction: Feminism and Psychoanalysis*.

16. Although 'identity' is often considered to be one of the key benefits of the women's liberation movement, it seems to me that the relationship between identity and liberation is much more problematic than we sometimes care to admit. To the extent that identity means being at-one with oneself, then it necessitates the repression of a difference within, a repression which Jacques Derrida sees as characteristic of the phallologocentric discourse of the West. However, even though I am not willing to equate identity with liberation, neither am I willing to claim that it is either possible or desirable to forgo identity; again, I ask only for a more skeptical approach to the issue of identity, an approach that refuses to accept wholeheartedly the notion that identity is liberating.

17. For a meditation on crypts and encrypting, especially as they relate to the psychoanalytic processes of introjection and incorporation, see Jacques Derrida's "Fors," translated by Barbara Johnson in *The Georgia Review*, 31 (1977), 64–116.

18. Dolores Hayden, *The Grand Domestic Revolution: A History of Feminist Designs for American Homes, Neighborhoods, and Cities* (Cambridge: MIT Press, 1981), pp. 182–277.

19. Some such discomfort may account for Gilbert and Gubar's defensive insistence that "we can be sure that Gilman . . . knew that the cure for female despair must be spiritual as well as physical, aesthetic as well as social" (*Madwoman*, p. 92).

An Unnecessary Maze of Sign-Reading

Mary Jacobus

"I may here be giving an impression of laying too much emphasis on the details of the symptoms and of becoming lost in an unnecessary maze of sign-reading. But I have come to learn that the determination of hysterical symptoms does in fact extend to their subtlest manifestations and that it is difficult to attribute too much sense to them" (SE 2:93n.).*

Freud's footnote to *Studies on Hysteria* amounts to saying that where hysteria is concerned it is impossible to overread. The maze of signs, his metaphor for the hysterical text, invokes not only labyrinthine intricacy but the risk of self-loss. What would it be like to become lost in the subtleties of sign reading? Charlotte Perkins Gilman's short story, "The Yellow Wallpaper," provides an answer of sorts. It would be like finding one's own figure replicated everywhere in the text; like going mad. This tale of hysterical confinement—a fictionalized account of Gilman's own breakdown in 1887 and the treatment she underwent at the hands of Freud's and Breuer's American contemporary, Weir Mitchell—could almost be read as Anna O.'s own version of "Fräulein Anna O." The

---

*Ed.: abbreviated references are to Sigmund Freud's *Studies on Hysteria*, vol. 2 of *The Standard Edition of the Complete Psychological Works of Sigmund Freud*, ed. James Strachey (London: Hogarth, 1955).

flower of fiction reproduces herself, hysterically doubled, in the form of a short story whose treatment by feminist readers raises questions not only about psychoanalysis, but about feminist reading.

Freud had favorably reviewed a German translation of Weir Mitchell's *The Treatment of Certain Forms of Neurasthenia and Hysteria* in 1887, the year of Gilman's breakdown, and himself continued to make use of the Weir Mitchell rest-cure alongside Breuer's "cathartic treatment." Gilman later wrote that after a month of the Weir Mitchell regimen ("I was put to bed and kept there. I was fed, bathed, rubbed, and responded with the vigorous body of twenty-six") she was sent home to her husband and child with the following prescription: "Live as domestic a life as possible. Have your child with you all the time. . . . Lie down an hour after each meal. Have but two hours' intellectual life a day. And never touch pen, brush or pencil as long as you live.'" Not surprisingly, she "came perilously near to losing [her] mind" as a result.[1] Mitchell, who apparently believed that intellectual, literary, and artistic pursuits were destructive both to women's mental health and to family life, had prescribed what might be called the Philadelphian treatment (a good dose of domestication) rather than the Viennese treatment famously invoked by Chrobak in Freud's hearing (*"Penis normalis dosim repetatur"*).[2]

Gilman, by contrast, believed that she only regained her sanity when she quit family life—specifically, married life—altogether and resumed her literary career. "The real purpose of the story," according to Gilman herself, "was to reach Dr. S. Weir Mitchell, and convince him of the error of his ways." Hearsay has it that he was duly converted: "I sent him a copy as soon as it came out, but got no response. However, many years later, I met someone who knew close friends of Dr. Mitchell's who said he had told them that he had changed his treatment of nervous prostration since reading 'The Yellow Wallpaper.' If that is a fact, I have not lived in vain."[3] Weir Mitchell figures in this autobiographical account from *The Living of Charlotte Perkins Gilman* (1935) as a surrogate for the absent father whom Gilman also tried to "convert" through her writing.[4] As Juliet Mitchell puts it, "Hysterics tell tales and fabricate stories—particularly for doctors who will listen."[5] But to read "The Yellow Wallpaper" as a literary manifestation of transference reduces the figure in the text to Gilman herself; recuperating text as life, the diagnostic reading represses its literariness. Gilman's is a story that has forgotten its "real purpose" (conversion), becoming instead a conversion narrative of a different kind—one whose major hysterical symptom is an unnecessary (or should one say "hysterical"?) reading of the maze of signs.

John, the rationalist physician-husband in "The Yellow Wallpaper," diagnoses his wife as suffering from "temporary nervous depression—a slight hysterical tendency" and threatens to send her to Weir Mitchell.[6] This hysterical tendency is shared not only by a story whose informing metaphor is the maze of sign reading figured in the wallpaper, but by the readings which the story generates. If Gilman creates a literary double for herself in the domestic confinement of her hysterical narrator, her narrator too engages in a fantastic form of re-presentation, a doubling like that of Anna O.'s "private theatre." Just as we read the text, so she reads the patterns on the wallpaper; and like Freud she finds that "it is difficult to attribute too much sense to them." Hers is a case of hysterical (over-)reading. Lost in the text, she finds her own madness written there. But how does her reading of the wallpaper differ from readings of the story itself by contemporary feminist critics?

Two pioneering accounts of the assumptions involved in feminist reading have used as their example "The Yellow Wallpaper"—by now as much part of the feminist literary canon as Freud's *Dora*. Both Annette Kolodny's "A Map for Rereading: Or, Gender and the Interpretation of Literary Texts" and Jean E. Kennard's "Convention Coverage or How to Read Your Own Life" focus on the feminist deciphering of texts which are seen as having deeper, perhaps unacceptable meanings hidden beneath their palimpsestic surfaces.[7] Kolodny's argument—that interpretative strategies are not only learned, but gender inflected—emphasizes the unreadability of texts by women embedded in a textual system which is controlled by men. Her own reading of "The Yellow Wallpaper" repeats the gesture of Gilman's narrator, finding in Gilman's story an emblem of women's dilemma within an interpretive community from which they are excluded as both readers and writers. For Kolodny, the doctor-husband's diagnosis anticipates the story's contemporary reception; male readers thought it merely chilling, while female readers were as yet apparently unable to see its relevance to their own situation. The "slight hysterical tendency" turns out to be, not that of Gilman's narrator or even of her story, but the hysterical blindness of Gilman's contemporary readers.

As Kolodny points out, John (the husband) "not only appropriates the interpretive processes of reading," determining the meaning of his wife's symptoms ("reading to her, rather than allowing her to read for herself"); he also forbids her to write. Kolodny's retelling of the story involves the selective emphasis and repression which she views as normative in any attempt to make meaning out of a complex literary text:

> From that point on, the narrator progressively gives up the attempt to *record* her reality and instead begins to *read* it—as symbolically adumbrated in her compulsion to discover a consistent and coherent pattern [in the wallpaper]. Selectively emphasizing one section of the pattern while repressing others, reorganizing and regrouping past impressions into newer, more fully realized configurations—as one might with any complex formal text— the speaking voice becomes obsessed with her quest for meaning. . . .[8]

"What [the narrator] is watching . . . is her own psyche writ large," Kolodny concludes. But whose obsessive quest for meaning is this? Surely that of the feminist critic as she watches her interpretive processes writ small, finding a figure for feminist reading within the text. The result is a strange (that is, hysterical) literalization; the narrator, we are told, "comes more and more to experience herself as a text," and ends by being "totally surrendered to what is quite *literally* her own text."[9] The literalization of figure (a symptom of the protagonist's hysteria) infects the interpretive process itself. Read as the case which exemplifies feminist reading, just as "Fraulein Anna O.," exemplifies hysterical processes for Breuer and Freud, "The Yellow Wallpaper" becomes, not the basis for theory, but the model on which it is constructed. Ostensibly, Kolodny emphasizes the need to re-learn interpretive strategies. But her reading ends by suggesting that re-vision is really pre-vision—that we can only see what we have already read into the text. Meaning is predetermined by the story we know; there is no room for the one we have forgotten.

As Kennard points out, surveying approaches such as Kolodny's, or Gilbert and Gubar's in *The Madwoman in the Attic*, readings that stress the social message of "The Yellow Wallpaper" (assuming both that the narrator's madness is socially induced and that her situation is common to all women) have become possible only as a result of "a series of conventions available to readers of the 1970s which were not available to those of 1892."[10] Kennard summarizes the concepts associated with these conventions as: *patriarchy, madness, space,* and *quest.* Feminist interpretations of "The Yellow Wallpaper" have tended, inevitably, to see the story as an updated fictional treatment of Mary Wollstonecraft's theme in her novel, *The Wrongs of Woman: or, Maria* ("Was not the world a vast prison, and women born slaves?");[11] mental illness replaces imprisonment as the sign of women's social and sexual oppression. But how justifiable is it to read into Gilman's story a specifically feminist tendency of this kind? And what is the tendency of such thematic readings anyway? We have learned not only to symbolize (reading the narrator's confinement in a former nursery as symbolic of her infantilization) but to read confinement itself as symbolic of her infantilization) but to read confinement itself as symbolic of women's situation under patriarchy, and to see in madness not only the result of patriarchal attitudes but a kind of sanity—indeed, a perverse triumph; the commonsensical physician-husband is literally floored by his wife at the end of the story. As he loses consciousness, she finds herself in the madness whose existence he has denied.

The "feminist" reading contradicts the tendency to see women as basically unstable or hysterical, simultaneously (and contradictorily) claiming that women are not mad and that their madness is not their fault. But a thematic reading cannot account for the Gothic and uncanny elements present in the text. The assumption of what Jacqueline Rose calls "an unproblematic and one-to-one causality between psychic life and social reality" not only does away with the unconscious; it also does away with language.[12] In the same way, the assumption of a one-to-one causality between the text and social reality does away with the unconscious of the text—specifically, with its literariness, the way in which it knows more than it knows (and more than the author intended). Formal features have no place in interpretations that simply substitute latent content for manifest content, bringing the hidden story uppermost. A kind of re-telling, feminist reading as Kennard defines it ends by translating the text into a cryptograph (or pictograph) representing either women in patriarchal society or the woman as writer and reader. If we come to "The Yellow Wallpaper" with this story already in mind, we are likely to read it with what Freud calls "that blindness of the seeing eye" which relegates what doesn't fit in with our expectations to the realm of the un-known or unknowable.

The "feminist" reading turns out to be the rationalist reading after all ("the narrator is driven mad by confinement"). By contrast, signs that might point to an irrationalist, Gothic reading ("the narrator is driven mad by the wallpaper") are ignored or repressed. Kennard admits that although the "feminist" reading is the one she teaches her students, "Much is made in the novella of the color yellow; feminist readings do little with this."[13] The color of sickness ("old foul, bad yellow things" p. 28), yellow is also the color of decay and, in a literary context, of Decadence (although the *Yellow Book* was not to appear until 1894). In America, it gives its name to "the yellow press" and to the sensationalism ushered in during the mid-1890s by color printing. Gilman's wallpaper is at once lurid, angry, dirty, sickly, and old: "The color is repellent, almost revolting; a smouldering unclean yellow, strangely faded by the slow-turning sunlight . . . a dull yet lurid orange . . . a sickly sulphur tint" (p. 13). The sensational ugliness of yellow is an unexplained given in Gilman's story. Yet the adjectival excess seems to signal not just the narrator's state of mind, but an inexplicable, perhaps repressed element in the text itself.

If feminist readings do little with the color of Gilman's title, they do even less with the creepiness of her story. Both Kolodny and Kennard ignore the uncanny altogether. Like the yellowness of the wallpaper, it is unaccountable, exceeding meaning; or rather, suggesting a meaning which resides only in the letter. The uncanny resists thematization, making itself felt as a "how" not a "what"—not as an entity, but rather as a phenomenon, like repetition.[14] A symptom of this uncanny repetition in the letter of the text is the word "creepy," which recurs with a spectrum of meanings spanning both metaphorical and literal senses (seeming to remind us, along with Freud, that figurative expressions have their origin in bodily sensations). Gilman's contemporary readers (to a man) found the story strange, if not ghostly. Her own husband thought it "the most ghastly tale he ever read."[15] The editor of *The Atlantic Monthly*, rejecting it, wrote that "I could not forgive myself if I made others as miserable as I have made myself!" and when he reprinted it in 1920, William Dean Howells called it a story to "freeze . . . our blood."[16] The *OED* reveals that the word "creepy" starts as "characterized by creeping or moving slowly," only later taking on the sense of chill associated with the uncanny ("creeping of the flesh, or chill shuddering feeling, caused by horror or repugnance"). Toward the end of the nineteenth century, the term came to be used especially in a literary context (*OED*: "A really effective romance of the creepy order"; 1892—the year in which "The Yellow Wallpaper" was finally published in the *New England Magazine*). If Gilman wrote a minor classic of female Gothic, hers is not only a tale of female hysteria but a version of Gothic that successfully tapped male hysteria about women. What but femininity is so calculated to induce "horror or repugnance" in its male readers?

The story's stealthy uncanniness—its sidelong approach both to the condition of women and to the unspeakably repugnant female body—emerges most clearly in the oscillation of the word "creepy" from figurative to literal. The link between female oppression, hysteria, and the uncanny occurs in the letter of the text; in a word whose meaning sketches the repressed connection between women's social situation, their sickness, and their bodies. A reading of the "slight hysterical tendency" displayed by "The Yellow Wallpaper" involves tracing the repression whereby the female body itself becomes a figure for the uncanny and the subjection of women can surface only in the form of linguistic repetition. A necessary first move would be to recover its lost literary and political "unconscious." The setting for Gilman's story is "a colonial mansion, a hereditary estate, I would say a haunted house, and reach the height of romantic felicity—but that would be asking too much of fate!" (p. 9). The trouble with the narrator is that her husband doesn't believe she's sick: the trouble with the text is its refusal of "romantic felicity." The narrator is no Jane Eyre (though the sister-in-law who is her "keeper," or "housekeeper," is named Jane) and her husband no Rochester ("John is practical in the extreme," p. 9); yet she must play the role of both Jane Eyre, who at once scents and represses a mystery, and Bertha Mason, who explodes it while refusing all attempts at sublimation—"I thought seriously of burning the house" (p. 29), the narrator confesses at one point.

In this prosaic present, romance can only take the form of hallucination (like Anna O.'s daydreaming); or perhaps, the form of a woman deranged by confinement. Female oppression has been de-eroticized, making the woman's story at best merely creepy and at worst sensational, just as the colonial mansion has been emptied of its romantic past. The empty house evokes romantic reading ("It makes me think of English places that you read about," p. 11), with its hedges and walls and gates that lock, its shady garden, paths, and arbors, and its derelict greenhouses. The rationalist explanation ("some legal trouble . . . something about the heirs and coheirs," p. 11) "spoils my ghostliness," writes the narrator; "but I don't care—there is something strange about the house—I can feel it. I even said so to John one moonlight evening, but he said what I felt was a *draught*, and shut the window" (p. 11). Like the coolly rational Dr. John in *Villette*, who diagnoses Lucy's hysteria as "a case of spectral illusion . . . resulting from long-continued mental conflict" (p. 330), John comes to stand not only for unbelief ("He has no patience with faith," p. 9), but for the repression of romantic reading. His "*draught*" is a literary breeze from *Wuthering Heights* ("the *height* of romantic felicity"?), and his gesture a repetition of Lockwood's in the nightmare that opens Emily Brontë's book. Indeed, like Lockwood confronted with the ghost of Cathy in his dream, John has "an intense horror of superstition" (p. 9) and scoffs at intangible presences ("things not to be felt and seen") as a way of shutting them out of house and mind. Hence his horrified loss of consciousness at the end of the story, when the narrator confronts him in all her feminine otherness.

Madness—the irrational—is what Doctor John's philosophy cannot dream of, and his repressive refusal of the unconscious makes itself felt in the narrator's inconsequential style and her stealthy confidences to the written page. But the same rationalist censorship also makes itself felt in Gilman's authorial relation to the uncanny. An age of doctors had made the tale of supernatural haunting a story about hysteria; no one dreamed of taking Anna O.'s death-head hallucinations seriously or believed that her "*absences*" or "split-off mind" were a form of demonic possession.[17] As Freud points out, literature provides a much more fertile province for the uncanny than real life. A deranged narrator is licensed to think irrational thoughts and confide the unsayable to her journal ("I would not say it to a living soul, of course, but this is dead paper and a great relief to my mind," pp. 9–10). Gilman herself only differs from the insane, in the words used by Alice James to describe the recollected torments of her own hysteria, in having imposed on her "not only all the horrors and sufferings of insanity but the duties of doctor, nurse, and straight-jacket."[18] Medical knowledge, in other words, straight-jackets Gilman's text as well as her narrator: "I am a doctor, dear, and I know," John tells his wife (p. 23). It is as if Gilman's story has had to repress its own ancestry in nineteenth-century female Gothic, along with the entire history of feminist protest. The house in "The Yellow Wallpaper" is strange because empty. An image of dispossession, it points to what Gilman can't say about the subjection of women, not only in literary terms, but politically—imaging the disinherited state of women in general, and also, perhaps, the symptomatic dispossession which had made Gilman herself feel that she had to take her stand against marriage alone, without the benefit of feminist forebears.[19] Lacking a past, privatized by the family, all she had to go on was her personal feeling. "*Personally*," the narrator opines near the start of the story ("Personally, I disagree with their ideas. Personally, I believe that congenial work . . .

would do me good," p. 10)—the subjection of women is also the enforced "subjectivity" of women, their constitution as subjects within an economy which defines knowledge as power and gives to women the disenfranchizing privilege of personal feeling uninformed by knowledge ("I am a doctor, dear, and I know"). In other words, an economy which defines female subjectivity as madness and debases the literature of the uncanny to the level of the merely creepy.

Mary Wollstonecraft's invective against the infantilization of women through sensibility and ignorance in *The Rights of Woman* becomes Gilman's depiction of marriage in terms of a disused attic room that has formerly been a nursery ("It was nursery first and then play-room and gymnasium, I should judge; for the windows are barred for little children, and there are rings and things in the walls," p. 12). But where Wollstonecraft had taken an enlightenment stance in her polemic (if not in her novel), Gilman is compelled to assume an irrationalist stance which she has no means of articulating directly; in her story, the irrational inhabits or haunts the rational as its ghostly other, hidden within it like the figure of a mad woman hidden in the nursery wallpaper. The site of repression, above all, the family is also the place that contains both strangeness and enslavement (as Engels reminds us in *The Origin of the Family, Private Property and the State*, the word "family," derives from "famulus," or household slave). For Freud, "*Heimlich*" and "*Unheimlich*" are never far apart; what is familiar returns as strange because it has been repressed. John may shut out the "draught," but the strangeness he fears is already within the home and creeps into the most intimate place of all, the marital bedroom—creeps in as both woman's estate and woman's body; at once timorous, stealthy, and abject; and then, because split off from consciousness, as alien.

The figure whom the narrator first glimpses in the wallpaper "is like a woman stooping down and *creeping* about behind that pattern," and by the light of the moon which "*creeps* so slowly" she watches "that undulating wall-paper till I felt *creepy*" (pp. 22–23; my italics). The meaning of the word "creep," according to the *OED*, like that of "creepy," starts from the body; and it too ends by encompassing a figurative sense: "1. To move with the body prone and close to the ground . . . a human being on hands and feet, or in a crouching posture"; "2. To move slowly, cautiously, timorously, or slowly; to move quietly or stealthily so as to elude observation"; and "3. *fig.* (of persons and things) a. To advance or come on slowly, stealthily, or by imperceptible degrees. . . . b. To move timidly or diffidently; to proceed humbly, abjectly, or servilely, to cringe." As "creepy" becomes "creep" we are reminded of Freud's formulation about the language of hysteria: "In taking a verbal expression literally . . . the hysteric is not taking liberties with words, but is simply reviving once more the sensations to which the verbal expression owes its justification" (SE 2:181). "Creepy" and "creep"—the female uncanny, the subjection of women, and the body—are linked by a semantic thread in the textual patterning of Gilman's story; only by letting ourselves become "lost in an unnecessary maze of sign-reading" like the narrator herself (and like Freud) can we trace the connection between female subjection and the repression of femininity; between the literature and the politics of women's oppression.

The narrator of "The Yellow Wallpaper" enacts her abject state first by timorousness and stealth (her acquiescence in her own "treatment," and her secret writing), then by creeping, and finally by going on all fours over the supine body of her husband. If she was Anna O., her creeping would be read as hysterical conversion, like a limp or facial neuralgia. At this point one can begin to articulate the relationship between the "feminist" reading, the hysterical reading, and the uncanny. The story is susceptible to what Kennard calls the "feminist" reading partly because the narrator herself glimpses not one but many women creeping both in and out of the wallpaper. But like the inconsequential, maddening pattern in the wallpaper—like a hysterical symptom—the repressed "creeping" figure begins to proliferate all over Gilman's text:

> It is the same woman, I know, for she is always creeping, and most women do not creep by daylight.
>
> I see her on that long road under the trees, creeping along, and when a carriage comes she hides under the blackberry vines.
>
> I don't blame her a bit. It must be very humiliating to be caught creeping by daylight!
>
> . . .
>
> I often wonder if I could see her out of all the windows at once.
>
> But, turn as fast as I can, I can only see out of one at one time.
>
> And though I always see her, she may be able to creep faster than I can turn!
>
> I have watched her sometimes away off in the open country, creeping as fast as a cloud shadow in a high wind. (pp. 30–31)

And finally: "I don't like to *look* out of the windows even—there are so many of those creeping women, and they creep so fast" (p. 35).

As the creeping women imprisoned both in and out of the wallpaper become the creeping woman liberated from domestic secrecy ("I always lock the door when I creep by daylight," p. 31) into overt madness ("It is so pleasant to be out in this great room and creep around as I please," p. 35)—as the "creeping" figure is embodied in the narrator's hysterical acting out—there emerges also a creeping sense that the text knows more than she; perhaps more than Gilman herself. At the culmination of the story, the rationalist husband tries to break in on his wife's madness, threatening to take an axe to her self-enclosure in the repetitions of delusion and language. The story's punchline has all the violence of his attempted break-in:

> "What is the matter?" he cried. "For God's sake, what are you doing!"
> I kept on creeping just the same, but I looked at him over my shoulder.
> "I've got out at last," said I, "in spite of you and Jane. And I've pulled off most of the paper, so you can't put me back!"
> Now why should that man have fainted? But he did, and right across my path by the wall, so that I had to creep over him every time! (p. 36)

The docile wife and compliant patient returns as a defiant apparition, her rebellious strength revealed as the other of domesticated invalidism. This time it is the doctor who faints on the floor. But the story leaves us asking a creepy question. Did she tear and score the wallpaper round her bed herself, or has her madness been pre-enacted in the "haunted" house? Who bit and gnawed at the heavy wooden bed, gouged at the plaster, splintered the floor? What former inmate of the attic nursery was confined by those sinister rings in the wall? As readers versed in female gothic we know that Bertha Mason haunts this text; as readers of the feminist tradition from Wollstonecraft on, we know that the rights of women have long been denied by treating them as children. The uncanny makes itself felt as the return of a repressed past, a history at once literary and political—here, the history of women's reading.

"Now why should that man have fainted?" The narrator's question returns us to male hysteria. The body of woman is hystericized as the uncanny—defined by Freud as the sight of something that should remain hidden; typically, the sight of the female genitals. The woman on all fours is like Bertha Mason, an embodiment of the animality of woman unredeemed by (masculine) reason. Her creeping can only be physical—it is the story that assumes her displaced psychic uncanniness to become "creepy"—since by the end she is all body, an incarnation not only of hysteria but of male fears about women. The female hysteric displaces her thoughts onto her body: the male hysteric displaces his fear of castration, his anxiety, onto her genitals. Seemingly absent from "The Yellow Wallpaper," both the female body (female sexuality) and male hysteria leave their traces on the paper in a stain or a whiff—in a yellow "smooch" and a yellow smell that first appear in metonymic proximity to one another in Gilman's text:

> But there is something else about that paper—the smell! I noticed it the moment we came into the room. . . .
> It creeps all over the house.
> I find it hovering in the dining-room, skulking in the parlor, hiding in the hall, lying in wait for me on the stairs.
> It gets into my hair.
> Even when I go to ride, if I turn my head suddenly and surprise it— there is that smell!
> Such a peculiar odor, too! I have spent hours in trying to analyze it, to find what it smelled like.
> It is not bad—at first, and very gentle, but quite the subtlest, most enduring odor I ever met.
> In this damp weather it is awful, I wake up in the night and find it hanging over me.
> It used to disturb me at first. I thought seriously of burning the house— to reach the smell.
> But now I am used to it. The only thing I can think of is that it is like the *color* of the paper! A yellow smell.
> There is a very funny mark on this wall, low down, near the mopboard. A streak that runs round the room. It goes behind every piece of furniture, except the bed, a long, straight, even *smooch*, as if it had been rubbed over and over. (pp. 28–29)

At the end of the story, the narrator's own shoulder "just fits in that long smooch around the wall" (p. 35). The mark of repetition, the uncanny trace made by the present stuck in the groove of the past, the "smooch" is also a smudge or smear, a reciprocal dirtying, perhaps (the wallpaper leaves "yellow smooches on all my clothes and John's" p. 27). In the 1890s, "smooch" had not taken on its slangy mid-twentieth-century meaning (as in "I'd rather have hooch/And a bit of a smooch"

[1945]).[20] The "smooch" on the yellow wallpaper cannot yet be a sexual caress, although dirty rubbing might be both Doctor John's medical verdict on sexuality and the story's hysterical literalization of it. As such, the dirty stain of smooching would constitute not just the unmentionable aspect of the narrator's genteel marital incapacity, but the unsayable in Gilman's story—the sexual etiology of hysteria, certainly (repressed in Gilman's as in Breuer's text); but also the repression imposed by the 1890s on the representation of female sexuality and, in particular, the repression imposed on women's writing.

And what of the "yellow smell"?—a smell that creeps, like the figure in the text; presumably the smell of decay, of "old foul, bad yellow things." *Studies on Hysteria* provides a comparable instance of a woman "tormented by subjective sensations of smell" (*SE* 2:106), the case of "Miss Lucy R.," an English governess secretly in love with the widowed father of her charges. Since, in Freud's words, "the subjective olfactory sensations . . . were recurrent hallucinations," he interprets them as hysterical symptoms. Miss Lucy R. is troubled first by "a smell of burnt pudding," and then, when the hallucination has been traced back to its originating episode, by the smell of cigar smoke. The episode of the burnt pudding turns out to be associated not only with her tender feelings for her employer's children but with tenderness for her employer ("I believe," Freud informs her, "that really you are in love with your employer . . . and that you have a secret hope of taking their mother's place," *SE* 2:117). The smell of cigar smoke proves to be a mnemonic symbol for a still earlier scene associated with the disappointing realization that her employer doesn't share her feelings. Here, hysterical smells function as a trace of something that has been intentionally forgotten— marking the place where unconscious knowledge has forced itself into consciousness, then been forcibly repressed once more. Freud does not pursue the question of smell any further in this context, although he does so elsewhere.

Jane Gallop's *The Daughter's Seduction* intriguingly suggests not only that smell is repressed by Freud's organization of sexual difference around a specular image ("sight of a phallic presence in the boy, sight of a phallic absence in the girl") but that smell in the Freudian text may have a privileged relation to female sexuality.[21] The female stench, after all, is the unmentionable of misogynist scatology. Two disturbing or "smelly" footnotes in *Civilization and Its Discontents* seem to argue, according to Gallop, that prior to the privileging of sight over smell, "the menstrual process produced an effect on the male psyche by means of olfactory stimuli" (*SE* 21:99n.) and that "with the depreciation of his sense of smell . . . the whole of [man's] sexuality" fell victim to repression, since when "the sexual function has been accompanied by a repugnance which cannot further be accounted for" (*SE* 21:106n.). In other words (Gallop's own), "The penis may be more visible, but female genitalia have a stronger smell"; and that smell becomes identified with the smell of sexuality itself.

Gallop connects Freud's footnotes with an essay by Michèle Montrelay associating the immediacy of feminine speech and what she terms, italianately, the "*odor di femina*" emanating from it. Montrelay is reviewing *Recherches psychoanalytiques nouvelles sur la sexualité féminine*—a book which, combining theory with case histories like *Studies on Hysteria*, "take[s] us to the analyst's: there where the one who speaks is no longer the mouth-piece of a school, but the patient on the couch. . . . Here we have the freedom to follow the discourse of female patients in analysis in its rhythm, its style and its meanderings." "This book," Montrelay concludes, "not only talks of femininity according to Freud, but it also makes it speak in an immediate way. . . . An *odor di femina* arises from it."[22] For Montrelay, feminine immediacy—predicated on the notion of an incompletely mediated relation between the female body, language, and the unconscious—produces anxiety which must be managed by representation; that is, by the privileging of visual representations in psychic organization. Or, as Gallop explicates Montrelay, "The '*odor di femina*' becomes odious, nauseous, because it threatens to undo the achievements of repression and sublimation, threatens to return the subject to the powerlessness, intensity, and anxiety of an immediate, unmediated connection with the body of the mother."[23] The bad smell that haunts the narrator in "The Yellow Wallpaper" is both the one she makes and the smell of male hysteria emanating from her husband—that is, fear of femininity as the body of the mother ("old, foul, bad yellow things") which simultaneously threatens the boy with a return to the powerlessness of infancy and with anxiety about the castration she embodies.

"The Yellow Wallpaper," like the Freudian case history or the speech whose immediacy Montrelay scents, offers only the illusion of feminine discourse. What confronts us in the text is not the female body, but a figure for it. The figure in the text of "The Yellow Wallpaper" is "a strange, provoking, formless sort of figure, that seems to skulk about

behind that silly and conspicuous front design" (p. 18). A formless figure? "*Absences*" could scarcely be more provoking. Produced by a specular system as nothing, as lack of absence, woman's form is by definition
formless. Yet both for the hysteric and for Freud, figuration originates in
the body—in "sensations and innervations . . . now for the most part . . .
so much weakened that the expression of them in words seems to us
only to be a figurative picture of them . . . hysteria is right in restoring
the original meaning of the words and depicting its unusually strong
innervations" (*SE* 2:181). The hysterical symptom (a smell, a paralysis, a
cough) serves as just such a trace of "original" bodily meaning. Figuration itself comes to be seen as a linguistic trace, a "smooch" that marks
the body's unsuccessful attempt to evade the repressiveness of
representation.

What is infuriating (literally, maddening—"a lack of sequence, a
defiance of law, that is a constant irritant to a normal mind," p. 25)
about the yellow wallpaper is its resistance to being read: "It is dull
enough to confuse the eye in following, pronounced enough to constantly irritate and provoke study, and when you follow the lame uncertain curves for a little distance they suddenly commit suicide—plunge off
at outrageous angles, destroy themselves in unheard-of contradictions"
(p. 13). A hideous enigma, the pattern has all the violence of nightmares
("It slaps you in the face, knocks you down, and tramples upon you. It is
like a bad dream," p. 25). But perhaps the violence is really that of
interpretation. The "figure" in the text is at once a repressed figure (that
of a woman behind bars) and repressive figuration. Shoshana Felman
asks, "what, indeed, is the unconscious if not—in every sense of the
word—a *reader*?"[24] Like the examinations undergone by Lucy Snowe and
Anna O., interpretive reading involves the specular appropriation or
silencing of the text. Only the insistence of the letter resists forcible
translation.

In Gilman's story, the narrator-as-unconscious embarks on a reading
process remarkably like Freud's painstaking attempts, not simply to
unravel, but, more aggressively, to wrest meaning from the hysterical
text in *Studies on Hysteria*: "by detecting lacunas in the patient's first
description . . . we get hold of a piece of the logical thread at the
periphery. . . . In doing this, we very seldom succeed in making our way
right into the interior along one and the same thread. As a rule it breaks
off half-way . . ."; and finally, "We drop it and take up another thread,
which we may perhaps follow equally far. When we have . . . discovered

the entanglements on account of which the separate threads could not be followed any further in isolation, we can think of attacking the resistance before us afresh" (*SE* 2:294). The language of attack entangles Freud himself in a Thesean fantasy about penetrating the maze to its center ("I *will* follow that pointless pattern to some sort of a conclusion," writes Gilman's narrator, with similarly obsessional persistence; p. 19).

The meaningless pattern in the yellow wallpaper not only refuses interpretation; it refuses to be read as a text—as anything but sheer, meaningless repetition ("this thing was not arranged on any laws of radiation, or alternation, or repetition, or symmetry, or anything else that I ever heard of," p. 20). Attempts to read it therefore involve the (repressive) substitution of something—a figure—for nothing. At first the pattern serves simply to mirror the narrator's own specular reading, endlessly repeated in the figure of eyes ("the pattern lolls like a broken neck and two bulbous eyes stare at you upside down. . . . Up and down and sideways they crawl, and those absurd, unblinking eyes are every-where," p. 16). But as the process of figuration begins to sprout its own autonomous repertoire of metaphors ("bloated curves and flourishes—a kind of 'debased Romanesque' with *delirium tremens*"; "great slanting waves of optic horror, like a lot of wallowing seaweeds in full chase," p. 20), it becomes clear that figures feed parasitically on resistance to mean-ing; the pattern "remind[s] one of a fungus. If you can imagine a toad-stool in joints, an interminable string of toadstools, budding and sprout-ing in endless convolutions—why, that is something like it" (p. 25). The function of figuration is to manage anxiety; any figuration is better than none—even a fungoid growth is more consoling than sheer absence.

Learning to read might be called a hysterical process, since it involves substituting a bodily figure for the self-reproducing repetitions of textuality. Significantly, the narrator's sighting of a figure in the text—her own—inscribes her madness most graphically. As the "dim shape" becomes clearer, the pattern "becomes bars! The outside pattern, I mean, and the woman behind as plain as can be. I didn't realize for a long time what the thing was that showed behind, that dim sub-pattern, but now I am quite sure it is a woman" (p. 26). The figure of bars functions in Gilman's text to make the narrator's final embodiment as mad woman look like a successful prison break from the tyranny of a meaningless pattern: "The woman behind shakes it! . . . she crawls around fast, and her crawling shakes it all over . . . she just takes hold of the bars and shakes them hard. And she is all the time trying to climb through" (p. 30). The climax of Gilman's story has her narrator setting to work to strip off the paper and liberate the figure which by now both she and we—hysterically identified with her reading—recognize as her specular double: "As soon as it was moonlight and that poor thing began to crawl and shake the pattern, I got up and ran to help her. I pulled and she shook, I shook and she pulled, and before morning we had peeled off yards of that paper" (p. 32). And finally, "I've got out at last . . . so you can't put me back!" (p. 36).

The figure here is the grammatical figure of chiasmus, or crossing (*OED*: "The order of words in one of two parallel clauses is inverted in the other"). "I pulled and she shook, I shook and she pulled" prepares us for the exchange of roles at the end, where the woman reading (and writing) the text becomes the figure of madness within it. Gilman's story hysterically embodies the formal or grammatical figure; but the same process of figuration dimly underlies (like the "dim shape" or "dim sub-pattern") our own reading. By the very fact of reading it as narrative, hysterical or otherwise, we posit the speaking or writing subject called "the narrator." "*Figure*" also means face, and face implies a speaking voice. In this sense, figure becomes the trace of the bodily presence without which it would be impossible to read "The Yellow Wallpaper" as a first-person narrative, or even as a displaced form of autobiography.

The chiastic figure provides a metaphor for the hysterical reading which we engage in whenever the disembodied text takes on the aspect of a textual body. Since chiasmus is at once a specular figure and a figure of symmetrical inversion, it could be regarded as the structure of phallogocentrism itself, where word and woman mirror only the presence of the (masculine) body, reinforcing the hierarchy man/woman, presence/absence. Is there a way out of the prison? The bars shaken and mistaken by the madwoman might, in a different linguistic narrative, be taken for the constitutive bar between signifier and signified. The gap between sign and meaning is the absence that the hysteric attempts to abolish or conceal by textualizing the body itself. Montrelay writes of the analyst's discourse as "not reflexive, but different. As such it is a *metaphor*, not a mirror, of the patient's discourse."[25] For Montrelay, metaphor engenders a pleasure which is that of "*putting the dimension of repression into play on the level of the text itself*"—of articulating or designating what is not spoken, what is unspeakable, yet incompletely repressed, about the feminine body. The ultimate form of this unmentionable pleasure would be feminine jouissance, or meaning that exceeds the repressive effects of interpretation and figuration. Montrelay's formulation risks its own literalness, that of (hysterically) assuming an unmediated relation between feminine body and word. But her story follows the same trajectory as Gilman's. The end of "The Yellow Wallpaper" is climactic because Doctor John, previously the censor of women's writing (as Felman demands, "how can one write *for* the very figure who signifies the suppression of what one has to say *to* him?"),[26] catches the text, as it were, *in flagrante delicto*. The return of the repressed, in Freud's scenario, always figures the sight of the castrated female body. What we glimpse in this moment of figuration is the return of the letter in all its uncanny literalness to overwhelm us with the absence which both male and female hysteria attempt to repress in the name of woman.

NOTES

1. *The Living of Charlotte Perkins Gilman: An Autobiography* (New York: Harper & Row, 1975), p. 96.

2. See *The History of the Psychoanalytic Movement, SE* 14:13–15.

3. *The Living of Charlotte Perkins Gilman*, p. 121.

4. See Mary A. Hill, *Charlotte Perkins Gilman: The Making of a Radical Feminist 1860–1896* (Philadelphia: Temple University Press, 1980), pp. 27–43.

5. Juliet Mitchell, "The Question of Femininity," *Women: The Longest Revolution*, p. 299.

6. Charlotte Perkins Gilman, *The Yellow Wallpaper*, Elaine R. Hedges, ed. (New York: The Feminist Press, 1973), p. 10. Subsequent page references in the text are to this edition.

7. Annette Kolodny, "A Map for Rereading: Or, Gender and the Interpretation of Literary Texts," *New Literary History* (Spring 1980), 11(3):451–67; Jean E. Kennard, "Convention Coverage or How to Read Your Own Life," *New Literary History* (Autumn 1981), 13(1):69–88.

8. Kolodny, "A Map for Rereading," pp. 457–58.

9. Ibid., pp. 457, 459; my italics.

10. Kennard, "Convention Coverage," p. 74.

11. Mary Wollstonecraft, *Mary, A Fiction and the Wrongs of Woman*, Gary Kelly, ed. (London and New York: Oxford University Press, 1976), p. 79.

12. See Jacqueline Rose, "Femininity and its Discontents," *Feminist Review* (June 1983), 14:17.

13. Kennard, "Convention Coverage," pp. 77–78.

14. See Neil Hertz's discussion of repetition and the uncanny in "Freud and the Sandman," *The End of the Line*, pp. 97–121.

15. See Hill, *Charlotte Perkins Gilman*, p. 186.

16. See Gilman, *The Yellow Wallpaper*, pp. 40, 37.

17. "The split-off mind is the devil with which the unsophisticated observation of early superstitious times believed that these patients were possessed" (*SE* 2:250).

18. *The Diary of Alice James*, Leon Edel, ed. (Harmondsworth: Penguin, 1982), p. 149.

19. See Hill, *Charlotte Perkins Gilman*, pp. 98–99; but see also pp. 144–45 for the course of feminist reading which Gilman undertook in 1887, the year of her breakdown.

20. "Once upon a time you 'spooned,' then you 'petted,' after that you 'necked' . . . but now you may 'smooch'" (1937); Harold Wentworth and Stuart Berg Flexner, *Dictionary of American Slang* (New York: Thomas Y. Crowell Co., 1975).

21. See Gallop, *The Daughter's Seduction*, pp. 27–28.

22. Michèle Montrelay, "Inquiry into Femininity," *m/f* (1978), 1:84; see also the discussion and critique of Montrelay by Parveen Adams, "Representation and Sexuality." ibid., 1:65–82.

23. Gallop, *The Daughter's Seduction*, p. 27.

24. See Shoshana Felman, "Turning the Screw of Interpretation," *Yale French Studies* (1977), 55/56:125.

25. Montrelay, "Inquiry into Femininity," p. 96.

26. Felman, "Turning the Screw of Interpretation," p. 146.

The Writing of
"The Yellow Wallpaper":
A Double Palimpsest

Catherine Golden

The first-person narrative of "The Yellow Wallpaper" unfolds as a diary written by a woman undergoing a three month rest cure for a postpartum depression.[1] Judith Fetterley has argued that the wallpaper functions as a text through which the narrator expresses herself; its pattern becomes the dominant text and the woman behind the pattern the subtext with which the narrator identifies.[2] To recall the terminology of *The Madwoman in the Attic*, the yellow wallpaper thus can be perceived as a "palimpsest." Similarly, Charlotte Perkins Gilman's story itself can be read as a palimpsest. The hallucinations and dramatic actions of tearing the wallpaper and creeping on the floor comprise the dominant text, but the writing comprises the second muted text, informing the narrator's final characterization. This muted text shows how the narrator fictionalizes herself as the audience of her story. Forbidden to write but continuing to do so in secret, the narrator comes to express herself by writing her own text. As she comes to see the wallpaper as a palimpsest, she presents herself on paper in a way that suggests that, although mad, she is not completely "destroyed"[3] by her patriarchal society. As the story unfolds, the narrator's writing ceases to match her thoughts and actions or to convey a cohesive characterization of a timid oppressed figure. The increased use of "I" and her syntactical placement of the nominative case pronoun within her own sentences demonstrate a positive change in self-presentation precisely at the point when her actions dramatically compromise her sanity and condemn her to madness.[4]

The narrator records her stay in a country ancestral hall through ten diary-like entries, each undated and separated only by several lines of blank space. The separateness of these units can be seen as a spatial indication of the narrator's own fragmented sense of self.[5] As Walter Ong notes, the audience of a diarist is oneself "encased in fictions. . . . The diarist pretending to be talking to himself has also, since he is writing, to pretend he is somehow not there. And to what self is he talking? To the self he imagines he is? Or would like to be?"[6] Although the narrator may in fact be writing for a fictional self, the way she imagines this self to be changes as the entries continue. The writing in her early entries matches the dominant text of her thoughts and actions. In the opening sentence the narrator introduces her husband before herself: "It is very seldom that mere ordinary people like John and myself secure ancestral halls for the summer."[7] Rarely used for self-expression, the reflexive case more effectively emphasizes an antecedent rather than replaces a subject. The narrator who claims she wants very much to write also hides her own belief that writing is "a great relief to my mind" (p. 10) by placing this insight in parentheses. Punctuation marks eclipse the forcefulness of this belief, which directly confronts the opinion of those who prescribe her rest cure: her physician-husband John, who "hates to have [her] write a word" (p. 13); her physician brother; the socially prominent nerve specialist S. Weir Mitchell, who is "just like John and [her] brother, only more so!" (p. 19); and even John's sister Jennie, an "enthusiastic housekeeper" who "thinks it is the writing which made [her] sick!" (pp. 17–18). At this point in the story the self-consciousness displayed through punctuational subordination keeps the narrator in a subordinate place within her sentences. The muted text matches the dominant text of her actions, which at this point reveals the narrator as fanciful and fearful. Even though her room initially repulses her, she rests in the former nursery because John chose it for her. The narrator prefers a room "that opened on the piazza and had roses all over the window, and such pretty old-fashioned chintz hangings!" (p. 12), yet she does not pursue her softly expressed conviction: " 'Then do let us go downstairs' " (p. 15). Asserting herself only through her secret act of writing, she hides her journal when she senses John's entry. Fear of detection restricts the amount she writes; she remains aware of her larger social reality at this point in the story and does not perceive of her private journal as a place for self-expression or a safe domain.

The dominant text of her actions and the muted text of her writing no doubt initially concur, in part, because the narrator is not only oppressed by those who forbid her to write but by language itself.[8] The language through which the narrator writes is imbued with a social, economic, and political reality of male domination of the late nineteenth-century that governs the way the narrator perceives language. The doctors pronounce the narrator "sick!" (p. 10). There is no escaping the words through which the doctors deliver their diagnosis, their prescription of a rest cure, or the language itself which the narrator must produce to maintain her sanity.

In the initial entry the narrator refers frequently to "Dear John" as well as what "John says" (p. 16). "John" appears four times on the opening page, the last three of which successively introduce a new paragraph:

> John laughs at me, of course, but one expects that in marriage.
>
> John is practical in the extreme. He has no patience with faith, an intense horror of superstition, and he scoffs openly of any talk of things not to be felt and seen and put down in figures.
>
> John is a physician, and *perhaps* — (I would not say it to a living soul, of course, but this is dead paper and a great relief to my mind) — *perhaps* that is one reason I do not get well faster (pp. 9–10).

Her husband appears ten times as "John" and eleven times as the forceful nominative "he" within the initial entry of thirty-nine short paragraphs. Reference and deference to her husband keep John firmly the subject of her sentences that describe how he "scoffs" and "laughs" at her and loses "patience" with her. Within her own journal of "dead paper" meant to be read by no "living soul" (except, of course, the narrator), she privileges the man who laughs at her, misunderstands her nature, and calls her, albeit affectionately, his "blessed little goose" (p. 15).

While she calls John by his proper name, the narrator elects to remain nameless until the very end of the story, where she hints that her name may be Jane.[9] Moreover, she rarely presents herself through "I." To recall the opening sentence of the story, "It is very seldom that mere ordinary people like John and myself secure ancestral halls for the summer" (p. 9). Herein "like" functions as a preposition meaning "similar to." Usage favors "me" rather than "myself" after a preposition; the reflexive case is heavier and more cumbersome in English than in other languages.[10] In introducing "myself" and "John," the narrator intensifies her awkward positioning in her sentence and society; she is not even on par with "ordinary people like John." Since the muted text of her writing initially concurs with her actions, it is not surprising that the narrator concludes at the end of the first entry: "There comes John, and I must put this away,—he hates to have me write a word" (p. 13). Using "I" becomes not an act of assertion but rather of acquiescence determined by John's authority. The blank space confirms that the narrator has put away her writing in compliance to John's prescription.

The narrator also elects to present herself anonymously as "one," "a kind of disguised *I*."[11] The narrator disguises her autonomy when she begins to question John's authority: "You see he does not believe I am sick! And what can one do?" (p. 10). "One" dominates the second page of the first entry (it occurs three times in close proximity). The syntactic positioning calls further attention to this pronoun. The expression "what is one to do" (p. 10) semantically conveys the narrator's helplessness and perceived inability to change her uncomfortable situation; the repetition of "one" creates a haunting echo of anonymity throughout this entry and the entire story.

As the entries unfold, the narrator comes to write for a different self hinted at on the opening page through her three-fold presentation of self as "I" (one time hidden in parentheses). To recall Ong once again, the narrator comes to write for the more forceful self she "would like to be." Simply by writing and exercising grammatical options within her patriarchal language, she writes in a way that questions and ultimately challenges the authorities that confine and oppress her. Her visible expansion on the sentence level[12] shows the muted text diverging from the dominant text. Learning to read the subtext of the yellow wallpaper, the narrator gives way to fancy and loses sight of her larger social reality. However, she concomitantly fictionalizes an identity overriding the fragmentation inherent within the discrete units of language she produces and the fragmentation she feels as a woman within her society. The narrator's greater self-awareness, emerging through her self-presentation beginning in the third entry, undermines her original compliance to John's orders to "lie down ever so much now" and "to sleep all [she] can" (p. 26).

When the narrator begins to cry uncontrollably at "nothing" (p. 19), to obsess with her reading of the shapes of the wallpaper's dominant and muted pattern, and to perceive that the muted text "is like a woman stooping down and creeping about behind that [dominant] pattern" (p. 22), she begins to write for a forceful fictionalized self, beginning successive sentences with "I":

> I don't know why I should write this.
> I don't want to.
> I don't feel able.
> And I know John would think it absurd. But I *must* say what I feel and think in some way—it is such a relief! (p. 21).

The contents of the "I" sequence records the narrator's vacillation and questioning of her own prescription of writing to improve her nervous condition. Janice Haney-Peritz even suggests that "such contradictions . . . betray the narrator's dependence on the oppressive discursive structure we associate with John."[13] But the clustering of "I," the italicized emphatic "must," and the exclamation point following "relief" convey an emerging sense of self and conviction precisely when she begins to have delusions leading to her final actions of tearing the wallpaper from the walls in order to free the woman and that part of herself trapped behind the restrictive bars of the dominant pattern of the wallpaper.

Appearing a total of seven times in this sequence, "I" introduces each of four consecutive sentences, three of which begin a new paragraph. No longer deferring to "John" or the social authority he represents, she conspicuously positions "I" in a configuration suggestive of a stronger albeit fictionalized self. The positioning and four-fold use of "I" most noticeably recalls the four-fold repetition of John on the opening page. However, in the third entry the narrator dramatically inverts her original pattern; by beginning the first three rather than the last three paragraphs with "I," the narrator gives heightened emphasis to self. The introductory positioning of the subject connotes power, and her use of "I" demonstrates a reversal of the dynamics of power between the narrator and John.

The narrator occasionally reverts to the reflexive case, such as within the fourth entry when she writes about solving the wallpaper's pattern: "I am determined that nobody shall find it out but myself!" (p. 27). In this sentence, however, the weight of the reflexive gives added force to her assertion, further accentuated through the surrounding words and the punctuation. A coordinating conjunction of contrast placed directly in front of the reflexive, "but" underscores her conviction and calls attention to "myself"; an exclamation mark reiterates this force. In the eighth, ninth, and tenth entries, the narrator uses "I" for self-presentation as well as to initiate short direct sentences, such as in the final entry when she tells John she cannot open the door to her room: " 'I can't,' said I" (p. 36). "I" becomes the first and the last word. The narrator syntactically occupies the two most powerful positions within her own sentence.

The choice and positioning of pronouns suggest a forceful sense of self complicating the narrator's final characterization. Independent of the muted text, the dominant text of her actions incrementally reveals her destruction. The later entries in which the narrator also comes to creep by daylight and to gnaw her bed in anger (pp. 34–35) demonstrate her delusional actions, which become increasingly dominant. In fact, "a slight hysterical tendency" (p. 10) grows into eventual madness as she gets in to the muted text of the yellow wallpaper. Given to fancy from the start, she begins to see the wallpaper come to life as she cries "at nothing . . . most of the time" (p. 19) and cannot sleep. Within the wallpaper she sees "strangled heads and bulbous eyes and wadded fungus growths" (p. 34). Personified midway through the second entry ("This paper looks to me as if it *knew* what a vicious influence it had!" [p. 16]), the muted side of the wallpaper assumes a human shape as the narrator sees within it "a strange, provoking, formless sort of figure" (p. 18). The muted figure within the wallpaper increasingly gains more definition for her. Although in the third entry she qualifies that the figure looks "like a woman" (p. 22), she confirms this perception in the fourth entry when she claims "now I am quite sure it is a woman" (p. 26). As the muted pattern becomes dominant to the narrator, her delusions translate into actions of madness that become most apparent during the final four entries. She sees the woman behind the wallpaper creeping and begins to creep herself, at first secretively just as she begins her writing: "I always lock the door when I creep by daylight. I can't do it at night, for I know John would suspect something at once" (p. 31). The dominant wallpaper pattern becomes prison bars, and the woman locked behind "just takes hold of the bars and shakes them hard" (p. 30). Sympathizing with the muted text, she writes more forcefully but acts more madly. She begins to peel the wallpaper from the walls to release that part of herself trapped by her own social condition as mirrored by the barred pattern of the wallpaper. The muted woman behind bars becomes a symbol and a message for women as the narrator sees outside the window "so many of those creeping women, and they creep so fast" (p. 35); in fact, she begins to "wonder if they all come out of that wallpaper as I did?" (p. 35).

Born of an hallucination, her identification leads the narrator to free herself from the restrictive pattern of her own society, and this liberation is conveyed on paper through her pronoun choice. Particularly the opening of the tenth entry celebrates the narrator's fusion of identity with the subtext of the wallpaper: "I pulled and she shook, I shook and she pulled, and before morning we had peeled off yards of that paper" (p. 32). But following her dramatic freeing of the woman behind the wallpaper, the narrator emerges independent and forceful. Hiding the key to her room under a plantain leaf, she seals herself in her room so that she can "creep around as I please!" (p. 35). The narrator tells her husband where he can find the key. Unlike the initial entry in which she senses John's entrance and puts away her journal, she does not allow his intrusion to disrupt her creeping in the finale. The narrator, mad, is no longer timid in her action. Echoing her use of "one" to avoid self-confrontation, the narrator now speaks with detachment of her husband: "Now why should that man have fainted? But he did, and right across my path by the wall, so that I had to creep over him every time!" (p. 36).

More than the tone of writing or pronoun usage, the placement of pronouns in this closing paragraph reveals the narrator's growing sense of awareness of her former submissive state and a reversal of the power dynamics of gender. Relegating John to a modifying phrase following an intransitive verb, the narrator assumes the subject position within the final clause. This sentence, in fact, exchanges the grammatical positions the narrator originally elected for each to occupy in a grammatically similar sentence on the opening page of "The Yellow Wallpaper": "John laughs at me, of course, but one expects that in marriage" (p. 9). In selecting an intransitive verb to convey John's abuse, the narrator in her early writing undeniably isolates herself from his emotional cruelty. The verb "to laugh" can only function intransitively and thus cannot possess or envelop the narrator, "me," as its object.[14] But, in doing so, the narrator relegates herself (and later John) to a weak position within the formal bounds of the sentence. Not a basic or essential sentence part, the prepositional phrase "at me" functions as a modifier embellishing the sentence (in this case adverbially).[15] Governed only by the preposition "at," the narrator in the first entry can be dropped from her sentence, which would thus read grammatically: "John laughs . . ., of course, but one expects that in marriage" (p. 9). With such a revision her presence would remain only through a disguised reference to self ("one"). However, by changing positions with John in the grammatically similar sentence in the tenth entry, the narrator now sends John—who has fainted to the floor—to a nonessential, powerless, syntactical place. Governed only by the preposition "over," John can be dropped from her final clause, which would thus read grammatically: "I had to creep . . . every time!" (p. 36). The narrator's actions are outside the realm of sanity, but the syntactic position she comes to occupy conveys her emerging sense of defiance against one of the forces in her patriarchal society that has fragmented her.

Other examples, particularly in the final four paragraphs of the tenth entry, join with this exchange of grammatical positions to affirm the narrator's newly imagined self:

> "What is the matter?" he cried. "For God's sake, what are you doing!"
> I kept on creeping just the same, but I looked at him over my shoulder.
> "I've got out at last," said I, "in spite of you and Jane. And I've pulled off most of the paper, so you can't put me back!"
> Now why should that man have fainted? But he did, and right across my path by the wall, so that I had to creep over him every time! (p. 36).

John's name seems conspicuously absent from these paragraphs. Four times the narrator substitutes the nominative case for John's name ("he cried" and "he did" within her narration and "you" twice in her dialogue). Within these paragraphs she thrice substitutes the objective case for John and further reduces his status by making each pronoun an object of a preposition ("at him," "of you," and "over him"). In the final paragraph she also uses the demonstrative pronoun "that" in "that man," a detached and generic reference to John. Unlike the demonstrative "this," "that" points the reader to something or someone who is respectively farther away in a spatial sense and thus works to distance the reader and the narrator from John and his authority, to which she once readily adhered. Used to direct the reader to a preceding rather than a subsequent reference, "that man" also orients the reader to the previous rather than the two future references to him, occurring in the final sentence; the wording anticipates John's disappearance from the final dramatic clause and close of "The Yellow Wallpaper," which leaves the narrator creeping flamboyantly in the daylight as she desires.

The narrator presents herself as "I" six times in the final four paragraphs, twice forcefully beginning her own paragraphs. She displays her growing sense of self, power, and confidence at the point at which she has uncoded the text of the yellow wallpaper and liberated its muted side. In addition, an exclamation point at the end of both the last and the penultimate paragraphs gives emphasis to her final sentences, in which she moves into the subject place initially reserved for John.[16] When referring to self, she uses the possessive case twice and the objective case once, but she no longer positions the objective case reference for self in a precarious place. Importantly, in the sentence "can't put me back," "me" functions as a direct object of the transitive verb "put." Securely positioned, "me" becomes essentially connected to the action verb. The use of negation in this sentence subtly undermines the contents of earlier sentences containing transitive verbs, such as "John gathered me up in his arms, and just carried me upstairs and laid me on the bed" (p. 21); while in both sentences "me" carries the force of her male oppressor, the negation in the later sentence equally negates his force and matches the writing in the finale, where the narrator is able to write a sentence that can function grammatically without "John."

Examining the muted text of the narrator's writing within this palimpsest in relation to the dominant text of her delusional actions permits the narrator a dubious victory. Her widening use of "I" and grammatical repositioning of "I" and "John" hint at a degree of personal liberation for her fictionalized self recorded within this tale of a woman's breakdown. The muted text of her writing comes to reflect her growing self-awareness as she moves beyond the prescription of healthy eating, moderate exercise, and abundant rest and chooses literal madness over John's prescription for sanity. As the narrator tears the paper to free the woman and that part of herself trapped within the story's mirrored palimpsest and creeps over her husband, she acts in a way that implies a cogent madness, rid of the timidity and fear that punctuate her earlier entries. Only at the point at which she acts out of madness does she find a place within the patriarchal language she uses, although not yet within her larger social reality. Creeping deeper into madness and her fictionalized self, the narrator writes in a defiant voice, circumvents John's force, and banishes "him" to the outer boundaries of her own sentence.

NOTES

1. In "Monumental Feminism and Literature's Ancestral House: Another Look at 'The Yellow Wallpaper,'" *Women's Studies*, 12, No. 2 (1986), 113–28, Janice Haney-Peritz calls the ten sections "diary-like entries" (p. 114). See also Paula A. Treichler's essay, "Escaping the Sentence: Diagnosis and Discourse in 'The Yellow Wallpaper,'" in *Feminist Issues in Literary Scholarship*, ed. Shari Benstock (Bloomington: Indiana Univ. Press, 1986), p. 63.

2. Judith Fetterley, "Reading About Reading: 'A Jury of Her Peers,' 'The Murders in the Rue Morgue,' and 'The Yellow Wallpaper,'" in *Gender and Reading: Essays on Readers, Texts, and Contexts*, ed. Elizabeth A. Flynn and Patrocinio P. Schweikart (Baltimore: Johns Hopkins Univ. Press, 1986), pp. 147–64. Fetterley advances that "blocked from expressing herself *on* paper, she seeks to express herself through paper" (p. 162). Although my reading concurs with and draws upon Fetterley's analysis, I would argue that the narrator does not experience writer's "block." While writing less and less frequently, she, in fact, writes more forcefully as she expresses herself through the paper and gets in to the subtext.

3. Elaine R. Hedges, "Afterword," *The Yellow Wallpaper* (New York: Feminist Press, 1973), p. 55. Hedges praises the late nineteenth-century work because it authenticates the experience of women restricted by a patriarchal society, but she concludes that the narrator's final actions confirm her destruction.

4. The relationship between language and the mental and social condition of the narrator has not gone undetected in previous literary and biographical criticism. See Hedges, pp. 48–49, on paragraphing and mental state; Annette Kolodny, "A Map for Rereading: Or, Gender and the Interpretation of Literary Texts," *New Literary History*, 11 (1980), 458–59, on pronouns and identity; and Treichler, p. 75, on the narrator as language user. These observations suggest a need for a systematic examination of the way the narrator writes to herself and for herself in her patriarchal society. Verb usage, discussed only briefly in this article, remains a rich field for systematic examination.

5. Akin to diary writing, the epistolary form divides writing into separate entities with discrete beginnings and endings and so accentuates the gaps inherent within all language. For more discussion, see Christina Gillis, *The Paradox of Privacy* (Gainesville: Univ. of Florida Press, 1984); Janet Altman, *Epistolarity: Approaches to a Form* (Columbus: Ohio Univ. Press, 1982).

6. Walter Ong, "A Writer's Audience Is Always a Fiction," *PMLA*, 90 (1975), 20.

7. Charlotte Perkins Gilman, *The Yellow Wallpaper* (New York: Feminist Press, 1973), p. 9. Further references will be included in the text and cited by page number.

8. For discussion of the relationship between language and social reality,

see, for example, Robin Lakoff, *Language and Woman's Place* (New York: Harper & Row, 1975) and two useful collections: Barrie Thorne, Chris Kramarae, and Nancy Henley, ed., *Language, Gender, and Society* (Rowley: Newbury House, 1983); Sally McConnell-Ginet, Ruth Borker, and Nelly Furman, eds., *Women and Language in Literature and Society* (New York: Praeger, 1980).

9. Hedges, pp. 62–63. The narrator's reference to "Jane" at the end of the story may be a printer's error, but it equally can be the narrator referring to her respectable and socially defined "Jane" self, of which she is also free at the end of the story. However, "Jennie" can also be a nickname for "Jane" and thus suggests she has freed herself despite John and Jennie.

10. For more explanation of the reflexive see Otto Jespersen, *Essentials of English Grammar* (University: Univ. of Alabama Press, 1981), p. 112.

11. Jespersen, p. 150.

12. For further discussion of deep surface structure, see Scott Soames and David Perlmutter, "Meaning and Underlying Structure," in *Syntactic Argumentation and the Structure of English* (Berkeley: Univ. of California Press, 1979), pp. 533–36.

13. Haney-Peritz, p. 116.

14. Although "laugh" is an intransitive verb, Jespersen points out that the sentence "everybody laughed at Jim" can be interpreted in two ways. Jim is governed by the preposition "at" and thus may be considered the object of the preposition. But "laughed at" can equally be considered a transitive verb phrase having Jim as its object. This latter interpretation explains the possibility of passivization for the sentence "Jim was laughed at by everybody" (pp. 122–23). This same reasoning can be applied to the sentences the narrator constructs in "The Yellow Wallpaper."

15. For more discussion of the roles of the prepositional phrase in sentence structure (passivization), see Soames and Perlmutter, pp. 552–68, and Jespersen, p. 121.

16. The narrator undeniably places an exclamation point following John's statement of outrage at her actions of tearing down the wallpaper, but her consecutive two-fold usage of this forceful punctuation mark weights the attention in favor of her own declaration.

Reader, Text, and Ambiguous Referentiality in "The Yellow Wall-Paper"

Richard Feldstein

A CRITICAL CONSENSUS

C ritics who have written on "The Yellow Wall-Paper" disagree on the most basic issues pertaining to the text. Is it a short story or a novella; should we underline its title or place it in quotation marks? The 1899 edition presents a novella format, but, in fact, "The Yellow Wall-Paper" first appeared as a short story in 1892.[1] There is also disagreement among critics about the writer's name: is it Charlotte Perkins, Charlotte Stetson, Charlotte Perkins Stetson, Charlotte Gilman, Charlotte Perkins Gilman, or Charlotte Perkins Stetson Gilman? Although each name relates to a phase in the writer's life, many commentators have arbitrarily chosen one designation to use normatively when discussing the writer's life and work. Ironically, this confusion over text's and writer's names was in part generated by Charlotte Perkins Gilman herself, who was anything but consistent in the names she used or the way she spelled *wall-paper*. If Gilman had the advantage of our perspective, she might have been pleased by this confusion of textual identity (is *wall-paper* one word or two] and amused by the critics' befuddlement over her name. Even without a historical perspective, however, she might have predicted such bafflement, possibly foresaw the manipulation of the names of the fathers—Perkins, Stetson, Gilman—as a means

307

of destabilizing the process of signification by presenting a proliferation of signifiers that ironically generate a paucity of signifieds.

Meanwhile, Gilman's editors have repeatedly altered the spelling of *wall-paper*, the overdetermined signifier that refers to both the title and the image of protean change featured in the story. The Feminist Press edition would have us believe that Gilman hyphenated the compound in the narrative but gave it in the title of the short story as *Wallpaper*.[2] But the original manuscript presents a different configuration: the use of *wall-paper* shifts arbitrarily, in defiance of any unvarying pattern of logic. The initial five references are *wallpaper, wall paper, wall-paper, wall paper, wall-paper*; its spelling then becomes more ambiguous because *wall-paper* then appears twice, hyphenated at the end of both lines; the final five references construct the indeterminate pattern of *wall-paper, wall paper, wall-paper, paper*, and *wall paper*.[3] Editors of the *New England Magazine*, where the story first appeared, could not abide such "confusion," so they altered the spelling to impose uniformity of textual reference. The title remained "The Yellow Wall-Paper," and the narrative reference still provided the ambiguous alteration of *wall-paper* and *wall paper*, but now there was a perceptible, though random, pattern of word usage: initially, there are three references to *wall-paper*; then, inexplicably, *wallpaper* appears five times before the pattern reverses itself and *wall-paper* is used four times. The next time the story was published, in 1899, Small, Maynard & Company consistently presented the compound as *wall paper*. Today, the version in *The Norton Anthology of Literature by Women* imposes the counterconsistency of *wallpaper*.[4] From Gilman's original manuscript, however, it is apparent that the word(s) *wall(-)paper* were conceived as a shifter calculated to create ambiguity about a referent that resists analysis, even as the narrator resists her husband's diagnosis and prescription for cure.

Despite such confusion, a critical consensus has developed on two issues central to "The Yellow Wall-Paper": John is the story's antagonist and the narrator/protagonist succumbs to a progressive form of madness. There is almost universal agreement that John is a turn-of-the-century patriarchal physician whose diagnosis of "a slight hysterical tendency" imprisons his wife within the prescription for her cure (10). Colluding with his brother and the likes of Weir Mitchell, John prescribes the placebolike "rest cure," which discourages work and isolates the patient from society. But the doctor who hypocritically pretends to be a neutral observer is emotionally implicated in the transference between husband and wife. Thus compromised, he relies on a realistic credo, openly scoffing "at any talk of things not to be felt and seen and put down in figures," a position he authorizes while policing his wife, making certain that her behavior complies with the regime suggested by his diagnosis (9). To counter these tactics, the narrator constructs representational strategies that privilege the spatial image over its analysis, modernist strategies that inform the imagist anthologies of the early twentieth century. Implementing this aesthetic through her writing and later through a purposeful acting out, the narrator produces a feminist counterdiscourse that opposes John's dualistic nineteenth-century empiricism with its dyads of good/evil, right/wrong, and, most relevant to this story, rational/irrational.

We can measure John's success in subjugating the narrator by the number of critics who direct our attention to the question of woman's madness as a central issue of the text. Critics generally agree that the narrator's condition deteriorates after she stops writing in her journal and becomes obsessed with the wall-paper. After the narrator substitutes a fixation with the wall-paper for her previous interests, she becomes protective toward the paper and the fantasized double(s) who inhabit it, eventually going so far as to threaten that "no person touches this paper but me, — not *alive*" (33). Because she recognizes these double(s) as fellow victims of a phallic system that resembles the wall-paper's restrictive outside pattern, the narrator believes that her projections might share a common psychogenesis with her: "I wonder if they all come out of the wall-paper as I did?" (35). Commentators who assert that the narrator's madness is genuine not only point to this quotation but to a list of other disconcerting facts to make their case — the narrator gnaws on her bedstead, crawls around the room with her shoulder against a long smooch in the paper, thinks about throwing herself out of a window, and determines that a rope is necessary to apprehend her double(s), who have escaped the wall-paper to creep over the lawn. Commentators who consider these actions conclusive evidence of madness find it difficult to accept Gilman's protagonist as a feminist, especially since she seems incapable of fending off insidious forms of surveillance.

In a recent issue of *Tulsa Studies in Women's Literature* there is a debate among three feminist critics — Paula Treichler, Karen Ford, and Carol Neely — which provides a representative sampling of critical opinion. Declaring that the narrator's final "confinement, infantilization, trivialization, banishment from discourse, [and] madness" are a triumph for patriarchy rather than a statement of feminism, Carol Neely argues that we should view that act of crawling at the end of the story not as "a victory for the narrator but as her defeat." As for the wall-paper itself, Neely considers that important symbol to be representative of patriarchal discourse "as perceived by women who look at it close up for [too] long."[5] Karen Ford also wonders what value the wall-paper holds for feminists; if it is "a new vision of women," she asks, "why is the narrator tearing it down?" Like Neely, Ford criticizes the narrator for "creeping as though she, like its [the wallpaper's] designs, is lame." On the question of madness, she concurs with Neely that no matter how "dignified and victorious these resolutions into madness and death may seem in relation to the compromised life of marriage and motherhood, they are not ultimately acceptable because suicide is not a viable alternative to a fulfilling life."[6] If one reads the short list of critical articles on "The Yellow Wall-Paper," it becomes apparent that on such issues Neely and Ford speak for the majority of critics who have analyzed the story.

In this issue of *Tulsa Studies*, Neely and Ford were responding to an essay written by Paula Treichler, "Escaping the Sentence: Diagnosis and Discourse in 'The Yellow Wallpaper,'" which appeared a year before.[7] Neely's and Ford's essays are followed by Treichler's rebuttal, "The Wall behind the Yellow Wallpaper: Response to Carol Neely and Karen Ford." Although Treichler concedes that both scholars' "interpretations of the yellow wallpaper metaphor are logical and persuasive," in an adept display of counterlogic, she notes that the text remains "an open and contested terrain" of language "which different people and groups inhabit, and 'work over' in many different ways." Treichler believes in an overdetermined conceptual space, in "multiple discourses," evolved in "multiple contexts," and thus she warns against an either-or reductionism, claiming that "women's discourse is never truly 'alternative' but rather inhabits the same terrain as the 'patriarchal discourse' it challenges." According to her reading, regression from linguistic expression to visual captation is not solely an act of compliance because it allows for the establishment of a counterdiscourse on "a highly policed terrain in which attempts at counterdiscourse are discouraged or forbidden."[8] This politicized regression through which the narrator endeavors to liberate the women of the wall-paper allows her to work through a conflict not previously visualized because of its unacceptability to consciousness. If we consider this important political dimension of the narrator's acting out, her "regression" can be framed by quotation marks to indicate the possibility of an ironic interpretation.

AN IRONIC READING OF THE WALL(-)PAPER

If we read "The Yellow Wall-Paper" ironically and not simply as a case history of one woman's mental derangement, the narrator's madness becomes questionable, and the question of madness itself, an issue raised as a means of problematizing such a reading. Reconfigured, the text becomes an allegorical statement of difference, pitting John, an antagonist and a proponent of realism who condemns his wife as a stricken romantic, against a nameless protagonist whose ironic discourse opposes the empirical gaze of the nineteenth-century American realist to a modern, not romantic, configuration—the wall-paper as gestalt—with its shifting significations born of the intermixture of figure and ground. The wall-paper is given to protean changes of shape from the sun- or moonlight reflecting on it. Combine this mutability with another variable: the wall-paper is a mirroring screen for the protagonist's projections, and the paper becomes an overdetermined construct destabilizing signification. Like the wall-paper, the text itself shifts, a signifier generating possibilities of interpretation while providing for a metacritique of its textuality.

From the standpoint of American realism, the narrator's obsession with the wall-paper constitutes a regression from a linguistic presentation, the one she would write if John would allow her "work," to an imaginary reconfiguration, an identification with mirror images in the paper as gestalt. From John's perspective, the narrator is a hapless romantic, a "little girl," a "blessed little goose," in other words, a regressed creature (23). Read ironically, however, her "regression" becomes purposeful—a cunning craziness, a militant, politicized madness by which the narrator resists the interiorization of authority. Through gestural comment, in a pantomime of subversion, the protagonist carefully enacts a series of reversals by exerting what little control she can as the madwoman in the nursery: she feigns sleep at night, sleeps during the day; she refuses to eat when eating is prescribed; she pretends not to write while writing a stratified discourse, literally a "writing" of the body, the sinuous crawl of an Eve/Satan composite commenting on the androcentric myth of the Fall. All the while the protagonist, though appearing to regress, maintains a level of ironic distance from her object of commentary.

From this point of view, the conclusion that the narrator of "The Yellow Wall-Paper" has a nervous breakdown, an oft-given answer to the difficulties posed by the text, becomes suspect. Although Gilman herself in *The Living of Charlotte Perkins Gilman* states that "The Yellow Wall-Paper" is a story about a woman's "nervous breakdown," later in her autobiography, she asserts another, more didactic purpose for having written the story: to prevent medical practitioners from prescribing "the rest cure" for "hysterical" patients.[9] In other words, Gilman consciously conceived "The Yellow Wall-Paper" from conflicting impulses; one accepted the narrator as simply "mad" and the other politicized the question of woman's madness and its "cure." Born of this conflict is a feminist text using modernist strategies in opposition to the prevailing literary theory of the period, American realism, which foreclosed examination of the complexities and inconsistencies posed by not only Gilman herself but a multilevel textuality that enunciates ambiguity. From this ironic perspective, to read "The Yellow Wall-Paper" as simply a flat representation of one woman's progressive descent into insanity is to diagnose the protagonist's case by means of the empirical ontology championed by the protagonist's doctor husband John, her doctor brother, and the *sujet supposé savoir*, Doctor Weir Mitchell.

Within the time frame of the story the protagonist comes to a modernist realization, that the field of representation is as important as that which is represented. This lesson is learned only after she pleads with John to acknowledge her illness as serious, but he dismisses her symptoms as the product of an overactive imagination. As physician and husband, John consolidates his authority to undermine the protagonist's confidence in her intuitive understanding of her illness. No matter how often she pleads for John's sympathy, once he claims that "she shall be as sick as she pleases," her case history is judged on the basis of his opinion and that of a consulting physician, if John decides that step is necessary (24). Once she understands this patriarchal logic, the nameless protagonist rechannels her effort into the symbolic sphere to counter John's simplistic notion of transparent reality.

We are then left asking if there is a therapeutic value in such acting out. More specifically, is there therapeutic value in the narrator's crawling as a means to shock her husband? To answer these questions, we need to consider the context. In most cases, patients who distrust their analysts terminate analysis. Unsatisfied Dora dumps Freud, who found it difficult to analyze the countertransference. But the protagonist in "The Yellow Wall-Paper" remains a captive to her husband, secluded in a room with barred windows, beyond a "gate at the head of the stairs," under the watchful eyes of John and Jennie (14). While other patients simply withdraw from analysis, the nameless protagonist must either file for divorce (as Gilman did in her lifetime) or find another effective means to register her dissatisfaction with the inequity of their relationship. Mindful of John's desire to misread her symptoms, the narrator chooses to act out, visualizing her experience, highlighting the common predicament she shares with other women victimized by patriarchy. She thus stages herself in the field of representation.

Within this context we observe the narrator creeping. Round a circle she goes, brushing against the paper that stains all who touch it. Prohibited from writing in her journal, the narrator embodies herself as a stylus writing the line, her body being written in the process. Round she goes, drawing the circle of certainty, diagrammatically constructing the binding process of obsession. When John discovers this activity, he faints. After he is revived, would he characterize her ritual as one of the narrator's many fixations with the wall-paper or with the women in it? If he did so, John's condemnation would not dissuade the narrator from recognizing that he exhibits his own fixations, especially the claim to a definitive diagnosis of her case, articulated with a fixed certainty that feigns objectivity while denying the countertransference. He thus constitutes an incontrovertible truth, a facet of the real he withholds from the symbolic order, dialectical transformation, and the network of free association.

The act of creeping is also a culminating illustration of the protagonist's disaffection with her husband. By the end of the story, she demonstrates the power to "see through" John when he pretends "to be loving and kind" (34). Her dissatisfaction with him becomes such that she wishes he "would take another room!" (31). Kept secluded for weeks on end in their country estate and banished for protracted periods to her bedroom, the protagonist decides to seek like revenge, if only for an instant, by locking John out of their bedroom. After fetching the key from under the plantain leaf, John goes to their bedchamber and enters an unidealized, contested space of intersubjectivity he finds confronting. John is confronted with the narrator's invocation of the Fall, in which woman works in tandem with Satan to violate knowledge. According to this myth, the fallen Eve/Satan composite combines to oust humanity from the garden, sentencing it, in Lacanian parlance, to a confrontation with its limitations as barred subjects forever separated from the Other. In the narrator's enactment of the Fall, woman is yet again blamed for the interpenetration of desire and knowledge. By creeping, the narrator draws attention to the misogynist nature of this condemnation, which presupposes that knowledge maintains a safe haven or conceptual space not permeated with desire.

AN ATTENDANT INCLUSIVENESS

It is of less consequence whether an interpretation is ironic if we conflate the identity of the narrator with that of the protagonist in the story. Until recently, critics have not distinguished between the protagonist who stops writing in her journal and the narrator who produces that journal, which becomes our narrative, an effective example of counter-discourse with political implications for feminists. If the protagonist and the narrator are one character, the narrator's journal poses a contradiction to the theory that the protagonist stopped writing when she regressed from the linguistic to the imaginary level of articulation. This problem, however, has been brushed over while critics place the narrator at an impossible interface: as an extension of the protagonist in the narrative and/or as a representation of the biological author, Charlotte Perkins Gilman. To accept the later conflation is to misread the symbolic for the real, a dimension that cannot be grasped through a dramatico-thematic explication.

An equation is made between the narrator and the protagonist early in "The Yellow Wall-Paper." At the end of the first segment the narrator writes, "We have been here two weeks, and I haven't felt like writing before, since that first day" (13). From this statement and others we are led to believe that we now read what she once wrote. Later in the story the narrator reinforces the impression that she is identical to the protagonist, explaining, "I am sitting by the window now, up in this atrocious nursery, and there is nothing to hinder my writing as much as I please, save lack of strength" (13). This set of quotations indicates that Gilman expended some effort to establish the link between the narrator/journalist and the protagonist in the story. As events unfold, however, John continues to debunk his wife's "imaginative power and habit of story-making" (15) so that she decides the effort needed to oppose her husband is "greater than the relief" she gets from writing (21). About two-thirds of the way through, the narrative records that the protagonist becomes too absorbed in her contemplation of the wall-paper to make reference to her need to write. It is this redirection of interest which leaves us with the seemingly irreconcilable contradiction I have described: if the protagonist stops writing, how do we explain the completion of her journal? To ask Paula Treichler's question: how do we understand a narrative that "is unfolding in an impossible form?"[10]

We could invent many conclusions to explain the radical disjuncture created by the characterological splitting of narrator/narrated. For instance, we could deny the split by concluding that after the protagonist creeps over her husband and the story ends, she writes her recollection of the final scene in her journal. We could also deny the narrator/narrated division by arguing for a chronological transposition in which the protagonist writes the second segment of her narrative after the fact, in effect providing us with documentation of her recovery. The last scenario most obviously parallels the accounts we have of Gilman's own life, how she divorced her husband, left her child with him, and then wrote "The Yellow Wall-Paper." If we reject a psychobiographical reading, however, and insist instead that the text be treated as a linguistic artifact, we are free to reconstruct traces of an ever-changing, inconsistent narrative in the same way that the protagonist grafts onto the wall-paper a gestalt with fluid boundaries.

The account the narrator provides is a written transcription inexplicably interrupted and succeeded by a spoken account in which she relates details of her life to a hypothetical audience of confidants. For as the story concludes, we confront yet another contradiction when the narrator asserts she is speaking to us, not writing in her journal, as she had previously explained: "I have found out a funny thing, but I shan't *tell* it this time!" (31, my emphasis). This statement, which equates narrative technique with a verbal recounting of events, is like a question asking how it should be read. It is especially significant because of the protagonist's previously stated concern for being allowed to write, a point of pique in the first half of the story, a mute issue in the second. No matter how we choose to read this contradiction, however, it will remain unassimilable to an interpretation of the text. Whichever reading we choose to affix univocal meaning onto a purposely ambiguous text will impose a thematic reduction that should be resisted, just as

Gilman resisted Weir Mitchell's diagnosis and her protagonist resisted John's phallocentric assessment of her situation.

The aim of this essay is to raise a feminist question cast in post-modernist terms: did Charlotte Perkins Gilman, grounding her critique in gender difference, use modernist techniques to form a disjunctive text that plays on the question of identity when emphasizing the narrator/narrated split that presents one entity as two? Could it be possible that Gilman intended the narrator to be both the same as and different from the protagonist, just as she believes the protagonist to be the same as and different from her double(s), the imprisoned other(s) in the wall-paper? From this perspective one slides into two with the shifting of signification. If we look back to the original manuscript of "The Yellow Wall-Paper," we are reminded that Gilman confused the issue of whether wall-paper was one word, two conjoined by a hyphen, or two separate words, whether this central referent—the paper—already a screen for the protagonist's projections, could become more ambiguous, a lure for transposition by critics and anthologists alike.

Besides foregrounding the modernist concern with self-reflexivity, Gilman's presentation of the wall-paper as mirror depicts the intra-psychic splitting and the consequent objectification of fantasy which produces what Lacan calls *méconnaissance*.[11] Lacan explains that in the mirror stage the child develops the ability to differentiate itself from its projective image, a developmental achievement of zero to one (aware-ness of "self") and one to two (distinction between subject and other). Like Lacan's infant, the creeping narrator is faced with overcoming a motor incapacity when she peers into the looking glass (actual or not), and like this infant, the reader faces a text that reflects itself as a literary artifact through the differentiation of the text's spelling from the wall(?)paper cited in the narrative. Like the infant and the narra-tor, we reassemble bits and pieces of perception into a unified configu-ration that fictionalizes analysis even as it calls attention to the stage where the first fictions were formed. Thus, we are left to *identify* with the object of our choice: with the protagonist, whose loss of boundaries causes us to experience a similar loss of identity, with the narrator, whose prose writes itself as a presence absent from most critics' deliber-ations, with both or neither of these narrative constructs. We con-figure our own fictions.

The use of text as mirror problematizes interpretation because it produces a doubling that, like the reductio ad absurdum of irony, resists the easy answer or definitive diagnosis. "The Yellow Wall-Paper," however, does not merely present a text that mirrors itself, since the story/novella also insists on its status as a question, a hesitation that replicates the narrative it recounts. In this way the text maintains a difference that remains unassimilable to a theoretical perspective that would reassemble it for its own advantage. This strategy of resistance is similar to the one Todorov describes as *fantastic* in a book by the same name.[12] The fantastic presents a textual resistance that induces us to suspend our judgment when interpreting an event as representative of either the supernatural (the women in the wall-paper are ghosts) or the uncanny (the protagonist projects self-aspects to form her double[s]). The fantastic exists, then, suspended between these dimensions, a contradiction to both, a pause or hesitation that, through its inconclusiveness, questions the validity of our assertions. If we apply Todorov's theory of the fantastic to "The Yellow Wall-Paper," we have yet another reason to suspend our judgment, especially since the protagonist acknowledges, as early as the second paragraph, the possibility of a supernatural interpretation—these "secure ancestral halls" are haunted (9). Such a conservative interpretation, which privileges the supernatural manifestation of gothic romanticism while discarding historical and cultural analysis, should not be confused with Todorov's notion of the fantastic, which delights in the ambiguity articulated in expressed difference.

Stated another way, "The Yellow Wall-Paper" is more a writerly than a readerly text, which Gilman designed to challenge her readers to produce, not merely consume. Gilman's protagonist, who configures a text from her vision of the wall-paper, illustrates a means of reading that allows for a play of difference, just as her protagonist allows for the play of sun and moon off the wall-paper's surface. This is how Gilman's text presents itself to us, an ambiguous, doubled referent, cast in the interrogative mode, a gestalt of changing patterns. Text as question formulates an inconclusiveness that attends enigma generated in part by the hyphen between wall and paper—a sign of difference and reminder of text as Other to which we look for closure, a means of satisfying unsatisfiable desires.

NOTES

1. Charlotte Perkins Gilman, *The Yellow Wall Paper* (Boston: Small, Maynard, 1899); Gilman, "The Yellow Wall-Paper," *New England Magazine* 5 (1891–92), 647–56.

2. Gilman, *The Yellow Wallpaper* (New York: Feminist Press, 1973). For ease of referral, all subsequent references, unless otherwise noted, are to this edition of the text.

3. Gilman, "The Yellow Wall-Paper," Schlesinger Library, Radcliffe College, Charlotte Perkins Gilman Collection, Folder 221.

4. Gilman, *The Yellow Wallpaper*, in *The Norton Anthology of Literature by Women*, ed. Sandra M. Gilbert and Susan Gubar (New York: Norton, 1985), 1148–61.

5. Carol Thomas Neely, "Alternative Women's Discourse," *Tulsa Studies in Women's Literature* 4 (1985), 316.

6. Karen Ford, " 'The Yellow Wallpaper' and Women's Discourse," *Tulsa Studies in Women's Literature* 4 (1985), 310, 311, 313.

7. Paula A. Treichler, "Escaping the Sentence: Diagnosis and Discourse in 'The Yellow Wallpaper,' " *Tulsa Studies in Women's Literature* 3 (1984), 61–77.

8. Paula A. Treichler, "The Wall behind the Yellow Wallpaper: Response to Carol Neely and Karen Ford," *Tulsa Studies in Women's Literature* 4 (1985), 324, 325, 327.

9. Gilman, *The Living of Charlotte Perkins Gilman* (New York: Arno-Hawthorne Books, 1972), 118–21.

10. Treichler, "Escaping the Sentence," 73.

11. See Jacques Lacan, "The Mirror Stage as Formative of the Function of the I as Revealed in Psychoanalytic Experience," in *Ecrits: A Selection*, trans. Alan Sheridan (New York: Norton, 1977), 1–7.

12. Tzvetan Todorov, *The Fantastic: A Structural Approach to a Literary Genre*, trans. Richard Howard (Ithaca: Cornell University Press, 1975).

"Out at Last"? "The Yellow Wallpaper" after Two Decades of Feminist Criticism

Elaine R. Hedges

"I've got out at last," said I . . . "And I've pulled off most of the paper, so you can't put me back!"

Since 1973, when I wrote the Afterword to the Feminist Press edition, "The Yellow Wallpaper" has become the Press's best-selling volume and one of the best-selling works of fiction by university presses in the United States. It has been reprinted in England, France, Spain, the Netherlands, Germany, Sweden, and Iceland, and it has inspired several film and dramatic versions, a television adaptation, and even an opera. It is of course regularly assigned in women's studies and literature courses and is by now firmly established in the literary canon, appearing in all of the major anthologies. Together with *The Awakening* it is probably the most well-known rediscovered work by a nineteenth-century American woman.

Since the story's republication, there have been more than two dozen critical studies of it, including biographical, genre, reader response, discourse theory, psychoanalytic, and new historicist and cultural studies readings. Collectively they offer a dazzling and significantly

A briefer version of this essay was presented at the Modern Language Association Annual Meeting in Washington, D.C., December 30, 1989.

disparate array of interpretations. The wallpaper, as the story's key metaphor, has been read as inscribing the medical, marital, maternal, psychological, sexual, sociocultural, political, and linguistic situation of its
narrator-protagonist; as an image of the situation of the woman writer
and hence a way of understanding the dilemmas of female authorship; as
revealing the relations between gender and reading and gender and
writing; and as a description of the problems of female self-
representation within both the Lacanian world of the Symbolic and the
capitalist world of the United States in the late nineteenth century.
Analyses of the story's formal and stylistic features have variously
argued for it as a realistic story, a feminist Gothic tale, and one of the
earliest modernist texts. The endlessly debated ending has been interpreted as the narrator's triumph and/or her defeat, with positions ranging along a spectrum that, at one end, sees her madness as a higher form
of sanity and her search for meaning in the paper as successful and
liberating, to the other end, that sees her as fatally retreating to a
condition of childishness, or infantilism, or animalhood, or even inanimateness. Her crawling, thus, is either a sign of rebirth or of regression; and her husband's fainting proof either that she has outwitted him
or that, by becoming unconscious, he's outwitted her, by refusing to
listen to her. Finally, critics have argued that Gilman's contemporaries
could not read the story because they lacked the necessary reading
conventions, and, on the other hand, that they in fact had such conventions but would not read it, for very fear of discovering what it really
said.

Such a synopsis might suggest that "The Yellow Wallpaper" has
become our white whale, or, as some recent critics would have it, our
feminist albatross, for by now not only the story's once roughly agreed-
upon meaning, but its privileged status as an exemplary text and a
feminist critical touchstone are being challenged. At the same time,
however, the story has been adopted by new historicist critics as one of
their exemplary texts, so that its continuing visibility and critical viabil-
ity seem assured. This would seem, then, to be a good moment for a
backward glance and a reconnoitering. What do the story's changing
interpretations, and the recent challenges to the earliest interpretations,
tell us about the trajectory of literary criticism, and particularly of feminist literary criticism, over the last twenty years?

The earliest studies of the story—and I'm referring to four that are
frequently grouped together—my Afterword, Sandra Gilbert and Susan

Gubar's treatment in *The Madwoman in the Attic*, Annette Kolodny's "A Map for Rereading: Or, Gender and the Interpretation of Literary Texts," and Jean Kennard's "Convention Coverage or How to Read Your Own Life"—read it, sympathetically, as the narrative of a woman's efforts to free herself from the confining social and psychic structures of her world, with the wallpaper interpreted as encoding those oppressive structures. The extent to which she was seen as succeeding was moot, with my arguing that she achieves temporary insight but is at the end defeated, totally mad, and Kolodny similarly concluding that she manages only to reencode her own unacceptable reality within herself. The readings of Gilbert and Gubar and Kennard showed the greatest investment in the narrator's success, with the former seeing her as "mad" only by society's standards but in fact moving into "the open spaces of . . . [her] own authority" (91), and the latter arguing that her madness could be seen as a higher form of sanity or truth. Other early, briefer, analyses were similarly split, with Loralee MacPike and Beate Schöpp-Schilling describing the narrator's insanity as, respectively, a creative act and a successful defiance, and Mary Beth Pringle on the other hand arguing that all she accomplishes is to shape the wallpaper into "the only thing she knows: a cage" (21). Despite what is roughly a fifty-fifty division here, the idea that its earliest critics saw an essentially or largely triumphant conclusion to the story, a victory for the narrator, has prevailed, with critical consequences that will be apparent later.

Although these studies, from 1973 to 1981, tended to read the wallpaper primarily in terms of the narrator's social situation, broadly defined, interest in describing her dilemma through reference to issues of textuality, language, and discourse was early evident, since, of course, the narrator in the story is crucially engaged both in writing—she tries to record her experience in her journal—and in reading—she tries to decipher the patterns in the paper. However, whose text she was reading—whether her own or her husband's—and how she read it, soon became as problematical as the degree of her success or failure. For Gilbert and Gubar, concerned as they were in *The Madwoman in the Attic* with the anxiety of female authorship, the wallpaper was "the facade of the patriarchal text" (90), which, by releasing the woman inside it, the narrator escapes, becoming ready to author her own. But for Kolodny the wallpaper was the narrator's own text, the text of herself, which could not get read or recorded. In 1985 Paula Treichler approached the story as a struggle over woman's right to author her own sentences, in opposition to her doctor-husband's medical "sentencing" of her, and found that the narrator did so, at least temporarily, through an "impertinent" language that defied male control, and through her relation to the wallpaper, which Treichler saw as a metaphor for women's discourse, "thick with life, expression, and suffering" (75, 73). The following year Judith Fetterley, also concerned with male control of textuality—of the scripts or stories through which women must try to define and understand themselves—found the narrator temporarily achieving the authority of her own script, but the wallpaper, as patriarchal text, eventually strangling the women who try to get through—a conclusion with which two other critics, Karen Ford and Carol Neely, who had written brief rejoinders to Treichler, generally agreed.

By 1986 this approach to the story, in terms of textuality and language, was producing readings that seemed to offer less and less autonomous or expressive space to the narrator. Two articles appeared that year that read the wallpaper, in Lacanian psychoanalytic terms, as the site of the narrator's struggle with self-representation through language. In "Monumental Feminism and Literature's Ancestral House: Another Look at 'The Yellow Wallpaper,'" Janice Haney-Peritz, arguing, as Treichler had, that the story should be approached not in terms of oppressive social structures, as earlier interpretations had approached it, but in terms of the oppressive structures of male discourse, could find less room for even the partial victory that Treichler and Fetterley, like most earlier critics, had tried to negotiate. For Haney-Peritz, once the narrator perceives a *real* woman as opposed to the *symbol* of a woman in the paper, she has surrendered all access to the Symbolic realm, the linguistic realm in which her identity as a speaking and writing subject must be constructed, and retreated into the realm of the pre-Oedipal Imaginary, where she becomes infantilized and hopelessly encrypted in fantasy. And Mary Jacobus, in her book, *Reading Woman*, by focusing on the narrator as an hysteric, saw her as engaged in a process of figuration, an hysterical overreading of the wallpaper, that trapped her in a maze of signs, where she becomes totally lost.

These readings, and especially Haney-Peritz's, were in turn given additional currency in a 1988 article by Diane Herndl, for whom the narrator is also an hysteric who, after failing in the Symbolic realm to find self-representation, retreats to the hallucinatory realm of the Imaginary. When, in that hallucinatory realm, she endows the wallpaper with life, she becomes herself an object, "just another of the indecipherable furnishings in her husband's house" (74). Although in 1988 in *Writing Beyond the Ending* Rachel Blau DuPlessis could suggest both possibilities—that the narrator's madness might be seen as "divinest Sense" or, from the "perspective of normalcy," as irrational and delusive behavior (92–93), and in 1989, in volume two of *No Man's Land*, Gilbert and Gubar could envision the narrator not only out on the garden paths beyond the house but "fleeing towards the . . . gardens of *Herland*" (77), Gilman's utopian world of liberated women, it was apparent that a new critical period had begun.

The new readings depended to a significant degree on foreground-ing elements in the story that, Jacobus argued, earlier critics had left unexamined: the disturbing yellow color of the wallpaper, and its smell. In her interpretation Jacobus had importantly relied on these elements, reading the yellow "stain" and the odor that the narrator ascribes to the paper as symbols of her repressed sexuality, denied representation by her culture. Embodied in her hysteric posture and erupting in her defensive and anxiety-induced overreading of the paper, this repression reduces her, at the story's end, to a creeping animal, "all body" (241), repugnant and terrifying to her fainting husband.

By the time of Jacobus's essay the wallpaper's yellow color and smell had in fact already begun to be examined, by Juliann Fleenor in 1983, and Jeffrey Berman in 1985. Both of these critics had also read the yellow color and smell as representing the narrator's sexuality, specifi-cally her sexual fear and disgust. For Fleenor, the yellow color implied "something strange and terrible about . . . female procreation, and about female physiology" (123), and for Berman the color and the smell also suggested fears of "uncontrolled reproduction" and "sexual defilement" (56). Three more recent readings have concurred. In 1988 William Veeder associated the yellow color and smell with the narrator's inability to handle adult sexuality; in 1989 Marianne deKoven saw the paper as "bloated" with denied sexual desire, its "waddling," "sprawling," "wallow-ing" qualities (31,32), as well as its smell, symbolizing the narrator's sexual self-disgust; and in the same year Linda Wagner-Martin also found the story conveying the "disgust . . . [the narrator] feels for herself as a sexual, procreative woman" (60).

As the quotations from Fleenor, Berman, and Wagner-Martin sug-gest, critics were also relating the narrator's sexual difficulties to her experience and attitudes as a new mother—another aspect of the story that its earliest critics had not extensively explored. Berman, who offered a Freudian interpretation of the story based on Gilman's own life—her unsatisfactory first marriage and her troubled childhood relationship to her parents—emphasized the narrator's fascination with the wallpaper's frightening ability to sprout into uncontrolled new growths—toadstools, seaweed, fungi—and found her projecting on to the paper her morbid fears of motherhood and reproduction. Veeder, reading the story in the light of psychological models taken from boundary and object relations theory and also using the facts of Gilman's own life, similarly found the narrator unable to deal with motherhood and, as a result, retreating to an infantile state, with the paper's repugnant yellow stain and smell becoming the infant's urine.

Meanwhile, the interpretations of Haney-Peritz and Jacobus not only disputed what they saw as the hegemonic reading of the story in my Afterword, and in Gilbert and Gubar, Kolodny, and Kennard; they also importantly challenged the interpretive practices on which those readings were based. Early interpretations, Haney-Peritz charged, citing especially Gilbert and Gubar's and Kolodny's, were essentialist: generalizing from the situation of one nineteenth-century woman, they read the story as "the" woman's story, as having some essential " 'female meaning' " (121, 122); and, she also argued, by encouraging readers to identify with the narrator, especially through a belief in the possibilities of her liberation, the critics had created and perpetuated an erroneous feminist critical assumption—namely, that women's literature contains "a really distinctive body" of meaning that can be discovered through such identification (123). Questioning whether we should identify with a narrator who may be reading her husband's text rather than her own, she therefore also warned against the assumption that such identification is necessarily liberating.

In 1990, in "Feminist Criticism, 'The Yellow Wallpaper,' and the Politics of Color in America," Susan Lanser reiterated and extended these charges. She, too, questioned the story's canonical status, the essentialist readings of some of its earliest critics, and their encouragement of reader identification with the narrator, while adding the observation that its interpreters have all been white academics, who have perhaps simply repeated the reading practice of the story's narrator, pursuing and finding in the text, as the narrator does in the wallpaper, only our own image reflected back. Emphasizing that both the story and its author are the products of their culture, Lanser urged us to recognize that not only men's writings, as feminist critics have long recognized, but women's, and feminist criticism as well, are all "collusive with ideology" (422), likely, that is, to embody and reflect the biases and prejudices of their times. In the light, especially, of current concern with differences among women, she therefore reads—or as she admits, provocatively overreads—the wallpaper, not, or not only, as either the patriarchal text or the woman's text, but as the culture's text. The result is that she finds in the paper's yellow color and smell and in its imagery a reflection of the nation's obsession, at the turn of the century, with issues of race, due to the massive immigration at the time from southern and eastern Europe and from Asia, an obsession which Gilman, as shown in her nonfictional writings, shared, and one which, according to Lanser, the word "yellow" came to convey, as connoting strangeness, ugliness, uncleanness, and inferiority. Where the wallpaper, for Jacobus, was the site of the sexual unconscious, it is now the site of the "political unconscious" (429), and what is found there is equally unsettling.[1]

But if some recent feminist critics are rejecting "The Yellow Wallpaper" as a paradigmatic or exemplary text, preferring to see it as at best (Jacobus) a "minor classic of female Gothic" (235) and at worst (Haney-Peritz) a "memento mori" (123), it seems to have found a new home among the new historicists, who, moreover, like Lanser, are interested in the text's complicitousness with ideology.[2] Two new historicist studies of the story that appeared in 1987 focus, as Jacobus and Herndl do, on the narrator's hysteria, but with hysteria now seen as a disease of capitalism. Walter Benn Michaels uses the story as the introduction to his study of the relation of late-nineteenth-century literary texts to American capitalism, *The Gold Standard and the Logic of Naturalism*, explicitly calling it his exemplary text. What it exemplifies now is the genesis of the marketplace, or the birth of the culture of consumption. In Michaels's reading, which is based on the Derridean idea of the self as an effect of writing, the narrator's nervous breakdown is "a function of her involvement in a certain political economy of selfhood" (27). Determined to produce herself through writing, she consumes herself in the process—a turn of affairs that of course undermines the gospel of production that Gilman preached, but that makes the narrator, as combined producer and consumer, the "efficient scene of [market] circulation" (13). Michaels's reading is extended and refined by Gillian Brown in "The Empire of Agoraphobia," which similarly sees the narrator as engaged in circulation—in, out, and around the walls of her room. But for Brown, such circulation, in both parodying that of the marketplace and protesting the immobility of domestic confinement, succeeds in making the story a feminist critique, one that anticipates Gilman's feminist redefinition of the home and women's role in her later, nonfictional works.

Where, then, are we, after almost two decades of reading "The Yellow Wallpaper," with its narrator described now as a "post-partum psychotic" or "schizophrenic" (Veeder, 63, 64), a child or infant, a disgusting body, a dead object; or, what may not be much better, a politically compromised but quite efficient member of the world of capitalism? To state the critical situation thus is of course to overstate it, since most of the newer critical interpretations still read the story as a feminist text. But it highlights what has been a major shift: the diminishment or even disavowal of the narrator's status as a feminist heroine.

What accounts for this shift are of course changes in the intellectual and critical climate since the story's first republication in the early 1970s. In her 1981 essay Kennard ably described much of that climate out of which the earliest readings emerged, especially the literary and extra-literary circumstances that enabled and encouraged us to read madness as a kind of sanity, or insight; to see the narrator as on a quest for her identity, or, as I described her, as "fighting for some sense of independent self" (51); and to see her husband as representing the patriarchal forces with which she had to contend. I should like now simply to elaborate a bit on what Kennard said, to talk in somewhat more detail about a few aspects of that intellectual climate.

Certainly the prior rediscovery and publication of Kate Chopin's *The Awakening* centrally mattered. The story of a woman who was questioning marriage and motherhood in the interest of her need for some greater fulfillment, its thematic appeal was strong at a time when we were posing the same questions about our own lives. "The Yellow Wallpaper" carried the same theme, with its important additional emphasis on the narrator's yearning for what she calls "congenial work" (Hedges 10). And both stories, of course, posed similarly problematic endings: whether the narrator's madness, like Edna Pontellier's drowning, was to be read as a victory or a defeat. To the extent that there was an early critical investment in finding some degree of triumph in the endings of both works, it was, I think, due not only to the textual clues that could support such readings, but also to our concern, in those years when the history of women's lives was being newly recovered, that that history not be read merely as one of victimization, the passive acceptance of subordination and suffering. As Elaine Showalter has noted, the image of "awakening" carried special resonance for women at the time (40), and so the narrator's growing awareness of her situation, her efforts to decipher, understand, and then question it—quite apart from the degree of her ultimate success or failure in changing it—were given important thematic weight. Kennard found "a sort of triumph" in the narrator's "understanding of her situation" (77), and I found her "heroism" residing "in her perceptivity and in her resistance" (53).

To a significant degree that resistance took the form of anger, as expressed for example in her defying both her husband's and the housekeeper's orders, or in tearing the paper, and this was important at a time when we were discovering, and wondering how to deal with, our own. Two years before the republication of "The Yellow Wallpaper" the poet Adrienne Rich had delivered a talk that would become one of her most influential pieces of writing. In "When We Dead Awaken: Writing as Re-Vision"—and the title's use of the image of awakening is of course further proof of its power in the early 1970s—she had linked women's anger to their victimization, encouraging its release into creative expression, thus validating what was considered an "unfeminine" emotion and supporting its discovery in women's texts.

In "The Yellow Wallpaper" the narrator's husband was also a doctor, important of course in many interpretations of the work. His occupation was yet another aspect of the story that in the 1970s carried a special force as we absorbed the implications of the discoveries then being made about the medical profession's treatment of women in the nineteenth century. Those reactions were best captured in the title of a later work on nineteenth-century medical attitudes toward women, G. J Barker-Benfield's *The Horrors of the Half-Known Life* (1976). Yet the work of researchers like Barbara Ehrenreich and Deirdre English in *Complaints and Disorders: The Sexual Politics of Sickness* and of Ann Douglas Wood in " 'The Fashionable Diseases': Women's Complaints and Their Treatment in Nineteenth-Century America," both published the same year as The Feminist Press edition of "The Yellow Wallpaper," provided a context that further committed us to the story's narrator in her struggle against a husband who could be seen as a doubly powerful antagonist. In the words of the title of the book published in 1971 by the Boston Women's Health Book Collective, at the beginning of the women's health movement, we, like the narrator, were trying to reclaim "our bodies, ourselves."

Finally, one cannot discount the political climate of the time. The year that saw the republication of "The Yellow Wallpaper" was the year of the *Roe v. Wade* Supreme Court decision, which climaxed a decade of legislative victories for women, from the Equal Pay Act of 1963 to Title VII of the Civil Rights Act to Title IX of the Education Act. This record of accomplishment created a sense of hope and expectation that could infuse the reading of women's texts, since their recovery, after years, decades and sometimes centuries of silence and neglect, was itself a "political" achievement. As Rich said in 1971, and as we believed, "hearing our wordless or negated experiences affirmed" in literature could have "visible effects on women's lives" (34).

In August 1973, shortly after The Feminist Press edition of "The Yellow Wallpaper" was published, I received a letter from writer Joanna Russ that described her experience teaching the story to her students. "I found myself emphasizing to the class (I'm not sure why) that although the protagonist is, of course, defeated at the end . . . some really extraordinary kind of positive things come out at the same time. Rage is one of them. And that lovely statement, 'Life is much more exciting now than it used to be.' And a genuinely eerie, ironic over-playing of her role into caricature, acting out (almost) the kind of questions her husband keeps asking her: But darling, what's *wrong*? Do be sensible! Her behavior in the last scene is a marvellously witty, wicked, loony way of doing the same to him, with its mock naivete, its addressing him as 'young man' (silly goose) and its triumphantly ghastly question, 'Now why should that man have fainted?' "

In asking why, in 1973, she found herself emphasizing the comic-triumphant aspects of "The Yellow Wallpaper," and clearly rooting for its heroine, Joanna wondered if it was "just a matter of temperament." I think it was more: our living in a historical moment when, as Kennard recognized, there was a community of readers sharing the same literary conventions, the same expectations of women's literature, and, I would add, the same political hopes. So Joanna found the story "wonderful to teach and the class loved it."[3]

The newer interpretations of "The Yellow Wallpaper" come out of a drastically changed intellectual and political climate and out of a myriad of new schools of critical thought whose methods and governing assumptions importantly differ, as Haney-Peritz, Jacobus, and Lanser make clear, from those that informed the story's earliest readings. If my Afterword appeared in the same year as *Roe v. Wade*, recent interpretations are appearing in the years that have seen increasing attacks on that decision, the failure of the Equal Rights Amendment, the erosion of affirmative action, and renewed, virulent racism, all leading to a skepticism or disillusionment about women's power to create and sustain significant political and social change, or at least to the recognition that change will be slower and more difficult to achieve. The new schools of critical thought are consonant with, although not the direct outgrowth of, this climate of reduced expectations. Post-structuralist, deconstructionist, psychoanalytic, and cultural studies critical theories—all of which have been brought to bear on "The Yellow Wallpaper"—newly problematize terms or concepts that were important to the thinking of the story's earliest critics and to the political activism of the time, such as "identity," "autonomy," and "liberation." Especially in retheorizing "identity"—seeing it as culturally or linguistically or textually constructed, and as fragmented and alienated from itself, even as fictitious—and in focusing on the narrator's unconscious, the new theories, from a pre–post-structuralist point of view, diminish her potential for understanding her situation, displace her from the heroic center of her tale, and drastically reduce the extent to which she can be seen as in control of the telling. Unconscious feelings, be they sexual, maternal, or racial, damage or even destroy her; her efforts to find her identity or subjectivity within the masculine signifying system of the Symbolic, the male realm of language, are almost always, given the sheer difficulty for all women of inserting themselves into that realm, likely to fail; and the story she tells unconsciously reveals meanings of which she is unaware, and which undermine faith in what Kennard had called the "triumph" of her understanding.

The story continues to be read as a feminist text. Many of its critics continue to find its narrator achieving a temporary insight into the nature of her oppression or a momentary victory over it; indeed, this tension between the degree of her success or her failure, dramatically unresolved in the narrative, continues to be the dynamic propelling many of the new readings. And in interpretations that see the narrator as defeated, the text itself still triumphs, makes its feminist point. For Jacobus, for example, the narrator's hysteria, and for Veeder her infantilization, are to be read as compelling critiques of her society's sexual or marital arrangements. For Jacobus the repugnant body to which the narrator is reduced becomes a figure for the repressions imposed both on representations of sexuality and on women's writing in the Victorian period; for Veeder, the story is a feminist cautionary tale that brilliantly exposes the inadequacies and infantilization of both men and women in Victorian marriage. While we may have lost a feminist heroine, we have retained a feminist text.[4]

To say that in their diminishment of the protagonist these new feminist readings are less empowering than earlier ones would probably be to misplace the locus of concern, implying that newer readings of the story should do for their time what our earlier readings did for ours. Critics like Haney-Peritz, for example, or Lanser, in warning against the tendency of earlier critics to identify with a narrator whom they see as seriously flawed or embedded in fantasy, are concerned, still, with the need for political and social change. Haney-Peritz's concluding argument is that only radical changes in "the material conditions of social life" will ultimately liberate the delusioned protagonist (124); and Lanser's caveat against assuming that the situation of one white woman can stand for the situation of all women reflects the greater sensitivity to issues of racial and ethnic diversity that has characterized the women's movement in the last decade, as well as her sense that feminism's identity today is more "precarious and conflicted" (425) than it was in the 1970s.

But warnings against essentializing the story of "The Yellow Wallpaper" and against identifying with its protagonist—if indeed she is allowed an identity to identify with—can also run the risk of depoliticizing it, stripping it of some of its imaginative—and political—power. Current suspicion or rejection of "essentializing" or "totalizing" words like "woman," as others have observed, seriously risks denying the existence of commonalities among women and of their group identity, rooted in subordination, whose recognition is essential to political action.[5] "The Yellow Wallpaper" is a story about a nineteenth-century white, middle-class woman, but it addresses "woman's" situation in so far as women as a group must still contend with male power in medicine, marriage, and indeed most, if not all, of culture. In so far as its earliest critics "identified," we identified, I believe, with that situation. As Diana Fuss has recently observed, the post-structuralist project to problematize and displace identity is difficult to reconcile with the feminist project to reclaim it (70). Whether newer readings of "The Yellow Wallpaper," as they continue to nuance both its narrator and her story, may help achieve that reconciliation remains to be seen.

NOTES

1. Barbara Johnson in 1989 also deals briefly with the race and class aspects of the story, arguing that "[t]he very equation of the woman's body with the blank page implies that the woman's body is white," and noting that "there are many other invisible men and women trapped in the wallpaper of the Western canon . . . that neither psychoanalytic nor feminist theory has taken sufficiently into account. . . ." (267, 268).

2. For Veeder, the story is still a major text, "one of the premier women's texts" (40).

3. Quoted by permission of the author.

4. Michaels would be an exception. In arguing that the narrator's commitment to work produces her madness he is not reading the story as a feminist text but seems, as a reviewer of his book has observed, "treacherously close to blaming a victim." Christopher P. Wilson, "Containing Multitudes: Realism, Historicism, American Studies," *American Quarterly* 41, no. 3 (September 1989): 475. Richard Feldstein, on the other hand, in an article published in 1989, argues for retrieving the protagonist as a feminist heroine by reading her regression ironically, as a "cunning craziness, a militant, politicized madness" (273), but he notes that this is, by then, a minority view.

5. See, for example, the article by Susan Bordo in Works Cited for an excellent discussion of this and related issues.

WORKS CITED

Berman, Jeffrey. "The Unrestful Cure: Charlotte Perkins Gilman and 'The Yellow Wallpaper.'" In *The Talking Cure: Literary Representations of Psychoanalysis*. New York: New York University Press, 1985.

Bordo, Susan. "Feminism, Postmodernism, and Gender-Skepticism." In Linda J. Nicholson, ed., *Feminism/Postmodernism*. New York: Routledge, 1990.

Boston Women's Health Book Collective. *Our Bodies, Ourselves: A Book by and for Women.* New York: Simon and Schuster, 1971.

Brown, Gillian. "The Empire of Agoraphobia." *Representations* 20 (Fall 1987): 134–57.

DeKoven, Marianne. "Gendered Doubleness and the 'Origins' of Modernist Form." *Tulsa Studies in Women's Literature* 8, no. 1 (Spring 1989): 19–42.

DuPlessis, Rachel Blau. *Writing Beyond the Ending: Narrative Strategies of Twentieth-Century Women.* Bloomington, Ind.: Indiana University Press, 1985.

Feldstein, Richard. "Reader, Text, and Ambiguous Referentiality in 'The Yellow Wall-Paper.'" In Richard Feldstein and Judith Roof, eds., *Feminism and Psychoanalysis.* Ithaca, N.Y.: Cornell University Press, 1989.

Fetterley, Judith. "Reading About Reading: 'A Jury of Her Peers,' 'The

Murders in the Rue Morgue,' and 'The Yellow Wallpaper.'" In Elizabeth A. Flynn and Patrocinio P. Schweickart, eds., *Gender and Reading: Essays on Readers, Texts, and Contexts*. Baltimore, Md.: Johns Hopkins University Press, 1986.

Fleenor, Juliann Evans. "The Gothic Prism: Charlotte Perkins Gilman's Gothic Stories and Her Autobiography." In Sheryl L. Meyering, ed., *Charlotte Perkins Gilman: The Woman and Her Work*. Ann Arbor, Mi.: UMI Research Press, 1989.

Ford, Karen. " 'The Yellow Wallpaper' and Women's Discourse." *Tulsa Studies in Women's Literature* 4 (Fall 1985): 309–14.

Fuss, Diana. *Essentially Speaking: Feminism, Nature and Difference*. New York: Routledge, 1989.

Gilbert, Sandra, and Susan Gubar. *The Madwoman in the Attic: The Woman Writer and the Nineteenth-Century Literary Imagination*. New Haven, Conn.: Yale University Press, 1979. pp. 89–92.

_____. *No Man's Land: The Place of the Woman Writer in the Twentieth Century*. Vol. 2. New Haven, Conn.: Yale University Press, 1989.

Haney-Peritz, Janice. "Monumental Feminism and Literature's Ancestral House: Another Look at 'The Yellow Wallpaper.'" *Women's Studies* 12, no. 2 (1986): 113–28.

Hedges, Elaine. Afterword. *The Yellow Wallpaper*. (New York: The Feminist Press, 1973).

Herndl, Diane. "The Writing Cure: Charlotte Perkins Gilman, Anna O., and 'Hysterical Writing.'" *NWSA Journal* 1, no. 1 (1988): 52–74.

Jacobus, Mary. "An Unnecessary Maze of Sign-Reading." In *Reading Women: Essays in Feminist Criticism*. New York: Columbia University Press, 1986.

Johnson, Barbara. "Is Female to Male as Ground Is to Figure?" In Richard Feldstein and Judith Roof, eds., *Feminism and Psychoanalysis*. Ithaca, N.Y.: Cornell University Press, 1989.

Kennard, Jean E. "Convention Coverage or How to Read Your Own Life." *New Literary History* 13 (Autumn 1981): 69–88.

Kolodny, Annette. "A Map for Rereading: Or, Gender and the Interpretation of Literary Texts." *New Literary History* 11, no. 3 (1980).

Lanser, Susan S. "Feminist Criticism, 'The Yellow Wallpaper,' and the Politics of Color in America." *Feminist Studies* 15, no. 3 (Fall 1989): 415–41.

MacPike, Loralee. "Environment as Psychopathological Symbolism in 'The Yellow Wallpaper.'" *American Literary Realism 1870–1910* 8 (Summer 1975): 286–88.

Michaels, Walter Benn. *The Gold Standard and the Logic of Naturalism*. Berkeley: University of California Press, 1987.

Neely, Carol Thomas. "Alternative Women's Discourse." *Tulsa Studies in Women's Literature* 4 (Fall 1985): 315–22.

Pringle, Mary Beth. " 'La Poetique de L'Éspace' in Charlotte Perkins Gilman's 'The Yellow Wallpaper.' " *The French American Review* 3 (1978): 15–22.

Schöpp-Schilling, Beate. " 'The Yellow Wallpaper': A Rediscovered 'Realistic' Story." *American Literary Realism 1870–1910* 8 (Summer 1975): 284–86.

Showalter, Elaine. "Women's Time, Women's Space: Writing the History of Feminist Criticism." In Shari Benstock, ed., *Feminist Issues in Literary Scholarship*. Bloomington, Ind.: Indiana University Press, 1985.

Treichler, Paula. "Escaping the Sentence: Diagnosis and Discourse in 'The Yellow Wallpaper.' " *Tulsa Studies in Women's Literature* 3 (1984): 61–77.

_____. "The Wall Behind the Yellow Wallpaper: Response to Carol Neely and Karen Ford." *Tulsa Studies in Women's Literature* 4 (Fall 1984–5): 323–30.

Veeder, William. "Who is Jane? The Intricate Feminism of Charlotte Perkins Gilman." *Arizona Quarterly* 44 (1988): 40–79.

Bibliography

BACKGROUNDS

Bernheimer, Charles, and Claire Kahane, eds. *In Dora's Case: Freud – Hysteria – Feminism*. New York: Columbia University Press, 1985.

Cobb, Stanley, M.D. "The Psychiatric Case History of Isabella Shawe Thackeray." Appendix 7. *The Letters of William Makepeace Thackeray*, ed. Gordon N. Ray, 518–20. Cambridge: Harvard University Press, 1946.

Conway, Jill. "Stereotypes of Femininity in a Theory of Sexual Evolution." *Suffer and Be Still: Women in the Victorian Age*, ed. Martha Vicinus, 140–54. Bloomington: Indiana University Press, 1972.

Earnest, Ernest Penney. *S. Weir Mitchell, Novelist and Physician*. Philadelphia: University of Pennsylvania Press, 1950.

Ehrenreich, Barbara, and Deirdre English. "The 'Sick' Women of the Upper Classes." *Complaints and Disorders: The Sexual Politics of Sickness*. New York: The Feminist Press, 1973. 15–44.

Gilman, Charlotte Perkins. *The Living of Charlotte Perkins Gilman: An Autobiography*. New York: D. Appleton-Century Company, 1935. Reprint. Madison: University of Wisconsin Press, 1991.

———. "Why I Wrote 'The Yellow Wallpaper.'" *The Forerunner* 4 (1913): 271.

Howells, William Dean, ed. *The Great Modern American Stories*. New York: Boni & Liveright, 1920.

Lane, Ann J. *To Herland and Beyond: The Life and Work of Charlotte Perkins Gilman*. New York: Pantheon Books, 1990.

334

Leavitt, Judith Walzer, ed. *Women and Health in America.* Madison: University of Wisconsin Press, 1984.

Mitchell, S. Weir. *Doctor and Patient.* Philadelphia: J.B. Lippincott & Co., 1887.

_____. *Fat and Blood: And How to Make Them.* Philadelphia: J.B. Lippincott & Co., 1877.

_____. *Lectures on Diseases of the Nervous System, Especially in Women.* Philadelphia: H.C. Leas's Son & Co., 1881.

_____. *Wear and Tear; or, Hints for the Overworked.* Philadelphia: J.B. Lippincott & Co., 1872.

Parker, Gail, ed. *The Oven Birds: American Women on Womanhood, 1820-1920.* Garden City, N.Y.: Doubleday & Co., 1972.

Poirier, Suzanne. "The Weir Mitchell Rest Cure: Doctor and Patients." *Women's Studies* 10 (1983): 15-40.

Showalter, Elaine. *The Female Malady: Women, Madness, and English Culture, 1830-1980.* New York: Pantheon Books, 1985.

Wood, Ann Douglas. " 'The Fashionable Diseases': Women's Complaints and Their Treatment in Nineteenth-Century America." *The Journal of Interdisciplinary History* 4, no. 1 (1973): 25-52.

CRITICISM

Bader, Julia. "The Dissolving Vision: Realism in Jewett, Freeman, and Gilman." *American Realism: New Essays,* ed. Eric J. Sunquist, 176-198. Baltimore, Md.: Johns Hopkins University Press, 1982.

Bassuk, Ellen L. "The Rest Cure: Repetition or Resolution of Victorian Women's Conflicts." *The Female Body in Western Culture: Contemporary Perspectives,* ed. Susan Rubin Suleiman, 139-51. Cambridge, Mass.: Harvard University Press, 1986.

Benn-Michaels, Walter. *The Gold Standard and the Logic of Naturalism.* Berkeley: University of California Press, 1987.

Berman, Jeffrey. "The Unrestful Cure: Charlotte Perkins Gilman and 'The Yellow Wallpaper.' " *The Talking Cure: Literary Representations of Psychoanalysis.* New York: New York University Press, 1985. 33-59.

Brown, Gillian. "The Empire of Agoraphobia." *Representations* 20 (Fall 1987): 134-57.

Bruno, Maria. "Teaching 'Women in America': Some Notes on Pedagogy and Charlotte Perkins Gilman." *Charlotte Perkins Gilman: The Woman and Her Work,* ed. Sheryl L. Meyering, 109-15. Ann Arbor, Mich.: University Microfilms International, 1989.

DeKoven, Marianne, "Gendered Doubleness and the 'Origins' of Modernist Form." *Tulsa Studies in Women's Literature* 8, no. 1 (1989): 19-42.

DeLamotte, Eugenia C. "Male and Female Mysteries in 'The Yellow Wallpaper.'" *Legacy* 5, no. 1 (1988): 3–14.

Doyle, Laura Anne. "Language and Materiality in Modern Women's Narrative." Diss. Brandeis University, 1987.

Fehr, Drude Daae von der. "Charlotte Perkins Gilman The Yellow Wallpaper: Ansatser til en semiologisk tekstanalyse." *Nordisk Tidsskrift for Litteraturforskning/ Scandinavian Journal of Literary Research* 1 (1982): 39–53.

Feldstein, Richard. "Reader, Text and Ambiguous Referentiality in 'The Yellow Wallpaper.'" *Feminism and Psychoanalysis*, eds. Richard Feldstein and Judith Roof, 269–79. Ithaca, N.Y.: Cornell University Press, 1989.

Fetterley, Judith. "Reading About Reading: 'A Jury of Her Peers,' 'The Murders in the Rue Morgue,' and 'The Yellow Wallpaper.'" *Gender and Reading: Essays on Readers, Texts and Contexts*, eds. Elizabeth A. Flynn and Patrocinio P. Schweikert, 158–64. Baltimore, Md.: Johns Hopkins University Press, 1986.

Fleenor, Juliann Evans. "The Gothic Prism: Charlotte Perkins Gilman's Gothic Stories and Her Autobiography." *The Female Gothic*, ed. Juliann Evans Fleenor, 227–41. Montreal: Eden, 1983.

_____. "Giving Birth: Images of Interior Space and 'For Eight Years I Did Not Do Anything I Thought Wrong.'" Diss. University of Toledo, 1978.

Ford, Karen. " 'The Yellow Wallpaper' and Women's Discourse." *Tulsa Studies in Women's Literature* 4, no. 2 (1985): 309–14.

Gilbert, Sandra, and Susan Gubar. *The Madwoman in the Attic: The Woman Writer and the Nineteenth-Century Literary Imagination*. New Haven: Yale University Press, 1979. 89–92.

_____. *No Man's Land: The Place of the Woman Writer in the Twentieth Century*. New Haven: Yale University Press, 1989. 71–76.

Golden, Catherine. "The Writing of 'The Yellow Wallpaper': A Double Palimpsest." *Studies in American Fiction* 17, no. 2 (1989): 193–201.

Haney-Peritz, Janice. "Monumental Feminism and Literature's Ancestral House: Another Look at 'The Yellow Wallpaper.'" *Women's Studies* 12, no. 2 (1986): 113–28.

Hedges, Elaine. Afterword. *The Yellow Wallpaper*. New York: The Feminist Press, 1973. 37–63.

Herndl, Diane. "The Writing Cure: Charlotte Perkins Gilman, Anna O., and 'Hysterical Writing.'" *NWSA Journal* 1, no. 1 (1988): 52–74.

Hill, Mary A. "Charlotte Perkins Gilman: A Feminist's Struggle with Womanhood." *Massachusetts Review: A Quarterly of Literature, the Arts and Public Affairs* 21, no. 3 (1980): 503–26.

Jacobus, Mary. "An Unnecessary Maze of Sign-Reading." *Reading Women: Essays in Feminist Criticism*. New York: Columbia University Press, 1986. 229–48.

Johnson, Barbara. "Is Female to Male as Ground Is to Figure?" *Feminism and*

Psychoanalysis, eds. Richard Feldstein and Judith Roof, 255–68. Ithaca, N.Y.: Cornell University Press, 1989.

Karpinski, Joanne, ed. *Critical Essays on Charlotte Perkins Gilman*. G. K. Hall. Forthcoming.

Kennard, Jean E. "Convention Coverage or How to Read Your Own Life." *New Literary History* 13, no. 1 (1981): 69–88.

King, J., and P. Morris. "On Not Reading between the Lines: Models of Reading in 'The Yellow Wallpaper.'" *Studies in Short Fiction* 26, no. 1 (1989): 23–32.

Knight, Denise. "The Reincarnation of Jane: Gilman's Companion to 'The Yellow Wallpaper.'" *Women's Studies* 20, nos. 3–4 (1991): 87–102.

Kolodny, Annette. "A Map for Rereading: Or, Gender and the Interpretation of Literary Texts." *New Literary History* 11, no. 3 (1980): 451–67.

Lanser, Susan S. "Feminist Criticism, 'The Yellow Wallpaper,' and the Politics of Color in America." *Feminist Studies* 15, no. 3 (1989): 415–41.

MacPike, Loralee. "Environment as Psychopathological Symbolism in 'The Yellow Wallpaper.'" *American Literary Realism 1870–1910* 8, no. 3 (1975): 286–88.

Masse, Michelle A. "Gothic Repetition: Husbands, Horrors, and Things That Go Bump in the Night." *Signs: Journal of Women in Culture and Society* 15, no. 4 (1990): 679–709.

Meyering, Sheryl L., ed. *Charlotte Perkins Gilman: The Woman and Her Work*. Ann Arbor, Mich.: University Microfilms International, 1989.

Mills, Sara, et al. *Feminist Readings, Feminists Reading*. Charlottesville, Va.: University of Virginia Press, 1989.

Neely, Carol Thomas, "Alternative Women's Discourse." *Tulsa Studies in Women's Literature* 4, no. 2 (1985): 315–22.

Nollen, Elizabeth Mahn. "The Gothic Experience: Female Imprisonment, Madness, and Escape in Selected Texts by Women Writers." Diss. Indiana University, 1984.

Payerle, Margaret Jane. " 'A Little Like Outlaws': The Metaphorical Use of Restricted Space in the Works of Certain American Women Realistic Writers." Diss. Case Western Reserve University, 1984.

Pringle, Mary Beth. " 'La Poetique de L'Éspace' in Charlotte Perkins Gilman's 'The Yellow Wallpaper.'" *The French American Review* 3, nos. 1–2 (1978): 15–22.

Scharnhorst, Gary. "Making Her Fame: Charlotte Perkins Gilman in California." *California History* 64, no. 3 (1985): 192–201.

Schöpp-Schilling, Beate, " 'The Yellow Wallpaper': A Rediscovered 'Realistic' Story." *American Literary Realism 1870–1910* 8, no. 3 (1975): 286–88.

Shumaker, Conrad. " 'Too Terribly Good To Be Printed': Charlotte Gilman's 'The Yellow Wallpaper.'" *American Literature* 57, no. 4 (1985): 588–99.

Treichler, Paula, "Escaping the Sentence: Diagnosis and Discourse in 'The Yellow Wallpaper.'" *Tulsa Studies in Women's Literature* 3, nos. 1–2 (1984): 61–77.

_____. "The Wall Behind the Yellow Wallpaper: Response to Carol Neely and Karen Ford." *Tulsa Studies in Women's Literature* 4, no. 2 (1985): 323–30.

Veeder, William. "Who is Jane? The Intricate Feminism of Charlotte Perkins Gilman." *Arizona Quarterly* 44, no. 3 (1988): 40–79.

Wagner-Martin, Linda. "Gilman's 'The Yellow Wallpaper': A Centenary." *Charlotte Perkins Gilman: The Woman and Her Work*, ed. Sheryl L. Meyering, 51–64. Ann Arbor, Mich.: University Microfilms International, 1989.

Permission
Acknowledgments

p. 55: Reprinted from the Introduction by William Dean Howells from *The Great Modern American Stories, An Anthology*, edited by William Dean Howells, vii. By permission of Liveright Publishing Corporation. Copyright 1920 by Boni & Liveright, Inc.; copyright renewed 1948 by Liveright Publishing Corporation.

pp. 58–65: From *The Living of Charlotte Perkins Gilman: An Autobiography*, 90–97 and 118–21, copyright © Radcliffe College. Reprint of the 1935 edition now published by The University of Wisconsin Press. Used by permission of the publisher.

pp. 67–70: "The Psychiatric Case History of Isabella Shawe Thackeray" by S. Cobb, M.D. is reprinted by permission of the publishers from *The Letters of William Makepeace Thackeray*, Gordon N. Ray, editor; Cambridge, Mass.: Harvard University Press, 518–20. Copyright © Thackeray Material 1946 by Hester Thackeray Ritchie Fuller, and © editorial matter 1946 by the President and Fellows of Harvard College; © renewed 1974 by Belinda Norman Butler and Gordon N. Ray.

pp. 71–82: Excerpt from "Stereotypes of Femininity in a Theory of Sexual Evolution" by Jill Conway. From *Suffer and Be Still: Women in the Victorian Age*, ed. Martha Vicinus, 142–52. Used with permission of Indiana University Press.

pp. 84–89: Excerpt from *The Oven Birds: American Women on Womanhood, 1820–1920* by Gail Parker, 49–56. Copyright © 1972 by Gail Thain Parker. Used by permission of Doubleday, a division of Bantam, Doubleday, Dell Publishing Group, Inc.

339

pp. 211–241: "The Unrestful Cure: Charlotte Perkins Gilman and 'The Yellow Wallpaper'" by Jeffrey Berman. Reprinted by permission of New York University Press from *The Talking Cure: Literary Representations of Psychoanalysis*, 33–59 Copyright © 1985 by New York University.

pp. 242–252: "'Too Terribly Good To Be Printed': Charlotte Gilman's 'The Yellow Wallpaper'" by Conrad Shumaker. Reprinted from *American Literature: A Journal of Literary History* 57, no. 4 (1985) : 588–99, with permission from the editors of *American Literature: A Journal of Literary History*.

pp. 253–260: "Reading About Reading: 'A Jury of Her Peers,' 'The Murders in the Rue Morgue,' and 'The Yellow Wallpaper'" by Judith Fetterley. Reprinted from *Gender and Reading: Essays on Readers, Texts, and Contexts*, 158–64. Copyright © 1986 by Elizabeth A. Flynn and Patrocinio P. Schweikert. Used with permission of Johns Hopkins University Press.

pp. 261–276: "Monumental Feminism and Literature's Ancestral House: Another Look at 'The Yellow Wallpaper'" by Janice Haney-Peritz. Reprinted from *Women's Studies* 12, no. 2 (1986): 113–28. Copyright © Gordon and Breach Science Publishers, Inc.

pp. 277–295: "An Unnecessary Maze of Sign Reading." Reprinted from *Reading Women: Essays in Feminist Criticism* by Mary Jacobus, 229–48. Used with permission of Columbia University Press.

pp. 296–306: "The Writing of 'The Yellow Wallpaper': A Double Palimpsest" by Catherine Golden. Reprinted from *Studies in American Fiction* 17 (1989): 193–201.

pp. 307–318: Reprinted from Richard Feldstein, "Reader, Text, and Ambiguous Referentiality in 'The Yellow Wallpaper'" in *Feminism and Psychoanalysis*, edited by Richard Feldstein and Judith Roof, 269–79. Copyright © 1985 by Cornell University. Used by permission of Cornell University Press.

New and Forthcoming Books from The Feminist Press

Eva/Ave: Woman in Renaissance and Baroque Prints, by H. Diane Russell. $59.95 cloth, $29.95 paper.

Here's to the Women: 100 Songs for and about American Women, by Hilda Wenner and Elizabeth Freilicher. Foreword by Pete Seeger. $49.95 cloth, $24.95 paper.

I Dwell in Possibility, a memoir by Toni McNaron. $35.00 cloth, $12.95 paper.

Intimate Warriors: Portraits of a Modern Marriage, 1899–1944, selected works by Neith Boyce and Hutchins Hapgood. Edited by Ellen Kay Trimberger. Afterword by Shari Benstock. $35.00 cloth, $12.95 paper.

Lion Woman's Legacy: An Armenian-American Memoir, by Arlene Voski Avakian. Afterword by Bettina Aptheker. $35.00 cloth, $14.95 paper.

Long Walks and Intimate Talks. Stories and poems by Grace Paley. Paintings by Vera B. Williams. $29.95 cloth, $12.95 paper.

Margret Howth: A Story of Today, a novel by Rebecca Harding Davis. Afterword by Jean Fagan Yellin. $35.00 cloth, $11.95 paper.

The Mer-Child: A Legend for Children and Other Adults, by Robin Morgan. Illustrations by Jesse Spicer Zerner. $17.95 cloth, $8.95 paper.

Now in November, a novel by Josephine Johnson. Afterword by Nancy Hoffman. $29.95 cloth, $10.95 paper.

On Peace, War, and Gender: A Challenge to Genetic Explanations, edited by Anne E. Hunter. Catherine M. Flamenbaum and Suzanne R. Sunday, Associate Editors. (Volume VI, Genes and Gender Series, edited by Betty Rosoff and Ethel Tobach). $35.00 cloth, $12.95 paper.

Women's Studies International: Nairobi and Beyond, edited by Aruna Rao. $35.00 cloth, $15.95 paper.

Women Writing in India: 600 B.C. to the Present, edited by Susie Tharu and K. Lalita. Vol. I: 600 B.C. to the Early Twentieth Century. Vol. II: The Twentieth Century. Each volume $59.95 cloth, $29.95 paper.

For a free catalog, write to The Feminist Press at The City University of New York, 311 East 94 Street, New York, NY 10128. Send book orders to The Talman Company, 150 Fifth Avenue, New York, NY 10011. Please include $3.00 postage/handling for one book, $.75 for each additional.